Religious Pluralism, State and Society in Asia

Taking a critical approach to the concept of 'religious pluralism', this book examines the dynamics of religious co-existence in Asia as they are directly addressed by governments, or indirectly managed by groups and individuals. It looks at the quality of relations that emerge in encounters among people of different religious traditions or among people who hold different visions within the same tradition. Chapters focus in particular on the places of everyday religious diversity in Asian societies in order to explore how religious groups have confronted new situations of religious diversity. The book goes on to explore the conditions under which active religious pluralism emerges (or not) from material contexts of diversity.

Chiara Formichi is Assistant Professor at the City University of Hong Kong. She holds a PhD in the History of Southeast Asia from SOAS (University of London). Her publications include *Islam and the Making of the Nation: Kartosuwiryo and political Islam in 20th century Indonesia* (2012) and the edited volume *Shi'ism and Beyond: Alid piety in Muslim Southeast Asia*.

Routledge religion in contemporary Asia series
Series Editor
Bryan S. Turner, Professor at the City University of New York and Director of the Centre for Religion and Society at the University of Western Sydney

1   **State Management of Religion in Indonesia**
     Myengkyo Seo

2   **Religious Pluralism, State and Society in Asia**
     Edited by Chiara Formichi

Religious Pluralism, State and Society in Asia

Edited by Chiara Formichi

LONDON AND NEW YORK

First published 2014
by Routledge
2 Park Square, Milton Park, Abingdon, Oxon OX14 4RN

And by Routledge
711 Third Avenue, New York, NY 10017

Routledge is an imprint of the Taylor & Francis Group, an informa business

© 2014 selection and editorial material, Chiara Formichi; individual chapters, the contributors.

The right of the editor to be identified as author of the editorial material, and of the authors for their individual chapters, has been asserted in accordance with sections 77 and 78 of the Copyright, Designs and Patents Act 1988.

All rights reserved. No part of this book may be reprinted or reproduced or utilised in any form or by any electronic, mechanical, or other means, now known or hereafter invented, including photocopying and recording, or in any information storage or retrieval system, without permission in writing from the publishers.

Trademark notice: Product or corporate names may be trademarks or registered trademarks, and are used only for identification and explanation without intent to infringe.

British Library Cataloguing in Publication Data
A catalogue record for this book is available from the British Library

Library of Congress Cataloging in Publication Data
Religious pluralism, state and society in Asia / edited by Chiara Formichi.
pages cm. — (Routledge religion in contemporary Asia series ; 2)
Includes bibliographical references and index.
1. Religious pluralism—Asia. 2. Religion and state—Asia. 3. Religion and sociology—Asia. 4. Asia—Religion. I. Formichi, Chiara, 1982- editor of compilation. II. Kersten, Carool. Urbanization, civil society and religious pluralism in Indonesia and Turkey.
BL1033.R46 2013
201'.5095—dc23
2013010147

ISBN: 978-0-415-83884-9 (hbk)
ISBN: 978-1-315-88756-2 (ebk)

Typeset in Times New Roman
by FiSH Books Ltd, Enfield

Printed and bound by CPI Group (UK) Ltd, Croydon, CR0 4YY

Contents

List of illustrations	vii
List of abbreviations	viii
Contributors	ix
Acknowledgements	xii

1 Religious pluralism, state and society in Asia   1
CHIARA FORMICHI

PART I
Pluralism and the state   11

**2 Urbanization, civil society and religious pluralism in
Indonesia and Turkey**   13
CAROOL KERSTEN

**3 Sacred sites and social conflict: Yasukuni shrine and
religious pluralism in Japanese society**   35
MARK R. MULLINS

**4 Hierarchical plurality: State, religion and pluralism in
southwest China**   51
LIANG YONGJIA

**5 Literacy wars: Children's education and weekend
madrasahs in Singapore**   71
PHYLLIS GHIM-LIAN CHEW

vi *Contents*

PART II
Conviviality in the city   91

6   **In the name of God: South Asian Muslims in a Chinese**
    temple fair in Hong Kong   93
    WAI-CHI CHEE

7   **Sweetness and light: The bright side of pluralism in a**
    Rajasthan town   113
    ANN GRODZINS GOLD

8   **Overcoming 'hierarchized conviviality' in the Manila**
    metropolis: Religious pluralism and urbanization in the
    Philippines   138
    MANUEL VICTOR J. SAPITULA

9   **Actually existing religious pluralism in Kuala Lumpur**   153
    YEOH SENG GUAN

PART III
Pluralism and individual identities   173

10 **Cosmopolitan Islam and inclusive Chineseness:**
    Chinese-style Mosques in Indonesia   175
    HEW WAI-WENG

11 **Ramadan in the newsroom: *Malaysiakini*, *Tempo*, and the**
    state in Indonesia and Malaysia   197
    JANET STEELE

12 **Pluralist currents and counter-currents in the Indonesian**
    mass media: The case of Anand Krishna   216
    JULIA DAY HOWELL

13 **A Sufi, Sikh, Hindu, Buddhist, TV Guru: Anandmurti**
    Gurumaa   236
    ANGELA RUDERT

    Index   258

Illustrations

3.1 The plaintiffs speak to reporters outside the Osaka District Court following the decision of the three judges on 26 February 2009   45
7.1 India's pluralism performed by Jahazpur school children on Republic Day   117
7.2 *Jhanki* of Krishna the Butter Thief, Janamashtami   121
7.3 Almond-Cashew Ganesh with neon Lakshmi, Ganesh Chaturthi   123
7.4 Men pray, children play, at the *Idgah*, Id   124
7.5 Crowd hands offerings for Tejaji into shrine, Teja Dashmi   126
7.6 Hindu deities pass through 'Mosque Gate', Jal Jhulani   127
7.7 Jain chariot outside temple, Anant Chaturdashi   129
7.8 Hindu woman makes offering to Muslim saint, Gaji Pir   135
10.1 The Surabaya Cheng Hoo Mosque   178
10.2 The Palembang Cheng Hoo Mosque   186
11.1 Arif Zulkifli, breaking the fast at *Tempo*   198
11.2 Hazlan Zakaria, breaking the fast at *Malaysiakini*   200
11.3 Pasar Ramadan, Bangsar   201
11.4 Vendors, Pasar Ramadan, Bangsar   201

Abbreviations

AKP	Adalet ve Kalkınma Partisi (Turkey)
BK	Brahma Kumaris
CCM	Council of Churches of Malaysia
CCP	Chinese Communist Party
CFM	Christian Federation of Malaysia
DP	Demokrat Parti (Turkey)
HDB	Housing Development Board (Singapore)
IAIN	Institut Agama Islam Negeri (Indonesia)
LDP	Liberal Democratic Party (Japan)
MCCBCHS	Malaysian Consultative Council for Buddhism, Christianity, Hinduism and Sikhism
MMDA	Metro Manila Development Authority (Philippines)
MUI	Majelis Ulama Indonesia
MUIS	Majlis Ugama Islam Singapura
NRI	Non-Resident Indian
NU	Nahdlatul Ulama (Indonesia)
PAS	Parti Islam Se-Malaysia
PITI	Persatuan Islam Tionghoa Indonesia
PKS	Partai Keadilan Sejahtera (Indonesia)
PRC	People's Republic of China
SARS	Severe Acute Respiratory Syndrome
UMNO	United Malays National Organization (Malaysia)

Contributors

Phyllis Ghim-Lian Chew has authored many books on language, education, women's studies and comparative religion. Her latest books are titled *Emergent Lingua Francas* (New York: Routledge, 2009) and *A sociolinguistic history of early identities in Singapore: from Colonialism to Nationalism* (Basingstroke: Palgrave, 2013). An applied linguist, she has served on the international advisory boards of such as *Teaching Education, Asian EFL Journal, Asia TEFL Journal* and *Gendering Asia*. She is the project advisor for Instep, the textbook and audio-visual series used in Singapore schools since 2001. She is currently Principal Researcher for the National Institute of Education project on Religious Ideologies and Literacy Practices.

Wai-chi Chee has a PhD in Anthropology from The Chinese University of Hong Kong, and currently teaches at the same department. Her research interests include migration, education, globalization, governance, grassroots activism, ethnicity, culture and identity, and youth. Geographical areas of her research include Mainland China, Hong Kong, and South Asia. Her dissertation addresses how Mainland Chinese and South Asian teenage migrant students adapt to schooling and life in Hong Kong. She has published articles in *Asian Anthropology, Ethnography and Education, Multicultural Education Review,* and *Taiwan Journal of Anthropology*.

Julia Day Howell has a doctorate in Anthropology from Stanford University, and is now Professor of the Sociology of Religion in the Centre for the Study of Contemporary Muslim Societies at the University of Western Sydney. She has worked for over thirty years on movements of religious reform in Indonesia, and on New Religious Movements both in Indonesia and the West. Her early research focused on conversions of Javanese people to the newly recognized Hindu and Buddhist religions, and on the eclectic mystical groups. In the 1990s she turned her attention to mainline Islam, pioneering studies of the urban Sufi revival and contemporary forms of spirituality among urban cosmopolitans, and contributing to emerging studies of Islamic televangelism and the marketing of Islamic personal and business development programs. Her edited volume, *Sufism and the 'Modern' in Islam* (with Martin van Bruinessen), has been translated into Indonesian, as have numbers of her articles and chapters.

x *Contributors*

Chiara Formichi is Assistant Professor in History and Religion at the Department of Asian and International Studies at City University of Hong Kong. Her recent publications include *Islam and the Making of the Nation: Kartosuwiryo and Political Islam in 20th Century Indonesia* (Leiden: KITLV, 2012) and *Shi'ism and Beyond: Alid Piety in Muslim Southeast Asia* (with Michael Feener [eds], forthcoming). She has published articles in *Indonesia, JSEAS*, and *Die Welt des Islams*.

Ann Grodzins Gold is the Thomas J. Watson Professor of Religion, and Professor of Anthropology at Syracuse University. During academic year 2010–11 she held a Fulbright-Hays Faculty Research Fellowship for fieldwork on landscape and identity in a small market town in North India. Her earlier research has focused on pilgrimage, gender, expressive traditions, and environmental history. Her publications include numerous articles and four books, including *In the Time of Trees and Sorrows: Nature, Power and Memory in Rajasthan* (2002, co-authored with Bhoju Ram Gujar) which in 2004 was awarded the Ananda Kentish Coomaraswamy Book Prize from the Association for Asian Studies.

Yeoh Seng Guan is Senior Lecturer at Monash University, Sunway Campus. He is an anthropologist who conducts research on cities, religion, media and civil society in Southeast Asia. He also produces ethnographic video documentaries. Recent publications include 'Holy Water and Material Religion in a Pilgrimage Shrine in Malaysia' in Julius Bautista (ed.) *The Spirit of Things: Materiality in an Age of Religious Diversity in Southeast Asia* (2012) and 'Malaysian Figures of Modernity' in Joshua Barker, Erik Harms and Johan Linquist (eds.) *Figures of Southeast Asian Modernity* (2013).

Carool Kersten is Senior Lecturer in the study of Islam and the Muslim World at King's College London. His research field is the contemporary intellectual history of the Muslim world, Islam in trans-regional contexts, and the history of Islam in Southeast Asia. He is the author of *Cosmopolitans and Heretics: New Muslim Intellectuals and the Study of Islam* (2011) and has co-edited volumes on alternative religious discourses in the contemporary Muslim world and present-day Islamic thinking about the caliphate. He is also the editor-in-chief of the Ashgate book series 'Contemporary Thought in the Islamic World'.

Mark R. Mullins is Professor of Japanese Studies in the School of Asian Studies, The University of Auckland, New Zealand. He is the author and co-editor of a number of works, including *Religious Minorities in Canada: A Sociological Study of the Japanese Experience* (1989), *Religion and Society in Modern Japan* (1993), *Perspectives on Christianity in Korea and Japan* (1995), *Christianity Made in Japan: A Study of Indigenous Movements* (1998), and *Religion and Social Crisis in Japan* (2001). He is currently writing a book on neo-nationalism and religion in contemporary Japanese society.

Contributors   xi

Angela Rudert holds a PhD in Religion from Syracuse University, and currently teaches at the Department of Philosophy and Religion, Ithaca College. Her research examines tradition and innovation in twenty first century guru devotion through a study of Anandmurti Gurumaa, a young, yet prominent and globetrotting north Indian female guru. Angela's work brings together ethnographic, religio-historical and textual research methods. A Doctoral Dissertation Research Award from Fulbright-Hays and a dissertation research award from FLAS supported Angela's fieldwork in India in 2008 and 2009.

Manuel Victor J. Sapitula has a PhD in Sociology from the National University of Singapore (NUS) and is currently Assistant Professor of Sociology at the University of the Philippines-Diliman (UPD). His fields of specialization are the sociology of religion and the study of Christianity in the Philippine context. He is currently completing his dissertation on the sociological study of the devotion to Our Mother of Perpetual Help, a form of Catholic popular religion that is widespread in the Philippines.

Janet Steele is an Associate Professor of Journalism at the School of Media and Public Affairs at George Washington University. She received her PhD in History from the Johns Hopkins University, and is especially interested in how culture is communicated through the mass media. Her book, *Wars Within: The Story of Tempo, an Independent Magazine in Soeharto's Indonesia*, focuses on *Tempo* magazine and its relationship to the politics and culture of New Order Indonesia. A former Fulbright professor at the University of Indonesia and the Dr. Soetomo Press Institute, her current work focuses on journalism and Islam in the Malay Archipelago.

Hew Wai-Weng recently graduated from the Australian National University, where he submitted his PhD thesis, 'Negotiating Ethnicity and Religiosity: Chinese Muslim Identities in Post-New Order Indonesia'. He is currently a Fellow at the Zentrum Moderner Orient (ZMO) in Berlin.

Liang Yongjia (PhD in Anthropology, Peking University) is now Professor of Anthropology at the China Agricultural University; he was Senior Research Fellow for four years in the Asia Research Institute, National University of Singapore. He has combined interests in the ethnographic and historical studies of popular religion and ethnicity in PR China. His papers are published on journals such as *The Asia Pacific Journal of Anthropology*, *Asian Journal of Social Science*, and *Chinese Sociology and Anthropology*. He is writing up a monograph on the religious and ethnic revival in southwest China to be published by Routledge.

Acknowledgements

It is only thanks to the efforts of several individuals and institutions that this volume could be completed. First of all my gratitude goes to Juliana Finucane, friend and colleague. It was our shared interest in investigating the junctures between religious pluralism, place, policies and social practices that brought us to organize the workshop 'Placing Religious Pluralism in Asia's Global Cities', hosted by the Asia Research Institute (ARI) of the National University of Singapore in May 2011.

We are most grateful to ARI for the financial and logistic support, and to all the participants for their stimulating contributions. In particular, I wish to thank Daniel Goh, Daniel Gold, Heidi Haugen, Ronie Parciack, Tony Reid, Kiran Shinde and Sherly Saragih Turnip for their participation to the workshop, and the discussants Julius Bautista, Tim Bunnell, Michael Feener, Andrea Pinkney and Vineeta Sinha for their valuable comments. In preparing the volume, I wish to thank all the contributors, and Routledge for their editorial support.

For their support throughout the preparation of the volume, I would also like to extend my thanks to Professor Bryan Turner and Peter Sowden as editors of the *Religion in Contemporary Asia* book series, to Helena Hurd, Asian Studies' Editorial Assistant at Routledge, and Mark Fisher, final copy-editor.

A special note of gratitude goes to Michael Feener, leader of the 'Religion and Globalization' research cluster at ARI, and mentor.

Chiara Formichi
Hong Kong

1 Religious pluralism, state and society in Asia

Chiara Formichi

In early October 2012 Ms Amy Cheong, assistant director with the NTUC Workers' Union of Singapore, complained on her personal Facebook page: 'How many *** days do Malay weddings at void decks go on for???...How can society allow ppl to get married for 50 bucks?', referring to the common practice for Malay families to hold wedding receptions in HDB public housing estate's void-decks, and hinting at Malays' lower socio-economic status. Ms Cheong was promptly fired within hours after the event (*Straits Times*, 9 October 2012).[1]

Such remarks, directed from a Chinese towards Malays, have been described as 'insensitive', 'ignorant', 'derogatory', 'racist' and 'profanity-laced', reviving the city-state's public debate on inter-ethnic relations. And government officials have used this event to make their statements on the importance and fragility of Singapore's social harmony: Law Minister K. Shanmugam expressed his concerns that such words 'reflect[ed] a deep seated racist attitude'; Deputy Prime Minister Tharman Shanmugaratnam commented that Ms Cheong had offended 'all the rest of us who value Singapore's multiracial spirit'; and as acting Minister for Manpower Chuan-Jin expressed his pride for Singapore's diversity,[2] PM Lee himself admitted 'how easily a few thoughtless words can...undermine our racial and religious harmony' (*Straits Times*, 8 October 2012).[3]

The storm had been stirred by cyber civil society, as Ms Cheong's comment had gone viral amidst support and heavy criticism, raising isolated concerns over the possibility for social mobilization of discontent[4] and arguably strengthening the decision of firing her (*Channel News Asia*, 8 October 2012). In the following weeks, public opinion remained vocal, with Malay as well as non-Malay netizens expressing their views on the 'Amy Cheong saga'. Many were simply outraged, some argued that a 'forgive and forget' approach would suit better the situation, and others tried to explain the cultural roots for holding Malay weddings at void-decks as a substitute for the *kampung*'s (village) common space for the bride's and groom's family to meet before the ceremony.[5]

The authors featured in this volume take Asia as a laboratory for the study of lived experiences of pluralism as well as state-orchestrated management of diversity. With an approach strongly grounded in empirical analysis, this volume participates in the theoretical debate on diversity and pluralism. All engage with legitimacy as a core aspect of the analysis of diversity as pluralism, with such

2 *Chiara Formichi*

concept transposed to identify situations where believers of different religious traditions, or followers of different understandings within one tradition, are equally legitimated in adhering to their beliefs and in performing their rituals.

As suggested by the Amy Cheong case in Singapore, the management of religious diversity involves the interaction of state and society through policies, but also calls into question daily practices of coexistence, and concerns over sharing common spaces. The following chapters investigate case studies from Turkey, India, China, Japan, Indonesia, the Philippines, Malaysia, and the two cities of Hong Kong and Singapore. In addressing multi-faith societies, these authors investigate ways in which states, cities, neighbourhoods, the media, or a single individual become spaces in which the boundaries of diversity are negotiated.

Negotiating the boundaries of diversity

The events illustrated above hit at the heart of Singapore's multi-ethnic, multi-cultural, and multi-religious society. British colonial policies of migration in the nineteenth and early twentieth centuries, and the politics of ethnicity that emerged in post-colonial Malaya (eventually leading to the establishment of Singapore as a state independent from Malaysia), have transformed concerns over negotiating differences in a modern city-state into a well-defined form of normative pluralism.

Singapore is representative of a state-directed effort to implement normative ideals of harmony and management of a diverse ethno-religious society. But neither is this the only option, nor are official policies advocating peaceful coexistence always successful. In a recently published volume, Michael Feener and Juliana Finucane have focused on one particular key fault-line of state pluralism: identifying the clash within various aspects of religious freedoms, they suggest that proselytization, for example, 'is both made possible by and simultaneously tests the limits of religious pluralism [as] [i]t assumes a situation of diversity in which individuals have the potential to change their religious identities and affiliations, while at the same time harbouring ultimate goals of overcoming that diversity through the eventual conversion of the rest of society to one's own religion' (Finucane and Feener 2013: 3).

It thus emerges as a priority to distinguish between empirical conditions of diversity, normative visions of pluralism, and experiences of everyday conviviality. In the intervening chapters, 'religious pluralism' is understood as the transformation of a mere condition of heterogeneity, into a reality where groups representative of this diversity are accepted and integrated as equals; in the development of the volume, we have engaged with Michael Peletz's definition of pluralism as diversity which is accorded legitimacy, thus pointing to pluralism as a condition of heterogeneity which has been vetted through a Weberian notion of group validation (Peletz 2009: 7). Yet this approach leaves untouched the issue of where the legitimacy emerges from, and the cases presented here point to the interplay of societal behaviour and government policies as a crucial factor in determining the outcome. On the one hand we look into cases where the state takes on the role of legitimizer, by establishing a set paradigm of normative

Religious pluralism, state and society in Asia   3

national pluralism; on the other hand, we investigate parallel cases where either it is a social group who creates pockets of conviviality – bringing into play Shail Mayaram's framework of 'living together' – or it is individuals negotiating their own boundaries between multiple religious understandings.

Yet, negotiating boundaries is a policy-endeavour as much as a metaphor and a physical reality. Investigating the intersection of official, societal, and individual practices in managing religious diversity, and creating spaces for legitimated religious diversity, this volume offers empirical analyses of political, legal, historical, cultural and social aspects of religious practices drawn from various Asian contexts. This multifaceted approach emerges as a useful path to explore modes of interaction which might (or might not) contribute to the shaping of an environment conducive for conviviality, or fuel the active structuring of specific models of normative pluralism.

Notions of pluralism have changed widely throughout time, mutating from observations of heterogeneity – previously referred to as empirical diversity – to reflections on how minorities are integrated and plural societies are managed, either through lived conviviality or the normative pluralism approach. This scholarly development can be traced through the work of a handful of scholars, who marked significant transitional moments in this scholarship. In the following paragraphs, we move from Tony Reid's historical reflections on Asia's pre-modern empirical condition of diversity onto Furnivall's observations of British and Dutch colonial 'plural societies'; then, onto Bob Hefner's work on multiculturalism and states' (mis)management of diversity which emerges from a contemporary reading of Furnivall, and capitalizes on the experience of Indonesia, Malaysia and Singapore as independent nation-states. The latest milestones on this path have been laid by Michael Peletz and Shail Mayaram, who engage with the concept of legitimacy, establishing the frameworks of pluralism that contributors to this volume have worked with.

Anthony Reid has made a historical argument to explain the conflictual perception of Asia as both religiously diverse and formally homogeneous, suggesting that an 'Asian pattern of diversity' grounded on the pragmatism of imperial world-conquerors (from Alexander the Great to Chenggiz Khan), the necessities of port-states' entrepôts, an 'animist experimentation' widespread across Hindu-Buddhist Asia, and the Indic tradition of inner monism, was successful in opposing exclusivist tendencies. A contemporary testimony to this approach can be found in spiritual leaders Anandmurti Gurumaa and Anand Krishna (see Angela Rudert and Julia Howell, respectively, in this volume), yet it appears that acceptance of 'multiple truths' is today an exception, rather than the rule, and one which can face strong opposition.

Reid explains the current climate of tension and apparent homogeneity of Asia's religious demographics by pointing at phenomena such as the pre-colonial states' tendencies to rely on externally validated forms of orthodoxy for the legitimation of their authority; anti-colonial religious-nationalist identities; the scarcity of institutionalized denominationalism; and the influence of faraway 'purist' movements (Reid 2011).[6] This historical perspective lays the foundation

4   *Chiara Formichi*

for a survey of theoretical considerations addressing the relation between diversity and pluralism as mediated by society (through experiences of collaboration and conviviality) or the state (in the form of management, assimilation, or inclusion of diversity).

In the early 1940s, J. S. Furnivall, economist and British colonial administrator, observed that the social economies of Malaya and the Netherlands East Indies were exemplars of a 'plural society', meaning one that comprises 'two or more elements of social orders which live side by side, yet without mingling, in one political unit' (Furnivall 1944: 446). Furnivall's statement was grounded on the indigenous *versus* colonial perspectives, and more broadly the insider *versus* outsider dichotomy, encompassing multiple indigenous groups. Most importantly, Furnivall could detect no 'common will' across the various social groups, thus predicting that with the end of colonialism and the emergence of nationalism and liberal democracies these new Asian nation-states would fall prey to inter-ethnic strife.

Observing post-colonial Southeast Asia, one could be tempted to agree with Furnivall: anti-Chinese violence had broken out in the early 1950s and again in 1965 in Indonesia (a pattern repeated at another crucial transitional time between 1996 and 2001); Singapore and Malaysia were both shaken by inter-ethnic riots in 1964–65 and 1969 respectively, with Singapore concurrently seceding from Malaysia on ethnic grounds; the Philippines have been torn by violence between Moro Muslims in the south and the Catholics in the north; while in Thailand the same geography is contended between Malay Muslims and 'Tai' Buddhists. Much scholarly effort has been dedicated to the issue of communal violence and social conflict in Asia, but research has also emerged on the constructive consequences of the upheavals, analysing civil society groups and state institutions set in place to moderate this diversity, manage minorities, and avoid potential conflict. The 1960s and 1990s incidents were to prompt national governments to develop new frames to manage citizenship in multi-ethnic and multi-religious countries; and each state implemented different models depending on their own historical and contingent circumstances.[7]

Pluralism and the state: Managing diversity

Shadowing Samuel Huntington's reframing of the modernization theory, in 2001 Freedom House and the International Monetary Fund had their representatives declare that 'democracy has been significantly more successful in monoethnic societies' and that 'fractionalization automatically translates into more conflict' (in Fish and Brooks 2004: 154–66).[8] Such a trend to argue that heterogeneity (of language, ethnicity, religion, class) hampers democratic politics and economic advancement is widely supported in developmentalist circles, but it has also been countered by political scientists, historians and sociologists.[9] And Asia offers a wide array of case-studies in this direction. In the first section of this volume, entitled 'Pluralism and the State', Carool Kersten, Liang Yongjia, Mark Mullins and Phyllis Chew focus on discourses of religious pluralism at the governance level, exploring the role of the state in managing situations of religious diversity, critically engaging the question of whether the state's actions foster either a climate of legitimation or rather exclusion of minority groups, and whether such initiatives are directed towards the protection of society or the state itself.

As noted at the very beginning of this chapter, Singapore is an exemplary case of state-involvement in managing a multi-ethnic and multi-faith society, and besides brokering relations between different religious groups, here the state also negotiates between religious and secular models, and ensures that differences internal to any given religion do not undermine social harmony. Phyllis Chew thus investigates these multiple levels of negotiations looking at the micro-reality of religious education, as she brings to our attention the variety of approaches in Islamic schooling, and the relation between three weekend madrasahs and week-day secular education.

Liang Yongjia puts forward a historical analysis of Dali, a multi-religious and multi-ethnic city in Southwest China, to show how it is the very role of the PRC's state in coordinating religious groups – whether through the Bureau of Religious Affairs, Cultural Affairs, or Public Security – that allows for the survival of religious pluralism. Exploring another key country in East Asia, Mark Mullins investigates the role of Yasukuni shrine in post-war Japan. As the 1947 constitution sanctioned both the separation of state and religion and wide religious freedoms, we find examples to confirm that in the East Asian paradigm, the state's priority in managing religious diversity is aimed at strengthening national identity (Baker 1997: 144–72). Mullins here illustrates the case of how despite the transformation of Yasukuni Shrine into a 'voluntary association', Buddhists, Christians and secularists are faced with legal obstacles in their effort to remove the names of their family members from the Shrine's list. In its strife to protect this symbol of national unity, the government is infringing citizens' constitutional rights in favour of 'the religious freedom of Yasukuni Shrine'. Shifting the geographical focus to Southeast Asia and the Middle East, Carool Kersten looks at the transnational parallel between Turkey and Indonesia, investigating the emergence of 'new' Muslim intellectuals and of a religious civil society at the same time as the states, in these two Muslim countries, managed the role of religion in the public sphere.

Negotiating the boundaries of religious identity

As suggested by the opening anecdote, sharing communal spaces can be a source of tensions, but also of positive exchanges. Looking at particular groups attempting to navigate the landscape of state legislation and management of religions, sections two and three of this volume engage critically with the state and suggest alternative ways in which society could grant legitimation to minority groups through interaction. The two paradigms for this analysis are Mayaram's framework of conviviality and Michael Peletz's embracing of the Weberian concept of group validation, whilst contributors to this volume continue to focus on the concept of place and social interaction.

6 Chiara Formichi

This second section is then titled 'Conviviality in the City', and explores the action of social groups in creating pockets of legitimation in operating against, and in spite of, states' policies and common social attitudes. Wai-chi Chee, Ann Grodzins Gold, Manuel Sapitula, and Yeoh Seng Guan's contributions reflect on Shail Mayaram's notion of conviviality, which indeed challenges scholarly traditions that 'prioritize binarism, given their emphasis on monadic selfhood, incommensurable identities, and boundaries around cultural isolates' (Mayaram 2005: 169).

These authors draw from Mayaram's analysis of global cities, and microcosms within the city, as hubs of 'associational forms of civic engagement' and of 'alternative cosmopolitanisms' that are not rooted in the state: this conviviality expressly focuses on a cosmopolitanism that does not relate to 'statist multiculturalism' (Mayaram 2009: 9–11). It is thus that Mayaram shapes a new methodology 'in order to write an ethnography of cultural encounter', one which she defines as 'living together' (Mayaram 2005: 149). Oftentimes identifying the state as the actor behind the creation of barriers, these authors focus on individuals and communities who succeed in overcoming formalistic sectarian boundaries through daily practices of 'pluralism', working against official policies aimed at separating and polarizing ethno-religious groups.

Wai-chi Chee investigates the shared space of a Chinese temple fair to talk more broadly about diversity in the territory of Hong Kong. Through her ethnographic study of a group of South Asian women who participate in a local fair, it emerges that although in the broader context of Hong Kong these Muslim migrants and their families are marginalized and discriminated against, it is still possible to find niches in which diversity is valued as cultural richness. In another chapter, Ann Grodzins Gold reflects on town festivals as experiences of conviviality in Jahazpur, Rajasthan, where the celebratory spirit is embraced by several communities creating 'performed and organic manifestations of plural society'. Echoing Mayaram's observation that government and citizens often have different views of how inter-communitarian interaction might turn out, Grodzins Gold juxtaposes officials' concerns over the sensitivity of the festivals with her interpretation of public celebrations as manifestations of 'ordinary pluralisms'.

Manuel Sapitula and Yeoh Seng Guan focus on different experiences of conviviality in two Southeast Asian cities, Manila and Kuala Lumpur. Manuel Sapitula focuses on negotiations of multi-ethnic and multi-religious coexistence within the boundaries of a neighbourhood in Manila which features a major Catholic shrine, the National Shrine of Our Mother of Perpetual Help, as well as a Moros migrant community. The struggle of Moro Muslims to retain their living space, mosque, and commercial activities needs to be contextualized in the broader historical relation between Christians and Muslims, the geopolitics of Mindanao Moros and Manila Muslim urbanites, as well as government policies to improve and develop the Baclaran district, where the shrine is located. Sapitula's reconstruction of this complex situation illustrates a picture characterized by urban social stratification, for which he uses the notion of 'hierarchized conviviality'.

Religious pluralism, state and society in Asia 7

Yeoh Seng Guan illustrates instead cases of 'actual pluralism' in Kuala Lumpur, contrasting the religious authorities' push to neatly define ethno-religious boundaries, and discusses the changes induced by recent plans for urban redevelopment aimed at absorbing decades of in-migration from the rural areas: while 'squatter colonies' allowed for ethno-religious homogeneity or community-directed negotiations of boundaries, forced relocation in high-rises has heightened the difficulty of 'conviviality'.

Investigating gender identities in Southeast Asia, Peletz suggests that 'gender pluralism' ought to be analysed through the lens of legitimation, the latter seen as a historically defined social and cultural process of group validation. Hence Peletz's approach differs from Mayaram's as he focuses on a legitimizing effort, which allows for the transition from a condition of diversity towards one of recognized and accepted pluralism. It is against this background that we can read the chapters included in the third section of this volume, titled 'Pluralism and Individual Identities'. These contributions focus on individuals' religious identities, and the process by which they might be seen as outliers by the rest of their communities, raising important issues about the relationship between state and society in matters of religious beliefs as well as calling into question governments' increased involvement in determining paradigms of orthodoxy, especially in Indonesia and Malaysia.

Individual identities are more complex than a religious denomination; Hew Wai-Weng investigates the negotiation of ethnic and religious identities amongst Chinese Muslims in Indonesia through mosque architecture, exploring the ways in which this community connects with the Chinese diaspora as much as with the *ummah* and Indonesia's national society. The multiplicity of Muslim identities, already highlighted in the context of Singapore's weekend madrasahs, emerges once more in Janet Steele's chapter. Steele compares practices related to the fasting month of Ramadan in two press-rooms in Kuala Lumpur and Jakarta, dwelling upon these two countries' believers' approaches to religious authority and pluralism, and individuals' relationship to perceived forms of 'correct religious behaviour'.

Julia Howell and Angela Rudert take the concepts of place, religious pluralism and individuals' negotiations of identities to a transcendental level, as they look at two charismatic figures' embodiment of religious pluralism and their relationship to their audiences, in Indonesia and India respectively. The trial of Anand Krishna, an 'eclectic spiritual development figure', is analysed here by Julia Howell as both a case of an individual's embrace of religious pluralism and as an expedient to assess the role of the media in disseminating the concerns of conservative religious groups and in shaping public opinion. An interesting comparison emerges with Angela Rudert's contribution, as she presents the case of another teacher inspired by multiple religious traditions, but in India. If in Indonesia the eclecticism of Anand Krishna is officially seen as blasphemous, Rudert argues that Anandmurti Gurumaa's refusal to be identified with any specific 'ism' becomes a manifestation of anti-exclusivism and itself a reflection, through her dress and body, of the complex networks that intertwine our contemporary world.

Notes

1 www.straitstimes.com/the-big-story/amy-cheongs-comments/story/ntuc-assistant-director-sacked-racist-remarks-20121009 (accessed on 3 December 2012).
2 Tan Chuan-Jin Facebook post, broadcast on 8 October 2012, and re-posted by *Channel News Asia*, available at www.youtube.com/watch?v=FtB0csoSnC8 (accessed on 3 December 2012).
3 www.straitstimes.com/the-big-story/amy-cheongs-comments/story/pm-lee-ministers-condemn-racist-remarks-facebook-20121008 (accessed on 3 December 2012).
4 By Monday morning, a new Facebook page had been started under the title 'Fire Amy Cheung', garnering thousands of supporters. *Channel News Asia*, available at www.youtube.com/watch?v=FtB0csoSnC8 (accessed on 3 December 2012). The secretary of Hougang's Inter-Racial and Confidence Circle had filed a police report, urging the police to act as Ms Cheong's comments would 'inevitably hurt the feelings of the Malays'. http://sg.news.yahoo.com/police-report-filed-against-amy-cheong-over-racist-facebook-post.html (accessed on 3 December 2012).
5 An interesting blog-entry explaining the practices of Malay weddings was posted by a Chinese Muslim, see http://wherebearsroamfree.blogspot.hk/2012/10/amy-cheong-malay-weddings-at-hdb-void.html (accessed on 3 December 2012).
6 I would like to thank Anthony Reid for his participation in the workshop 'Placing Religious Pluralism in Asia's Global Cities'. The text is extracted from his keynote speech 'Many but one: The paradox of religious pluralism in Southeast Asia'.
7 Studies investigating multi-ethnic and multi-religious contexts in contemporary Asia mostly delve into instances of violence (see for example Das 2006; Hefner 2001; McCargo 2008; McGilvray 2008; Sidel 2006; Wilson 2008). Or they analyse systems set in place to avoid potential conflict (see Lai 2008; Lee 2010; Nedilsky 2009).
8 See also Huntington (1968). Pluralism, as inclusion of diversity, is seen by many scholars as a key aspect of liberal democracies; see also Flathman (2005), and Connolly (2005).
9 An interesting counterargument has been put forward by Steven Fish and Robin Brooks who have challenged this assumption and proved it wrong using data from Freedom House itself and the National Bureau of Economic Research. Their quantitative analysis shows indeed that in none of the models 'is ethnic fractionalization statistically or substantially significant' to limited democracy (Fish and Brooks 2004: 159). Here ethnic diversity, together with language and religion, is also used to determine diversity. From another study by the same Steven Fish it also emerges that in Eastern Europe, for example, diversity has actually positively contributed to creating mechanisms of inclusion and management of diversity that promote democracy (Fish and Kroenig 2006).

References

Baker, D. (1997) 'World Religions and National States: Competing Claims in East Asia', in Rudolph, H. and Piscatori, J. (eds), *Transnational Religions and Fading States*, Boulder, CO: Westview Press.

Connolly, W.E. (2005) *Pluralism*, Durham, NC: Duke University Press.

Das, V. (2006) *Life and Words: Exploring Violence and the Descent into the Ordinary*, Ewing, NJ: University of California Press.

Finucane, J. and Feener, R.M. (eds) (2013) *Proselytizing and the Limits of Pluralism in Contemporary Asia*, Singapore: Springer.

Fish, M.S. and Kroenig, M. (2006) 'Diversity, Conflict and Democracy: Some Evidence from Eurasia and East Europe', *Democratization*, 13(5): 828–42.

Fish, M.S. and Brooks, R.S. (2004) 'Does Diversity Hurt Democracy?', *Journal of Democracy* 15(1): 154–66.

Flathman, R.E. (2005) *Pluralism and Liberal Democracy*, Baltimore, MD: The Johns Hopkins University Press.

Furnivall, J.S. (1944) *Netherlands India: A Study of Plural Economy*, Cambridge, UK: Cambridge University Press.

Hefner, R. (ed.) (2001) *The Politics of Multiculturalism: Pluralism and Citizenship in Malaysia, Singapore, and Indonesia*, Honolulu: University of Hawai'i Press.

Huntington, S. (1968) *Political Order in Changing Societies*, New Haven, CT: Yale University Press.

Lai, A.E. (ed.) (2008) *Religious Diversity in Singapore*, Singapore: Lee Kuan Yew School of Public Policy, National University of Singapore, Institute of Policy Studies: Institute of Southeast Asian Studies.

Lee, J. (2010) *Islamization and Activism in Malaysia*, Singapore: ISEAS.

Mayaram, S. (2005) 'Living Together: Ajmer as a Paradigm for the (South) Asian City', in Hasan, M. and Roy, A. (eds), *Living Together Separately*, New Delhi: Oxford University Press.

Mayaram, S. (2009) 'Rereading Global Cities: Topographies of an Alternative Cosmopolitanism in Asia', in S. Mayaram (ed.) *The Other Global City*, London: Routledge.

McCargo, D. (2008) *Tearing Apart the Land*, Singapore: NUS Press.

McGilvray, D. (2008) *Crucible of Conflict: Tamil and Muslim Society on the East Coast of Sri Lanka*, Durham, NC: Duke University Press.

Nedilsky, L.V. (2009) 'Institutionalizing the Representation of Religious Minorities in Post-1997 Hong Kong', in Cheung, S.-K., Lee, J.T.-H. and Nedilsky, L.V. (eds) *Marginalization in China: Recasting Minority Politics,* Palgrave Macmillan.

Peletz, M. (2009) *Gender Pluralism: Southeast Asia since Early Modern Times,* New York: Routledge.

Reid, A. (2011) 'Many But One: The Paradox of Religious Pluralism in Southeast Asia', paper presented at the workshop 'Placing Religious Pluralism in Asia's Global Cities', Asia Research Institute, University of Singapore, 5–6 May.

Sidel, J. (2006) *Riots, Pogroms, Jihad*, Ithaca, NY: Cornell University Press.

Wilson, C. (2008) *Ethno-Religious Violence in Indonesia: From Soil to God*, London and New York: Routledge.

Part I

Pluralism and the state

2 Urbanization, civil society and religious pluralism in Indonesia and Turkey

Carool Kersten

This comparative study is part of a broader intellectual history of the Muslim world involving the formulation of alternative Islamic discourses by contemporary Muslim intellectuals. I have identified Indonesia and Turkey as two new cardinal points in the cartography of this innovative contemporary Muslim thinking, because both countries evince an important and perhaps crucial transformation in the outlook of religious intellectuals. Here I will primarily concentrate on the parallels between Indonesia and Turkey regarding new engagements with religion in the public sphere as a part of articulations of civil society in the Muslim world, which have begun to emerge at the close of the second and the beginning of the third millennium.

The choice of the term 'parallel' is deliberate, because tracing parallels strikes me as less reductionist than a search for similarities or commonalities. It will leave the most room for specific trajectories within culturally particular contexts of the two countries that are accommodative of a plurality of manifestations of religiosity and the simultaneous recognition of universal values, which characterizes the dispositions, attitudes, practices and modes of expression of these contemporary Muslim intellectuals. In spite of their wide geographical separation, vast cultural differences, and variance in religious factors influencing the establishment of the Turkish and Indonesian republics, I suggest that – between the mid-1980s and 1990s – it has become increasingly manifest that the divergent political-historical experiences of these two Muslim countries are converging onto closer parallel tracks in terms of redefining and expressing the role of religion in public life.

In the wake of the 1997 'Post-Modern' Coup in Turkey and in the course of Indonesia's Post-Suharto *Reformasi* era (begun in 1997–98), new Muslim or religious intellectuals in both countries have re-invented themselves yet again along alternative discursive lines. In Indonesia these ideas are presented under the rubrics of cultural, civil or cosmopolitan Islam predominantly by young cadres of the traditionalist Islamic mass organization the Nahdlatul Ulama (NU) or its youth wing, Anak Muda NU. Their newly formulated discourse is referred to as *Post-Traditionalisme* – or *Postra*, for short. The Turkish parallel is formed by a 'Post-Islamist' discursive formation articulated by religious intellectuals who have left behind their political agendas of the 1980s and early 1990s.

14   *Carool Kersten*

The efforts of these intellectuals have shaped an environment that is open to the creativity and capable of accommodating the plurality expected by upwardly mobile middle class Muslims as they explore their individual religiosity in the urban environments of megacities like Istanbul and Jakarta, as well as the smaller cities in the provinces. This finds its expression in new strands of Islamic thinking and a concomitant social activism.

A news website dealing with the contemporary Muslim world refers to both Turkey and Indonesia as 'laboratories' for experimentation in innovative interpretations of Islam, which can accommodate the cultural and religious diversity of an increasingly interconnected world (Parker 2011; Stahr 2009). In the wake of the seismic shifts in the political landscape during the Arab uprisings of 2011, Turkey, governed by the Justice and Development Party (Adalet ve Kalkınma Partisi, AKP) since 2002, has been turned into the new point of reference for the political future of the southern shores of the Mediterranean. These are not merely the conjectures of political pundits and Middle East watchers; also newly emerging activists and returning opposition leaders in Egypt and Tunisia have explicitly invoked Turkey as a source of inspiration.[1]

While it is understandable that only Turkey is invoked in projections of a so-called 'third way' – an alternative to both the deposed secular autocracies and the spectre of the rise of Islamist regimes in the Arab world – because of its proximity to the affected region, it makes sense to bring Indonesia into the picture as well. Detractors of the Turkish example reject the country's experimentation with combining democratization, economic development and religiously inspired social conservatism on the basis of the so-called Turkish exceptionalism thesis (Mardin 2005). They argue that Turkey's present political course is the outcome of the country's unique historical experience which cannot be replicated anywhere. This thesis can be undermined by pointing to the parallels between developments in Turkey and Indonesia, countering the proposition that Turkey forms the lone exception to the rule that Islam and democracy are not compatible. Developments in Indonesia offer yet another example of the transformative potential of religious intelligentsias throughout the Muslim world.

Geo-spatial and historical dimensions of contemporary parallels

An intellectual history of the contemporary Muslim world from an inter-regional perspective requires not only a timeline, but must also account for the spatial dimensions of the parallels it seeks to identify. Aside from an appreciation for the need to localize a world religion such as Islam through acculturation, it is also important to go beyond these confines and account for Turkey and Indonesia's geographical positioning in the wider Muslim world. Both countries find themselves on the peripheries of the *dar al-Islam*. Turkey is situated on the interstices of the Eastern Orthodox and Roman Catholic domains of historical Christendom, but also the nexus of the Shi'ite and Persianate worlds. It acts as a bridge between the Eastern Mediterranean and the Middle East, and – via the Black Sea and

Caucasus – a gateway into Central Asia. Indonesia takes up most of the Malay-Indonesian archipelago, an equatorial island world adjacent to Buddhist mainland Southeast Asia. Via the Indian Ocean and the South China Sea it is also directly connected to the provenances of the region's Indic traditions, its Confucianist-Taoist legacies, and the colonial Christian heritage of the Philippines, not to mention its direct exposure to missionary activities which continued into the post-colonial era. Thus both countries form nodal points in what some global historians have called the 'European and Asian Mediterraneans' (Guillot, Lombard and Ptak 1998).

While the developments of the last twenty-five years are key to explaining Post-Islamist and Post-Traditionalist discourses in today's Turkey and Indonesia, it is important to realise that their respective genealogies can be traced back to 'new opportunity spaces' that were created before that (Yavuz 2003: 25). Conceived as intellectual environments conducive to alternative Islamic discourses rather than a narrow understanding of a particular physical place, their contours can already be discerned in the 1950s and 1960s. Therefore, it is necessary to take a brief look at the formative years of the Turkish and Indonesian republics and political experiences in the middle of the twentieth century in order to appreciate the historicity of the shift from divergent trajectories onto parallel tracks from the 1980s onwards. Recognizing the potential volatility of the combustible ethnic and cultural-religious mixes of their respective populations, the infant Turkish and Indonesian republics opted for constitutions that kept religion at bay or defined it in neutral terms.

Turkey opted for a radically secular nationalist ideology generally referred to as Kemalism, which only allows a carefully circumscribed 'Lausannian Islam' (Yilmaz 2005: 285). Perceptive commentators note that this did not mean banning religion from the public sphere along the lines of French laicism, but rather bringing it under government control. In 1924 and 1925, the new regime abolished the caliphate, disbanded Sufi orders (*tariqa*) and closed traditional religious schools (*medrese*), but it also established a Presidency of Religious Affairs (*Diyanet*). These measures were accompanied by other legal reforms introducing European codes, the replacement of Arabic with Latin script, removal of references to Islam as the state religion and the prohibition of parties and societies on religious or sectarian bases (Yavuz 2003: 48–9).

During the Interbellum, Kemalist ideology had also exercised a considerable influence on secular nationalists fighting for independence of the Dutch East Indies (on this see also Formichi 2013). However, their leader Sukarno looked for a different accommodation of religion in post-colonial Indonesia. In 1945, he proclaimed the Pancasila, the 'Five Principles', as the new state's core political ideology. The first principle prescribes the obligation of a belief in 'One Supreme God', neutrally defined as *Ketuhanan Yang Maha Esa*. It retains religion as part of the public sphere, but limits recognition to major religious traditions, which were only in a later instance explicitly restricted to Islam, Catholicism, Protestantism, Buddhism, Hinduism and Confucianism, while denying Islamic law any official status. This remained so throughout the first two decades of independence. *Masyumi* (Majelis Syuro Muslim Indonesia), Indonesia's main

16   *Carool Kersten*

political Islamic party, campaigned in vain for the integration into the constitution of the so-called Jakarta Charter, stipulating that Muslim citizens were bound to by Islamic law, and was eventually disbanded in 1960 as part of Sukarno's 'Guided Democracy'. Any hopes for re-establishing the party after the 1965 coup against Sukarno and the take-over by the army-led *Orde Baru* or 'New Order' regime under Suharto, were quickly dashed. The new government's priority was to repair Indonesia's dismal economic situation and there was no place for political Islam in this policy.

Following the introduction of a multi-party system and the electoral victory of the Democrat Party (Demokrat Parti, DP) in 1950, post-war Turkey too entered an ambiguous period during which 'the reinfiltration of Islam into public life became quite apparent' (Yavuz 2003: 59). It was not so much the DP leadership as its grassroots support base that used the structural transformations affecting Turkish society, such as urbanization and educational reforms, to pursue a vernacular Islam expressing itself in the form of a 'spiritual or inward looking Islamic movement', predominantly inspired by Bediüzzaman Said Nursi. This former soldier turned Sufi had suffered brutal persecution during the first twenty-five years of the republic, but his writings had continued to circulate underground. Under the relatively liberal years of DP rule, his followers known as Nurcus turned these into a 'print-based Islamic discourse' that has continued to colour the religious outlook of subsequent generations of Turkish Muslims (Yavuz 2003: 151). The backlash came in the form of a military coup in 1960, which saw DP leaders not merely ousted from power and arrested, but eventually pay with their lives. For the two ensuing decades, there was 'a constant ambiguity and tension' in the republic's attitude towards Islam (Yavuz 2003: 64). The result was a fragmentation of the political field into the Kemalist 'deep state' with its paramount security concerns, an increasingly assertive leftish camp, Kurdish separatists, dissatisfied Alevis, and an increasingly alienated conservative sector of society.

In the face of the political repression throughout the twentieth century, Turkish and Indonesian Muslim activism in this time frame was therefore primarily found in the interstices of state and society. I am referring here to the formation of an Islamic education system under the auspices of designated government agencies such as Turkey's Diyanet and the Indonesian Ministry of Religious Affairs, as well as the activities of Islamic social movements.

Having closed the traditional *medreses*, the Law of Unification of Education of 1924 foresaw in the establishment of a limited number of so-called Imam-Hatip schools and a Faculty of Divinity to train functionaries for Diyanet's central organization and local mosques. In spite of the state's attempts to stamp out the Sufi infrastructure in the Turkish Republic, the Nakşibendi Order managed to survive by adapting itself to the new realities. Having accommodated themselves to the national-secular philosophy of the state, affiliates of what was formally a forbidden organization dominated religious positions on all levels in Diyanet. This way, the order provided 'the intellectual and historical groundwork for a new urban Islamic intellectual discourse' and the 'matrix of the majority of contemporary Turkish Muslim socio-political movements' (Yavuz 2003: 140).

The Indonesian situation is different. There, two Muslim mass organizations (the modernist Muhammadiyah, founded as early as 1912, and the traditionalist Nahdlatul Ulama, established in 1926) had already actively engaged in providing a religious education for Muslims as an alternative to colonial and post-independence secular state education. Between 1945 and 1960, the government – in cooperation with these two organizations and with Masyumi – introduced a number of initiatives to provide Indonesian Muslims also with a religious higher education system. By the 1960s, the country had two State Institutes of Islamic Studies (Institut Agama Islam Negeri, IAIN) in Jakarta and Yogyakarta modelled after Egypt's reformed al-Azhar University (Saeed 1999: 177–91).

There is another difference between the Turkish and Indonesian systems. Although the Turkish Imam-Hatip Schools constituted an alternative space and 'vital bridge between traditional Anatolian Society and the emergence of a confident and dynamic modern Islamic-oriented intellectual and business class', unlike Indonesia's IAINs they were not allowed to 'become sites for critical thinking and appreciation of divergent sub-Islamic cultures' (Yavuz 2003: 122). This situation would only change with the opening up of private education opportunities in the late 1990s.

From divergent trajectories towards convergent experiences: The Indonesian track

The ambitious economic development policy of Indonesia's army-controlled New Order regime foresaw a prominent non-martial role for the military referred to as *dwifungsi* – or 'double function'. It resembled the involvement of Turkey's top brass in lucrative business ventures generated by the étatist approach of Kemalist ideology towards industrialization, except that the Indonesian junta preceded its Turkish counterparts by more than a decade in finding a *modus vivendi* with a segment of the country's Muslim intelligentsia. The trio most prominently associated with this rapprochement were Mukti Ali, Harun Nasution, and Nurcholish Madjid. Their involvement heralded the shift from advocacy of an Islamic state by Masyumi's old guard towards a less doctrinal, more pragmatic, and certainly much intellectualized, redefinition of the relationship between state and religion in Indonesian society at the hands of a new generation of Muslim intellectuals.

Mukti Ali had received a combined Islamic and secular state education before leaving for postgraduate studies in Pakistan and Canada in the 1950s (Munhanif 1996: 85–91). Upon his return he became professor of comparative religion at IAIN Yogyakarta where he also ran a discussion group for budding Muslim intellectuals. When he was appointed Minister of Religious Affairs in 1971, Mukti Ali began formulating a 'Weberian' religious policy in which all religions would become involved in the socioeconomic development of the country (Steenbrink 1999: 185). In the face of a spectacular growth in conversions to Christianity during the 1950s and 1960s, he initiated an interfaith dialogue by establishing a Musyawarah Antar-Umat-Beragama, or Forum for Inter-Religious Consultation,

18   *Carool Kersten*

in 1972 (Munhanif 1996: 106–7). Mukti Ali was able to facilitate the educational reforms that provided the necessary preconditions for the emergence of a new Muslim intellectual capable of elaborating what in the Indonesian context is variably referred to as cultural, civil or cosmopolitan Islam. The concomitant redefinition of the IAIN curriculum fell to the newly appointed rector of IAIN Jakarta, Harun Nasution – like Mukti Ali, an alumnus of McGill University in Montreal. The programmatic transformation of Indonesia's Islamic higher education system was geared towards better preparing Muslims for participation in a rapidly changing and increasingly prosperous society – not only in terms of professional skills, but also to harness them mentally and spiritually.

As Mukti Ali and Nasution established themselves as the nestors of an inclusivist, pluralist Islam based on an open understanding and study of Muslim civilization, the most influential Muslim intellectual from the 1970s until the new millennium was Nurcholish Madjid, or Cak Nur as he is affectionately known. Born in the NU heartland of rural East Java, he moved to Jakarta to become a promising Muslim student leader. Initially regarded as the anointed successor of Masyumi leader Muhammad Natsir, he was soon vilified for his proposed radical renewal of Islamic thinking. This bold initiative advocated rationalization and secularization, but without equating that with Westernization, or falling into the trap of secularism. Nevertheless, he was disowned by the conventional Islamic modernists around Natsir and in the mid-1970s Madjid left Indonesia for postgraduate studies in America. Upon his return in 1984, he was an acknowledged scholar of Islam, and became a prolific writer, educationist, and public intellectual. By the time of his death in 2005 he was regarded as a *guru bangsa* or 'teacher of the nation' (Kersten 2011a: 45–89).

In Madjid's absence, significant changes had been set in motion in Indonesian society. In contrast with the political turmoil that began affecting the wider Muslim world between 1978 and 1988, Indonesia witnessed a further retreat of Islamism combined with a 'great leap forward in the social and intellectual vitality of the community' (Hefner 1997: 86). Much improved socioeconomic conditions had given a renewed drive to the activities of the Department of Religious Affairs. The policies from the mid-1980s onwards must be regarded as a response to an important side-effect of the economic boom: the emergence of a sizeable and now relatively prosperous urban Muslim middle class. Becoming increasingly uncomfortable with what they regarded as the narrowing or 'privatization' (*pribadisasi*) of moral concerns in the 1970s, the search for a new moral anchor in religion brought about a broad Islamic resurgence in civil society. It was in these circles that civil or cultural Islam began to manifest itself most spectacularly (Hefner 1997: 90–2). This led the then Minister of Religious Affairs (1983–93), Munawir Sjadzali, to draw up the so-called 'Reactualisation Agenda'. This approach envisaged giving the country's development policies a 'new theological underpinning' by emphasizing 'the holistic nature of Islam' and the 'dynamism and vitality of Islamic law', while at the same time taking account of 'Indonesia's own local and temporal particularities' (Effendy 1995: 110–11). With the booming metropolitan regions of Indonesia at the centre of this advancing cultural Islam, and the

Indonesia and Turkey: urbanization and pluralism 19

universities acting as its vanguard, it is not surprising that a further expansion of the country's Islamic higher education system formed an important part of Sjadzali's programme. A crucial new dimension was added by the decision to use the financial windfall of the 1970s oil boom to send substantial numbers of talented Muslim students overseas for postgraduate studies in North America, Australia and Europe, as well as the Middle East (including Turkey). By the late 1980s, the number of young scholars returning from abroad with advanced degrees in Islamic or religious studies was surging, creating a new Muslim intellectual elite concentrated at the IAINs in Jakarta, Yogyakarta and new campuses established throughout the country (Hefner 1997: 86–9).

In spite of Indonesia's political homogenization following New Order's 1984 reaffirmation of the Pancasila, the combined effect of a slightly more relaxed political climate, economic affluence, and a reawakened religious awareness also led to the formation of a new political–Islamic paradigm, under which approved political parties and the top brass of the military hierarchy began establishing their piety (Abdullah 1996: 53–63). In 1991 even President Suharto joined in, demonstrating his own commitment to Islam by making the pilgrimage to Mecca. Green being the symbolic colour of Islam, this process was called the 'greening' (*penghijauan*) of Indonesian society. The renewed salience of Islam in Indonesian public life and its acceptance in government circles was formalized through the establishment of the Indonesian Muslim Intellectual Association or Ikatan Cendekiawan Muslim se-Indonesia (ICMI), under presidential patronage and chaired by Suharto's protégé and successor, B. J. Habibie.

The two key domestic social phenomena that have conditioned Indonesia's Islamization are growing prosperity and urbanization. With the economic boom, increasing numbers of peasants left the rural areas for the cities in search of education and jobs. Those who managed to acquire the necessary skills began entering a burgeoning middle class. However the benefits of greater material wealth were offset by the stress of professional competition, high-density urban living, and tensions between the traditional rural lifestyle and exposure to diverse cultural interactions. 'For the middle classes, cities were at once stimulating, broadening and enriching, but also unsettling, threatening and alienating' (Fealy 2008: 27). At the same time, the external element that 'added frisson' to this mix was globalization. It was in particular this emergent class of relatively well-to-do and technologically literate city dwellers who had the greatest exposure to globalizing forces, through access to new information sources such as satellite television and the internet, their opportunity for regular interaction with a wide array of individuals, groups and movements found in large, internationally connected metropolises, and – finally – thanks to their opportunities to travelling abroad. This too 'has a profound effect on identity formation and consumption patterns in urban area' (Fealy 2008: 27).

The ensuing socioeconomic, cultural, and technological changes are responsible for what is called the commodification of Islam: a process that has been characterized as 'strengthening an individualised form of Islam in which established institutions or figures are less influential than they once were' (Fealy 2008:

20　*Carool Kersten*

16). This is only partially so. The new opportunity spaces are not only filled by new exponents of religiosity, such as televangelists and the commercialization of religion; well-established organizations such as the Muhammadiyah and the NU have managed to reinvent themselves and remain relevant. More importantly, especially younger cadres from these organizations responded proactively, tapping into this market of rapidly changing 'new cultural forms and intellectual trends' (Fealy 2008: 27).

Even the old Islamist establishment has been able to make a comeback of sorts through the expanding activities of the religious propagation organization Dewan Dakwah Islamiyah Indonesia (DDII), or Indonesian Council for Islamic Propagation. Initially led by Muhammad Natsir and later by Muhammad Rasjidi, the organization benefitted from the old Maysumi's excellent international network and close connections with the Saudi Arabia-based World Muslim League. The Dewan Dakwah has exercised considerable influence on the emergence of the 'so-called "Campus Islam" phenomenon', its key exponent being the Salman Mosque of the Bandung Institute of Technology (Hasan 2009). These proponents of Salafi-inspired Islamism were also hostile to the reform of the IAIN curriculum and the policy of sending Muslim students to universities in North America, Europe, and Australia for further study. Thus they succeeded in turning Islamic education, once again, into a contentious issue. In 1996 they successfully lobbied the government, obtaining both a Memorandum of Understanding for student exchanges with Saudi Arabia, and securing approval for the opening of branches of al-Azhar University on IAIN campuses. However, given the decline of al-Azhar's reputation, the government decided also to explore alternative forms of Islamic education in India, Iran, and Malaysia.

While these advocates of an overt Islamist agenda are very vocal, stressing the outward manifestations of the Islamic revival, such as the performance of obligatory rituals and close observance of other religious prescriptions (including dress codes), Julia Howell has rightly pointed to the fact that this has drawn much attention away from the parallel increased popularity of spiritual expressions of Islamic religiosity (Howell 2001). Sufi-inspired piety and devotionalism is not only alive and well within traditional contexts, but – as an integral part of the commodification of religion – has also been repackaged as neo-Sufism, urban Sufism, *tasawuf positif*, practical Sufism and this-worldly mysticism (Howell 2001: 721–2).[2] The outlets for this intellectualized Sufism were 'adapted to a variety of new institutional forms in urban settings', utilizing 'such international cultural forms' as foundations, institutes, seminars, courses and workshops (Howell 2001: 718). The Muslim intellectual *avant-garde* associated with Nurcholish Madjid played a prominent role in the dissemination of this new breed of Sufism. Some of them belonged to the *Mazhab Ciputat*, or Ciputat School, a reference to the suburb where Jakarta's IAIN is located. Among its members was the university's present rector, the philosopher Komaruddin Hidayat, who had obtained his doctorate from Middle East Technical University in Turkey (Kull 2005: 210–12).

In this highly competitive environment, Madjid had managed to remain at the forefront of this robust cultural Islam, fine-tuning his renewal thinking from the

1970s by introducing a more sophisticated and confidently assertive anti-hegemonic subculture more firmly grounded in the Islamic tradition. His ideas from the late 1980s, and throughout the 1990s, strike a balance between the universal aspects of Islam's doctrinal teachings and the Muslim world's cosmopolitanism, consisting in a civilization that was capable of accommodating the cultural particularities of its various composite regions. His initiatives were designed to subvert the dominant position of the Javanese *priyayi* aristocratic elites and their relative disregard for the Islamic components of Javanese culture. For this purpose, Madjid began extending his activities outside academia, focusing on the increasingly affluent urban Muslim middle class professionals and government technocrats. As a vehicle for this proselytization among the elites he founded in 1986 the Yayasan Paramadina, or Paramadina Foundation. The choice of name was deliberate as it conjures up associations with both a generic urban polity and the historical pluralist community arising in the city of the Prophet, Medina on basis of the so-called 'Medina charter', which Madjid frequently invokes when discussing Indonesian pluralism (Kull 2005: 164). A special unit within the foundation, called the Klub Kajian Agama, or Religious Study Group, became the vehicle for religious seminars targeting Indonesia's Muslim elites.

From divergent trajectories towards convergent experiences: The Turkish track

In the Turkey of 1960s, another Nakşibendi sub-branch known as the Gümüşhaveni Nakşibendi led by Shaykh Mehmet Zahid Kotku rose to prominence. In spite of the fact that he was a traditional Islamic establishment figure, to some degree Kotku's views resonated with those of worldly intellectual Nurcholish Madjid, because he too regarded Islam as 'a repository of moral arguments' and stressed 'both religious (*uhrevi*) and worldly liberation (*felah*)' (Yavuz 2003: 142). But there were also differences – Madjid's associates became involved in government policy-making or providing spiritual training to bureaucrats and technocrats, whereas Kotku encouraged his followers to opt for mercantile careers rather than joining government service, creating the conditions for transmitting Nakşibendi Sufism to the new urban culture and turning his order into 'the incubator of the post-war generation of prominent Islamist intellectuals' (Yavuz 2003: 141). Although he kept a distance from politics, some of his followers played a crucial role in the formation of the pro-Islamist National Outlook Movement or Milli Görüş Hareketi. The Gümüşhaveni branch can be considered as a kind of matrix of contemporary Turkish-Islamic social-political movements and a string of Islamist parties led by the engineer Necmettin Erbakan.

The Milli Görüş Hareketi played a vital role in integrating large, marginalized sections of Anatolian Turkish society into the political processes by catering to their inclusive identity, which remained rooted in a more pluralist Ottoman-Islamic tradition as opposed to the homogenizing Kemalist state ideology (Yavuz 2003: 208). Nowhere was this marginalization and alienation felt more acutely than among rural and small-town migrants to major cities such as Ankara and

22   Carool Kersten

Istanbul. Living in satellite squatter-towns known as *gecekondu,* these places became the geo-cultural spaces for new mixed rural-urban subcultures, which not only contrasted sharply with the lifestyles of the Westernized urban elites shaped by decades of exposure to Kemalism and in their view not yet integrated rural 'newcomers', but also reflected the ideological fragmentation of Turkish society into leftist, right-wing, socially conservative, and ethnic-religious Kurdish and Alevi camps (Karaosmanoğlu 2005: 81; Yavuz 2003: 83).

Faced with increasingly violent political activism from various directions, the military, then led by General Kenan Evren, decided to step in, leading to the 1980 *coup d'état.* This military intervention can be considered the watershed event in the convergence of the Turkish and Indonesian Islamic discourses in the last quarter of the century. Evren was the first senior military officer to present Islam as a 'legitimizing counterweight' to the ideological fragmentation of Turkish society or, more specifically, as the 'antidote to communism'. Underlining the rational nature of Islam, this religion was capable of promoting modernity and acting as a 'unifying agent or social cement' (Yavuz 2003: 69–70). The new military-dominated regime translated this new salience of religion into a 'Turkish-Islamic Synthesis' through which it sought to 'diffuse the growing conflict between Sunnis and Alevis on the one hand and Kurdish nationalists and the state on the other' (Yavuz 2003: 69–70).[3] Although one could argue that the armed forces in Turkey preceded their Indonesian counterparts by having a military strongman flaunt his personal piety, they lagged behind their Southeast Asian peers in terms of making a liberal economic policy an integral part of the Islamization of Turkish society.

That component was only added with the rise to power of Turgut Özal, an American-trained engineer and civil servant who was put in charge of economic policy, first as deputy prime minister and prime minister, and then, in 1989, as successor of Evren to the presidency. A technocrat, Özal was also a pious Muslim with close links to Mehmet Zahid Kotku (Özal 1999). Emphasizing 'the merchant ethics of the Prophet Muhammad and try[ing] to fuse these with the values of modern capitalism', he became the architect of a highly successful neoliberal economic policy founded on privatization and support for entrepreneurship (Yavuz 2003: 95). This hybrid background enabled him to define new opportunity spaces mixing free enterprise with Islamic morality, and thus turn 'the market into a space for identity formation' (Yavuz 2003: 92). Forging an alliance between new Anatolian industrialists, intellectuals and Islamic groups, Özal was instrumental to the formation of MÜSAID, the Independent Industrialists' and Businessmen Association. As manifestations of a Turkish version of cultural Islam, they represented a nascent civil society, while their economic independence enabled them 'to offer diverse and original interpretations of Islam to the public' (Yavuz 2003: 96).

The combined effect of this military-supported recalibration of Turkish politics and the replacement of state capitalism with a market-driven economy with the financial backing of 'green capital' was the emergence of a 'postmodern urbanism' reflected by the rise of global cities and the formation of new cultural identities (Karaosmanoğlu 2005: 3, 83, 136–8).

The outcome of this process is manifested in four new phenomena: the increased visibility of religious and ethnic elements in these global cities; the fragmentation of the once official, homogenous centre of the republic; the proliferation of media outlets and emergence of new media; the enormous expansion of private education initiatives. The most successful operator in these last two areas is the rather amorphous neo-Nur *Cemaat* or Gülen movement – a loose network of individual initiatives, associations and foundations named after a former Diyanet imam and preacher, Fethullah Gülen, which has become the subject of growing outpour of scholarly writings (Yavuz 2003: 189–94).

The common denominator in all this is the central place allocated to human agency. The negotiations surrounding this search for new cultural identity or alternative identity formation place the onus on the individual urban Muslim. Individualism implies choice and decision-making under conditions of a plurality of both meaning and options for social action, because aside from the social aspects identified earlier, this pluralization also extends to what Appadurai calls the 'ideoscape' (Appadurai 1996: 33–7).

Özal's entrepreneurial flair and anti-bureaucratism, combined with a pro-Islamic attitude and personal charisma, foreshadowed the arrival of a new type of Turkish Muslim intellectual. An earlier generation had still received their religious formation in the underground Sufi networks and retained a quietist political attitude. The new generation, referred to in Turkey as 'modern Islamic intellectuals', differs from the traditionalist religious scholars because – like secular intellectuals – they draw on the critical traditions of both the West and the Islamic world to challenge the established political and social order. Thus, these 'Islamic intellectuals act like cultural entrepreneurs in the construction and externalization of an Islamic political consciousness in Turkish society' (Yavuz 2003: 112).

Like Indonesia's new Muslim intellectuals, the modern Islamic intellectuals in Turkey began advocating a vernacularization of Islam into the country's social, cultural and political context. However, unlike Indonesians such as Mukti Ali, Harun Nasution, Nurcholish Madjid, and the *Mazhab Ciputat*, one segment of the emergent Turkish Muslim intelligentsia was associated with the Islamic parties led by Erbakan, while others continued to hold on to the quietist attitudes of the Nakşibendis. Engaged in the literary field, poets and novelists – as well as founders and contributors of new periodicals – were inspired by earlier figures such as Necip Fazil Kisakürek, Nurettin Topçu. Young intellectuals such as Sezai Karakoç, Hayderrin Karaman and Nuri Pakdil wanted to demonstrate that Islam was not from the 'backward periphery', and pursued this goal modifying Islamic concepts and reformulating them in line with modern demands of identity and ethics, using the collective memory of Islamic tradition and history. Using the Ottoman past as their frame of reference, 'they did not treat Islam strictly as a religion but rather as a civilization' (Yavuz 2003: 114). Very similar to the attempts of Indonesia's Islamic *avant garde* to recast Sufism as this-worldly mysticism, in Turkey too, a new Muslim literary elite began to develop who 'created a language that merged Islamic esoteric traditions of inner dimensionality with the outward modern idiom of individuality' (Yavuz 2003: 115).

24   *Carool Kersten*

Subsequently, there emerged what Yavuz has dubbed the 'Islamic Skeptics' or 'post-modern' Muslims because of their comprehensive epistemological critique, which simultaneously challenges the Kemalist project and the glorification of the Ottoman past by their Islamic intellectual predecessors (Yavuz 2003: 118). Instead, these religious intellectuals who include such figures as Rasim Özdenören, İsmet Özel, and Ali Bulaç, offer an alternative vision for a new future in which individual Muslims act as individual agents for positive change and self-liberation. It is because of this emphasis on human agency that the accuracy of the characterization post-modern can also be called into question, because the focus of both Foucauldian discursive formations and Derrida's post-structuralist deconstruction of texts often does away with autonomous actors. It might there-fore make more sense to qualify them as post-colonial thinkers or even – as Cemil Aydin has suggested – Occidentalists (Aydin 2006: 456).

Illustrative of this new strand of Turkish Islamic thinking is the work of Ali Bulaç, who is generally regarded as the most influential representative of his generation (Guida 2010: 348; Lapidot 1995: 145; Yavuz 2003: 119). With first-hand experience of the changes brought about by Turkey's rapid urbanization and the impact this had on society at large, but especially on its individual members, Bulaç described this migration to the major cities as 'the biggest trauma of recent history for Turkey' (Guida 2010: 354). Born into an Arabic-speaking family in Mardin, he received his primary education at an illegal Qur'an school and then went on to study at an Imam-Hatip high school. During his advanced studies in sociology at Istanbul University he became acquainted with the writings of Muhammad Iqbal, Maududi, and Sayyid Qutb, but he was especially influenced by Ali Shariati (Aydin 2006: 454; Guida 2010: 353). Also other Iranian thinkers such as Jalal Al-e Ahmad, Daryush Shayegan and Seyyed Hossein Nasr had a strong impact on Turkey's new Muslim intellectuals. Together they were very important for the development of a comparable anti-Western Occidentalist discourse.

In spite of being the co-founder of *Düşünce*, a magazine affiliated with Erbakan's National Salvation Party and sympathetic to Egypt's Muslim Brotherhood, already by the mid-1980s Bulaç was becoming disenchanted with this strand of Islamism. In his view, 'the Arab world produced only militancy that does not really fit the post-1980 Turkish democratic trend' (Guida 2010: 354). Thus Bulaç moved into a similar direction as thinkers such as Mohammed Arkoun and Hasan Hanafi by becoming engaged in 'a double critique of both the Islamic legacy and the dominant Western culture' (Lapidot 1995: 149).[4] On the back of the earlier noted commodification of Islam which began to affect Turkey too, Bulaç similarly became an Islamic entrepreneur. He was involved in the foundation of the publishing house *Insan* and the *Zaman* newspaper, before joining the publisher *Birleşek* as an editor for one of its magazines (Guida 2010: 352; Lapidot 1995: 146). This enabled Bulaç to become one of the relatively few Turkish intellectuals who can make a living solely from his writings (Yavuz 2003: 111).

In spite of including Western culture in his overall critique, Bulaç is not entirely dismissive of what he calls the other 'invitational' religions – Judaism

Indonesia and Turkey: urbanization and pluralism   25

and Christianity – although he insists that, in contrast to the other two, Islam 'has never abandoned its struggle against the corrupt and unjust status quo' (Lapidot 1995: 155). In another instance, his writings betray a perennialist streak, as he 'recognized that Islam and all other religions, traditions and cultures were equally *hikmets* (wisdoms), virtues and truths' (Guida 2010: 355). While seemingly counterintuitive, Bulaç uses the core Islamic dogma of *tawhid* (unity) as the root for all other principles to argue for both social and ideological pluralism (Lapidot 1995: 164–5). Like Nurcholish Madjid, Bulaç frequently invoked the Medina Constitution or Medina charter as a blueprint for political and social transformation, 'paving the way to a pluralist accord (Kadioğlu 1998: 16). However, Bulaç's main concern remains with 'the present state of Islamic thought and Muslim intellectuals', and the fact that not until the 1960s, was there a discernable return to the Qur'an and the Sunna and purification from Westernized ideas. An affirmation of authentic Muslim identity meant therefore a rejection of 'man-made systems of control such as imperialism, colonialism and nationalism' (Lapidot 1995: 167).

And yet, although critical of Western thinking, Bulaç is sympathetic to Marxist and socialist ideas. The writings of one of Bulaç's students suggest that his thinking can be characterized as a form of Islamic Liberation Theology, because the four themes of the Latin American Christian counterpart – ideology critique, dependency theory, humans as the subject of history, and a focus on the poor and oppressed – are all present in Ali Bulaç's work (Lapidot 1995: 149).[5] He also agreed with Shariati that 'leadership should be transferred to the "enlightened thinker" from within the people and not necessarily from the ranks of the *ulema*' (Lapidot 1995: 168–9).

In the course of the last decade or so, Bulaç's thought has undergone yet another transformation which brings him, and other new religious intellectuals in Turkey, closer to the outlook of Indonesians such as Nurcholish Madjid, Abdurrahman Wahid, and representatives of ensuing generations, who are unequivocally propagating that Islam is compatible with universal values of human rights and democracy, regardless of the provenance of their initial formulation. Instrumental to this reorientation of Turkish Muslim intellectuals such as Bulaç, and to the spread of this transformed interpretation of Islam, was the re-emergence of the Nurcus, and in particular the plethora of Neo-Nur organizations gravitating around the figure of Fethullah Gülen, on the back of the introduction of the Turkish-Islamic Synthesis in 1983.

Whereas the custodians of Said Nursi's immediate legacy had turned the publication of his writings into a vast printing and new media enterprise, his adept Fethullah Gülen reworked the Nurcu legacy in his own particular fashion. From its modest beginnings in the late 1960s at a privately-run *Kestanepazari Qur'an* (Qur'an study centre *cum* dormitory), sympathisers and followers of the *Hoçaeffendi* turned the movement into a key provider of quality private education from pre-school to the tertiary level, in both Turkey and abroad. This was regarded as an integral part of Gülen's 'activist pietism' or 'theology of action' translated into the principles of *Hizmet* (service to religion and state), *Himmet*

26   Carool Kersten

(donations and good works), and *İhlas* (seeking God's appreciation for every action) (Yavuz 2003: 185–7). Aside from education, the two other fields of action are the market and the media. Starting with the purchase of *Zaman* newspaper (in 1986), activities have since expanded into specialist periodicals and academic journals, TV and radio stations (in 1993), as well as think-tanks and discussion formers, such as the Writers and Journalists Association (in 1994), the Abant Platform and the Intercultural Dialogue Platform (in 1997) (Ebaugh 2010: 83–101; Yavuz 2003: 188–92).

Turning points for a new future? The aftermath of Turkey's post-modern coup and the fall of New Order in Indonesia

At the dawn of the new millennium, the late 1990s heralded the latest crucial turn in the way the role of religion has been interpreted in contemporary Turkey and Indonesia. The turmoil affecting Turkey's political landscape in the aftermath of the military intervention against the coalition government led by Necmettin Erbakan in February 1997 and the collapse of Indonesia's New Order Regime after Suharto's resignation on 20 May 1998, created a very fluid situation in both countries as they were led into the twenty-first century. In Turkey coalition governments came and went, while an equally instable Indonesian government led by the former leader of the Nahdlatul Ulama, the mercurial intellectual Abdurrahman Wahid, failed to restore law and order. His premiership saw bloodshed between Muslims and Christians in Moluccas, Javanese trans-migrants and autochthonous populations of other outer Islands, and violence by radical Islamic vigilantes against perceived deviant sects. In both instances it showed how delicate was the balance that kept both countries tilted towards a degree of tolerance even in the face of an increased salience of Islam in the public sphere.

Eventually Turkey underwent a political sea change. The main reason for this was a drastic rethinking and restructuring within the Islamist camp. This was necessitated by what researchers have called the 'securitization of Islam' (Yavuz 2003: 239). Between April 1997 and January 1998 the military introduced a major reorientation of its strategic concept, shifting from fighting Kurdish separatism and defence against interstate warfare to declaring 'reactionary Islam' as the main enemy of the state. In first instance, this decision resulted in 'the shrinking of political, economic, and cultural opportunity spaces' (Yavuz 2003: 245–6).

Consequently, by the late 1990s two camps were clearly discernible within the besieged Virtue Party (*Fazilet Partisi*) as the successor of the outlawed Welfare Party (Refah Partisi): (1) an old guard around Necmettin Erbakan, which wanted to stay on the old course, and (2) an upcoming younger generation of politicians gravitating around the former mayor of Istanbul Recip Tayyip Erdoğan and the parliamentarian Abdullah Gül. These 'Young Turks' of the twenty-first century wanted to navigate a different course. Instead of the conventional Islamist agenda, stressing Islamic symbolism and formal aspects of Islamic law, they emphasized universal democratic values and standards of human rights, combined with a neoliberal economic policy reminiscent of the Özal years. In

Indonesia and Turkey: urbanization and pluralism 27

2001 a split became unavoidable; while the conservative faction founded the Felicity Party (*Saadet Partisi*), the reformists led by Erdoğan and Gül established the Justice and Development Party (AKP). The party's electoral successes since 2002 took all observers by surprise: political pundits and other Turkey watchers often seem still at a loss and frequently disagree on how to assess the AKP and what to make of its agenda.[6] Not fitting into the neat categories defining Turkish politics since the 1970s, the AKP's hybrid identity 'is a sign of the constitution of a new social center and the socialization of the political center with the new hybrid ideas of nationalism, Islam, and Westernism' (Yavuz 2003: 259).

Like Turkey after the 'post-modern coup' of 1997, post-New Order Indonesia has also seen a pluralization of political actors, accompanied by the undeniable polarization of the political arena. At the turn of the century, voters in both countries were spoilt for choice: In the three elections since the fall of Suharto five different parties running on an Islamic ticket have managed to make the threshold for obtaining seats in Indonesia's parliament. Although small in absolute numbers, the most interesting to watch is the Prosperous Justice Party (*Partai Keadilan Sejahtera, PKS*). Although more Islamist in orientation and allegedly having Muslim Brotherhood connections, its very name is remarkably similar to the Justice and Development which created the seismic shift in Turkey's political landscape. Moreover, the observation by one international relations' specialist that the rise of the PKS 'terrified the secular as well as moderate Islamic parties' mirrors the concern of both Kemalists and conservative Islamists in Turkey (Soğuk 2011: 160).

Amidst all the political uncertainties, and somewhat away from the fracas, the 'urban rehabilitation of Sufism' has managed to sustain itself (Howell 2001: 710). On the one hand, it has resulted in a further diversification and the deepening of its intellectual dimensions. On the other hand, this-worldly spiritualism also has been further commodified, especially as the further advancement of information technology has widened the scope for televangelism, the emergence of religiously coloured media conglomerates, and a massive expansion of private Islamic education as a result of liberal and open mark economic policies.

Almost coinciding with the dismantling of the New Order Regime following the resignation of President Suharto, Nurcholish Madjid extended the ambit of the Paramadina Foundation by establishing a private university under the name Universitas Paramadina Mulia. Individuals from Madjid's entourage began deploying their own initiatives to corner what was becoming a lucrative 'spiritual' or 'divine supermarket'. Ahmad Gaus, a communications specialist and former chief publishing editor with the Paramadina Foundation, helped establish the Intensive Course and Networking for Islamic Sciences, which operated from within Syarif Hidayatullah Islamic State University in Jakarta (Hasan 2009: 239; Howell 2001: 720). For many years he worked closely together with the already mentioned Komaruddin Hidayat, a former member of the Ciputat School who had studied philosophy in Turkey.

After serving as executive director of Madjid's Paramadina Foundation, Hidayat rose through the ranks of academia and the religious bureaucracy, working his way up to Professor of Philosophy at both Driyarkara School of

Philosophy and the State Islamic University of Jakarta. He also served as head of the university's centre for Contemporary Islamic Development Studies, and as director of tertiary education at the Ministry of Religious Affairs. In 2006 he became the university's rector and a patron of the Paramadina Foundation. Aside from his work in higher education administration, he remains a prolific writer, working as a columnist for *Kompas*, contributor to a host of other periodicals, and editor of books on perennial philosophy, hermeneutics and comparative religion and interfaith dialogue. Making frequent appearances on television, individuals such as Hidayat represent an Indonesian Televangelism 'in a Higher Register' than that of celebrity media personalities such as Aa Gym or Arifin Ilham. In a study of contemporary expressions of Islamic piety in Indonesia, Hidayat was foregrounded as one of the country's leading 'professor-preachers', alongside Quraish Shihab and Jalaluddin Rakhmat (Howell 2008: 48).

Emulating the pioneering efforts of Nurcholish Madjid, in 1997, Dr Jalaluddin Rakhmat, an Australian-educated academic based in Bandung and director of the Mutahhari Foundation, founded *Tazkiya Sejati*, which incorporated aspects of Shi'a Islam in its theosophist interpretation of Sufism (Hasan 2009: 239; Howell 2001: 721). Other spin-offs also include organizations that have translated this-worldly salvation into agendas of social and political activism. In fact, in the last twenty years, Indonesia has witnessed a proliferation of think-tanks, research institutes, and NGOs catering to ever better educated and well-to-do urban Muslims.

One such initiative is the Liberal Islam Network or Jaringan Islam Liberal. It was established in 1999 by two young scholars, Ulil Abshar-Abdalla and Luthfi Assayaukanie, with the objective to safeguard the legacy of Nurcholish Madjid and defend his interpretation of a pluralist Islam against the challenges of Islamist discourses (Harjanto 2003; Nurdin 2005). In 2003, the International Center of Islam and Pluralism (ICIP) was founded with a mission to establish a network of Islamic Non-Governmental Organizations and progressive-moderate Muslim activists and intellectuals' from Indonesia, Malaysia, Bangladesh, Thailand and the Philippines (interview with Syafii Anwar, Director of ICIP, Jakarta, 12 May 2011). A year after the death of Nurcholish Madjid in 2006, Anas Urbaningrum was appointed the new chairman of the Paramadina Foundation. Urbaningrum started his public career in 1997 in the same function as Madjid had thirty years earlier: as chairman of the Islamic Students Society (HMI). After shepherding the organization through the tumultuous transition from New Order to *Reformasi*, he turned his interest to politics, serving on several commissions preparing free elections. Since then he has become one of the leading members of President Susilo Bambang Yudhoyono's Democratic Party, ascending to the position of chairman in 2009 at the relatively young age of forty.

Other intellectuals with close links to the Nahdlatul Ulama have established institutions and NGOs that seek to preserve the legacy of their former chairman and president of the Republic, the late Abdurrahman Wahid, as well as coordinate grassroots level initiatives for the betterment of living conditions of less prosperous Muslims. These include the Wahid Institute and the US-supported LibforAll Foundation, as well as the NU-affiliated NGOs Human Resources Development

Indonesia and Turkey: urbanization and pluralism 29

and Study Institute (Lakpesdam), and the Center for Pesantren and Community Development (P3M) (Sirry 2010).

Closely associated with these latter two bodies is a new generation of intellectuals, who are referred to as Anak Muda NU or Post-Traditionalists, mentioned at the beginning of this chapter. They include individuals, such as Ahmad Baso, Ahmad Rumadi, and Zuhairi Misrawi, who have begun to critically examine and reformulate the ideas of their former mentors. Conversant with post-modern and post-colonial thinking, as well as philosophers and text critics from elsewhere in the Muslim world, such as Muhammad Abed al-Jabiri, Abdullahi an-Na'im and Nasr Hamid Abu Zayd, their critiques not only challenge the inconsistent argumentations and lack of academic rigour in the work of their predecessors, but even accuse them of complacency and complicit post-colonialism, which has enabled the political elites to perpetuate the *status quo* that is hampering true progress in the Muslim world (Kersten 2010, 2011b).

Against the background of the earlier sketched reconfiguration of the political arena, Turkey's Islamic intellectual scene was also transformed. On the back of the penetration of the Gülen Movement into Turkish civil society starting in the 1980s and the political success of the AKP, the new religious intellectuals who had formulated the Occidentalist narratives of Islamism from the mid-1980s onwards were forced to reinvent themselves as 'post-Islamists' advocating universal standards of human rights and democracy grounded in a rethinking of the role of the West as the best guarantee for safeguarding the particularities associated with Muslim religiosity (Aydin 2006; Daği 2004, 2005).

This hermeneutical turn is reflected in the changed attitude of Ali Bulaç. After initial disagreements with the editorial policies at *Zaman*, following the conglomerate's take-over by Alaattin Kaya (a businessman with ties to the Gülen *Cemaat*), Bulaç temporarily left to work for other newspapers. However a few years later he 'went back to *Zaman* and became closer to Fethullah Gülen's organization, as evidenced by his recent writings' (Guida 2010: 352). In 2003, he published a book entitled *Blessed Tree: Fethullah Gülen in the World of Intellectuals*, and in a 2005 editorial, he presented him as an 'enlightened alim' of the same standing as Said Nursi, Maududi and Sayyid Qutb (!) because of his profound knowledge of Islamic and Western sciences (Guida 2010: 352, 368). While still reflecting an admixture of his earlier Islamist convictions, Ali Bulaç's new post-Islamist positions seem to gel much better with the advocacy of liberalism, secularization, and pluralism by Indonesia's Post-Traditionalist intellectuals and their mentors. Whereas in Turkey, the AKP government and its civil society support base are engaged in a constant and very precarious balancing act with the constitutional heritage of Kemalism, Indonesia's Muslim intellectuals are joining a broad spectrum civic coalition that unequivocally reaffirmed the republic's foundational ideology of Pancasila. On 1 June 2006, they delivered the *Maklumat Keindonesiaan* or 'Declaration of Indonesian-ness' in front of President Susilo Bambang Yudhoyono who responded by stating that the 'Pancasila is not to be disputed or challenged', but also that 'Indonesia is a state "with God" [...] [where] religion is practised in a civilized manner' (Raillon 2011:101)

30   *Carool Kersten*

Conclusion

The dialectical relationship between the salience of religion and the concomitant commodification of Islam applies in equal measure to the situations in both Indonesia and Turkey. As 'both a product of and causal factor in accelerating religiosity', this commodification is characterized by a set of differing features and consequences. Whereas the ethical certitudes and safe comfort associated with the lives of earlier generations in the small towns and villages of rural Turkey and Indonesia have been eroded by modern urban lifestyles and have led to cultural alienation and even a kind of religious disorientation – what Turner has called the 'destabilisation of religious identity' – it has certainly also contributed to new identity formations along the lines of increasingly individualized and intellectualized ways of expressing Islamic religiosity (Turner 2007: 35). Obviously, this appears to affect more heavily those who have only recently joined the upward socially mobile middle classes in metropoles, rather than established elite urbanites.

This sense of alienation is further exacerbated by the sheer complexity of the ideological ramifications, as existing organizations such as Nakşibendis and NU, Muhammadiyah and Nurcus are joined by Salafis of various provenances. In spite of growing competition, the identification of a resilient inward-looking yet this-worldly spiritual Islamic movement by Howell, a decade ago, also seems still valid. In *Expressing Islam*, Greg Fealy noted that the dominance of 'pluralist patterns of Islamic consumption' in Indonesia is also found in 'other rapidly modernising and Islamising societies'. Invoking Jenny White's assessment of the situation in Turkey, which suggests that commodification has 'led to the "Muslimisation" rather than "Islamisation" of public life, with the middle classes increasingly concerned to present themselves as Muslim rather than Islamist', is very similar to what has transpired in Indonesia (Fealy 2008: 35). The Turkish Islamist movement has transformed into a 'hybrid modern urban – community – and value-based political process' (Smith 2005: 318). In the same vein, Turkish analysts have noted a transmutation in the identification and self-referencing among young Turkish Muslims from *dinci,* meaning 'religionist' (read: Islamist), to *dindar* or 'devout'. Both are presented in contrast to the somewhat archaic *mütedeyyin*, 'denoting elderly, wise, and apolitical pious Muslims' (Saktanber 2007: 419; Genel and Karaosmanoğlu 2006: 478).

There has also been a critique as to whether the commodification of Islam, which accompanied the 'Greening' of Indonesian society, has resulted in a shallower or richer Islam. Intellectuals and traditional Islamic scholars shared a certain disdain for the new manifestations of Islamic practice and identity exemplified by TV preacher such as Aa Gym. For example, the former Muhammadiyah chairman Ahmad Syafii Maarif once commented that 'the "new" pious (*santri*) Muslims are more concerned with *looking* Islamic than they are with *being* Islamic' (Fealy 2008: 36). Notwithstanding such concerns and reservations, the young Muslim intellectuals who are now questioning traditional interpretations of Indonesian Islam, whether they advocate Islamist or liberal Muslim agendas, 'are part of a worldwide Islamic opening or liberalization', reading Salafi literature

Indonesia and Turkey: urbanization and pluralism 31

alongside philosophy, science, technology and global history (Soğuk 2011: 159). While it may not qualify as a univocal acceptance or embrace of religious pluralism, it certainly is a manifestation of religious and intellectual plurality.

Notes

1 See Tunisian's *Ennahda* Party leader Rachid Ghannoushi's interviews with the BBC on 30 January 2011, www.bbc.co.uk/news/mobile/world-africa-12318824, and with *al-Jazeera* on 7 February, 2011, http://english.aljazeera.net/news/africa/2011/02/2011233464273624.html
2 Cf. also Burhani (2002).
3 For a detailed discussion of the Turkish-Islamic Synthesis, cf. Cetinsaya (1999).
4 For Arkoun and Hanafi as 'double critics' (cf. Kersten 2011a: 10, 122, 154, 165, 177, 184, 194–5).
5 For a detailed discussion of Dependency Theory in Turkey, cf. Gulalp (1998).
6 There is a rapidly growing literature on these developments (cf. Atasoy 2009; Çavdar 2006; Cinar 2006; Criss 2010; Patton 2009: Quinn 2004; Şen 2010; Tepe 2005; Yildirim, Inaç and Özler 2007).

References

Abdullah, T. (1996) 'The Formation of a New Paradigm? A Sketch on Contemporary Islamic Discourse', in Woodward, M.R. (ed.) *Toward a New Paradigm: Recent Developments in Indonesian Islamic Thought*, Tempe: Arizona State University Program for Southeast Asian Studies.

Appadurai, A. (1996) *Modernity at Large: Cultural Dimensions of Globalization*, Minneapolis: University of Minnesota Press.

Atasoy, Y. (2009) *Islam's Marriage with Neoliberalism: State Transformation in Turkey*, New York: Palgrave MacMillan.

Aydin, C. (2006) 'Between Occidentalism and the Global Left: Islamist Critiques of the West in Turkey', *Comparative Studies in South Asia, Africa and the Middle East*, 26(3): 446–61.

Burhani, A.N. (ed.) (2002) *Manusia Modern: Mendamba Allah: Renungan Tasawuf Positif*, Bandung, Indonesia: Mizan.

Çavdar, G. (2006) 'Islamist New Thinking in Turkey: A Model for Political Learning?', *Political Science Quarterly*, 121(3): 477–97.

Cetinsaya, G. (1999) 'Rethinking Nationalism and Islam: Some Preliminary Notes of the Roots of the "Turkish-Islamic Synthesis" in Modern Turkish Political Thought', *The Muslim World*, 89 (3–4): 350–76.

Cinar, M. (2006) 'Turkey's Transformation under AKP Rule', *The Muslim World*, 96(3): 469–86.

Criss, N.B. (2010) 'Dismantling Turkey: The Will of the People?', *Turkish Studies*, 11(1): 45–58.

Daği, I.D. (2004) 'Rethinking Human Rights, Democracy and the West: Post-Islamist Intellectuals in Turkey', *Critique: Critical Middle Eastern Studies*, 13(2): 135–51

Daği, I.D. (2005) 'The Transformation of Islamic Political Identity in Turkey', *Turkish Studies*, 6(1): 21–37.

Ebaugh, H.R. (2010) *The Gülen Movement: A Sociological Analysis of a Civic Movement Rooted in Moderate Islam*, Dordrecht, The Netherlands: Springer.

32 *Carool Kersten*

Effendy, B. (1995) 'Islam and the State in Indonesia: Munawir Sjadzali and the Development of a New Theological Underpinning of Political Islam', *Studia Islamika*, 2(2): 97–121.

Fealy, G. (2008) 'Consuming Islam: Commodified Religion and Aspirational Pietism in Contemporary Indonesia', in Fealy, G. and White, S. (eds) *Expressing Islam: Religious Life and Politics in Indonesia*, Singapore: ISEAS.

Formichi, C. (2013) 'Mustafa Kemal's Abrogation of the Ottoman Caliphate and Its Impact on the Indonesian Nationalist Movement', in al-Rasheed, M., Kersten, C. and Shterin, M. (eds), *Demystifying the Caliphate: Historical Memory and Contemporary Contexts*, London and New York: Hurst and Columbia University Press.

Genel, S. and Karaosmanoğlu, K. (2006) 'A New Islamic Individualism in Turkey: Headscarved Women in the City', *Turkish Studies* 7(3): 473–88.

Guida, M. (2010) 'New Islamists' Understanding of Democracy in Turkey: The Examples of Ali Bulaç and Hayder Karaman', *Turkish Studies*, 11(3): 347–70.

Guillot, F., Lombard, D. and Ptak, R. (eds) (1998) *From Mediterranean to the China Sea: Miscellaneous Notes*, Wiesbaden, Germany: Harrassowitz Verlag.

Gulalp, H. (1998) 'The Eurocentrism of Dependency Theory and the Question of "Authenticity": A View from Turkey', *Third World Quarterly*, 19(5): 951–61.

Harjanto, N.T.B. (2003) 'Islam and Liberalism in Contemporary Indonesia: The Political Ideas of *Jaringan Islam Liberal* (The Islamic Liberal Network)', unpublished MA Dissertation, The College of Arts and Sciences of Ohio University.

Hasan, N. (2009) 'The Making of Public Islam: Piety, Agency and Commodification on the Landscape of the Indonesian Public Sphere', *Contemporary Islam*, 3(3): 229–50.

Hefner, R.W. (1997) 'Islamization and Democratization in Indonesia', in Hefner, R.W. and Horvatich, P. (eds), *Islam in an Era of Nation-States: Political and Religious Renewal in Muslim Southeast Asia*, Honolulu: University of Hawai'i Press.

Howell, J.D. (2001) 'Sufism and the Indonesian Islamic Revival', *Journal of Asian Studies*, 60(3): 701–29.

Howell, J.D. (2008) 'Modulations of Active Piety: Professors and Televangelists as Promotors of Indonesia "Sufism"', in Fealy, G. and White, S. (eds) *Expressing Islam: Religious Life and Politics in Indonesia*, Singapore: ISEAS.

Kadioğlu, A. (1998) 'Republican Epistemology and Islamic Discourses in Turkey in the 1990s', *The Muslim World*, 58(1): 23–41.

Karaosmanoğlu, K. (2005) '*Beyond the Nation: Minorities and Identities in Urban Turkey*', unpublished PhD Thesis, Goldsmith's College.

Kersten, C. (2010) 'Islamic Post-Traditionalists and Liberal Muslims: Alternative Islamic Discourse in Indonesia', paper presented at XX Quinquennial Congress of the International Association for the History of Religions (IAHR), Toronto, August 2010.

Kersten, C. (2011a) *Cosmopolitans and Heretics: New Muslim Intellectuals and the Study of Islam*. London and New York: Hurst and Columbia University Press.

Kersten, C. (2011b) 'Mohammed Abed al-Jabiri, Mohammed Arkoun, and Nasr Hamid Abu Zayd in Indonesia: A Study in Reception Theory', paper presented at the Annual Meeting of the American Academy of Religion (AAR), San Francisco, November 2011.

Kull, A. (2005) *Piety and Politics: Nurcholish Madjid and His Interpretation of Islam in Modern Indonesia*, Lund, Sweden: Department of History and Anthropology of Religions, Lund University.

Lapidot, A. (1995) '*Islam and Nationalism: Contemporary Islamic Thought in Turkey 1980–1990*', unpublished PhD Thesis, University of Durham, UK.

Mardin, Ş. (2005) 'Turkish Exceptionalism Yesterday and Today: Continuity, Rupture and Reconstruction in Operational Codes', *Turkish Studies*, 6(2): 145–65.

Munhanif, A. (1996) 'Islam and the Struggle for Religious Pluralism in Indonesia: A Political Reading of the Religious Thought of Mukti Ali', *Studia Islamika*, 3(1): 79–126.

Nurdin, A.A. (2005) 'Islam and State: A Study of the Liberal Islamic Network in Indonesia 1999–2004', *New Zealand Journal of Asian Studies*, 7(2): 20–39.

Özal, K. (1999) 'Twenty Years with Mehmed Zahid Kotku: A Personal Story', in Özdalga, E. (ed.) *Naqshbandis in Western and Central Asia*, Istanbul: Swedish Research Institute.

Parker, L. (2011) 'Indonesia's "Multicultural Laboratories"' *Qantara.de Website.* Available from http://en.qantara.de/wcsite.php?wc_c=8425 (accessed 17 November 2012).

Patton, M.J. (2009) 'The Synergy between Neoliberalism and Communitarianism: "Erdoğan's Third Way"', *Comparative Studies of South Asia, Africa and the Middle East*, 29(3): 438–49.

Quinn, M.R. (2004) 'From the Ashes to Virtue, a Promise of New Light: The Transformation of Political Islam in Turkey', *Third World Quarterly*, 25(2): 339–58.

Raillon, F. (2011) 'The return of Pancasila: Secular vs Islamic Norms, Another Look at the Struggle for State Dominance in Indonesia', in Picard, M. and Madinier, R. (eds) *The Politics of Religion in Indonesia: Syncretism, Orthodoxy, and Religious Contention in Java and Bali*, London and New York: Routledge.

Saeed, A. (1999) 'Towards Religious Tolerance through Reform in Islamic Education: The Case of the State Institute of Islamic Studies in Indonesia', *Indonesia and the Malay World*, 27(79): 177–91.

Saktanber, A. (2007) 'Cultural Dilemmas of Muslim Youth: Negotiating Muslim Identities and Being Young in Turkey', *Turkish Studies*, 8(3): 417–34.

Şen, M. (2010) 'Transformation of Turkish Islamism and the Rise of the Justice and Development Party', *Turkish Studies* 11(1): 59–84.

Sirry, M. (2010) 'The Public Expression of Traditional Islam: The *Pesantren* and Civil Society in Post-Suharto Indonesia', *The Muslim World*, 100(1): 60–77.

Smith, T.W. (2005) 'Between Allah and Atatürk: Liberal Islam in Turkey', *Journal of Human Rights*, 9(3): 207–25.

Soğuk, N. (2011) *Globalization and Islamism: Beyond Fundamentalism*, Lanham, MD: Rowlands and Littlefields.

Stahr, V.S. (2009) 'Turkey as a Laboratory of Islam? Synthesis of Islamic Thought, Secularism, and Modernity', *Qantara.de Website*, Available from http://en.qantara.de/ Synthesis-of-Islamic-Thought-Secularism-and-Modernity/9500c9599i1p224/ index.html (accessed 17 November 2012).

Steenbrink, K. (1999) 'The Pancasila Ideology and an Indonesian Muslim Theology of Religions', in Waardenburg, J. (ed.) *Muslim Perceptions of Other Religions: A Historical Survey*, New York and Oxford: Oxford University Press.

Tepe, S. (2005) 'Turkey's AKP: A Model "Muslim Democratic" Party?', *Journal of Democracy*, 16(3): 69–82.

Turner, B. (2007) 'New Spiritualities, the Media and Global Religions: *Da Vinci Code* and *The Passion of Christ*', in P. Kitiarsa (ed.) *Religious Commodifications in Asia: Marketing Gods*, London and New York: Routledge.

Yavuz, M. H. (2003) *Islamic Political Identity in Turkey*, Oxford and New York: Oxford University Press.

34 *Carool Kersten*

Yildirim, E., Inaç, H. and Özler, H. (2007) 'Sociological Representation of the Justice and Development Party: Is It a Political Design or a Political Becoming?', *Turkish Studies*, 8(1): 5–24.

Yilmaz, I. (2005) 'State, Law, Civil Society and Islam in Contemporary Turkey', *Muslim World*, 95(3): 385–411.

3 Sacred sites and social conflict

Yasukuni shrine and religious pluralism in Japanese society[1]

Mark R. Mullins

The free practice of religion has been a prominent feature of Japanese society since the end of World War II. The disestablishment of State Shinto by the Occupation government, the abolishment of the wartime laws regulating religion, and the post-war Constitution of 1947 created a free-market religious economy in which all forms of religion were allowed to exist without interference from agents of the state. In this new environment, legally registered religious organizations (*shūkyō hōjin*) were defined by the government as 'public benefit organizations' (*kōeki hōjin*) and accorded special treatment and tax benefits. It was understood that diverse expressions of religion could co-exist and contribute in some positive way to a democratic and peaceful society.

Religious pluralism has flourished in the post-war environment and today there are 182,310 religious bodies registered with the government.[2] This number includes Shinto shrines (46.7 per cent), Buddhist temples (42.5 per cent), Christian churches (2.3 per cent), and New Religions (8.9 per cent). In addition, there are close to 25,000 propagation centres across the country (roughly 80 per cent belong to one of the New Religions). The older established Shinto and Buddhist institutions still clearly dominate the religious landscape and the 'late-comers' – both Christianity and new religious movements – represent only a small portion of organized religion in contemporary Japan.

While these figures indicate a strong institutional presence and variety in the contemporary Japanese religion, it should be noted that there is a serious discrepancy between the membership statistics claimed by these institutions and the self-understanding of the vast majority of Japanese. The total number of religious adherents for all of these religious bodies exceeds the population of Japan (127 million) by some 84 million people. Individuals are clearly being counted by more than one institution, which reflects the fact that many Japanese are at least loosely affiliated with both Buddhist temples and Shinto shrines and typically participate in annual events, festivals, and family rituals associated with multiple religious traditions.

While such religious diversity has been a part of Japanese society and culture for centuries, it did not constitute 'religious pluralism' in the modern sense of the term. As Winston Davis explains: 'Pluralism is a differentiated system of genuine religious and/or cultural alternatives. I say "genuine" because in this case society

36   *Mark R. Mullins*

recognizes that adherence to one alternative may legitimately make commitment to other alternatives impossible'. The notion of religions as 'alternatives' is not a natural one in the Japanese context. Here, there has been a general tendency for individuals to be embedded in a system of 'layered obligations that has little to do with personal beliefs or convictions' (Davis 1992: 30–1). Individuals normally participate in rituals appropriate to the social groups to which they belong (Buddhist household rituals, Shinto community rituals) with little or no consciousness that the practices are associated with a distinctive religious tradition.[3] While 'religion as obligation' has certainly weakened in the post-war period due to demographic changes (i.e. the shift of the masses from rural communities to urban areas), the notion of religious commitment and affiliation based on conscious choice and understanding of religious alternatives is still not that common.[4]

Survey research over the past several decades has consistently discovered that only about 30 per cent of the Japanese population claim to have a 'personal faith'. The vast majority profess to be 'without religion' (*mushūkyō*), which essentially means that they are without an exclusive commitment to one particular religion. While some 30 per cent may claim a personal faith of some kind, survey research also reveals that less than 10 per cent of the population claims to actually 'belong' to a religious organization (Ishii 2007 [1997]: 142).[5] For most Japanese, in other words, organized religion appears to be something best avoided.

Due to a number of controversial incidents and court cases related to religion over the past several decades, a serious 'gap' has emerged between the 'official' post-war understanding of religion as something beneficial for society and the public perception of religion as a 'problem' and in need of more serious scrutiny and regulation. For several decades, survey research has indicated that many Japanese perceive religions as something 'dark and gloomy' (*kurai*), 'closed' (*heisateki*), and 'dangerous' (*abunai*). In recent years, in fact, the concern for religious freedom, which many were preoccupied with in the early post-war period, has been overshadowed by a concern for 'protection from' religion. Media preoccupation with problematic religious groups – often referred to as 'cults' – has been evident throughout the post-war period, but has been particularly prominent since 1995, the year when some followers of Aum Shinrikyō perpetrated the sarin gas attack on the Tokyo subway system (Kisala and Mullins 2001).

It is not just the new religions that are a cause for concern. Even a 'traditional' religion like Shinto, which includes a diverse range of shrines and sects, has faced serious criticisms and legal challenges, particularly in relation to Yasukuni Shrine, the controversial site dedicated to Japan's military war dead. Why is it that this particular shrine – which represents itself today as the foundation for a 'peaceful nation' – has become such a source of social conflict and the focus of legal battles in post-war Japan? This is the basic question I seek to address in this study. Following a brief overview of Yasukuni Shrine's place in Japanese history, I will focus on the concern of some bereaved families for protection from the shrine's unilateral enshrinement of their deceased family members without permission or regard for their religious faith.

Historical background

Yasukuni Shrine, a sacred site in Tokyo's Kudan district – only a short distance from the Imperial Palace – has been an important part of Japan's religious landscape since the late nineteenth century. Initially established in Kyoto by Emperor Meiji in 1868 as Shōkonsha, it was relocated to Tokyo the following year. Although it began as a shrine dedicated to those who had sacrificed their lives in the Boshin War (1868–69) on behalf of the Emperor, it quickly became the central shrine for memorializing all of Japan's war dead for the next century. It was renamed Yasukuni or 'peaceful country' in 1879, and the following year was given a special rank (*Bekkaku-kanpeisha*) in the new system of national shrines established by the Meiji government.

Yasukuni Shrine – along with other 'state-protecting shrines' (*gokoku jinja*) – were central to what came to be known as 'State Shinto'. In order to deal with the problems of internal chaos and the threat of Western imperialism, the restoration government pursued a policy of uniting the people of Japan under the canopy of a state-sponsored and Emperor-centred civil religion. From the Meiji Restoration until the end of World War II, the government used existing Shinto shrines and created new shrines – such as Yasukuni – to unify and integrate the heterogeneous population and mobilize the people for nation-building, modernization, and military expansion. In order to shift the allegiance of the majority of the population from particularistic local communities with their distinctive clan gods (*ujigami*) to the Emperor and the national community, a major effort of re-socialization was required on the part of the government. Eventually this transformation was achieved through the effective use of the public school system, military conscription, and control of mass media.[6]

During this period, Yasukuni Shrine was under the direct administration of the Ministries of the Army and Navy and financially supported by the government. Although Shinto priests conducted rites of deification and pacification of the deceased, the government defined these ceremonies as 'non-religious' patriotic or civil ceremonies and clearly distinguished them from the 'religious' rituals conducted by followers of Buddhism, Christianity, and various new religions. By defining what went on at Yasukuni and other Shinto shrines as 'non-religious', the government was able to require all of its citizens to participate in such ceremonies as a part of their patriotic duty.[7] In this way, sacred sites such as Yasukuni Shrine became the symbolic focus of a new Japanese identity based on the ideal of self-sacrifice for the nation and Emperor.

All of this changed abruptly in August 1945 with the Japanese surrender and the arrival of the Occupation Forces. The Allied Occupation brought about a major restructuring of Japanese religion and society, including the place of Shinto institutions. Although there were some loud voices calling for the 'razing' of Yasukuni and other 'national shrines', which they thought would be necessary to destroy the central pillars of Japanese militarism, those actually involved in the planning and implementation of the State Department's policies for post-defeat Japan were cautious and pragmatic. In fact, not one Shinto shrine was destroyed

38   *Mark R. Mullins*

or closed during the Occupation. Nevertheless, the Supreme Commander for the Allied Powers issued directives that radically transformed the place of Shinto in Japanese society.[8]

It was the Directive for the Disestablishment of State Shinto issued by Supreme Commander on 15 December 1945 that set in motion policies that effectively reduced Shinto to the status of a voluntary organization. In accordance with the Directive, the wartime laws regulating religion were subsequently abolished and all religious groups, including Shinto shrines, were placed on equal footing as 'voluntary' organizations. The overall aim of the Directive was to establish the free practice of religion, and it was assumed that this required a clear separation of religion and state. In addition to ending government support and administration of Shinto shrines, the Directive instructed the Japanese government to remove Shinto elements from all public institutions.

The Directive assured 'complete religious freedom' to the Japanese people, which included the practice of Shinto. It indicated, however, that certain conditions would need to be met:

> Shrine Shinto, after having been divorced from the state and divested of its militaristic and ultra-nationalistic elements, will be recognized as a religion if its adherents so desire and will be granted the same protection as any other religion insofar as it may in fact be the philosophy or religion of Japanese people.
>
> (Woodard 1972: 298)

Given this policy, all Shinto shrines – including the controversial Yasukuni Shrine (and other *gokoku* shrines) were allowed to register as religious corporations. Yasukuni Shrine completed this registration process and was officially recognized as a religious organization on 7 September 1946. It was removed from the administration of the Army and Navy and brought under the control of shrine priests. Yasukuni lost its official status as a national shrine and was reduced to a voluntary religious organization (*shūkyō hōjin*).

The problems associated with Yasukuni Shrine in the post-war period are related to the fact that Shinto leaders redefined it as a 'religious' institution in 1946. Articles 20 and 89 of the 1947 post-war Constitution, likewise, provided unambiguous statements that defined the relationship between the state and religion (i.e. separation) and the rights of individuals to freely practice (or not) a religion of their choice. The policies of the Occupation authorities and the new Constitution worked together to clearly establish religious freedom and liberate Japanese from civil or national religious obligations connected with State Shinto and the Emperor system. The controversies and legal battles surrounding Yasukuni Shrine today are related to claims that either the principle of separation has been violated or the rights of individuals with regard to religion have been constrained in some way.

Post-Occupation developments

Yasukuni Shrine has become the focus of public concern and debate on a number of occasions since the Occupation period. Debate regarding the future of Yasukuni Shrine began in the Diet in the mid-1950s. One key figure involved in these discussions was Kanemori Tokujirō (1886–1959), a politician who served in the first cabinet of Yoshida Shigeru. He argued that the new Constitution's articles on the separation of religion and state could only permit State support for Yasukuni to be restored if the religious elements of the shrine were removed. In the committee's debates and discussions about this, many of his opponents followed the pre-war view that the shrine was essentially a 'non-religious' patriotic site. Kanemori maintained that this view was no longer a tenable one since the shrine had registered as a religious corporation and had spent over a decade emphasizing its 'religious character'.

The early proposal debated in the Diet required the secularization of the shrine as a condition for securing State support, and was opposed by both Shinto leaders and the Japan Association of War-bereaved Families (*Nihon Izoku Kai*). This opposition was expressed in a resolution passed by the priests from the 'state-protecting shrines' (*gokoku jinja*) at a special meeting held on 9 March 1956, which stated that the traditional Shinto rites could not be abandoned. In short, a 'non-religious' (or religiously neutral) memorial site for the war dead was viewed as unacceptable.[9] Due to the lack of consensus in these early debates, the issue of Yasukuni Shrine was pushed to the side for over a decade.

Efforts to re-nationalize the shrine were resumed in the late 1960s. From 1969 to 1974, leaders of the Liberal Democratic Party (LDP) tried to pass the *Yasukuni jinja hōan*, a bill that would restore direct government support to the shrine. During this period, in fact, the LDP presented six bills to the Diet for the re-nationalization of Yasukuni Shrine. Proponents of the bills maintained that the Shrine is a national site for remembering the war dead and should not be regarded as 'religious' (Jinja Shinpōsha 1971: 158; Haruyama 2006: 65). They argued, furthermore, that 'official visits' (*kōshiki sanpai*) by government representatives and officials should be fully supported and recognized as a matter of civic duty and an example of patriotism. Critics of these bills, on the other hand, claimed that Yasukuni Shrine was clearly a 'religious' site that was monopolized by the priests of one religious tradition – Shinto.[10] Any direct support, they argued, would violate the constitutional separation of religion and state. The bills promoting the restoration of state support to Yasukuni Shrine were defeated each time and faced strong opposition from various Buddhist, Christian, and secular groups, who shared the common concern to preserve the freedom guaranteed by the post-war Constitution.

A decade later the shrine attracted attention again when Prime Minister Nakasone Yasuhiro and other government leaders made 'official visits', particularly the visit on 15 August 1985. On that occasion Nakasone made an offering of 30,000 JPY from public funds, which was interpreted by many observers as a highly symbolic act done to promote the reinstitution of government support for

40   *Mark R. Mullins*

the shrine. It quickly generated a critical response. Within Japan many intellectuals and religious leaders expressed their strong opposition to the prime minister's initiative. International criticism also appeared in newspapers and media reports in China, North Korea, South Korea, Singapore, and the Soviet Union. The negative press and reaction was such that Nakasone cancelled his planned visit to the shrine the following year, and his administration organized a study group to review the issue and provide recommendations for future government policy. As a result, 'official' prime ministerial visits to the shrine were avoided for over a decade, and the debate subsided through the 1990s.

Prime Minister Koizumi Jun'ichirō reignited the public controversy by following through on a campaign promise he made in 2001 when running for the presidency of the ruling Liberal Democratic Party that he would visit Yasukuni Shrine in his official capacity, which he did a number of times between 2001 and 2006. There was considerable domestic opposition to Koizumi's visits, and eight different court cases were launched against him across the nation. Over 900 plaintiffs claimed that his behaviour violated the constitutional separation of religion and state, caused them mental anguish, and demanded compensation. Although some district courts dismissed these lawsuits, both the Fukuoka District Court in April 2004 and the Osaka High Court in September the following year ruled that the Prime Minister's visits did violate the constitution, but denied compensation for damages.

Koizumi's behaviour also provoked widespread international concern. The governments of South Korea and the Peoples' Republic of China issued strong official statements and criticisms of his actions. It did not escape notice in the US either. At a hearing before the House of Representatives Committee on International Relations on 14 September 2006, Republican Henry Hyde and Democratic member Tom Lantos, a holocaust survivor, both expressed their concerns about Japan's 'historical amnesia'. In their statements they urged future prime ministers to avoid visits to the shrine out of concern for peace in the region, and urged them to do something about Yūshūkan, the museum adjacent to the shrine, which promotes a revisionist history that especially disturbs Japan's nearest neighbours. Lantos explained:

> For the survivors of World War II in Asia and America visits to the Yasukuni Shrine where 14 Class A war criminals are interred would be the equivalent of laying a wreath at the graves of Himmler, Rudolph Hess and Herman Greer in Germany. My message to the incoming Japanese prime minister is very simple; paying one's respects to war criminals is morally bankrupt and unworthy of a great nation such as Japan. This practice must end.

Both Hyde and Lantos are now deceased.[11] Because of the negative reaction to Koizumi's initiative, in any case, the LDP prime ministers who followed him – Abe Shinzō, Fukuda Yasuo, and Asō Tarō – avoided visiting Yasukuni Shrine during their brief tenures.

Some observers thought that the landslide victory of the Democratic Party in

Sacred sites and social conflict in Japan 41

the August 2009 election, which essentially ended half a century of domination by the Liberal Democratic Party, would have some significant implications for Yasukuni Shrine. Even before assuming the office of Prime Minister, Hatoyama Yukio made it clear that he thought it was inappropriate for government officials to visit Yasukuni and indicated that he was in favour of re-starting discussions about the creation of an alternative memorial site, one that would be religiously neutral and unencumbered by the negative history and association with Class-A war criminals.[12] Hatoyama was preoccupied with other matters during his brief time as Prime Minister and his successors, Kan Naoto and Noda Yoshihiko, have been overwhelmed by the 11 March 2011 earthquake and nuclear disaster, which makes it unlikely that the Yasukuni Shrine problem will receive serious attention in the near future.

My interest here, however, is not so much with the question of prime ministerial visits to Yasukuni, but the way in which the war dead have been unilaterally enshrined in the post-war period without regard for the wishes or feelings of many bereaved families. Given the media preoccupation with politically significant figures, the more fundamental conflict over post-war enshrinements of the war dead has not received the attention it deserves. In recent years, Japanese Buddhists and Christians, as well as some foreigners (citizens of South Korea and Taiwan), have initiated lawsuits against Yasukuni Shrine and the Japanese government for the alleged violation of the Constitution (Articles 20 and 89) and appealed to have the names of their family dead removed from the shrine register.[13] It is this particular problem that I want to consider in more detail here.

Enshrinement as a religious problem

Although enshrinement has only become a serious public concern over the past two decades or so, it is hardly surprising that it would become a problem in the context of a religiously plural society. In the early months of the Occupation, in fact, the issue was already raised by Miyaji Naokazu (1886–1949), a leading scholar who occupied the Chair for Shinto Studies at the Imperial University in Tokyo.[14] In a 1946 interview, which was conducted soon after Yasukuni Shrine had registered as a religious organization under the new Religious Corporations Ordinance, Miyaji recognized that enshrinements could very well become a contentious issue:

> Now that Yasukuni has become a religion, Buddhists and Christians may not want to be enshrined there. This is quite a natural phenomenon, for the shrine has become connected with religion. This problem will arise concerning Gokoku Shrines too. Those who fail to understand the fact that the shrine has become religion may feel unpleasant, due to misapprehension because of the existence of the Buddhists and Christians who refuse to be treated as kami of Yasukuni.[15]
>
> (Miyaji 1966: 149)

42 Mark R. Mullins

The phrase 'Yasukuni has become a religion' should not be misunderstood here. Miyaji is referring to the fact that the shrine had become clearly defined as a *shūkyō hōjin* (religious corporation). He is not denying the shrine's 'religious' character prior to this post-war change in legal status. Earlier in the same interview he stated: 'In my opinion religion is intercourse between human beings and what is superhuman. Therefore, all shrines naturally fall into the category of religion.... The government did not negate the religious activities of the shrines even when it did not regard the shrines as religion' (Miyaji 1966: 143). This is a striking statement coming from someone who just a decade earlier had headed the Research Department of the Shrine Bureau of the Ministry of Home Affairs.

Although State Shinto was disestablished by the Occupation authorities at the end of the war, Yasukuni Shrine survived in the post-war period as a voluntary religious organization supported by the faithful and without direct financial aid from the government. In some respects, however, it has operated 'as if' nothing had been changed by the Occupation policies or the post-war Constitution, which established religious freedom and the clear separation of religion and state (Articles 20 and 89). Given the post-war legal framework, one might assume that those among the bereaved families who wished to have a family member enshrined would indicate this to Yasukuni and request that the ritual be conducted. In fact, however, Yasukuni Shrine officials contacted the Ministry of Health and Welfare – without consulting any families – to request assistance in the preparation of lists for all of the war dead so that enshrinement rituals could be completed. After the war, this ministry was responsible for veterans' affairs, repatriation of Japanese from overseas, and Yasukuni Shrine, which had been managed by the Army and Navy. The paper trail revealing cooperation between Yasukuni Shrine and government offices stretches back to 1956. That year the Ministry of Health and Welfare sent instructions to city and prefecture offices to assist with Yasukuni Shrine's administrative needs related to enshrinement plans. At least twenty meetings between shrine representatives and government officials occurred over the years to discuss and arrange for the paperwork required. Extensive documentation that reveals the extent to which government offices were involved in assisting with this process is now preserved in the National Diet Library.[16]

While those who belong to the Japan Association of War-bereaved Families (Nihon Izoku Kai) are strong supporters of Yasukuni and pleased about the enshrinement, there are many who belong to alternative associations of bereaved families – the Shinshū Izokukai (Buddhist) and Heiwa Izokukai (Christian), for example. They are appalled that their family members have been enshrined and deified, and are now worshipped as a 'kami' (god) along with the Class A war criminals enshrined several decades ago. Over the years, a number of individuals have made personal visits to Yasukuni Shrine and requested that enshrinement be cancelled and the names of their family dead be removed from the shrine register. In addition to appeals from Japanese families, there are also Koreans and Taiwanese who have been dismayed and angered to learn that Yasukuni's generous enshrinement policy extended even to individuals from former colonial domains who had been conscripted and mobilized for Japan's war efforts and later died 'on behalf of the Emperor and nation'. While Shrine representatives no doubt believe they are honouring their memory and sacrifice, these Korean and Taiwanese families feel they have been exploited by Japan in both life and death, with their ancestors still spiritually under 'colonial rule' symbolized by enshrinement in Yasukuni.

In spite of their numerous personal appeals, Yasukuni priests have insisted that 'de-enshrinement' is impossible. Families have never been consulted in advance, they explain, since all are enshrined according to the 'will of the Emperor' and the tradition established in the early Meiji period. It has nothing to do with the will or desires of the deceased or the bereaved families. In other words, Yasukuni is engaged in 'business as usual', and 'usual' here means according to the norms established in the pre-war period. The 'will of the Emperor', according to priestly interpretation at Yasukuni Shrine, still trumps individual choice and family religious tradition.

Much to the dismay of many Yasukuni supporters, however, it was revealed in 2007 that even Emperor Hirohito was not pleased with the shrine's handling of the war dead in the post-war decades. According to the diaries of Chamberlain Urabe and Chief Steward Tomita, both of whom served the late Emperor, he was opposed to the plan to enshrine Class A war criminals (Breen 2008: 3–5). No doubt nervous about being too closely associated with those held responsible for Japan's wars of aggression, he even stopped making visits to the shrine. While many Japanese may be offended that their relative has become part of such a questionable pantheon, those who belong to the alternative associations of bereaved families are opposed to all that Yasukuni Shrine stands for, particularly the glorification of so many tragic deaths and promotion of the view that Japan's past wars were all about liberating Asia from Western colonialism and oppression.

Legal action against Yasukuni Shrine and the Japanese government

Since Yasukuni Shrine has been unwilling to comply with requests for cancellation of enshrinement and removal of names from the register, a number of individuals decided to pursue legal action against both Yasukuni Shrine and the Japanese government. Several years ago lawsuits were launched almost simultaneously by three different groups and are now being processed by the courts in Tokyo, Osaka and Okinawa. Unlike the issue of prime ministerial visits to Yasukuni, these court proceedings have received minimal media coverage. Here I turn to a brief review of the ruling handed down by the Osaka District Court on 26 February 2009.

The nine plaintiffs in the Osaka case are an ecumenical group of seniors – ages ranging from 64 to 82 – and include several Buddhists and one Christian. Two have written extensively about their personal struggle with Yasukuni Shrine over the years. Sugahara Ryūken, a Jōdo Shinshū priest (Honganjiha) and head of the Shinshū Izokukai, provides a critical Shinshū perspective in his *Yasukuni to iu ori kara no kaihō* [Liberation from the Cage of Yasukuni] (2005).[17] In the same vein, Nishiyama Toshihiko, a Catholic priest of the Osaka Archdiocese, records his unsuccessful efforts to have his father's enshrinement revoked in an interim report published in 2006.[18] While their philosophical and theological reasons for opposing Yasukuni Shrine may differ, the plaintiffs are united in their view that ritual enshrinement without permission is a violation of their personal right to remember the deceased without interference from a third party. Individuals and families, the plaintiffs maintain, should be protected from actions and labelling that bring dishonour to a person's name and memory.

Although Buddhist and Catholic anti-Yasukuni activists are not that common, both Jōdo Shinshū denominations and the Catholic Church in Japan have issued critical statements for decades regarding the LDP efforts to re-nationalize Yasukuni and expressed strong opposition to prime ministerial visits (*kōshiki sanpai*). In connection with this most recent Osaka court case, a representative of the Japan Catholic Council for Justice and Peace, Bishop Matsuura Gorō, also wrote a letter in 2006 to express support for Fr. Nishiyama and his legal struggle, which was published in *The Catholic Bishops' Conference of Japan Yearbook* (2008). In this document, Bishop Matsuura recognizes that Yasukuni Shrine – as an independent religious organization – has every right to conduct religious activities as long as it remains separate from the government. He also maintains, however, that 'the unilateral enshrinement of people of other religions and creeds against their will is not proper conduct'.[19]

While the plaintiffs made it clear that they were opposed to their family members being 'used' by Yasukuni Shrine to legitimize and beautify Japan's past wars of aggression, they were primarily concerned in this case with the actions Yasukuni took with regard to people who do not belong to the Shrine. The plaintiffs demanded that the enshrinement be cancelled and the names of the family members be erased from the shrine register. The judges regarded the plaintiffs' claim that the self-image and memory of the deceased was damaged by Yasukuni's actions to be too 'subjective' and 'abstract' to be taken seriously by the Court, and their demands for compensation were denied.

The plaintiffs also argued that the enshrinement of their relatives was an illegal action carried out with close cooperation between the government and Yasukuni Shrine, which is clearly prohibited by the post-war Constitution. In their view, the government violated their right to privacy and provided information to the shrine, which enabled it to proceed with the enshrinement ritual. The judges ruled, however, that the government could not be held responsible for the enshrinements, reasoning that the Health and Welfare Ministry routinely provided information regarding the deceased to various parties (in connection with pension inquiries, for example), and it would have been discrimination against a religious organization if the government offices refused to provide the requested information to Yasukuni. Although the government did provide information, in the end the decision to enshrine was made by Yasukuni officials according to their accepted tradition and practice, and did not involve the government (see Figure 3.1).[20]

Sacred sites and social conflict in Japan 45

Figure 3.1 The plaintiffs speak to reporters outside the Osaka District Court following the decision of the three judges on 26 February 2009 (photo by Mark Mullins).

The Osaka District Court dismissed the case as 'groundless' and reduced it to the issue of religious freedom. In addressing this issue, the judges clearly followed the precedent established by the 1988 Supreme Court decision regarding a similar case, which involved the enshrinement of Nakaya Takafumi, a Self-Defense Force officer, in the *Yamaguchi Prefecture Gokoku Jinja* ('state-protecting shrine') in 1972. The Self-Defense Force Veterans Association had the enshrinement conducted in spite of opposition from the surviving spouse, Nakaya Yasuko. Nakaya filed a civil law suit against the government for violating both her religious rights and Article 20 of the Constitution, which prohibits government involvement in religion. She also sought compensation 'for mental damages allegedly caused by the enshrinement of her dead spouse'. Although Nakaya won her case at the Yamaguchi District Court in 1979, and again at the Hiroshima High Court in 1982, these earlier decisions were overturned by the Supreme Court in 1988. The Court ruled that the Veterans Association was not a 'State Agency' and, therefore, no violation of the separation of religion and state could have occurred. Furthermore, Nakaya's religious rights had not been violated since she was not required to participate in the enshrinement ritual. Finally, the judges found no legal basis 'for giving priority to a surviving spouse over surviving parents or children with regard to mourning and honoring the memory of the

46 *Mark R. Mullins*

deceased'. In the end, Nakaya was required to repay with interest the 1 million JPY that had been awarded by the Yamaguchi Court.[21]

Following the logic of the Supreme Court decision, the judges in the Osaka case concluded that the religious freedom of both parties – Yasukuni Shrine and bereaved families – must be protected. Yasukuni Shrine's 'freedom' to remember and worship the dead according to their own tradition must be recognized. The Court is not in a position, they argued, to interfere with a religious organization and dictate what is appropriate belief and practice. While the judges conceded that it is clearly advisable to have the permission of the bereaved families, they concluded that the enshrinement did not violate their rights in any way since they were not forced to participate. Each party must allow the other to freely memorialize the dead in their own way and according to their respective faith tradition. Representatives of Yasukuni Shrine and the government were obviously pleased with the Court's decision, but the plaintiffs vowed to carry on their struggle to liberate their family members from the 'cage' of Yasukuni Shrine.

Hishiki Masaharu, a Buddhist priest and scholar, and leader of the support group for the plaintiffs in the Osaka case, finds it ironic that Articles 20 and 89 of the post-war Constitution, which were meant to establish religious freedom and 'protect' people from the coercive practices of State Shinto – such as forced shrine visits during the war – are today being used to 'protect' the religious freedom of Yasukuni Shrine over the rights of individuals. In stark contrast to the judges' perspective and reasoning, Hishiki argues that religious organizations do not have unlimited freedom. The government can intervene without violating the constitutional separation of religion and state if a religious organization is involved in illegal activities. In fact, the courts have intervened in cases of tax evasion, fraudulent fund-raising activities, harassment of individuals through high-pressure membership recruitment activities, and when religious groups engage in acts of violence and murder (the most extreme example in recent Japanese history is the Tokyo subway gas attack by Aum Shinrikyō members in 1995, which was legitimized by religious doctrine). All of these cases reveal that the courts and the Japanese public recognize there are some 'limits' to the freedom of religion. In spite of all this, Hishiki maintains that the courts have given Yasukuni Shrine a 'free pass' to conduct business as usual even though their activities bring dishonour and shame to the name of the deceased and contribute to the suffering of the bereaved families con cerned.[22] The 'politics of inclusion' as practiced by Yasukuni Shrine reveals the limits of religious pluralism and represents a harsher reality that still faces individuals and minorities in contemporary Japan.

Conclusion

During Japan's modern century – at least until the end of World War II – Yasukuni Shrine was a national institution and sacred site that provided one important symbolic focus for Japanese identity and contributed to the forging of a strong connection between the people of Japan and the Emperor and Imperial Household.

Sacred sites and social conflict in Japan   47

With Japan's defeat and the Allied Occupation, the status of Yasukuni was transformed from an institution of the state into a voluntary association. The Shinto Directive, issued by the Occupation authorities on 15 December 1945, privatized the shrine and removed its special status and government support. The principles of religious freedom and the separation of religion and state laid out in the Shinto Directive were also institutionalized in the post-war Constitution. It is not surprising that under these new social and legal conditions the role and meaning of Yasukuni Shrine have been seriously contested by Buddhists and Christians, as well as secular intellectuals and activists, during the post-war period.

We have only reviewed here the results of one legal challenge over post-war enshrinements, but there are a number of cases involving plaintiffs in Okinawa, as well as many Koreans and Taiwanese, still before the courts at various stages of appeal. To date the courts have concluded that neither Yasukuni Shrine nor the Japanese government has acted in a manner that violates either the principle of religious freedom or the separation of religion and state. It seems unlikely that future deliberations will lead the courts to reach a different decision. One possibility, however, is that the emerging transnational anti-Yasukuni movement in East Asia, which includes activists and bereaved family members from Taiwan and South Korea, will bring greater international attention to the fate of religious minorities and pressure the Japanese government and its courts to take these appeals more seriously.[23] This movement has already undertaken campaigns in the US, which included a march to the United Nations building in New York, where it appealed to the Human Rights Commission for an investigation, and a press conference in front of the Japanese Consulate. It has also sought to bring the issue to the wider public through academic conferences, film screening events, and art exhibitions, including the work of Korean artists and cartoonists depicting the meaning of Yasukuni for Japan's neighbours.[24] At the moment, it does not appear that this movement is gaining serious traction, but it does reveal an emerging clash between the values of global civil society that give priority to individual rights and freedoms and those values embraced by political and religious leaders in some national contexts, which regard the rights of the individual to be secondary and subservient to the needs of the nation or group.

Notes

1 This chapter draws on some material from earlier articles; see Mullins (2010a) and (2010b).
2 These statistics are for 2007, which are the latest figures provided by the Agency for Cultural Affairs, Ministry of Education, Culture, Sports, Science and Technology. Available from www.mext.go.jp/b_menu/toukei/001/index39.htm (accessed 30 January 2010).
3 The 'combinatory' character of Japanese religiosity has a long history. For one important study of its early formation, see Grapard (1992).
4 A case could be made that this is a religious orientation rooted in Western traditions and fundamentally at odds with what is usually found in Japan and East Asia. There are examples, however, of 'home-grown' Japanese expressions of Buddhism (Nichiren and Sōka Gakkai) that tend to cultivate a similar religious orientation.

48 *Mark R. Mullins*

5 Japanese names in the text are given in the Japanese order – surname first, then given name.

6 The role of public education was particularly important in the forging of a new national identity connected to the imperial household and symbolized by the new national shrines (Murakami 1982: 46–9). For a more focused treatment of the place of Yasukuni Shrine in textbooks for elementary school children during this period, see Irie (2001: 73–8).

7 It is worth noting here that Article 28 of the Meiji Constitution (1889) guaranteed citizens religious freedom 'within limits not prejudicial to peace and order, and not antagonistic to their duties as subjects'. Under State Shinto, however, it became obvious that 'duties as subjects' would be in conflict with and override individual freedoms during the wartime period.

8 For a detailed examination of the treatment of Shinto institutions during the Occupation period, see Mullins (2010b: 89–136).

9 Debates regarding an alternative memorial site have resumed in recent years. It is clearly a complicated issue that is unlikely to be resolved in the foreseeable future. The issue was the focus of a 2002 symposium, the results of which were published in Inoue and Shimazono (2004). This volume provides a wide range of pro and con views on proposals for an alternative to Yasukuni Shrine.

10 An examination of Yasukuni's own website (www.yasukuni.or.jp/) as well as a number of scholarly studies reveal the distinctively Shinto and 'religious' nature of the rituals that occur in the shrine's precincts (see, for example, Breen 2004).

11 The statements of Hyde and Lantos are available on the U.S. government House of Representatives homepage in the Hearing Record entitled 'Japan's Relationship with its Neighbors: Back to the Future', 14 September 2006. Available at http://commdocs.house.gov/committees/intlrel/hfa29883.000/hfa29883_0f.htm.

12 Reported in the *Asahi Shimbun*, 11 August 2009.

13 These lawsuits are known in Japanese as *gōshi torikeshi soshō*.

14 Prior to his faculty appointment in 1938, Miyaji had served in the Ministry of Home Affairs as head of the Shinto Bureau's Research Department (*Jinjakyoku Kōshōka*). Although the university abolished the Chair for Shinto Studies in early 1946 in response to a recommendation from the CIE Religions Division staff, Miyaji was allowed to remain as a member of the faculty until his retirement shortly thereafter. He subsequently served as an adviser to Jinja Honchō (Association of Shinto Shrines), the main umbrella shrine organization of the post-war period, which was established in 1946.

15 Miyaji's remarks are from an interview conducted by Woodard on 15 October 1946, and recorded by Dr. Hiyane Antei (1892–1970), a Protestant scholar who later taught the history of religion at Aoyama Gakuin University and Tokyo Union Theological Seminary. The interview was published two decades later in *Contemporary Religions in Japan*, a journal edited by Woodard.

16 For an English overview of the Yasukuni-related materials preserved in the National Diet Library, see: www.ndl.go.jp/en/news/fy2007/1173395_903.htm; and for a helpful introduction to these materials, see Haruyama (2006).

17 More recently, Sugahara has published an additional short booklet *Gōshi torikeshi: Yasukuni mondai no kakushin o tou* (2007).

18 See his *Yasukuni Gōshi Torikeshi Soshō no Chūkan Hōkoku: Shinkyō no Jiyū no Kaifuku o motomete* (Tokyo: San Paulo, 2006).

19 See the 'Statement on Filing a Suit by Fr. Toshihiko Nishiyama Demanding Revoking Enshrinement in Yasukuni Shrine, 11 August 2006', in the *Nihon Katorikku Shikyō Kyōgikai Iya-bukku 2008* (Tokyo: Katorikku Chūō Kyōgikai, 2008), 108–10.

20 Here I am only summarizing some key points elaborated by the Osaka District Court judges in their final decision (81 pages) on 26 February 2009.

21 For helpful overviews of the Nakaya case, see Hardacre (1989: 153–7) and Reid

Sacred sites and social conflict in Japan 49

(1991: 52–4). The full statement of the Supreme Court decision (1 June 1988) may be found in *Minshu* (1988).

22 This brief synopsis draws on an interview with Hishiki Masaharu (22 October 2008) and personal conversations following the Osaka High Court decision (26 February 2009). For a more detailed treatment of his views regarding Yasukuni Shrine and religion-state issues, see his *Shiminteki jiyū no kiki to Shūkyō: Kenpō, Yasukuni Jinja, Seikyō bunri*, (Tokyo: Shirasawa, 2007).

23 For one useful resource on this development, see Chueiling (2008).

24 The 2005 documentary, *Annyong Sayonara*, directed by Tae-il Kim, has been used at film screening events. This work examines Yasukuni Shrine from the perspective of Heeja Lee, a Korean woman who lost her father after he was drafted by the Japanese army and killed in action.

References

Breen, J. (2008) 'Introduction: A Yasukuni Genealogy', in Breen, J. (ed.) *Yasukuni, the War Dead and the Struggle for Japan's Past*, New York: Columbia University Press.

Breen, J. (2004) 'The Dead and the Living in the Land of Peace: A Sociology of Yasukuni Shrine', *Mortality*, 9(1): 76–93.

Chueiling, S. (2008) 'Network-Building: Development of Anti-Yasukuni Transnational Advocacy Network, 2002–2007', *Issues & Studies,* 44(4) (December): 167–99.

Davis, W. (1992) *Japanese Religion and Society*, New York: SUNY Press.

Grapard, A. (1992) *The Protocol of the Gods: A Study of the Kasuga Cult in Japanese History*, Berkeley, CA: University of California Press.

Hardacre, H. (1989) *Shinto and the State: 1868–1988*, Princeton, NJ: Princeton University Press.

Haruyama, M. (2006) 'Yasukuni jinja to wa nanika: Shiryō kenkyū no shiza kara no joron' [What is Yasukuni Shrine? A Bibliographical Introduction]. *The Reference*, 56(7): 49–75.

Hishiki, M. (2007) *Shiminteki jiyū no kiki to shūkyō – kenpō, Yasukuni Jinja, seikyō bunri* [Religion and the Crisis of Civic Freedom: Constitution, Yasukuni Shrine, and Separation of Religion and State], Tokyo: Shirasawa.

Inoue, N. and Shimazono S. (eds) (2004) *Atarashii tsuitō shisetsu wa hitsuyō ka?* [Is a New Memorial Institution Needed?], Tokyo: Pelican.

Irie, Y. (2001) *Nihon ga "kami no kuni" datta jidai: Kokumin gakkō no kyōkasho o yomu* [The Period When Japan Was the 'Kingdom of God': Reading the Textbooks of Public Schools], Iwanami Shoten.

Ishii, K. (2007 [1997]) *Da-ta bukku: Gendai Nihonjin no Shukyo* [Data Book: The Religion of Modern Japan], Tokyo: Shinyosha.

Jinja Shinpōsha (ed.) (1971), *Shintō Shirei to sengo no Shintō* [The Shintō Directive and Postwar Shintō], Tokyo: Jinja Shinpōsha.

Katorikku Chuō Kyōgikai (2008) *Nihon Katorikku Shikyō Kyōgikai Iya-bukku 2008* [The 2008 Japan Catholic Yearbook], Tokyo: Katorikku Chuo Kyōgikai.

Kisala, R. and Mullins, M.R. (eds) (2001) *Religion and Social Crisis in Japan: Understanding Japanese Society Through the Aum Affair*, Basingstoke, UK: Palgrave and St. Martin's Press.

Minshū (1988) no. 42(5).

Miyaji, N. (1966) 'An Interview with Dr. Naokazu Miyaji' (by William P. Woodard on 15 October 1946, and recorded by Dr. Hiyane Antei), *Contemporary Religions in Japan*, 7(2): 143–53.

50   *Mark R. Mullins*

Mullins, M.R. (2010a) 'From "Departures" to "Yasukuni Shrine": Caring for the Dead and Bereaved in Contemporary Japanese Society', *Japanese Religions*, 35(1–2): 101–12.

Mullins, M.R. (2010b) 'How Yasukuni Shrine Survived the Occupation: A Critical Examination of Popular Claims', *Monumenta Nipponica*, 65(1): 89–136.

Murakami, S. (1982) *Kokka Shintō to Minshū Shūkyō* [State Shintō and Popular Religion], Tokyo: Yoshikawa Kōbunkan.

Nishiyama, T. (2006) *Yasukuni gōshi torikeshi soshō no chūkan hōkoku – shinkyō no jiyū no kaifuku o motomete* [An Interim Report on the Lawsuit Against Yasukuni Shrine for De-Enshrinement – Seeking the Recovery of Religious Freedom], Tokyo: San Paulo.

Reid, D. (1991) *New Wine: The Cultural Shaping of Japanese Christianity*, Berkeley, CA: Asian Humanities Press.

Sugahara, R. (2005) *Yasukuni to iu ori kara no kaihō* [Liberation from the Cage of Yasukuni], Kyoto: Nagata Bunshōdo.

Sugahara, R. (2007) *Gōshi torikeshi: Yasukuni mondai no kakushin o tou* [Cancellation of Enshrinement: Probing the Core of the Yasukuni Problem]. Booklet printed by the author.

Woodard, W.P. (1972) *The Allied Occupation of Japan 1945–1952 and Japanese Religions*, Leiden: E.J. Brill.

4 Hierarchical plurality

State, religion and pluralism in southwest China

Liang Yongjia

During a small workshop on Chinese Christianity, two American scholars present findings on when and how the Chinese state 'intrudes' into society by 'harassing' house churches, and how Christians are 'scared', suffering from severe trauma to the extent that, even after being evacuated to California with the help of under-ground asylums, they are still afraid of praying in public. However, when the Chinese state is mentioned, the scholars do not seem interested in explaining why the state regulates house-churches so strongly. Instead, they repeat for a dozen times the word 'harassment'. This lexical shortage suggests a conceptual one in regard to describing the empirical data of state–religion relations in contemporary China, a topic dominated by a set of terms laid out by the universal-in-disguise standard of religious freedom based on individualism and state–church separa-tion. This standard also implies that religious freedom will prevail once the state is removed, and that religious adherents should be left alone, free to choose among religions in the way similar to customers in a shopping-mall where the state is nothing but a negligible security guard, as suggested by the term 'religious marketplace' (Yang F. 2010a). With these assumptions, religious pluralism is premised by religious organizations being free from state 'harassment'.

State–church separation, state–society dichotomy, and religious freedom based on individual choice are not fixed categories, but provincial experiences that have undergone a long process of contention, re-interpretation, and indigenization, in a particular spatial-temporal setting. The reason for its universalistic claim is in itself interesting, and deserves a stronger methodological caution than merely transplanting the given categories to non-Western contexts. If one distils Chinese 'facts' with these categories, one is methodologically going nowhere other than the office desktop, and China will continue to remain a mysterious exception. By so doing, one is not comparing but inventing 'cases' with categories non-existent in the societies in question, and there will always be some 'residual' that eventu-ally escapes from the analysis. The consequence of such analysis may be politically pressing but academically it is insignificant.

Several chapters in this volume suggest that religious diversity in the Asian context is in itself plural, and something must be done to correct the conceptual shortage, such as the workshop example I mentioned. Mark Mullins provides an example of the Yasukuni Shrine that turns from state-cult into private shrine,

52 *Liang Yongjia*

inducing domestic and international controversies in the context of legally sanctioned religious pluralism and the separation of religion and state. Carool Kersten also explores the variation of pluralist policies in Turkey and Indonesia. All of them deal with situations where state presence is (or was) strong. Rather than dismissing the state-presence as an annoying 'harassment', these authors explore the potential for comparative concepts capturing the particular state–religion relations in salient settings in Asia.

In this chapter, I provide an example from Dali, a multi-ethnic, multi-religious city in northwestern Yunnan province, in southwest China. Based on empirical data set against historical records, I explore the state's relation with religion in the post-Mao era. I argue that we can't understand religious pluralism without appreciating the religiosity of the state itself – the transcendence of the state, which provides a context of pluralism under strong regulatory measures, a context I propose to call 'hierarchical plurality'. I will explore the religiosity of the Chinese state, and assess state regulations and their operation in Dali, with an example of commodification.

Post-imperial China: atheism, state religion and hierarchy

The Chinese state's hostility toward religion is often explained as caused by the Chinese Communist Party's (CCP) ideology of atheism. Yang Fenggang, for example, writes that

> almost as soon as it took power in 1949, the CCP followed the hard line of militant atheism. Within a decade, all religions were brought under the iron control of the Party [...] Religious believers who dared to challenge these policies were mercilessly banished to labor camps, jails, or execution grounds.
>
> (Yang F. 2004: 103)

This 'ideological atheism' culminates in the Cultural Revolution, where almost any religious activity was pushed underground. One of the current problems with Chinese religiosity, he observes, is that the Party-state still 'clearly reaffirms the atheist doctrine: religion will eventually wither away and atheist propaganda should be carried out unremittingly' (Yang F. 2004: 105).

It is true that China under the CCP declares its ideology to be atheism, and hopes it will succeed in eliminating religion. Yet, to say that the state's hostility toward religion is based on its atheism might be too quick an acceptance of the state's formal standpoint, and thus involve 'seeing like a state', to use the expression of James Scott (1998). The 'atheism argument' seems to me misleading because it contradicts the historical and comparative reality. Historically, as Anthony Yu observes, 'there has never been a period in China's historical past in which the government of the state, in imperial and post-imperial form, has pursued a neutral policy toward religion. Let alone encouraged, in terms dear to American idealism, its "free exercise"' (Yu 2005: 3). In post-imperial China,

Hierarchical plurality in southwest China 53

campaigns against religion were quite strong under late Qing and the nationalist governments, as in the cases of Hebei and Jiangsu (Duara 1997: 85–114), as well as in the case of regulatory measures to get rid of the so-called wasteful and harmful 'popular religions' by creating a 'superstitious regime' (Nedostup 2009). Comparatively, the 'atheism argument' starkly constitutes an unnecessary 'third type' in addition to the theocracies and secularist states, respectively exemplified by the case of Taliban dynamiting the Buddha of Bamiyan and Iran persecuting the Baha'i on the one hand, and the privileged status of Hinduism in India, Theravada Buddhism in Thailand, and Islam in Malaysia on the other. The Chinese state, if understood merely in terms of atheist ideology, seems to find no counterpart except for North Korea and, to a lesser extent, the changing Vietnam, which has been working on religious pluralism for more than two decades (see Bouquet 2010). Such 'atheism type' is unnecessary because it encourages China's exceptionalism, and there is little difference between ideology and state religion in the case of China.

The Chinese state's hostility toward religion, manifested in strong regulatory measures, has not so much to do with its atheist ideology. On the contrary, it does so precisely because the state itself assumes a religious aura – a unique promise of delivering utopia, a particular claim to universal transcendence, and an enduring attempt to encompass other religions. If we move away from the indulgence in accusing Chinese 'atheism', a Eurocentric category having trouble even with legitimizing great religions such as Hinduism, Jainism and Buddhism (see, for example, Durkheim 1995: 27–33), we are able to see state relations with religion through the lens of a state religion that persists in post-imperial China.

Similar to the denial of the imperial court's own religiosity, post-imperial China never described its ideology – nationalism or communism – as religious. However, the CCP and its predecessor, the Kuomintang Nationalist Party, never received enough legitimacy by virtue of the people's mandate. Both seek legitimacy through a discourse of transcendence that paradoxically keeps religions away. Actually, the word 'religion' (*zongjiao*) was introduced into China precisely for the state to separate itself from it so that it could exercise regulatory measures. This is what lies behind the post-colonial explanation by Vincent Goossaert (2008) on why national associations of different religions were created, roughly at same time, by China's nationalist leaders. Anthony Yu believes that for the Chinese state,

in imperial and post-imperial form [. . .] [t]he impetus to engage religion, on the part of the central government, stem[s] first of all from its own subscription to a specific form of religiosity that, most appropriately, should be named a state religion. For more than two millennia, the core ideological conviction shaping and buttressing imperial governance also direct correlatively the purpose and process to regulate, control, and exploit all rivalry religious traditions whenever it is deemed feasible and beneficial to the state.

(Yu 2005: 3)

54 *Liang Yongjia*

In this respect, regulating religions was not the invention of the Chinese Communist Party, who but pushed the measures to the extreme. The CCP's hostility to religions was not entirely about the worry of the subversive power of the 'redemptive societies' such as the Yiguandao or the infiltration potential vested in Christianity. It regulates religions by virtue of an over-optimistic conviction that even if religious freedom is constitutionally guaranteed, religions will wither away and religious adherents will die out in the face of orthodox 'scientific communism'. As Adam Chau suggests,

> one should not exaggerate the impact of the period of supposed irreligiosity, for the most uncompromising anti-traditionalism lasted less than ten years, from the Socialist Education era of the mid-1960s to a little after the most radical phase of the tradition-smashing Cultural Revolution era was over (i.e. late 1960s and early 1970s).
>
> (Chau 2011: 5)

This optimism persisted for quite a long time, and in 2001 – after two decades of relative tolerance – the CCP publically admitted that religion would last for a very long period of time.

With the decline of communist Utopia, the post-Mao state does not abandon its quest for transcendence and works out a new form of 'state religion': nationalism. Indeed, both Marxism and nationalism, according to Bruce Lincoln (2006: 5–6), could be and should be understood in terms of religion, because 'should they ground their views in Scripture, revelation, or immutable ancestral traditions, in that moment their discourse becomes religious because of its claim to transcendental authority.' In practice, the speakers 'make claim to absolute truths without explicit gestures to the transcendent, as in the case of Marxists with extreme confidence in historic dialectics', and 'similar points can be made about varying forms of nationalism' (Lincoln 2006: 115).

This is almost exactly what the post-1949 Chinese state has been doing, except that it does make explicit gestures to the transcendent – a communist utopia, followed by a claim to a universal deliverance to 'the great revival of the Chinese nation' (*zhonghua minzu de weida fuxing*), two essential parts of the Party's 'Construction of the Spiritual Civilization' (*jingshen wenming jianshe*). In a speech delivered at the ceremony marking the centennial of the 1911 revolution, Chinese then president Hu Jintao mentioned 'the great rejuvenation of the Chinese nation' (*zhonghua minzu de weida fuxing*) twenty-three times! In other words, despite efforts to separate state from religion, the post-imperial state seems to never achieve secularism, and it somehow still feels obliged to be transcendental. The transcendence is intended to be all-encompassing over alternative transcendental claims made by Christianity, Buddhism, Daoism, and other religions. It would therefore be oversimplifying to take state–church separation as given and to attribute the lack of religious freedom to CCP's atheism. Such views will not see the religious aspect of the state, or understand the logic behind the power operations – the logic of imperial legacy that the state is trying to reclaim,

Hierarchical plurality in southwest China   55

a logic embedded in the conviction that the state has to be able to retain proper transcendence, more 'truthful' than the other religions. It is in the terms of state religion, not in the terms of free exercise of religions – 'terms dear to American idealism' – that the contemporary Chinese state's relation with religion should be understood.

The question is, then, under such a system, is pluralism possible? If so, how does it work in practice? Pluralism, as Michael Peletz argues, is not simply the state of diversity, but

> two or more principles, categories, groups, sources of authority, or ways of being in the world are not only present, tolerated, and accommodated, but also *accorded legitimacy* in a Weberian sense [...] pluralism is a feature of fields, domains, and systems in which diversity is ascribed legitimacy, and, conversely, that diversity without legitimacy is *not* pluralism.
>
> (Peletz 2009: 7)

The definition emphasizes Weberian legitimacy, and may be too easily understood as the condition in which different religions accord legitimacy to each other under an egalitarian social milieu in which certain values, norms, principles and social practices are taken to be 'equally' legitimate, as Peletz himself may also imply. However, the Weberian legitimacy also involves non-egalitarian societies where traditional authorities penetrate discretely in the legal, political and social life, like the Chinese state I suggested above. Not to mention the charismatic authority. At stake is the fact that under the contemporary Chinese state, which shares much of the imperial legacy of state religiosity claiming transcendence over other religions, and accommodating religions in a limited but not unaccountable or incomprehensible way, we can see that a kind of legitimacy among religions, as well as between religion and state, is indeed taking shape, though this is from time to time subjected to bitter struggles and controversies. To capture this kind of pluralism, I propose to epitomize this situation as 'hierarchical plurality', by which I mean a transcendence monopolized under the state; a kind of pluralism which exists, in actual practice, at the empirical level – however contested and unpleasant this is – in the form of hierarchical relations of a state encompassing all religions, and the accordance of legitimacy between state and religions, as well as among religions.

Dali and the state's state of mind

The Dali Bai Autonomous Prefecture is one of the many regions under the jurisdiction of ethnic regional autonomy (*minzu quyu zizhi*). As such, the prefecture is more often represented as a Bai prefecture, though there are other ethnic populations such as the Hui, the Yi, the Hani, the Miao and the Han which altogether constitute the majority. The prefectural capital – the city of Dali – is one of the few Chinese cities with walls which largely date from the Ming period (1368–1644), though for administration purposes, the city cluster goes well

56   *Liang Yongjia*

beyond the walled area. The 2008 census indicates a total population of 68,900 individuals. No municipal census on religious affiliation is released, but according to the prefectural statistics 15 per cent of the total population is religious; yet, there are good reasons to believe that there are higher rates of religious adherents in the city, as the government only recognizes the five religions under the control of state-sanctioned religious organizations.

The city was built in the seventh century and had been the capital of the kingdoms which had consolidated in the region (Yang B. 2009). After Kublai Khan's conquest in 1254, the relatively detached polity was gradually incorporated into imperial China. The Ming rulers made of Dali one of the most strategic fortresses and administrative centres in southwest China, which functioned to control the multi-ethnic and multi-religious population at the imperial periphery. In 1956, shortly after the CCP government had officially classified many peripheral peoples into ethnic minorities, the Dali Bai Autonomous Prefecture was created, along with several other autonomous areas, also with the intention of containing the multi-ethnic and multi-religious landscape of southwest China.

Contrary to what might be the general impression on the controversial situations in Tibet and Xinjiang, Dali and its region, packed with all major world religions and popular cults, are relatively under-reported internationally in regard to Chinese religious and ethnic issues. However, as Koen Wellens (2009: 436) comments, 'ethnic minorities in this region enjoy a relatively high level of religious freedom, not in opposition to the party-state but with its full blessing', and it is possible to observe here how a particular kind of pluralism is available together with a strong state presence, a situation desired by the state itself. It's true that the state exercises tremendous authority over the religious, and any other kind of, local affairs, and many times this control is no less than that in other non-ethnically autonomous areas. It is also true, however, that religious adherents have easy access to rituals, beliefs, scriptures and ceremonies as they desire, without causing personal or familial troubles. The local state agents are also keen in maintaining the prosperity of religion for various reasons, including the incentive to stimulate the local economy.

At the state level, post-Mao religious policies have been continuous and increasingly accountable (Yang F. 2010b). There is no Law of Religion, but most religious affairs are regulated by the CCP's official documents and State Council's regulations. The CCP Document 19 released in 1982 re-states that Buddhism, Daoism, Islam, Catholicism, and Protestantism are the only recognized religions, and their activities must be confined in self-managed, government-overviewed 'religious sites and places'. CCP members and underage juniors are forbidden from taking part in religious activities. However, implementation of these regulations fluctuates over time and across places. For example, the controversial house-churches are not formally allowed, but they are not entirely banned either. Document 19 laid out the principle for the 1982 Constitution, in which religious freedom is guaranteed under the condition that religious engagement should not 'disrupt public order, impair the health of citizens or interfere with the educational system of the State', as well as it should be free from 'foreign domination'.

CCP Document 6 of 1991 carries on the 1982 policy but for the first time tries to 'adapt religions to socialist construction'. The slogans publicized now, were conceived after this document. Since Document 6, religions are viewed not as 'survival' of a 'backward ideology', but constructive components of the 'socialist building-up of the nation'. The state has accepted the fact that religions will be around for a very long time still. The 1994 'Regulations on Managing Places for Religious Activities' issued by the State Council, revised in 2005 as 'Regulations on Religious Affairs' (*Zongjiao shiwu tiaoli*) makes further attempts to contain and regulate religions in a more accountable way. To date, the state has established a complete regulatory system that brings about three major changes: first, regulating recognized religions but suppressing heterodox 'cults'. Second, subsidizing recognized religions in terms of infrastructure, education, and management, and encouraging them to contribute to the nation-building. Third, maintaining religious pluralism by encompassing the religious worldview within the nationalist ideology.

The city of Dali is one of the thousands of the low-level state agents responsible for regulating 'religious affairs'. As such, different bodies are supposed to coordinate their activities here to ensure the implementation of successful regulations, rather than representing competing interest groups. The regulation of religious affairs is carried out by two sets of bodies: first, the Bureau of Religious Affairs – responsible to the government but also reporting to the Department of United Front of the Dali CCP headquarters – looks after various 'religious affairs'. These include the mandatory registration of sites and activities, the appointment and patriotic education of the clerics, the approval and inspections of religious activities, and the implementation of measures against 'foreign infiltration'. In Dali, as in most Chinese administrative units at this level, the bureau is merged with the Commission of Ethnic Affairs, which is responsible for issues concerning ethnic minorities. The second level of regulating bodies are the various 'religious organizations', one for each of the five major religions, headed by religious figures such as monks, priests, fathers, elders and Imams, who obtained official certificates from the government and hold political positions in the local People's Consultation Conference, one of the organs of the state structure that symbolizes the CCP's United Front – thus 'uniting' peoples of 'all walks of life'. These organizations bear different names in respective religions, and are further complemented by the 'democratic management committee' installed at each religious site, like temples and churches.

These two bodies create a structure of cooperation between the government and religious associations. They meet regularly on a variety of occasions, including one annual meeting, several religious festivals, training of clerics, organized study of new policies, and politicians' speeches. In ceremonies held to inaugurate a mosque, consecrate a monk, or promote a bishop, representatives of the government and the respective 'religious organizations' should be both present for authorization. For example, in a meeting of the prefectural Buddhist association, the board members of the association, abbots, influential monks, nuns, and lay Buddhists, would all meet to discuss the association's affairs. It is mandatory that

58 *Liang Yongjia*

the meeting also features politicians representing the Department of the United Front of the prefectural CCP committee, the prefectural Bureau of Religious Affairs, and the provincial government. The ceremony would usually start with government agents re-stating old and new policies, followed by the chief and board members of the association reporting on their study of new speeches by state leader (who might happen not to address religious affairs), expressing their determination to follow the guideline of 'love the country, love religion' (*aiguo aijiao*), as well as contributing to the state's effort to build a harmonious society. It is like a theatre in the sense of Goffman (1963), as the players are playing their expected roles on the public stage.

The centrality of patriotism has been a persistent and overarching value for the state's regulatory measures. In the 1950s, patriotism served as the major discourse to nationalize religion by re-structuring grassroots organizations and creating national associations. As a result, foreign clerics were expelled from their churches and deported; adherents were encouraged to 'reform', and pro-government clerics seized the power; the dissidents among the adherents were gradually marginalized, sometimes arrested and sent to labour camps. The most palpable change was the re-orientation of each religion's theologies toward a value hierarchy of the state over religion, as reflected in the enduring slogan of 'love the country, love religion' (*aiguo aijiao*). My survey of the Dali archives from the 1950s shows that patriotism was always the paramount excuse for the state's interference in the affairs of religious groups. Since 1982, after the failed attempt to eradicate religions, patriotism was again put at the centre of regulatory policies. In Dali, the implication of patriotism is two-fold: firstly, religions should subscribe to nationalism, which is officially defined as 'to love the socialist motherland' (*re'ai shehui zhuyi zuguo*). Secondly, religious activities should be alert to infiltration from foreign organizations in religious or non-religious disguise.

Though the regulatory system is carefully designed, its local agents – the government, the Party Committee, and the legislation – also act for their own interest, sometimes against the state. The local interests span from careerist desire for 'merit' (*zhengji*), to extra-duty income. In 1994, the Chinese state installed a new revenue system, putting local governments in serious financial difficulty (Zhou 2006). At about the same time, China also switched the development gear from command economy to market economy, which creates immense rent-seeking opportunities for politicians, whose promotion, apart from nepotism, relies heavily on how fast the economy of the area of their responsibility grows. Therefore, finding a 'growing point' has become the most important manifestation of a politically tailored 'local economy', also called GDP-ism. Starting from the year 2000, after a decade of rapid growth of the tobacco industry for example, the CCP authority of Yunnan province decided to shift from a 'major tobacco province' to a 'major culture province', or 'from a smoking industry to a smokeless one'. Yunnan is proud of being the most ethnically diversified province of China, with tremendous 'deposits of cultural resources ready for development', namely, the tourist industry.

Under the rubric of developing the tourist industry, officially recognized

Hierarchical plurality in southwest China 59

religions and unofficial religions are both subject to commodification. However, it is not an economic process in a free market. Rather, it is initiated, choreographed, and overseen by the political authority, which controls a large amount of resources and seeks its own interests. For example, if the development of the tourist industry involves the renovation of religious sites or the holding of events at these sites, investors must obtain official approval from the Bureau of Religious Affairs, the legal owner of religious sites – temples, cathedrals, churches, mosques. With this power, state-agents are able to decide on matters as to what, when and how religions are commodified. In the case of Dali, Buddhism, Daoism and the so-called 'ethnic religions' are turned into objects of commodification, while Islam, Christianity and Catholicism are not.

As a prefecture under the jurisdiction of ethnic autonomy, the government's commodification is often promoted under the umbrella of 'developing ethnic culture' to play with 'the politics of difference', in reaction to the Han culture (Harrell 1995). In this sense, the CCP's interest in containing religion is largely ignored if 'harmless' religious activities may contribute to developing tourist projects. As a result, various practices in folk religions have become major sources of 'invented traditions'. Folk religion only came to the attention of the Bureau of Religious Affairs quite recently, and it is not formally recognized yet. In this regard, folk religions are mostly 'administered' by the Bureau of Culture, which is instrumental for fabricating an ancient and mysterious ethnic Bai culture, to cater to the rapidly growing consumerism. Under the rubric of reviving ethnic culture, many temples, practices and ritual specialists are represented as bearers of ethnic traditions. Some of them have successfully entered the list of Intangible Cultural Heritage at various levels, with Buddhism, Daoism and popular religions having become the major resource for these developments.

Since only state-sanctioned religions are protected, activities legitimized as religious practices in other countries are here not considered by the Chinese state as religion, and might thus be subject to measures ranging from disinterest to repression. Such practices include ancestral veneration, geomancy, fortune-telling, physiognomy, and glyphomancy; interestingly, these traditions are often ignored by the state, even though its agents sometimes get involved in these practices themselves, consciously or unconsciously. For example, burning incense and paper-money at certain festivals is a regular practice for most residents of Dali, including civil service personnel. This practice, intended to send offerings to the dead in the hope of benevolent reciprocity, is clearly a religious act seldom questioned by the authority. The Baha'i faith is also considered as 'harmless' and its spread is largely tolerated. However, when some unregistered religious movements become 'too' organized, like Falun Gong, house-churches or Christ's Disciple (*mentu hui*), the state will consider them as threats and declare them 'heterodox cults', which leads to formal repression. These practices will not be called 'religions' and will be handled by the Bureau of Public Security.

A curious phenomenon has occurred in the post-Mao era: religions are subjected to three governmental departments: Bureau of Religious Affairs, Bureau of Cultural Affairs, and Bureau of Public Security. But this seemingly

60 *Liang Yongjia*

'chaotic' order is instead desirable for the state: the state actively functions as an arbitrator to decide which practices are 'religious', 'cultural', or 'heterodox'. Therefore, instead of providing a secular context for religious practices, the state, by emphasizing its orthodoxy of 'rejuvenating the Chinese nation', monopolizes a paramount transcendence, which encompasses the values of each religion, manifested in the slogan of 'love the country, love religion'.

Religious pluralism under differentiated regulations

From a bottom-up perspective, the state presence in the landscape of Dali religions can be political or economic. Politically, the state regulates religions according to the 'potential threat' it thinks might be coming. Economically, the state uses the power of capital to commodify religious materials and practices. The former tends to undermine pluralism with its preferential differences toward religions, but the latter helps to create a platform to entertain all religions. Both political and economic engagements involve official and unofficial religions, who are faced with regulatory measures disproportionally accorded.

Christianity, Catholicism, and Islam are somehow taken as 'politically sensitive' religions. In a sense, the mentality is that these religions are originally 'foreign', and therefore prone to infiltration. Measures against 'foreign' influences are strongly implemented, especially toward 'unregistered' clerics and groups. They are also less promoted towards tourists, and this approach is shared by both government and adherents. For example, Muslim community leaders turned down several times the proposal of identifying certain mosques as tourist destinations, and up until now non-Muslims have been discouraged to visit the mosques. In July 2010, the First Yunnan Sports Games of Religious Communities (*Yunnan Zongjiao Yundonghui*) was held in Dali, bringing registered clerics and adherents to play some light, amateur sports together. On an online forum, there were debates about whether such a Games should take place at all. Some say 'What a joke! In the Christians' eyes, the other believers are "evil". How do you expect the good and evil living harmoniously?' while others say 'People find their own ways to salvation, and it should not be singled out for blame.' Whatever the debate, the sensitivities around Abrahamic religions are felt by the non-religious populations.

Christianity was introduced in Dali by the British Inland Mission in 1888. In 1952, all foreign clergymen were forced to leave, and the two existing congregations were merged into the 'Dali Christian Church.' Activities in most churches were halted by the Land Reform and Suppressing Anti-revolutionaries Campaign in 1950, but resumed in 1953, being incorporated into the 'Three-self Movement' (see, Bays 2011). The same groups were forced underground during the Cultural Revolution (1966–76). The activities resumed again in the early 1980s, overseen by the 'two organization' (*lianghui*) system. There are several hundred believers by estimation, one church in Dali and another in the Xiaguan town. There are several house-churches in Dali, led by local Christians, and their followers – despite being hard to estimate in numbers – are often raided by the authorities.

Hierarchical plurality in southwest China 61

Christian organizations introduced modern education, hospitals, and orphanages to Dali, but all of these were confiscated and turned into public institutions. The government emphasizes that Christian organizations should not be involved in public affairs, and should reduce their activities to a minimum. However, in Xiaguan, Christians – about 1,000 believers – are actively involved in 'evangelical rehabilitation' and AIDS care. Their church was demolished during the Cultural Revolution, and after 30 years of attempting to reclaim the confiscated land, they were given half an acre to rebuild the church themselves. It should be kept in mind that most Christians are low paid or laid-off workers, and the rebuilding project is now facing a serious fund shortage. Unlike other religious or quasi-religious practices, the government not only refuses to fully return the confiscated land, but is also reluctant to subsidize the community's activities, which lack economic value and are, presumably, 'subversive'.

A magnificent Catholic cathedral was built in 1927 on one of the major roads, and this constitutes the Diocese of Dali. After nationalization, which followed the rubric of 'one association, one college' (*yihui yituan*) system, the church's grandiosity dramatically declined, but it has been slowly revived in recent years. Gathering only a few hundred followers, this is one of the largest catholic churches in southwest China. The church is now run by a government-administered committee created in 2008. According to a 102-year-old nun, she and a 90-year-old nun went on a hunger strike in late 1984 in front of the government building, to request that the church were re-opened for religious service. The government then agreed to subsidize the renovation of the church, which was in turn declared 'municipal level ancient relic' in 1985, and thus subject to legal protection. However, the reclaiming of other confiscated properties through lawsuit was never successful. The church came under serious financial difficulties for the renovation work, as with the exception of very few tourists and a handful of Catholics who live in the vicinity, people seldom visit. Father Tao – who looks after the Diocese's affairs – comments on their activities as significantly contributing to the well-being of western Yunnan. However, the government is not interested in their contributions and creates 'too much hindrance' (interview with Father Tao, June, 2005). He also appeals to Catholic communities to help relieve the financial expenses related to the up-keeping of the church, especially the renovation debt (Tao 2008).

Muslims arrived as early as the thirteenth century, along with the Mongolian conquerors. After centuries of localization, Dali's Muslims scattered in different settlements. In the last century, Islam has been considered by the state as one of the most serious 'headaches'. In 1856–73, the Muslim Panthay Rebellion led by Du Wenxiu swept across western Yunnan (Atwill 2006). It was caused by the imperial government's hidden agenda of massacring Muslim communities in Yunnan, and the rebellion culminated in the formation of an Islamic state centred in Dali, which lasted 16 years. Two mosques were founded in Dali, as more than 5,000 Hui Muslim live in the city and its vicinity.

The Bureau of Religious Affairs is responsible for organizing the annual *hajj* pilgrimage to Mecca, and the local Muslim association is responsible for locating

62 *Liang Yongjia*

those who are both qualified and financially empowered to do so. There is a ceremony for seeing the pilgrims off, and on this occasion representatives of the government re-affirm the religious policy, and remind all pilgrims to 'follow strictly the discipline, guard against infiltration, and ensure their safety' (Gazetteer-Compiling Committee 2011: 265). These pilgrims are then sent to join the provincial authority, having dispatched some 'administrator' to lead the groups all the way to Mecca. During the pilgrimage, contact with foreign Islamic groups is not allowed.

The Muslim population is often identified as Hui. But informants of different ethnicities would tell me that they are different from the Hui because, according to an informant, 'after all, we are two ethnicities'. This is like Jewish identity in the US which is religious rather than ethnic, in the sense that, according to Hiroko (1990), the Hui identity in Dali is mainly religious. There are reasons to think so, as the Hui tend to live in a cluster around the mosque, sometimes separated from the other communities, and regularly practice Islam. However, this does not mean they are living entirely in isolation. On the contrary, cultural, ethnic and religious diversity provides a context for them to make sense of the world. For example, some of the Hui business persons run the marble factories for carving and preparing tombstones important to the local Bai and other ethnic people for their ancestor worship. A quick trip through Dali will easily reveal how important marble is, as this is a lucrative business particularly to the city, which received its Chinese name from the stone itself (*dalishi*), and it is indeed famous for its high quality quarries.

The Muslim population in Dali is also famous for their enterprises in restaurants and long-distance transportation (Hill 1998). Among the non-Muslim population, their restaurants are popular not because of the *halal* food, but for their good hygiene. Local, non-Muslim residents and tourists frequent Muslim restaurants because of their 'cleanliness', which the Muslims are very proud of, too. When I conducted my first fieldwork in Dali, one of the suggestions from my Bai landlady was to buy cakes from the Hui bakery, 'because they use clean, vegetable oil'. According to the Bai custom, neighbours should be invited at weddings or funerals for a meal that usually involves pork. Muslim neighbours are often invited at such occasions, and served *halal* food at separate tables, and they seldom decline such invitations, also reciprocating such openness, and inviting non-Muslim neighbours and friends at their weddings or funerals.

Buddhism in Dali is a major religion which has undergone several incarnations. It was adopted in the ninth century as the state-religion for the local kingdoms. During the following seven centuries, Dali developed a localized form of esoteric Buddhism centred on the emperor, the Chakravatin; he was then assisted by his ministers of Acarya masters on the ceremonial aspects of state affairs, and by Zen ministers who wield 'real' power (Liang 2011). Therefore, the esoteric Acarya Buddhism and Zen Buddhism had both been strong in Dali, to the extent that according to a fourteenth-century report, the people in Dali upheld Buddhism: 'Every family, rich or poor, never fails to install a Buddhist shrine in their house. No one, old or young, ever fails to carry in hand a string of chanting beads. The days of observing vegetarianism, prohibiting eating meat and drinking alcohol, amount to more than half a year. Countless temples have been built along the mountains' (Guo 1986: 22–3). The Zen sect dominated Dali Buddhism since the seventeenth century, when esoteric Buddhism was banned under an edict of Emperor Kangxi for unknown reasons. As a result, formal Buddhist adherents in Dali's temples are Zen monks, including the Guanyin Tang temple, and the magnificent Chongsheng Temple which was founded in the ninth century as an esoteric centre.

The Buddhist tradition is so strong that Dali is often depicted as a Gandahar (a Buddhist country, *miaoxiang foguo*) (Lian 2007: 1). And this is naturally subjected to strong commodification, with most of its temples being renovated and turned into tourist destinations. This process is probably best illustrated with the case of the Chongsheng Temple, a temple built in the ninth century and widely famous for its pagodas. The temple structure was demolished during the Cultural Revolution, and only the pagodas – too strong to be destroyed – remain today. In 1994, the prefectural government created a cultural relic station and a park, covering the site. In the following years, it invested about 80 million RMB (12.5 million USD) to cast an iron bell, a giant bronze image of Avalokiteśvara, and a cauldron: three items of an invented tradition, not necessarily relevant to Buddhism. The government then created large patches of greenery, built a hotel, and turned the complex into a holiday resort whilst still preserving its status as a site of 'culture relics' (*wenwu*). The government never attempted to hide the goal of using the pagodas to develop the tourist industry. The site was handed over to the government-sponsored Dali Tourist Corporation, which facilitated its passing of the ISO9001 examination, and the 4A level of 'National Tourist Resort' certified by the State Bureau of Tourism. In 2005, the government decided to contribute another 182 million RMB (20 million USD) to create a new set of temple structures 'to end the history of a temple with nothing but pagodas' (Dali Tourism Group 2007).

The project was aimed at attracting more tourists, but this time with a new mission – turning the 'relic site' into a real temple, that is, to make it a religious site for Buddhist activities. To the government, it is obvious that a temple without monks or religious activities cannot be attractive to tourists who most likely come to seek a 'spiritual enclave' from the turmoil of urban life. After a year of highly complicated coordination, a grand inauguration ceremony was held at the temple upon completion of the infrastructural works, where a number of monks, including a prominent abbot, were appointed at the presence of high monks and politicians from the national, provincial and prefectural levels. The abbot was then appointed chair of the prefectural Buddhist association, and the temple was quickly qualified to provide comprehensive religious services, including full ordination of monks.

In July 2011, the Chongsheng Temple was certificated with 5A level 'National Tourist Resort', the highest rank authorized by the State Bureau of Tourism. However, the religious aspect of the temple is largely separated from its tourist function. The monks and abbots are not able to collect the high-priced admission

64   *Liang Yongjia*

tickets paid by the tourists, as the income is shared by the local government and the developers, who give limited financial benefits to the monks. It is for the strong incentive of developing tourism that the local government patronizes Buddhism, and creates additional religious sites. It is starkly in contrast with the government's suspicion of Abrahamic religions, towards which it has little interest in providing financial help.

Among the five recognized religions, Daoism is the least influential, and there is no temple or organization in Dali. However, many people believe that this is because the state's classificatory system doesn't count popular religion as Daoism. This is certainly true, since in the city temporally ordained masters send petitions to various gods on behalf of temple visitors, possessed spiritual-mediums release heavenly revelations at intervals, and proud literates gather regularly for the cult of Wenchang and Guandi.

A sophisticated network of patron-god system, *benzvt*, also has several 'franchised' temples in the city. *Benzvt*, or *vuzeng*, means 'my master' or 'our master'. Every Bai community has at least one, and sometimes two, of these temples. The deity in the centre of the shrine is a local historical figure, who has a particular legend, character, and family. The *benzvt* temple is the symbol of a community, and gives an identity to each household in terms of alliances, residence, and most other concerns of life. The temples were taken care of by the women of the Old Women's Association who maintain the primary symbol of community, and see themselves as community representatives. Most of the Bai households visit their *benzvt* temples whenever important events take place at home, or at festivals. Many rituals and practices of the ancient esoteric form of Buddhism had merged with Daoist rituals in the *benzvt* cult (Liang 2005).

The state's presence in religious issues is two-fold: political and economic. Such presence provides the context for different religions to be co-opted. Certainly, it could be described as 'limited tolerance' (Yang F. 2010b), particularly in the case of Abrahamic religions. However, it is equally fair to say that different religions have to participate in, or even are actively involved in, cooperation, recognition, legitimization and toleration of each other, for good and bad reasons. Then this is what can be described as secularism in the third sense suggested by Charles Taylor (2007), that secularity is the condition in which different religions and non-religion are aware of, and accommodate, each other. Accommodation involves common submission to state power in the Political Consultation Conference led by the Party's United Front Department, as well as everyday activities pursued to endorse each other's position in reference to the state. The state plays the role of encompassing all religious beliefs, which it takes advantage of, to meet its own ends: developing the tourist industry. The differentiated regulation is very conspicuous in the economic aspect. The condition of diversity in which legitimacy is accorded is indeed present, though it is not the kind of pluralism present in an egalitarian context. It is hierarchical plurality.

Commodifying Gwer Sa La

Gwer Sa La is a large-scale, grassroots practice that involves a legend, a pilgrimage, fertility rituals and temple fairs, best described as a popular religious event. In this sense, it does not have a legal status as religion from the viewpoint of the state. However, in recent years, the prefectural state agencies – the government, the congress, and the Political Consultation Conference – launched a campaign of commodification of Gwer Sa La by applying for Intangible Cultural Heritage status. Through this case, we can examine how the state appropriates religious practices and maintains hierarchical plurality in practice.

Gwer Sa La ('visiting three places') is an annual pilgrimage which takes place from the 22nd to the 25th of the fourth month of the lunar calendar. During this time-span, people visit three places in the Dali basin, one after another. It is a carnival-like festival where non-marital or pre-marital relations are tolerated. Men and women in Gwer Sa La may *bir sai bair vux*, or 'engage in furtive relations', becoming lovers (*jani*). The relation is mostly established through song duets at nights. However, it is not supposed to go beyond Gwer Sa La. The baby born through this extra-marital relation will be considered legitimate, and credited as the blessing of the White King, the main god in one of the temples not far from the city of Dali.

Members of village ritual societies, such as the Old Women's Association, assume the ritual responsibility of the festival. These people – mostly women – believe themselves to be devoted Buddhists, but they are not affiliated with Buddhist temples. Nor they have anything to do with the state. They are obliged to follow the entire itinerary and pray for benevolence on behalf of their families and villages. The members claim to be Buddhists, though neither the government nor the Buddhist associations recognize them as such. During the Gwer Sa La, they will visit many key temples and send the legendary Princess Jingu and her husband off, at the City-god Temple of Dali, burning offerings at various occasions. A variety of people participate in the event in one way or another. Vendors sell snacks and drinks, music CDs and ritual consumables, while local officials regulate and observe. Beggars line on the road, many of them disabled, asking for rice and money. Domestic and international tourists come to observe the 'authentic' Bai culture, expecting exotic scenes or romantic encounters. Most of the visitors spend the whole day at the fair, enjoying the food, watching the dances, and buying items. All of them seem to wear their best clothes, looking cheerful.

Officially recognized religions take part in this 'unorthodox' pilgrimage. The Buddhist temple (Sacred Source Temple) nearby the pilgrimage destination (Capital of All Gods dedicated to the White King) will accommodate pilgrims, as they make no difference between a 'popular religious temple' and a registered Buddhist Temple. Members of the Old Women's Associations, after paying homage to the Capital of All Gods, will visit the Sacred Source Temple, forming a procession consisting of two leaders, a group of dragon dancers, and other members of the association. The procession, together with musical instruments and dances, is said to be able to solicit rain for the crop as well as to help people

66   *Liang Yongjia*

multiply. This 'eccentric', fertility-soliciting procession will *kowtow* before each image and ask the monks to pray on their behalf. These practices are totally irrelevant to the Buddhist tradition, but the monks are happy to see them coming, and offer due assistance as they will do for any other visitors.

On the eve of Gwer Sa La in 2002, a monk from the Sacred Source Temple paid a visit to the small police station where I stayed. The monk humbly spoke before a group of policemen and a few cadres from the municipal government, who were too uninterested to give him an attentive ear,

> I come over to thank the government who provides order and security to Gwer Sa La. As an old, ordained monk, it is my fortune to live in a time of the Party's wise policy to let us have religious freedom. The Dali people also 'settle in and enjoy their ways of living' (*anju leye*). My best wishes go with each of you, who spare your precious time for the order and peace of the festival. I will never forget how good the government is.
>
> (fieldwork notes)

Though this 'speech' is not a surprising one, given the fact that the monks often have to recite the political script, it is rare to hear it in a dark night in a village centre full of low-ranked, wage-earning policemen. What I learned later on, is that the monk came over with this speech because he wanted to make sure that the paid service of 'burning the high incense' his temple offers to the pilgrims would go smoothly without being questioned by the police.

Compared to the Buddhist program of 'burning the high incense', the Daoist participation to the Gwer Sa La is coordinated by the Bureau of Cultural Affairs, which brings several Dongjing music bands to the Gwer Sa La sites, playing the 'Scripture of the Great Grotto' (*dadong xianjing*). Unlike the Old Women's Associations, the Dongjing bands are composed of male elders who distinguish themselves as 'community moral exemplars' by playing the music eligible only to the literate. A variety of Daoist rituals and liturgical practices characterize these bands, but most of them are enlisted by the Bureau of Cultural Affairs as preservers of the 'traditional musical art'. The event evolves into competition over time, but the performances have been always paid by the government.

As a festival in which most of the Bai-speaking people participate, Gwer Sa La has become one of the targets of commodification for the purpose of developing the tourist industry. In 2005, the Bureau of Culture of the Dali Bai Autonomous Prefecture submitted an application through the provincial Bureau of Culture to the State Ministry of Culture, requesting to include Gwer Sa La in the national representative list of Intangible Cultural Heritage. The application was made at the moment that 'cultural heritage' had become one of the most popular topics in the Chinese media, and heritage safeguard was well-known and heart-felt.

In the application booklet, the Gwer Sa La is essentialized in many ways, including being given historical roots, religious reasons, and specific meanings which involved craft, literature, dress, and beliefs – all of them accredited to the Bai *minzu*. Gwer Sa La was thus represented as a signature 'culture item' of the

Bai. It has a materialistic origin, arising from 'rice-cultivation', and a religious nature (to 'amuse gods and men'), but it represents Bai-ness in an encompassing way ('hosting a spectrum of cultural activities'). Its 'original meaning' is 'to visit three "Public houses"' (*gong fang*), which allures to the fictive primitive promiscuity. Finally, Gwer Sa La honours three gods of *benzvt*, a territorial-cult system that has been held as the Bai's 'ethnic religion'.

The application booklet goes on to enumerate more Bai cultural 'items' and activities found in Gwer Sa La. It took place in the central area of the Bai's prefecture. The 'sun patch', the willow, the gourd, the dancing stick ('tyrant's whip'), and the drums ('golden coin drum' and 'double-swallows') are found nowhere else but among the Bai. Some standard Chinese musical instruments such as *suona* (Chinese shawm) and *sanxian* (Chinese lute) are described with 'Bai' as modifier. The overall feature of the festival is 'a folk carnival entertaining gods and men, *solely owned [duyou]* by the Bai'. Three legends are provided as possible origins of the Gwer Sa La, each of which tells how the Bai king ruled his Bai subjects. It seems that once you see Gwer Sa La, you are surrounded exclusively by authentic Bai culture.

The application turned out to be successful. Gwer Sa La was officially included in the national list in May 2006, and the application booklet was widely circulated as the 'model text' for future applicants. A Gwer Sa La 'master' was quickly located, and subsequently authorized by the Ministry as the 'representative transmitter' (*daibiaoxing chuanchengren*) for this national intangible cultural heritage. Before long, another man was nominated for the same position.

In 2009, after much lobbying, the State Ministry of Culture decided to nominate Gwer Sa La for candidacy to UNESCO's 'representative list' of Intangible Cultural Heritage. Scholars were invited for conferences; a team of specialists from the Ministry of Culture was sent to Dali to 'instruct' related works; media coverage was coordinated at municipal, prefectural, provincial and national levels. The prefectural governor's report to the local legislation emphasized the need to 'accelerate the application of Gwer Sa La to world intangible cultural heritage'. A committee composed of various political bodies was created to make sure Gwer Sa La would be looked after. In addition to upgrading the infrastructure, the committee mobilized a large team to create a stage-show performed at the first day of the Gwer Sa La festival, displaying this intangible cultural heritage in a very tangible way.

Gwer Sa La illustrates how non-Abrahamic religions – popular religions, Buddhism, Daoism – may be carefully orchestrated by the state's power, which has strong incentives to appropriate popular religion for commercial ends. According to a local newspaper, after Gwer Sa La was conferred the national Intangible Cultural Heritage status, tourists to Dali increase by 2 per cent each year during the festival, generating a total GDP of 1.1 billion RMB (about 174 million USD). By authorizing the Intangible Cultural Heritage status, the state has legitimized a religious practice without legally recognizing it as a religion. In other words, in the case of Gwer Sa La, the religious plurality the state desires goes beyond the realm of state-sanctioned religions. Examining the imperial

68   *Liang Yongjia*

state's authorization of the God of War, Prasenjit Duara (1988) suggests that authorization is a process of superscription, in which the state legitimizes a popular religious practice by declaring given aspects of the practice as consistent with state-sanctioned morality, while leaving the practitioners alone with unorthodox, 'superstitious' aspects of the practice. I argue that Intangible Cultural Heritage status has become a superscribing tool by which the state continues to maintain its encompassing power through its authority to legitimize some practices of popular religions, and reifying its superiority to religion.

Conclusion

The multi-ethnic, multi-religious city of Dali has a long tradition of entertaining Buddhism, Daoism, Islam, Catholicism, Christianity, and popular religions. For the last 30 years, it has experienced a vibrant religious revival of all these faiths and practices. The state has been active in regulating religions, through its Bureau of Religious Affairs, the Bureau of Cultural Affairs, and sometimes, the Bureau of Public Security. The state's presence in religious issues is thus two-fold: political and economic. This presence provides the context for different religions to be co-opted, creating a space where different religions have to – or even want to – cooperate, recognize, legitimize and tolerate each other. Given political control and state-led commodification, the state's presence, though seemingly illegitimate, has been central in maintaining the context of religious pluralism.

More than atheism, the state's strong engagement with religions is an imperial legacy characterized by the religiosity of the state itself. The transcendence that the state sanctions, constitutes a kind of orthodoxy that maintains the 'truth' of the cosmos. However, the orthodoxy does not intend to eliminate other, alternative, transcendences revealed in non-state religions. On the contrary, the state contains them, regulates them, and tolerates them by maintaining a hierarchical relation with them. This is part of the famous argument of the 'imperial metaphor' (Feuchtwang 2001) that wields a 'superscribing power' over different popular religious practices. The state's religiosity, and its symbolic superiority over religions, arguably persists in post-imperial, contemporary China, as the state decides whether a set of beliefs and practices is a religion or not, and brings them under effective control with different state organs. As Tim Oakes and Donald Sutton (2010: 15) observe, in contemporary China, '[t]he gods and churches are sponsored and in principle subsumed within the party-state – much as approved gods and religious institutions in imperial times were subsumed ideologically within the imperial metaphor and bureaucratically within the official system.'

This is the context the Chinese state provides for religious pluralism in the city of Dali, which I propose to call a scheme of 'hierarchical plurality'. The state never allows the free exercise of religions. Instead, it only recognizes five major religions, subjected to strong regulations and nationalization, while leaving other 'religious practices' either with the hands of Public Security or, as in the case of the immense scale of popular religions, to the practitioners themselves. Moreover, the state also promulgates differentiated regulations according to its political or economic interests. The incentive of religious commodification is so strong that local state-agents often act on their own interests, like the case of Gwer Sa La. The traditional authority – the reincarnated imperial state – is central in discussing religious pluralism in contemporary China, which is neither egalitarian freedom nor authoritarian atheism, but hierarchical plurality under the transcendence of the state.

References

Atwill, D. (2006) *The Chinese Sultanate: Islam, Ethnicity and the Panthay Rebellion in Southwestern China, 1856–1873*, Stanford, CA: Stanford University Press.

Bays, D. (2011) *A New History of Christianity in China*, Malden, MA: Wiley-Blackwell.

Bouquet, M. (2010) 'Vietnamese Party-State and Religious Pluralism since 1986: Building the Fatherland?', *Sojourn: Journal of Social Issues in Southeast Asia,* 25(1): 90–108.

Chau, A. (ed.) (2011) *Religion in Contemporary China: Revitalization and Innovation*, London: Routledge.

Dali Tourism Group (2007) 'The Destruction and the Re-building of the Chongsheng Temple', available from www.dalisanta.net/publish/chinese/show.php?itemid=1956, (accessed on 20 July 2011).

Duara, P. (1988) 'Superscribing Symbols: The Myth of Guandi, Chinese God of War', *The Journal of Asian Studies,* 47(4): 778–95.

Duara, P. (1997) *Rescuing History from the Nation: Questioning Narratives of Modern China*, Chicago: University of Chicago Press.

Durkheim, E. (1995) *Elementary Forms of Religious Life*, New York: The Free Press.

Feuchtwang, S. (2001) *Popular Religion in China: The Imperial Metaphor*, Richmond, UK: Curzon.

Gazetteer-Compiling Committee (2011) *Dali Zhou Tongzhi Nianjian* [Annuals of the Dali Prefecture], Dali Bai Autonomous Prefecture, Kunming: Yunnan Minzu Chubanshe.

Goffman, E. (1963) *Behavior in Public Places; Notes on the Social Organization of Gatherings*, New York: Free Press of Glencoe.

Goossaert, V. (2008) 'Republican Church Engineering. The National Religious Associations in 1912 China', in Mayfair Mei-hui Yang, (ed.), *Chinese Religiosities: Afflictions of Modernity and State Formation*, Berkeley: University of California Press.

Guo, S. (1986 [14th century]) *Dali Xingji ji Qita Wuzhong* [The Dali Travelogue and Other Five Pieces], Beijing: Zhonghua Shuju.

Harrell, S. (ed.) (1995) *Cultural Encounters on China's Ethnic Frontiers*, Seattle, WA: University of Washington Press.

Hill, A.M. (1998) *Merchants and Migrants: Ethnicity and Trade among Yunnanese Chinese in Southeast Asia*, New Haven, CT: Yale University Southeast Asia Studies.

Hiroko, Y. (1990) 'Ethnic Groups in the Dali Basin', In Fei Xiaotong (ed.) *Zhonghua Minzu Yanjiu Xintansuo* [New Explorations of Chinese Ethnic Studies], Beijing: Zhongguo Shehui Kexue Chubanshe.

Lian, R. (2007) *Yincang de Zuxian: Nanzhao Miaoxiangguo de Chuanshuo yu Shehui* [The Hidden Ancestors: the Gandahar Legend and Society of Nanzhao], Beijing: Sanlian Shudian.

Liang, Y. (2005) *Diyu de Dengji* [Territorial Hierarchy], Beijing: Sheke Wenxian Chubanshe.

Liang, Y. (2011) 'Stranger-Kingship and Cosmocracy; or, Sahlins in Southwest China', *Asia Pacific Journal of Anthropology,* 12(3): 236–54.

70 *Liang Yongjia*

Lincoln, B. (2006) *Holy Terrors: Thinking about Religion after September 11*, Chicago: University of Chicago Press.

Nedostup, R. (2009) *Superstitious Regimes: Religion and the Politics of Chinese Modernity*, Cambridge, MA: The Harvard University Asia Center.

Oakes, T. and D. Sutton (2010) 'Introduction', in Oakes, T. and Sutton, D. (eds) *Faiths on Display: Religious Revival and Tourism in China*, Lanham, MD: Rowman and Littlefield.

Peletz, M. (2009) *Gender Pluralism: Southeast Asia Since Early Modern Times*, London: Routledge.

Scott, J. (1998) *Seeing Like a State: How Certain Schemes to Improve the Human Condition Have Failed*, New Haven, CT: Yale University Press.

Tao, Z. (Fr.) (2008) 'Report on Applying for Funding to Compensate for the Construction Work of the Church and Places of Praying', available from http://immensee.blogbus.com/logs/29586062.html (accessed on 18 June 2011).

Taylor, C. (2007) *A Secular Age*, Cambridge, MA: Harvard University Press.

Wellens, K. (2009) 'Negotiable Rights: China's Ethnic Minorities and the Right to Freedom of Religion', *International Journal on Minority and Group Rights,* 16(3): 433–54.

Yang, B. (2009) *Between Winds and Clouds: The Making of Yunnan*, New York: Columbia University Press.

Yang, F. (2004) 'Between Secularist Ideology and Desecularizing Reality: The Birth and Growth of Religious Research in Communist China', *Sociology of Religion,* 65(2): 101–19.

Yang, F. (2010a) 'Religion in China under Communism: A Shortage Economy Explanation', *The Journal of Church and State,* 52(1): 3–33.

Yang, F. (2010b) 'Religious Awakening in China under Communist Rule', in Turner, B. (ed.), *The New Blackwell Companion to The Sociology of Religion,* Singapore: Wiley-Blackwell.

Yu, A. (2005) *State and Religion in China: History and Textual Perspective,* Chicago: Open Court.

Zhou, F. (2006) 'Rural Fee Reform and the Changing Relationship between State and Peasant', *Shehuixue Yanjiu* (Sociological Studies), 21(3): 1–38.

5 Literacy wars

Children's education and weekend madrasahs in Singapore[1]

Phyllis Ghim-Lian Chew

For historian Anthony Reid (2011) Southeast Asia is the great laboratory of religious pluralism. It is not difficult to understand this viewpoint since there is an extraordinary abundance of languages, ethnicities, modes of production, beliefs and cultural patterns existing in close proximity in this part of the world. Pluralism is also a constant feature of everyday life in view of the profusion of ethnic, religious and linguistic groups, creating a form of 'unity in diversity' (Chew 2009). While diversity has its advantages as an accelerator of social change (Moore 2007), its downside is that this diversity needs to be 'managed'. For example, the plural state needs to protect religious tolerance since not all expressions of religion are 'moderate' or safe. Some forms of religion, especially if they belong to the minority, may be seen as 'toxic' as they may reduce the numbers of other groups in the society, erode community spirit and impair the ability of different groups to live together in peace and mutual respect. It is unwise to ignore the possible harm generated by some expressions of religious life. Hence, we see states grappling with the means to manage diversity through various measures, be it parliamentary, the courtroom or the classroom. In Singapore, my site of analysis, the 1990 Maintenance of Religious Harmony Act, which comes under the aegis of the Minister for Home Affairs, in turn advised by a Presidential Council for Religious Harmony, makes it an offence to cause ill-feelings between different religious groups.

Singapore is a nation that has successfully crafted a distinct group of people through highly focused multiracial and multilingual practices, and perhaps pluralism is nowhere as evident in Southeast Asia as it is here (Chew 2013). One may suppose that in a 'competitive, lean and modern state' on 680 square kilometres of land with a relatively high per capita gross domestic product, and a reputation for efficiency and enterprise, religious aspirations would be secondary to material ones. But such a presupposition would be untrue. Religion is alive and well in the lives of Singaporeans and freedom of worship is enshrined in the Singapore constitution. The Inter-religious Council is an officially recognized and supported Non-Governmental Organization as well as one which actively promotes activities such as the annual celebration of World Religion Day, whereby representatives from the ten religions of Singapore (Baha'i Faith, Buddhism, Christianity, Jainism, Judaism, Hinduism, Islam, Sikhism, Daoism, and

72 *Phyllis Ghim-Lian Chew*

Zoroastrianism) come together to commemorate a day of diversity and tolerance in religious beliefs.[2] For many people, religion is a source of spiritual, social and even cultural nourishment. In addition, for the Sikhs, Malays and Parsis of Singapore, religion is a definition of their identity. For the Chinese and Indians, it is a major part of their cultural life, as seen in their practice of annual local festivals such as the Moon Cake Festival and Thaipusam.

Singapore is also characterized by internal religious pluralism (cf. Tong 2002). The Chinese religion for one is extremely difficult to characterize not least because of its eclecticism. Nevertheless, within its wide umbrella, one discerns Confucianism (in its various orders), Shenism and Daoism, each including smaller groups, with their own canonical traditions (e.g. *Tuapekong* and *Tien Fei*). Buddhists are also pluralistic in rituals, practices, and certain canonical beliefs and this is manifested through their multiple denominations, such as Mahayana, Theravada, Nichiren Shoshu association and Soka. So too, Hinduism is distinctly 'pluralistic' as revealed by the temples, which are distinguished not just in design but also separate priesthood and segregated patronage. There are also various Hindu-inspired movements such as Sai Baba and Brahma Kumaris. As for the Christians of Singapore, they are divided among the Catholic Church and a great variety of other Christian denominations including the Baptists, Brethens, Presbyterians, Lutherans, Anglicans, Adventists and Methodists. Muslims are divided into various schools such as the Sunni and the Shi'a, and each in turn also have their own various distinctive schools. For example, Sunni jurisprudence is divided into four schools of jurisprudence (*fiqh*): Shafi'i, Hanafi, Maliki and Hanbali. Finally, one notes that adherents to all these religions mentioned above also display evidence of infusion of beliefs and practices of local traditions (such as animistic beliefs) or are influenced by religious practices of other world religions.

Such internal religious pluralism is not widely known among believers themselves, and this is true for the Malay Muslim community (the focus of this study) as it is for the Chinese and Indian communities in Singapore. A common perception is that the Malay Muslim community is more tightly drawn in than the rest, a perception helped by the fact that the Malays of Singapore, unlike those in Malaysia and Indonesia, are a cultural minority. As a community, they are 'doubly marked' by the sense of 'Malayness' and a common faith (Chua and Kwok 2001). Doubtless, the Islamic notion of *ummah* as a universal community of believers who voluntarily profess one faith, also provides a rallying point for unification. However, in reality, the *ummah* has been fragmented over many centuries into denominations, parties, and movements, some of them denying each other the status of true believers. The *ummah* is also fraught with ambivalence as shown in this study of the three groups of children. While 90 per cent of Muslims in Singapore belong to the Shafi'i school, there are distinctive differences within these schools, as will be evident in this study of weekend madrasahs. This study of weekend madrasahs discerns a desire to preserve traditions on the one hand, and the need to open the community to new bodies of knowledge and economic opportunities on the other.[3]

The focus on weekend madrasahs is an attempt to shed light on Muslims who are neither activist nor religiously visible. It is meant to be a balanced response to the many volumes on activist Muslims, which are ostensibly 'attractive' to researchers because of their visibility and activism. However overexposing this particular group leaves other groups of Muslims underexposed, and eventually risks becoming hegemonic 'evidence' of political and public understandings of Muslims as particularly (and dangerously) religious (Schmidt 2011). Thus, my objective here is to examine everyday religious practices of 'lived Islam' (cf. Jeldtoft 2011). While these types of practices are not solely bound to the private sphere because 'the everyday' is constituted by many different aspects and spaces of people's lives, they seem to be under-represented in published studies.

Literacy and children's classes

The 'literacy' and 'literacies' that surround a child from the moment he is born is worthy of study, not least because literacies are used by various groups to produce, maintain and control knowledge. Literacy practices may take place in or out of school. Where school is concerned, in Singapore there is usually the week-day 'mainstream' school which is 'secular', and the weekend 'peripheral' religious school which is 'sacred'. These literacies are usually kept apart, for they are entirely different in orientation and practice; and hence is the origin of what I have termed 'literacy wars' fought for the hearts and minds of the children. The child's association or exposure to these dynamics will of course be of great influence, not least because children have an extremely absorbent mind and are spontaneous learners.[4]

In this study 'literacy' is not defined as an autonomous set of skills, decontextualized from society and culture, without links to ideology, knowledge and power. On the contrary, 'literacy' is intimately associated with ways of thinking; believing and valuing that is connected with group membership. Often, literacy is mastered not so much by overt instruction but by apprenticeship and guided participation in social practices with people who have already mastered such literacies.[5] A child, or any individual, may thus move through and participate in a number of literacies every day, each of which is, in reality, a discoursal ritual or genre with particular ways of talking, dressing, reading, and writing. The term, 'Literacy wars', is used here to refer to the plurality of Literacies practiced in each madrasah. Although all three schools in my study belong to the Shafi'i school of Sunni Islam, it would be erroneous to assume that the schools are homogenous. Indeed, no single voice or trend predominates even within clearly demarcated schools (Saeed 2009). Their members are at best a mosaic and their literacies are as wide as the many sub-ethnicities, such as Boyanese, Bugis, and Javanese, in the Malay community. There are, for example, traditionalists and reformists, fundamentalist and moderates, the English-educated and the Malay-educated. This mosaic includes Muslims who are practising and devout, as well as a large number whose relationship with their faith is largely nominal. Every madrasah has its own history, aims and orientation. And each madrasah has its own set of

74 *Phyllis Ghim-Lian Chew*

guidelines of what it means to be a member in good standing. Part-time or week-end madrasahs organize their curriculum differently, choose their own textbooks and are said to be fiercely independent (Muklis 2006).

Where Muslim education in general is concerned, anthropologists and religious historians have already recounted the pedagogies that shaped it and the intellectual, moral and affective spiritual effects attributed to it (Boyle 2004; Brenner 2001). Researchers in these areas have produced rich accounts of elementary Islamic education using a wide range of methods such as interviews, questionnaires, participant observation, archival research, psychological experiment as well as fine-grained analysis of video (cf. Moore 2008). In Singapore itself, there has also been a recent spate of publications on madrasah education, for example Noor and Lai (2006), Alatas (2006), Saeed (2009) and Saeda (2010). However, very little has been written about part-time or weekend madrasahs even though it is attended by at least 40 per cent of young people aged 5 to 24 (MUIS 2007: 51).[6] These weekend schools take place outside school hours, usually on a Saturday or Sunday, for a few hours each week. A Muslim child would attend such a school for an average of two to four hours per week, and for an average of six years (Chee 2006).

It should be noted from the onset that children's classes have always been popular in Islam not least because Islam is first and foremost a religion centred on literacy. The first word revealed by the Prophet Mohammed is the imperative *iqra* (read, recite): 'Proclaim (or read) in the name of your Lord and Cherisher, Who created . . . ' (Qur'an, 96:1). Hence, verses are read aloud to accompany birth and death and in times of distress or joy. The Koran, as Islam's sacred book, is used most extensively in the liturgy in mosques and in private devotion. In almost every sermon and religious talk, Koranic verses are quoted and explained. Chapters and verses from the Qur'an are used regularly in congregational and individual prayers and indeed, it is impossible for a Muslim to pray without reading the Qur'an's first chapter which is entitled 'The opening'.[7]

At the simplest level of weekend education, it is common for students to move from teacher to teacher to further their spiritual education, and payment to such teachers may be in the form of cash or a gift. At the more complex level, religious education may take place in the mosque or on the premises of a religious association. Such weekend classes comprise the 'common face' of Islam that the majority of Muslim children and youth will ever be acquainted with. Traditionally, such classes were supported and run by community members and in larger cities by the wealthy. They may be described as genuine community institutions, which are responsive to community needs and values without being highly centralized or overly bureaucratic. They also descend from a long and loosely organized tradition of schools which stretches back to the seventh century and which has since then provided elementary education in calligraphy, poetry, grammar, arithmetic, penmanship, etc. (Hefner 2001). Weekend classes may also be said to originate from the small *maktab* or *kuttab* (writing schools) or *suraus* (a small building in a village used for religious purposes but not normally a mosque) in the Middle East which catered to children, providing them with skills to read, perform basic Islamic rituals, and recitation of the Qur'an. The main objective of such schools is to inculcate values that would produce good Muslims and to train future clerics for the community.

These weekend madrasahs are popular with parents keen to equip their children with religious values. Most of the parents interviewed in my study cited madrasah culture as offering a 'safe' environment in which their children can be insulated from the influence of negative social values associated with drug abuse, sexual permissiveness, youth gangsterism and consumerism, in the face of rapid globalization. Some of the parents look to the weekend madrasah as the ideal instrument that provides for an integration of both secular and religious knowledge. The principal of WM2 (Weekend Madrasah no.2), one of the madrasahs involved in this study, said that the children in her school 'belong to parents who have a conscience, who know about religion'. According to her, some put their child in 'as early as 3 years old' with many 'regretting not putting them in earlier'. Typical reasons given for placement are: 'I want them to attend so as to balance what they learn in [mainstream] school' (WM2 P1 line 40–41). Or, '[It is] very difficult to control my children. They love to go shopping watch movies. I am afraid of all this bad influence' (WM2 P2 line 340–2411). 'Character training is the most difficult – not school work. My daughters know what is *haram* but still they are always tempted to do it' (WM1 P3 line 98).

In brief, families send their children to weekend madrasahs to study the Qur'an, to develop competence in reciting, reading and writing the sacred text, and they hope that this will also help them develop good moral character and proper religious feelings. And, in fact, weekend schools are not just conducted by the Muslim community, but also by other faith groups such as Christians, Buddhists and Sikhs. Indeed, their presence in Singapore is a taken-for-granted part of the pluralistic landscape, a contribution to the relationship between religion and racial-cultural identity and which may be viewed as part of the self-perpetuating institutional narrative promoted by the Singapore government (Goh 2009). WMs not only contribute and maintain the pluralistic options available to the multiracial, multicultural, and multilingual population, but are seen as providing 'a balance' to the alienation so often found in a capitalist-industrial society.

This chapter outlines the literacy practices of three weekend madrasahs which may be said to range from 'traditional' to 'moderate' to 'liberal', referred to as WM1, WM2 and WM3, respectively in this chapter.[8] The methodology used includes ethnographic research methods such as field notes, participant observation, audio and video tape analysis, and interviews with teachers and parents. The study uses as its theme, the less-known Literacies wars within the weekend madrasahs, as well as the more obvious 'war' between the weekend and the weekday school; between the sacred and the secular or the peripheral and the mainstream. Each of the three madrasahs is examined in terms of three main criteria: classroom semiotics, pedagogical practices and the medium of instruction. Classroom semiotics refer to individual sounds or letters that humans use to form words, body movement to show attitude or emotion or something as general as the clothes that one wear. I will define it broadly as an approach that seeks to

76 Phyllis Ghim-Lian Chew

interpret messages in terms of their signs of patterns of symbolism; and the relationship among these signs. Keane (2007) terms it as 'a way of eating, sitting, playing games and building houses'. Where pedagogical practices are concerned, we may think of them as a kind of 'patterned social acts' (Street 2005). It assumes that in learning to read and through reading itself, children acquire socio-culturally appropriate information, values and ways of thinking and doing that teachers normally assume children should have (Pike 2006). 'Pedagogical practices' depend on textbooks to introduce the child reader to cultural knowledge considered legitimated or valued (Curdt-Christiansen 2008). An examination of curriculum materials is therefore an examination of the construction of cultural knowledge and of what is considered primary or secondary knowledge. Finally, we examine the medium of instruction not least because 'the world and the word' (Freire and Macedo 1989) involves not just the script but also the subtle socio-cultural historical knowledge associated with the script. Each language carries the particularities of its socio-cultural and historical contexts, and cuts markers on the landscapes, whereby we habitually traverse. In brief, the way we experience the world is determined by our choice of language.

WM1 (traditional mosque)

Of the three weekend madrasahs under study, WM1 may be said to be the most traditional, and this is gleaned by a remark made by a grandparent, whose job it was to accompany his grandson to class every week: 'I was taught in this mosque. Here they teach exactly the same. Very good – no change to the past.' (WM1 GP1 lines 56–7).

WM1 is part of a handful of madrasahs affiliated to a traditional Muslim association which views child education as an activity of supreme importance. It admits school-going children aged 7 to 16 for a nominal fee. The classes are held in the main hall of a small private mosque every Saturday and Sunday morning. The child's syllabus and curriculum is formulated by a committee of adult volunteers, all members of the association. They are then given honorary designations such as 'treasurer', 'discipline master', 'ladies coordinator', 'events coordinator', 'parents coordinator', and so forth and their tasks are to administer the classes. The primary objective of WM1 is teaching the children to recite the Qur'an, as 90 per cent of curriculum time is dedicated to achieve this goal. Their main textbook is the series *Buku Iqro; cara cepat belajar membaca al-Quran* in six volumes, authored by Kiyai Haji Asad Human, and which is imported from Jakarta. The teachers for the male pupils are recruited from abroad, mostly from India, to teach Arabic and Qur'an recitation. This is because the association is unable to find suitable male Singaporeans who are able to do so at competitive wages. However, the teachers for the female pupils are local volunteers, usually mothers. The curriculum for male and female children is slightly different, and here there are female teachers for the girls, and male teachers for the boys.

The mosque is a sacred space and there is a rarefied atmosphere as one enters it. Every child has to display the appropriate emotions such as respect, reverence and prayerfulness, as he or she enters. The main hall of the mosque is given to the education of the children for a particular period of time. There is a quarter section of the hall partitioned off with a high screen, and this is where the girls gather with their female teachers for their own education. The girls have to cover themselves modestly except for their face and hands. The gowns they wear are loosely cut so that the shape of the body is not apparent and/or distracting to others. They all wear the *tudong* (head covering), which is white in colour. The teachers are also dressed in this same fashion, that is, a loose white gown crowed with a white *tudong*. The girls' education seems to be given less attention – these groups were bigger, double the size of the boys', and I was told it was so because it was difficult to find suitable female teachers to conduct classes. I was also informed, however, that where education for girls was concerned, there has been 'a lot of progress', as girls were until recently only given religious instruction at home. The attire of the boys is slightly different from that of the girls: they wear a loose flowing white upper shirt matched with black trousers and a Muslim cap, marking a clear differentiation of gender forms and roles.

Each child 1) enters the mosque with a respectful bow, 2) recites a memorized short prayer, and then 3) proceeds to find their own group, all seated on the floor of the mosque. Groups are segregated according to their age, gender and ability. The groups are in different stages of a planned lesson and are doing different kinds of activities. Some are practising reading the Qur'an, in which case it will be one pupil at a time practising with the teacher, while the others, all lined up in rows, await their turn. As each pupil recites personally for the teacher's ear, the teacher will correct the parts that have been wrongly recited or pronounced. Others are memorizing prayers by themselves. In one group, a teacher reads a prayer line-by-line and the pupils recite after him. The children speak very softly when talking to the teacher and often the teacher has to ask them to speak up. In another group, a lesson on 'proper prostration posture' is going on with a group of boys. The teacher is seated with folded legs on the floor and holds a short stick which he uses to direct the boys to do what he wants them to do. Occasionally he would use the stick to gently reprimand the child for not doing the exercise well. In this particular mosque, I have seen it used lightly on young boys who were not able to recite the Qur'an to the teacher's expectation or on those who did not complete their assigned homework.

The main pedagogy in WM1 is recitation and memorization, in keeping with the memorizing tradition of *tahfiz ul-Qur'an* from the days of the Prophet. This practice is reminiscent of a 'religious classical' situation and shares a similar sociolinguistic position with other denominations, such as Biblical Hebrew and Ecclesiastical Greek in some Jewish and Greek communities. Here, the child is placed in an environment whereby he has to learn not just to pray but also to respond properly to the use of Koranic verses in sermons, ceremonies, conversations, etc. In other words, a child is expected to learn to recite the Qur'an from memory, and perform Koranic recitation with proper speech, demeanour and effect. I observed that the younger children learnt the Qur'an through imitation, intensive listening, repetition, memorization, and the copying of texts.

78   *Phyllis Ghim-Lian Chew*

Where the role of the teacher was concerned, he is a giver of knowledge and a figure of authority, not to be challenged. These teachers would expound verses from the Qur'an and excerpts from the sayings of the Prophet (*hadith*) as these are regarded as foundational texts. Students were regarded much like empty receptacle ready to receive knowledge. For the youths, the teacher might explain and elaborate difficult Arabic words, phrases and passages. The students would then memorize and copy the texts of each lesson. The procedure was repeated until the text was completed.

The medium of instruction is Arabic, although some Malay is used as well. Arabic is believed to be the actual words of God – being able to decode and reproduce it becomes critical. Hence, more emphasis is placed on accuracy in pronunciation and in reading aloud, rather than on meaning and understanding. Generally, loudness and clear articulation are seen as mirrors of sincere individual intentions (Hashim 1996).[9]

WM2 (Housing Development Board void deck)

WM2 is a madrasah for children aged 6 to 16. It was founded by an individual with a firm belief in child education. With a group of like-minded individuals, he organized a non-profit school in a relatively poor neighbourhood and recruited some teachers and a principal so as to make it a viable enterprise. The fees charged are slightly lower than what WM1 charges, probably because there are no imported and professional teachers to support. Indeed, I was informed that it is one of the 'most affordable' private madrasahs. There are many other similar 'private' schools in the void deck space, run in the same manner, but these tend to be more expensive – probably twice or up to five times as much. WM2 classes are large, with an average of 25–35 pupils in each class. The madrasah opens all-day on Saturday and Sunday. The teachers are all salaried and permanent staff, mostly graduates from the full-time local madrasahs in Singapore.[10] Most of them are not trained in the education of children, but through the years they have gained practical teaching experience. Teachers take Mondays and Tuesdays off in lieu of their weekends, when they have to teach, and spend Wednesday to Friday at the madrasah planning lessons, liaising with parents, marking, grading, and pursuing other administrative duties. There are also tests and examinations at the end of each semester. There is a report card to fill at the end of each semester for each pupil, which must be duly signed by the parent concerned. There are also prizes for top students, accompanied by graduation certificates given at the end of each year for good attendance and content mastery.

The madrasah takes place in a void deck of an HDB (Housing Development Board building, which refers to public housing) block which has been simply renovated to house the children. The pupils are from the surrounding neighbourhood – many play in the same playground and attend the same schools. Most of them will walk with their backpacks to the madrasah from their HDB apartments. WM2 does not quite have the rarefied mosque atmosphere of WM1; and indeed it is much noisier with the heavy prattle of feet and chatter of children's voices.

The teachers, all of whom are women, are very nurturing in their manner with hardly a harsh word. There were efforts to hire male teachers but the salaries are too low, hence the reason for an all-female staff. The class is divided into two distinct halves – the girls on one side and the boys on the other, but with no physical screening. Hence, unlike WM1, the two groups are able to see each other, sharing the same space. The children do sit, but not on the floor with neatly folded legs, rather on chairs in front of a desk facing the teacher, much like what we may expect in a typical classroom. Children are streamed to different classes according to their age and ability. The uniform which the children wear is a brown loose tunic from neck to foot with a matching head covering for the girls. Boys are dressed in a short-sleeved brown top and matching long trousers, topped with a *songkok* (hat). The female teachers are attired in the traditional loose Muslim garment, but unlike WM1 where the colour is white, they may elect to dress in any colour they wish, as long as it is not patterned, or of bold design or of a nature which others may construe as distracting.

In terms of pedagogical practice, attendance records are kept as seen from the roll call which begins each lesson. Pupil absences from class have to be explained either through a medical certificate or a letter from a parent. There were some attempts at group work but generally the teacher sits and speaks from behind her desk. The pupils will then listen, take out their exercise books and either refer to them or make notes as the teacher goes along. After the teacher's explanation of the topic at hand, there is a typical follow-up activity such as writing, or filling-in the-blanks. Sometimes, the same text might be read a second or third time, should the teacher deem it necessary. In general, the teacher does not encourage questions or discussions from the pupils, perhaps because there is a lot to cover. As classes are large, I observed that some of the more boisterous children, especially the boys, tend to talk among themselves, or engage in private activities of their own. In the teaching of morals, the teacher uses stories from the textbook, followed by exercises on reading comprehension. In brief, pedagogical practice is focused mainly on teacher-talk and seat-work.

All pupils had to buy a prescribed set of books for the different subjects. A fuller range of subject is taught in WM2 relative to WM1 and they include:

- *aqidah* (faith) and *fiqh* (jurisprudence);
- *akhlaq* – character and life skills;
- *sirah* and *tarikh* – social history and Islamic civilization; and
- *Iqra*/Qur'an reading – Koranic literacy.

The memorization of key verses of the Qur'an and key prayers remains important, but this takes up only 25 per cent of curriculum time, not 90 per cent. Here, the phonic approach is preferred and the Arabic syllabary is introduced primarily through a chalk and talk method.[11] The children are required to commit selected Arabic syllables to memory and then to recognize the syllables through simple words such as 'cat' and 'mat', moving from one- to two-syllable words, and eventually to longer words. Children also participate in group writing activities,

80 *Phyllis Ghim-Lian Chew*

watching their teacher write as they learn to identify the alphabet and the spelling system. When they pray, they use the liturgical language which is Arabic but this is not always said aloud, as was the case in WM1; but may be intoned silently, according to the child's (or teacher's) variable preference.

The lesser emphasis on Arabic and the relative liberal treatment of pupils also meant the tolerance of a lower achievement threshold in the reading of Koranic verses. The teacher explains:

> Most are weak. I have to do spot check, one by one. I have to teach them the phonics. I have to make the parents involved. Malay is easy but Arabic is difficult. I will recommend students to do extra Arabic classes – they have to pay extra. Full time madrasah students are of course better in Arabic. Part-time is difficult.
>
> (WM2 T1 lines 300–3)

The medium of instruction is Malay and the atmosphere in the madrasah is reminiscent of a Malay-medium school. The use of Malay helps promote a generally relaxed atmosphere in the school, enabling most children to treat the madrasah as their 'second home' and their teachers, including the principal, more as 'substitute mothers' rather than as professional religious teachers. A little English is used and only when the child is not able to understand Malay:

> Now, if there is someone who cannot understand Malay, then we speak in English; otherwise we can speak in both English and Malay. It's good to have balance in English and Malay – because many students have friends who are Chinese and Indian who will ask them about religion in English. Last time, they just say 'I don't know' – if they don't know how to answer in English. 'Mengapa kita chakap Ingerris' – sometimes when I teach and share stories of the past, I do say in Malay – so that the acceptance is more deep.
>
> (WM2 T2 lines 333–8)

While compulsory prayers have to be learnt in Arabic, other *do'a* (prayers) are allowed to be learnt in English – a strategy to lighten the cognitive load of the child. Nevertheless, interjections in Arabic such as *as-Salamu 'alaykum* (Peace be upon you), *al-hamdu lillah* (thanks be to God), *subhan Allah* (glory to God) and *astagh-firullah* (may God forgive us) are often heard.

WM3 (the mosque-madrasah)

WM3 is one of the madrasahs involved in the 'Kids aL.I.V.E.' and 'Teens aL.I.V.E.' (Learning Islamic Values Everyday) programmes for pupils aged 5–8 years old and 13–16 years old, respectively. This is a holistic and comprehensive Islamic education system organized by the Islamic Religious Council of Singapore (Majlis Ugama Islam Singapura, MUIS) located in mosques throughout Singapore. It is an outcome of the Singapore Islamic Education System,

Weekend madrasahs in Singapore 81

which was introduced in 2004 to address the overall need of part-time religious education (MUIS 2007). It grew out of a concern to combat the focus on rituals as opposed to ethical aspects of religion, and otherworldly concerns at the expense of problems of life, and attention to dogmas and practices at the expense of universal values (cf. Noor and Lai 2006). Unlike WM2, most of the teachers of WM3 are part-timers, rather than full-timers. Another difference is that these part-timers are also graduates of the Specialist Diploma in Teaching and Learning, following a tie-up between MUIS and the National Institute of Education (NIE).

Semiotically, the classes take place in 'mosque-madrasahs' – multi-functional buildings which are also educational institutions, spiritual centres, council chambers for the deliberation of community affairs, community service centres, secretariat offices, etc. While serving as a focal point for prayers, they are also usually equipped with libraries, computer rooms, conference rooms for discussion of religious studies, a multipurpose hall, underground car parks and a room for the *jenazah* (corpse) where preparations can be made for burial. Such mosques also conduct regular activities such as marriage counselling, exhibitions on drug abuse, and child education at the mosque madrasah. The WM3 that I visited was held in a classroom in one of these mosque-madrasahs. The classroom is of a good size with movable chairs and tables which may be arranged either facing the teacher or in groups. There are usually educational posters and samples of students' work affixed on the walls as well as other learning materials, such as a small class-library where learning materials are made accessible. The classrooms are also equipped with technologies such as internet connection, video projectors and a sound system for the teacher's use. Just like WM2, both boys and girls attend the same lessons by the same teacher, and are exposed to the same curriculum. They are also conspicuously seated on separate sides of the classroom. Boys and girls are also dressed differently: the girls may be in the loose Muslim tunic or in jeans with long-sleeved blouses. All girls wear a *tudong*, but this is likely to be not only shorter but also of various hues and shapes, perhaps more 'fashionable' than those worn in WM1 and WM2. The teacher may also be dressed in the same way – bottom half jeans with a long-sleeved blouse; unless they are elderly, in which case they may dress a little more traditionally, like the teachers in WM2. The boys are in trousers and a long-sleeved shirt, topped with a *songkok*. Generous funding from MUIS ensures a smaller teacher–pupil ratio of 1:20; rather than the 1:35 that we see in WM2.

Students are given every opportunity to discuss religious issues individually with the teacher or in groups with one another. The following quotes are typical feedback from two supportive parents of the programme:

> Usually, I just listen, never have a chance to ask questions, and we have great respect for teacher. Today, children go on talking when teacher is speaking and not afraid to speak with themselves and ask questions.
>
> (WM3 P2 Lines 456–9)

82   *Phyllis Ghim-Lian Chew*

Now it's more interactive and there's the web children can find out from. Usually, we cannot ask *ustaz* [teacher] any kind of question – now everybody can ask anything.

(WM3 P6 Lines 234–5)

There is a well-designed and extremely attractive series of textbooks, which contain stories from the Qur'an as well as classroom activities on key Islamic topics such as: a) knowing God and relationship with Allah; b) Islamic identity; c) knowledge and interest in the prophet; d) knowledge and interest in the Qur'an. There are also self-reflective, self-appraisal sections entitled 'my training log book' and 'novel' features such as 'Parents' observation pages'.

Indeed, the pedagogical processes observed in WM3 are quite similar to mainstream day-school pedagogy. There is a resistance to break down words into component letters and sounds as in WM1 and WM2. Instead, there is an emphasis on holistic learning, that is, encouraging pupils to understand whole passages of writing before thinking about individual words. Pupils are also exposed to problem-solving skills through role play, case studies, project work, quizzes and other hands-on activities which are believed to enhance their learning and discovery. The Islamic worldview of *iman* (faith), *ilmu* (knowledge) and *amal* (action) are integrated and stressed. Indeed, the syllabus views Muslim pupils as needing the necessary spiritual and emotional guidance to face modern and global challenges such as school work, examinations and peer expectations (MUIS 2007).

With regards to the medium of instruction, pupils may opt to attend the lesson in either English or Malay, but about two-thirds of attendees prefer Islamic teachings to be delivered in English, as they find it 'easier' to understand. English language has become a tool to teach key concepts and prayers found in Arabic,[12] yet this is not without its attendant difficulties. For one it is not merely the tongue of the colonial masters but one associated with Christianity (Goh 2009). Just as the replacement of Arabic (WM1) by Malay (WM2) requires a mental shift historically and culturally, the English language poses a challenge to the delivery of Islamic concepts not least because language is never a-cultural or apolitical. Hence, some parents continue to choose madrasahs, such as WM2, which teaches in Malay; or madrasahs such as WM1, where more Arabic is used.

One notes that the English used by the teachers in WM3 is often interspersed with Malay expressions and Arabic quotations. Code-switching is rife in this context and may take two forms: switching languages within the same sentence (intra-sentential) and switching of languages in whole sentence chunks (inter-sentential), as evidenced in the following teacher's speech:

Aaah, siapa yang masih perlu betulkan bacaan Tajuib, bacaan Al Quran tu nak betulkan balik, minta phone daripada Ustazah. *(Aah, those of you who still need practice and guidance on Quran prayers, get the phone number from teacher.)* $18 awak attend . . . ada sixteen sessions throughout the whole month tu. *(For $18, you attend...sixteen sessions throughout the whole month.)* So you can attend from 9 am to 11 am from Thursday to Friday. Ok?

(WM3 T4 lines 144–50)

This hybrid form of speech is dominant in the context of WM3 and gives the madrasah a more 'modern' and 'trendy' face, attractive to many youths.

Weekend vs. weekday literacies

My ethnographic visits to WM1, WM2 and WM3 over a period of six months shows that Shafi'i weekend madrasahs are not as homogenous as one might imagine. Indeed, all three madrasahs may be put on a cline where literacy practices are concerned. There are differential classroom semiotics, literacy processes and media of instruction. The pupils who attend these madrasahs reflect not only the pluralistic landscape, but also the subtle 'literacy wars' that take place in these educational institutions. However, while the madrasahs in our study have claimed a few hours of a Muslim student's life, the 'real' madrasah, which is the secular weekday one, takes up 90 per cent of their school-time.[13] This situation arises because the mainstream 'day' school derives from the most powerful dominating group in society. As Marx puts it: 'The ideas of the ruling class are in every epoch the ruling ideas. The class which is the ruling material force of society is at the same time its ruling intellectual force' (Marx and Engels 1976 [1846]: 67).

In many children's lives there are, then, often enough, two mutually independent systems, upholding mutually exclusive and usually contradictory educational philosophies which operate independently (Hashim 1996). Here, the existence of oppositional literacy practices in areas such as objectives, pedagogical processes and language choices often give rise to a conflict of identities within the child, a negotiation process which remains unstable even after graduation.

The first oppositional factor is that weekday schooling or mainstream literacies do not recognize the comprehensive Islamic belief system rooted in *tawhid*, the oneness of God. Indeed, the relationship between God and human beings, so central in madrasah culture, is intellectually or socially irrelevant in secular schools. The Singapore mainstream school is in essence a pragmatic one, embedded with 'materialist' values such as competitiveness, independence and self-interest. Singapore textbooks (as with textbooks from other 'capitalist' societies) portray a world of global consumerism related indirectly to clothing, grooming, music, communication technology (notably the mobile phone) and entertainment. The backdrop of culture is urbanization, formal education, wider adult literacy, mass-media and communication technology, new methods of production, the industrialization of agriculture, consumerism and a growing sense of national, regional and world-community membership. Mainstream culture is also embedded with a heavy dose of popular culture, which is driven by countries such as America, Britain and Europe and which includes music, film, literature and sports. Oppositional images such as these exist not least because while the aim of the weekend school is to construct a Muslim (religious) identity, that of the

84 *Phyllis Ghim-Lian Chew*

mainstream school is to construct a Singaporean (national) identity. While the madrasah concentrates on the inculcation of virtues such as modesty as seen through their attire, courtesy as seen through the use of respectful language, respect for all and especially for the teacher and the guests; secular day schools tend to prize other kinds of virtues more, for example assertiveness, independence, initiative, and creativity (Chew 2006).

The second oppositional factor is pedagogy. In the madrasah, the common pedagogical practice is to decode Arabic through the phonic method, often without the use of any pictures, syntactic, semantic or contextual clues as is the case in WM1. This method relies to a great extent on memory. Memorization is a technique that is unnamed and outside the boundaries of current English teaching. However, in mainstream schools, it is neither well-practised nor well-utilized. Neither is it given a pedagogical status in the English class unlike in mathematics where the importance of 'mental' skills is emphasized.[14] Obviously then, the different cultural capital which children bring to a classroom has different sociocultural-linguistic values, and only some of them are ranked with privileges and power.[15] The Muslim child is therefore disadvantaged since most mainstream teachers are unaware of the cultural resources that the Muslim child brings to school, and even if they are aware of the child's unique resources, they do not recognise or appreciate its value.

The 2010 Ministry of Education Syllabus for Singapore Primary and Secondary School is influenced by many principles underlying what has hitherto been called the 'Whole language approach'. Here, there is a stress on the teaching of language through engaging and interactive lessons leveraging on project work, speech and drama, and oral presentation, much like what WM3 is trying to achieve (Stellar 2010). The main purpose of reading engaging stories in class is to build confidence for students in speech and writing, and enhance their learning of the language. There is also a drama technique called 'hot seating' where a pupil in the hot-seat takes on the role of a character and answers in a spontaneous manner the questions posed by his peers. Teachers are encouraged to incorporate drama and music in a mini-musical using stories from the STELLAR Books. Parents are also enlisted to support their children in learning English through a range of everyday activities such as reading together, playing simple language games, going to libraries or having a conversation on a familiar topic or favourite past-time (Tan 2009). Last but not least, pupils are given opportunities to speak extensively, and to discuss and share views with the teacher and their peers.

While the weekend schools aim to teach accurate recitation in the reading class, the weekday schools emphasize silent meaning and comprehension. The weekday reading class aims to build on young learners' psycholinguistic knowledge and on the ability to guess and predict unfamiliar words and events based on culturally loaded expectations. In other words, the pupils who will achieve high grades in school are those who will read widely during their weekends so that they may acquire the skills of guessing and predicting much like a 'western' reader. This understanding presupposes familiarity with written English texts, fictional stories, and knowledge about book language, which are all culture-specific. Frank Smith

Weekend madrasahs in Singapore 85

(2004), a reading specialist, reminds us that exclusive attention to the phonic dimension of reading, as observed in WM1 and WM2 is literally 'barking at print'. Yet it must be said that millions of children, together with their supportive parents and teachers, participate in this type of literacy in weekend madrasahs and do not perceive their practice to be 'meaningless'.

Finally, we examine the medium of instruction in which religious instruction is given, not least because language is a 'mirror of traditionalism and modernization' (Tay 2004). In Singapore as elsewhere, language choice is largely determined by political, economic and social factors and has significant consequences in later life (Chua 2004). Therefore, despite efforts to maintain the Malay language in religious classes in the weekend, we find that when given a choice as to the medium of instruction in WM3, more Malay children opt to learn Islam through English rather than in their mother tongue, Malay (MUIS 2007). This may be because Malay children have grown accustomed to speaking English in the mainstream school and may not wish to appear 'different' from other English-speaking Singaporeans (cf. Pagett 2006). Another reason is the realization that the social capital of Malay in relation to English in a globalized world leaves much to be desired (Saeda 2010).

The fact that both English and Malay use the Roman script in relation to Arabic which uses the Arabic script, may also explain why the majority of pupils find it easier, or less daunting, to study in Malay rather than Arabic. Nevertheless, it should be noted that rather than being merely recording devices, scripts are also tools of symbolic, psychological significance which helps in the creation, shaping and maintenance of identities (Unseth 2008). While mastery of the Roman script has meant greater accessibility to modernization and westernization where the interpretation of Arabic texts and Koranic verses are concerned, it has also had the power to 'soften' the face of Islam to one which is less oppositional, thus secular and 'westernized'.[16]

Conclusion

Becoming literate is a process of not just learning to read or write but of becoming socialized into a particular culture's way of knowing and being. It is not, as is commonly supposed, an attribute or a skill but rather a social practice and communal resource (Gee 2005). The knowledge, values and behaviour that a child comes to imbibe are therefore not simply the products of his or her own self, unique, and independent, psychological interactions with the world. Instead, they are the products of interactions and experiences with the various pluralities and ideological groups of which the child is a part. We have seen how children read, write, and think in ways that reflect their social and religious identities on each weekday and/or weekend; wars are fought for their allegiance through the 'cover' of literacy practices. In addition, we have examined 'Literacy wars' as seen in the semiotics of the classrooms, pedagogical practices and medium of instruction; all social resources allowing pupils to construct the cultural knowledge that their parents deem important. While the war between weekday (mainstream) and

86 *Phyllis Ghim-Lian Chew*

weekend (peripheral) children's education is well known, and commonly seen as the proxy war for the 'secular' and the 'sacred' in the world at large, what is less known are the mini wars fought within each denomination of Islam. The existence of these literacy wars do not merely reveal the existence of religious pluralism but also reveal a pluralism that is passively acknowledged and thus, is accorded legitimacy by the state.

This study shows that weekend schools themselves do not normally acknowledge the differences in opinions or 'wars' within Islam. Weekend schools tend to take into account only their own group's perspective and are desirous to shield their children from the existence of other perspectives. Yet there are fundamental differences of opinion on central moral problems and controversial ethical issues, such as the treatment of women, dress and certain ritualistic practices. The second point that weekend religious schools do not address with their congregation, is the acknowledgement of the plurality of differing practices which is prevalent in multi-faith globalized societies. Hence, they tend to be subjected to the belief of exclusivism.

Most mainstream school textbooks in pluralistic capitalist societies offer a depiction of the world from a secular, liberal perspective (rather than a particular faith viewpoint) and it is therefore important for children in plural, multicultural, global society to be 'critically' educated to discern the 'literacy wars' underlying whatever they read. In developing critical literacies in young children in an amorphous pluralistic landscape, it is important that they be helped to understand not only explicit meanings but also the more subtle and nuanced messages, positions and stances that literacy or literacies present or assume. In other words, the educator should always discern and convey, with due respect to the respective child's ethnic and religio-cultural background, the interpretation of values underlying texts and symbols, no text being neutral (Pike 2006). Equally important, parents and pupils have a responsibility to re-examine their own commitments in the face of an ever-advancing 'global' religious pluralism.

Notes

1 This project is funded by the National Institute of Education AcRF Research Grant 'Religious Ideologies and Literacy Practices', 2009–12.
2 See e.g. 'Singapore first World Religion Day draws 1000', *Straits Times*, 16 January 1995, p. 19.
3 Madrasah is an Arabic word that means 'school' but in the present context a madrasah means an 'Islamic religious school'.
4 Indeed, up to the age of 6, children have been found to have intense concentration and are able to do non-stop repetition of a particular activity, which will form the basis of their later characters (Montessori 1997).
5 Literacies (with the capital L) is opposed to literacy without the capital letter; as it is connected with longer stretches of language and signifies more potently the way life is lived within a particular setting and social group.
6 Singapore encourages the moral development of children as a way to combat the encroachment of 'undesirable' foreign values that come with the capitalist development and modernization of the city-state.

Weekend madrasahs in Singapore 87

7 'The opening' begins: 'In the name of God, Most Merciful, Most compassionate, praise be to God, Lord of all worlds, the Merciful, the compassionate, the King of the Day of Judgment. It is you we worship and it is from You we seek help . . . '
8 The research ethics code does not allow me to name the madrasahs nor the participants observed or interviewed.
9 Many academics and journalists usually show their distaste for liturgical literacy with value-laden words such as 'stringent discipline', 'laborious work' and 'long-term commitment' (Bledsoe and Robey 1993: 116).
10 One of the teachers is, however, a graduate of a foreign madrasah based in Egypt.
11 The phonic method grouped the letters according to sounds and taught children to recognize the relationship between letters and sounds. The look-and-say method taught children to recognize simple words as a whole unit and then individual letters.
12 An accompanying book to learn Arabic is entitled *Panduan Musafir Solat Jama dan Qasar* by Hj Johari Hj Alias, published by Negri Sebilan: Percetakan Putrajaya Sdn Bhd. (Entirely in Malay interspersed with Arabic quotations).
13 When we make a distinction between secular and religious education, this is actually a 'western' concept because traditionally Muslim schools and colleges, similar to Confucian philosophy, make no distinction between the religious and the secular. Rather the distinction then was between the traditional and intellectual sciences (cf. Alatas 2006).
14 This is so even if the teacher uses memorization techniques such as naming the letter of the alphabet, teaching phonic awareness and phonic words (Robertson 2002).
15 In other words; rote learning is discounted in mainstream school, although it may have some benefits. For example, Wagner (1983: 87) cites evidence from work he has done with the Morocco Literacy Project and which suggests that prior memorization is helpful to reading acquisition in Arabic. He also cites work by Chomsky which suggests that being able to orally recite passages before having to decode them helped children who normally had trouble with reading fluency.
16 A similar dilemma in the same period can be found in Turkey where in 1928 the Arab-based writing system in use was replaced by a Latin-based writing system, signifying a 'modern' rather than a 'traditional' Islam.

References

Alatas, S. F. (2006) 'Knowledge and Education in Islam', in Abdul Rahman, N. A. and Lai, A. E. (eds) *Secularism and Spirituality: Seeing Integrated Knowledge and Success in Madrasah Education in Singapore,* Singapore: Institute of Policy Studies, pp. 166–9.

Bledsoe, C. H. and Robey, K. M. (1993) 'Arabic Literacy and Secrecy among the Mende of Sierra Leone', in Street, B. (ed.) *Cross-Cultural Approaches to Literacy,* Cambridge, UK: Cambridge University Press, pp. 110–34.

Boyle, H. (2004) *Quranic Schools: Agents of Preservation and Change,* New York/London: Routledge Falmer.

Brenner, L. (2001) *Controlling Knowledge: Religion, Power and Schooling in a West African Muslim Society,* Bloomington, IN: Indiana University Press.

Chee, M. F. (2006), 'The Historical Evolution of Madrasah Education in Singapore', in Abdul Rahman, N. A. and Lai, A. E. (eds), *Secularism and Spirituality: Seeing Integrated Knowledge and Success in Madrasah Education in Singapore,* Singapore: Institute of Policy Studies.

Chew, P. (2006) 'Language Use and Religious Practice: The Case of Singapore', in Omoniyi, T. and Fishman, J. A. (eds) *Explorations in the Sociology of Language and Religion* Amsterdam: John Benjamins.

88 *Phyllis Ghim-Lian Chew*

Chew, P. (2009) *Emergent Lingua Francas and World Orders: The Place of English in the World Today,* New York: Routledge.

Chew, P. (2013) *A Sociolinguistic History of Early Identities in Singapore,* Basingstoke, UK: Palgrave Macmillan.

Chua, B. H. and Kwok, K. H. (2001) 'Social Pluralism in Singapore', in Hefner, R. W. (ed.) *The Politics of Multiculturalis: Pluralism and Citizenship in Malaysia, Singapore and Indonesia,* Honolulu: University of Hawaii.

Chua, S. K. C. (2004) 'Singapore's Literacy Policy and Its Conflicting Ideologies', *Current Issues in Language Planning,* 5(1): 64–76.

Curdt-Christiansen, X. L. (2008) 'Reading the World through Words: Cultural Themes in Heritage Chinese Language Textbook', *Language and Education,* 22(2): 95–113.

Freire, P. and Macedo, D. P. (1989) *Literacy: Reading the Word and the World,* Westport, CT: Bergin and Garvey.

Gee, J. (2005) *An Introduction to Discourse Analysis Theory and Method,* New York: Routledge.

Goh, R. (2009) 'Christian Identities in Singapore: Religion, Race and Culture between State Control And Transnational Flows', *Journal of Cultural Geography,* 26: 1–23.

Hashim, R. (1996) *Educational Dualism in Malaysia,* Kuala Lumpur: Oxford University Press.

Hefner, R. W. (ed.) (2001) *The Politics of Multiculturalism: Pluralism and Citizenship in Malaysia, Singapore and Indonesia,* Honolulu: University of Hawaii Press.

Jeldtoft, N. (2011) 'Lived Islam: Religious Identity with "Non-Organized" Muslim Minorities', *Ethnic and Racial Studies,* 34(7): 1134–51.

Keane, W. (2007) *Christian Moderns: Freedom and Fetish in Mission Encounter,* Berkeley, CA: University of California Press.

Marx, K. and Engels F. (1976) [1846] *The German ideology,* Moscow: Progress Publications.

Moore, K. M. (2007) 'Muslims in the United States: Pluralism under Exceptional Circumstances', *American Academy of Political and Social Sciences,* 612: 116–32.

Moore, L. C. (2008) 'Body, Text and Talk in Maroua Fulbe Quranic Schooling', *Text and Talk,* 28(5): 643–65.

Montessori, M. (1997) *Basic Ideas of Montessori's Educational Theory: Extracts from Maria Montessori's Writings and Teachings 1870–1952,* Oxford, UK: Clio Press.

MUIS (2007) *Building Resilient Youth* [Papers from the 2007 Mosque madrasah convention], Singapore: MUIS.

Muklis, A. B. (2006) 'Between State Interests and Citizen Rights: Whither the Madrasah?', in Abdul Rahman, N. A. and Lai, A. E. (eds) *Secularism and Spirituality: Seeing Integrated Knowledge and Success in Madrasah Education in Singapore,* Singapore: Institute of Policy Studies.

Noor, A. A. R. and Lai, A. E. (eds) (2006) *Secularism and Spirituality: Seeking Integrated Knowledge and Success in Madrasah Education in Singapore.* Singapore: Institute of Policy Studies & Marshall Cavendish Academic.

Pagett, L. (2006) 'Mum and Dad Prefer Me to Speak Bengali at Home: Code-Switching and Parallel Speech in a Primary School Context', *Literacy,* 40(3): 137–45.

Pike, M. (2006) 'From Beliefs to Skills: The Secularization of Literacy and the Moral Education of Citizens', *Journal of Beliefs and Values,* 27(3): 281–9.

Reid, A. (2011) 'Many But One: The Paradox of Religious Pluralism in Southeast Asia's History', paper presented at the workshop 'Placing Religious Pluralism in Asian Global Cities', Asia Research Institute, National University of Singapore, 5–6 May.

Robertson, L. H. (2002) 'Parallel Literacy Classes and Hidden Strengths: Learning to Read in English, Urdu and Classical Arabic', *Reading Literacy and Language,* 36(3): 119–26.

Saeda, B. (2010) 'Muslim Education and Globalization: The Re-(de)positioning of Languages and curriculum Content in Southeast Asia', in Vaish, V. (ed.) *Globalization of Language and Culture in Asia: The Impact of Globalization Processes on Language,* London: Continuum.

Saeed, A. (2009) 'Muslims in Secular States', *MUIS Occasional Paper, No 1*, Singapore: MUIS.

Schmidt, G. (2011) 'Understanding and Approaching Muslim Visibilities: Lessons Learned from a Fieldwork-based Study of Muslims in Copenhagen', *Ethnic and Racial Studies*, 34(7): 1216–29.

Smith, F. (2004) *Understanding Reading: A Psycholinguistic Analysis of Reading and Learning to Read*, 6th edn. Mahwah, NJ: Lawrence Erlbaum Associates.

Stellar (2010) www.stellarliteracy.sg/cos/o.x?c=/wbn/pagetree&func=view&rid=20786

Street, B. (2005) 'New Literacies Studies and Literacies across Educational Contexts', in Street, B. (ed.) *Literacies across Educational Contexts: Mediating Learning and Teaching*, Philadelphia PA: Carlson.

Tan, L. (2009) Stellar Literacy*, Challenge,* Sep–Oct, 12–13, available from www.challenge.gov.sg.

Tay, M. W. J. (2004) 'Language as a mirror of Traditionalism and Modernization', in Yong, M. C. (ed.) *Asian Traditions and Modernization: Perspectives from Singapore*, Singapore: Marshall Cavendish International, pp. 89–118.

Tong, C. K. (2002) 'Religion', in Tong, C. K. and Lian, K. F. (eds) *The Making of Singapore Sociology: Society and State*, Singapore: Times Media Pte Ltd.

Unseth, P. (2008) 'The Sociolinguistics of script Choice: An Introduction', *International Journal of Sociology of Language,* 189(2): 1–4.

Wagner, D. (1983) *Literacy, Culture and Development: Becoming Literate in Morocco*, New York: Cambridge University Press.

Part II
Conviviality in the city

6   In the name of God

South Asian Muslims in a Chinese temple fair in Hong Kong

Wai-chi Chee

Globalization and transnational flows of religious groups may mean negotiation and contestation for religious spaces, especially in cities (Geoffroy 2004). While some scholars argue that, as a consequence, sociability has become a casualty in capitalist modern cities (Marty 2007; Niebuhr 2007), others contend that the acquired cosmopolitan worldview has encouraged accommodation of differences (Garces-Foley 2007; Moore 2007; Roof 2007; Williams 2007). Adding to this conversation, I put my focus on Hong Kong, which claims to be 'Asia's world city', and which is well known for increasingly crowded public spaces. This research explores how religious spaces are created, negotiated, and contested between a migrant ethnic-religious minority group and the local dominant group by looking into the active participation of some fifty South Asian women and children, predominantly Pakistani Muslims, in a Chinese temple fair (Tai Kok Tsui Temple Fair).

This group's participation is remarkable because it contradicts the usual perception that Muslims are subject to strict religious rules and therefore do not participate in Chinese popular religion. It also problematizes the general claim that South Asians in Hong Kong, especially women, are subject to institutionalized discrimination and social exclusion (City University of Hong Kong and Unison Hong Kong 2003; Frost 2004; Ku 2006; Ku *et al.* 2003, 2005, 2006, 2010; Loper 2004; Plüss 2006). Above all, these Muslims' involvement in the Chinese temple fair demonstrates the permeability of religious boundaries and the creation of new spaces for religious pluralism.

According to Michael Peletz (2009), pluralism is more than diversity. Pluralism, he maintains, refers to 'social fields, cultural domains, and more encompassing systems in which two or more principles, categories, groups, sources of authority, or ways of being in the world are not only present, tolerated, and accommodated, but also *accorded legitimacy* in a Weberian sense' (Peletz 2009: 7). Put differently, diversity without legitimacy is not pluralism. Thus, the central question is how diversity is ascribed legitimacy. By looking at the religious and social spaces inhabited by Islamic women and children in a Chinese temple fair, this chapter seeks to inform how people make sense of and handle variation among one another, and how, in the process, they negotiate pluralism. I analyse in particular the social, cultural, political, and economic factors that are

94 *Wai-chi Chee*

at force. In Hong Kong, South Asians' ethnic and religious identities are almost inseparable and hence they will be discussed as an intertwined entity for most part of this contribution.

Tai Kok Tsui Temple Fair

Tai Kok Tsui Temple Fair (The Fair) is an annual event held in Tai Kok Tsui, a lower-middle class residential area in Hong Kong, to pay tribute to Hung Sing (God of the Sea). It is also a fair where visitors can enjoy cultural activities and shopping. The 2011 Fair attracted more than 130,000 visitors. Five streets are closed for twenty-four hours to the traffic to make room for the outdoor temporary stage, seventy plus booths, and the parade. After the opening ceremony, at about 10:30 am, the parade begins. The highlights of the parade include lion dance, Chinese traditional puppetry floats and Chinese cultural performances like drum dance, Chinese ethnic dance, Chinese kung fu (martial arts), Chinese acrobatic performance, and traditional Sichuan face-changing (*bian lian*).[1] When the parade is in progress, the organizing committee members and guests sit on the makeshift stage. Each performing group halts in front of the stage and performs briefly for a few minutes as a prelude before marching on. It is a reversal that the audience is on the raised platform while the performers are down in the street. After the parade, which lasts for about an hour, the guests leave the stage and each performance group takes turns to perform on it. Along the route of the parade, on both sides of four streets, there are about seventy booths of various types: handicrafts, palm reading, Chinese tea, Chinese calligraphy, Chinese painting, old toys, and snacks, just to name a few. At 6:30 pm, the booths gradually close to make room for the *puhn choi* feast in the open air.[2] Guests include organizing committee members, residents of Tai Kok Tsui, and tourists. The highlight before the closing is the 500-feet luminous night dragon dance, which casts a very bright fluorescent glow against the dark background as all the street lights are switched off.

The South Asian women and children I work with have participated for six consecutive years, with increasing involvement, ranging from raising funds, joining the parade, selling South Asian food, and drawing henna patterns for visitors, to performing ethnic dances, dragon-dance and Chinese kung fu. While their number may seem negligible among the numerous participants and performers, their different appearance and distinct ethnic costumes are enough to make them stand out in the Fair where they are the only non-Chinese.[3] Their ethnic dances are the only non-Chinese performances; their two food booths (one selling South Asian snacks like samosa; the other masala tea) are the only non-Chinese food stalls. And more importantly, they are the only Muslims.

The setting

South Asian Muslims in Hong Kong are both an ethnic and religious minority. According to the 2011 Population Census, Hong Kong has a population of over seven million, 94 per cent of which is ethnically Chinese. South Asians, including

Indians, Nepalese and Pakistanis, comprise about 15 per cent of the ethnic minority population with a total of around 63,000 (Census and Statistics Department 2012). The Information Services Department reported that Hong Kong has about 90,000 Muslims, of which approximately 30,000 are Chinese, with the rest mainly from Pakistan, India, Malaysia, Indonesia, and Middle Eastern and African countries.[4]

Chinese popular religion encompasses the worship of ancestors and protective deities in domestic shrines and community temples (Overmyer 2003). It is a flexible and highly adaptable cultural institution with elements from Buddhism, Daoism and other socio-cultural institutions, and there is no clear boundary between Buddhism, Daoism, and local religious practices (Liu 2003). Unlike many organized religions, Chinese popular religion is institutionalized in the midst of ordinary social life rather than through formal organizations or scriptures (Overmyer 2003). There is no official record on the number of Chinese popular religion worshippers; nonetheless, the existence of more than 600 Chinese Buddhist and Taoist temples in the territory – as opposed to five principal Islamic mosques – is suggestive of its overwhelming dominance.

Data for this research are largely drawn from my involvement in the Fair for four years from 2009 to 2012, as a visitor in the first year and a helper in the subsequent three years, and from my participation in the South Asian women's cooking and Cantonese classes. I conducted semi-structured interviews with the participating South Asian women and children, their friends and relatives who came to join the Fair as visitors, and the social workers of Chan Hing Social Service Centre. Each of the South Asian women in this research came to Hong Kong as a bride at different times, ranging from a few years to more than ten years ago; and all children were born in Hong Kong.

I have witnessed the expansion of the Fair in scale in the course of my research. From 2009 to 2012, the number of visitors has surged from 90,000 to 150,000; the parade participants from 500 to 1,000; and the *puhn choi* feast from 100 to 170 tables. The budget for the 2012 Fair was 1.5 million HKD (190,000 USD). As mentioned, South Asian women and children began to participate in the Fair in 2007: the children usually join the parade and perform ethnic dances, mini-dragon dance and Chinese kung fu; the women organize four booths: two South Asian food booths, a henna booth drawing patterns on visitors' hands, and a booth selling South Asian clothing and accessories.

Chan Hing Social Service Centre (the Centre) is a major organizer of the Fair and also the channel through which the South Asians join the Fair. The following paragraphs trace briefly the historical development of the Fair and the Centre. The first Tai Kok Tsui Temple Fair, held in 2005, was the result of a proposal by the Yau Tsim Mong District Office of the Home Affairs Department to the Mongkok Kai Fong Association Ltd (the Association) after the SARS (Severe Acute Respiratory Syndrome) epidemic in 2003 so as to promote tourism and to boost the sluggish economy.[5] To this day, the Association remains the main organizer of the Fair, the co-organizer being the Yau Tsim Mong District Office, and the main sponsors being the Yau Tsim Mong District Council and the Kowloon Chamber of Commerce. The aims of the Fair, as stated in the official website, are to cultivate community interest in Chinese culture, arts and performances, to foster community support for tourism, to promote the development of the local community economy and to enhance the sense of belonging of the residents.[6]

Kai fong is a Cantonese term meaning 'long-term neighbours'. The Association was established in 1951 to provide relief measures for the needy in the neighbourhood, such as temporary shelter, medical services, and funeral services. Since the 1960s, as the Hong Kong Government began to take a more prominent role in providing public welfare, the Association has shifted from providing relief measures to social services.

In 1975, the Government granted ten thousand square feet of land, in Tai Kok Tsui, to the Association to build the Centre. Since its opening of operations in 1980, the Centre has been expanding from a youth centre to a comprehensive and integrated social service centre,[7] with thirty registered social workers, and receiving an annual government subvention of 30 million HKD (3.9 million USD).

With a mission of 'Mutual Help, Mutual Care, Mutual Support and Advocat[ing] for Change', the Centre reacts to the changing needs of its community. A social worker that I interviewed said that about seven years ago, the outreach team began to notice the increasing number of South Asian residents,[8] and hence took the initiative to provide services for them to achieve community inclusion. At the beginning, they visited every household in the community and invited South Asian residents to join the Centre. They also set up booths in the streets to promote activities and services. As some South Asians began to join the Centre, they gradually brought friends and relatives. Now most new members are referred to the Centre by old members. The social worker said:

> At first, they didn't know why they should join the Centre, but since some joined and found the services relevant to their needs, they advertised for us. One member has returned to Pakistan but still recommends his friends who come to Hong Kong to join our Centre. Some old members come back to join outings and gatherings even after they have moved to another district.

The social worker went on to elucidate that the specialized team serving South Asians aims to enhance their adaptability and competitiveness, build up their sense of belonging to the community, eliminate racial discrimination, and establish an ethnically harmonious community. The services for South Asians include homework tutoring, South Asian women's mutual help group, South Asian Cub Scout, spoken Cantonese classes, outings, joint activities with other organizations, consultation and counseling.

Why join the Fair?

This article offers a ground-level, actor-oriented view to delineate why the South Asian women and children participate in the Fair. I argue that the participation of South Asian Muslims in this Chinese religious fair is made possible when

Muslims in a Chinese temple fair in Hong Kong 97

different people make sense of their participation in their own ways and downplay the elements of religion. In discussing how the South Asians perceive their involvement, I first describe how they see joining the Fair as a way to reciprocate the help given by the Centre and to contribute to the community. I move on to suggest that participation in the Fair has become an important means for them to perpetuate and widen their social circle. Hence, I propose that South Asian women's participation should also be understood as a means of empowerment, as some are then able to gain economic benefits and, more notably, as all of them enjoy the social life of the Fair, get a sense of satisfaction and take pride in helping others.

I then shift my discussion to how the organizers understand the participation of South Asian Muslims in the Fair. Although the official organizers and the South Asian participants may have different understandings of the presence of Muslims in this Chinese temple fair, the disparity is filled by the mutual understanding that one's religious or ethnic identity does not necessarily go against one's place as a member of a diverse community, in terms of both obligations and rights. Their mutual effort to downplay theological doctrines has enabled them to transcend the boundary of religion.

Reciprocal relations

I contend that one important reason for the South Asians' involvement in the Temple Fair is that they see joining the Fair as a way to reciprocate to the Centre. Almost invariably all the women and the children at the Centre told me that they first decided to join the Fair because the social workers invited them to, and they felt glad that they could do something for the Centre. I believe they saw it as a chance to reciprocate the help they got. Fatima,[9] a Pakistani woman who helped at the masala tea booth at the Fair, said:

> The social worker is very helpful. She helps us with our English and Cantonese. She translates and reads letters for us. She organizes a lot of activities for us. We don't know the way and don't have the money to travel around Hong Kong. When we join activities organized by the Centre, they pick us up at the Centre and bring us back to the Centre. We have been to Lantau Island and seen the big Buddha. When she asked us to join the Temple Fair, we were glad to help.

Tania, another Pakistani woman who cooked food for the Fair, also emphasized the reciprocal relations of the people in the Centre:

> In the Centre, people get along very well. South Asian women and Chinese women invite each other to their homes to have gatherings. Although I have moved out of Tai Kok Tsui, I still come back for activities. When the social worker asked me and my children to join the Fair, we were glad to help. I am also glad to teach the cooking class for the Centre.

98   Wai-chi Chee

Tania teaches a Pakistani cooking class joined by eight Hong Kong Chinese women. As such, she not only joins activities run by Hong Kong Chinese, but also runs activities *for* Hong Kong Chinese residents. This is a clear reciprocal relationship and a shift of roles. She also earns respect from the participants. At her cooking class, the Hong Kong Chinese women listened attentively and praised her as an excellent cook. Some of them cooked the newly learned dishes for their friends and family, and in the following meeting, shared with the whole group the sense of satisfaction they got, or the funny mistakes they made in cooking the dishes. And they often remarked that they did not make the dishes as well as Tania; at this point, Tania usually gave a humble but confident grin. She also told me proudly that she was the champion of last year's cooking competition.

A social circle round the Centre

As most of the South Asian women do not have their natal family in Hong Kong and do not work, the Centre has become an important place for them to socialize, to learn useful skills, and to have access to information on other resources. Tania says:

> The first few years in Hong Kong were very hard for me. I had no children yet and after my husband went to work, I was left alone at home. I didn't know anyone, nor did I know the way or the language. When I was bored, I went to the small park near my home and that was where I met Fatima. We have become close friends since then. Before we [Pakistani women] joined the Centre, we made friends with fellow Pakistani women when we happened to see each other in the street. But now at the Centre we can meet a lot of friends. I also bring my friends who are new to Hong Kong here. There are many activities for me and my kids, like cooking class, Cantonese, computer, Cub Scout. The social workers also help us with public housing application. My kids have joined many activities here. The social workers help them with their Chinese homework, and they have a lot of fun joining the activities.

Not only for children, but also for women, fun is a central reason to join the activities. In the spoken Cantonese class taught by volunteer Hong Kong Chinese undergraduate students, the women laughed at each other's intonations as they practiced Cantonese conversation but at the same time helped each other with the class assignments. They attended the class while their older children were at school and brought with them the pre-school children. When the mothers were learning Cantonese, the babies slept in the baby carriage; the toddlers ran around the classroom and played with each other. The mothers occasionally intervened when the toddlers fought or cried; otherwise they could enjoy their lesson which was full of laughter. They also took the class as an opportunity for them to meet and to discuss other matters. For instance, before the cooking competition, they talked about what dishes to cook, what ingredients to prepare etc., and before the visit to Disneyland, they bargained as a group with the social worker for more free tickets.

The cooking class and the Cantonese class have demonstrated well the personal relationship between South Asian women and Hong Kong Chinese women. This social circle helps to alleviate their experience of discrimination by the larger Hong Kong public. In general, the South Asian women I talked to have experienced a certain degree of social exclusion, but they emphasized it was mainly from those who had no personal relationship with them and hence did not understand them. In their intimate social circle which is around the Centre, they feel accepted by the local Hong Kong Chinese who treat them as friends. Fatima said:

> Some Chinese people are good to us, but some Chinese people seem to hate us. When I go to the market, I pick and choose, but sometimes people may say, 'Don't touch. *Zau laa, zau laa* (Go away, go away)'. I feel bad about it. Maybe because we're dark; maybe because they don't understand us. For instance, there are criminals among both Chinese and Pakistanis. But if there's one criminal who is Pakistani or Sri Lankan, Hong Kong people will talk about it as if we were all doing bad things. But some Chinese people are very good to us. For example, after giving birth to my baby, my breasts were heavy and in pain; my Chinese landlady advised me on what to do. She went to buy me a pump but took no money from me. She's like an old grandmother to my four children. Now I have moved but I still sometimes bring fruit to visit her and she'll be very happy. At Chinese New Year she gives red packets to all of my four sons, even if I bring only one son to visit her.
> [...]
> In general the local Hong Kong Chinese respect our religion and know that we don't eat pork. Sometimes they may give us food with pork inside, but only because they don't know. The educated people are very good. For example the social workers understand us. In every country there are some bad people and some good people. Even in Pakistan, there are some good people and some bad people. [*Then she stretched out her hand and made an analogy*] Our five fingers are not all the same, right?'[10]

Huma, a Pakistani teenage girl who helped at the henna booth, said:

> I don't like some rude Chinese. For example some old people in the market yell at us. I don't have this experience but mom said that sometimes people yell at her and she doesn't understand. She doesn't speak Cantonese. She doesn't know why other people are angry with her, but at the Centre South Asians and Hong Kong Chinese get along well with each other.

One may think that the social worker is only doing her job, but I believe their relationship is beyond social worker and client, well into the realm of personal friendship. In Tania's first cooking lesson, she and the social worker thought the other one would prepare the ingredients for the chapatti, so no one brought anything. The social worker immediately went to the home of a Pakistani woman living nearby and in less than fifteen minutes she returned with all the necessary ingredients. In the second class, the pot at the Centre was not big enough for the chicken curry, and again, the social worker got a huge pot from another Pakistani woman in no time. Given the strict food taboo of Pakistani Muslims, the woman must trust the social worker well enough to let her use her cooking utensils.

The social worker also said she sees the South Asian women more like friends than clients:

> The South Asians trust us and believe we can help them, and we mustn't abuse their trust.
> [...]
> When they buy things, or when they need to change goods, they will ask me to talk to the shopkeeper. For example once a South Asian woman bought a can of paint but wanted to change the colour. The shopkeeper refused because it was opened. I went to the shop to see how I could help.
> [...]
> After Ramadan they have a party and ask us to let them use a room in the Centre. There are more than 100 women plus children from 20 to 30 families. We try our best to accommodate them.
> [...]
> Some children need homework help and their parents may not speak Chinese and can't help them. We help them. The Centre is also like a playground for them. Their home is small. They can play with other children here.

If the Centre is the core of their social circle for the South Asian women, it is a second home for the South Asian children. They go to the Centre four days a week regularly to finish homework and play games together. The children who performed at the Fair said that they joined it because the social workers asked them to and they could have fun together. As the Fair approached, they practiced the ethnic dances six days a week for three weeks. They said they would finish their homework quickly so that they could have more time to practice. They even designed their own steps. About a week before the Fair, the social workers took them to Star Avenue in Tsim Sha Tsui, one of the busiest areas in Hong Kong, to have a dress rehearsal to perform to the public in the street, so as to gain stage experience. Then they realized they did not dance very well and therefore practiced harder. The children were still very excited about the performances when they talked about them two weeks after the Fair. They said when they practiced they had a lot of fun together, and the best part was after the performances they all went to McDonald's to celebrate. Some of them have participated in the dance performances for multiple years. And most of them participated in more than one performance in both 2011 and 2012, usually a dance plus Chinese kung fu. Some girls even join the regular Chinese kung fu class and seem to love it. I found it fascinating because this is contrary to the stereotypical image of Muslim females.

Muslims in a Chinese temple fair in Hong Kong   101

While Muslim females are perceived to be oppressed, marginalized, and submissive, Chinese kung fu is connected to masculinity, self-defence, and power.

Empowerment through helping others

As I have suggested, most of the South Asians may have started to participate in the Fair as a gesture of reciprocity to the Centre, but I believe it was the sense of satisfaction out of the successful experience that has kept them on. The sense of satisfaction comes not only from being able to reciprocate to the Centre, but more importantly, from being able to contribute to the community, and from feeling accepted by their neighbours. Tania's satisfying experience in the cooking class is a good example, as the social worker explained, 'Why do we join the Temple Fair? Slogans are meaningless. If they [South Asians] can do something that the neighbours appreciate, they'll feel part of the community.'

In general the South Asian women whom I interviewed are from lower socio-economic backgrounds. Mona, a Sri Lankan woman who helped at the food booth, is divorced with two daughters and lives on Comprehensive Social Security Assistance.[11] Huma's father is over the official retirement age of sixty but still needs to work as a security guard, earning a monthly salary of 4,000 HKD (500 USD), which is not enough to support a family of six. They also need Social Security as supplement. Tania had to move to another flat recently because of 'family problems' that she would not elaborate on. Fatima can afford only a one-bedroom unit of about 300 square feet with her husband and their four sons.

The Fair should be understood as a means of female empowerment for them, as the women took pride and achieved a sense of satisfaction in contributing to make the Fair a success, and to help others. In this year's Fair, money raised by the food booths went to the Temple Fair; money raised by the henna booth went to the South Asian Women Force (a mutual help group under the Centre organizing activities for South Asian women); money raised by the jewellery booth went to the sellers, who were unemployed. Financial gain is undoubtedly empowerment, but intangible gains like confidence building may even be more important forms of empowerment. The social worker said:

> This activity [joining the Fair] is especially good for the Pakistani women, because most of them don't work. They stay at home to take care of their children. In comparison to the Nepalese, Filipina and Indian women, the Pakistani women don't feel at ease going out to work. Before we ever joined the Fair, we organized activities for them to sell snacks in the Centre (not in the street) to raise money. Money was a secondary issue; it was more important to build their confidence. When the business was good, they would have more confidence. We had small booths on a weekday inside our Centre, with only a small number of customers. With the experience, they are now confident enough to sell snacks in the street to the public. Their sense of satisfaction is also greater. At this year's Fair, we used 600 HKD [77 USD]

as capital for the food booths and earned about 2000 HKD [260 USD]. Everybody was happy. The money will be donated to the Tai Kok Tsui Temple Fair.

[...]

Both the women and the children were eager to volunteer to help at the Fair and to introduce friends to help. For example one Pakistani girl passed by and volunteered to help to paint henna tattoo when she saw a long queue waiting at the booth. The henna booth raised 600 HKD [77 USD]. The money will go to the South Asian Women Force to organize activities for the women. This is important because some money can't be claimed from government funding. For instance when they have cooking activities at the Centre, they may need to buy a new pan just to make sure it hasn't been used to cook pork.

South Asian participants who helped raise money in the Fair generally had a great sense of satisfaction. Mona said:

At the Temple Fair I sold fish cutlets and raised more than 100 HKD [13 USD]. I was very happy about it. I made the food not so spicy because I understand we need different tastes for different people. I was happy to see that a lot of customers were Chinese. Even four Europeans bought from me. When we first joined the Fair five years ago [in 2007], half and half Pakistani and Chinese bought from us. But now most customers are Chinese, and this is very satisfying. I like the feeling of being able to help. I was very happy when the food I cooked finished first. Before the Fair we discussed what food to sell, and had tasting parties. Next year I will try some new dishes.

Fatima said:

I was responsible for milk tea. I said in Cantonese 'Naai caa, naai caa, hou leng' [Milk tea, milk tea, very good] to attract customers [she laughed at her own Cantonese as she repeated the words, but she took pride in being able to help]. Two of my sons performed in the dragon dance. My husband gave me 20 HKD [2.60 USD] to donate to the Fair. He said people with power should help the poor; if you earn two thousand, two hundred must go to charity. And God will be happy. My husband just asked me to put the money into the box and didn't take any food. I'm lucky to have a good husband.

She was very proud that her husband supported the Fair and supported her participation in the Fair. She was particularly happy when Hong Kong Chinese bought her food, which was a sign of support and acceptance.

To ensure success, the South Asian women were very serious in preparing for the Fair. They had meetings to discuss what to cook, tried different dishes and different tastes, and drew on their previous experience to make the Fair a success. They had a great sense of satisfaction when the food sold well and they could

Muslims in a Chinese temple fair in Hong Kong   103

raise money for the Centre and the needy. And when Hong Kong Chinese bought food from them, they felt they were accepted. For the South Asian women, the Fair and the Centre are both a place for the perpetuation and widening of their social circle, as well as a means of empowerment, to show that they are valued members of the community.

A porous religion boundary

When Fatima told me her husband donated money to the temple fair, I asked whether donation to a Chinese temple fair was against their religion, Islam. She assured me that as long as the money went to the needy, it would make no difference. She used the Islamic concept of *zakat*, or alms-giving, as her principle to donate, not in the context of Islam, but rather to a Chinese temple fair.[12] I argue that the participation of these Muslim South Asian women and their children in this Chinese 'religious' fair was made possible as they downplayed the elements of religion and made sense of the participation in their own ways. Huma said:

> I know it is a religious event. I know there's a Chinese temple. But there's no problem. This event is like a festival party. We also have our festival parties, like after Ramadan we have Eid. We celebrate by putting on henna and we have new clothes and jewellery. We visit every house. The elderly give money to children. And we put oil lamps in the street.

Mona said:

> I know there is a small temple, but it is not against our religion [Islam]. If you're forced to do something, it's no use. It's not from the heart. There's only one God and we're in the same family. Maybe you go to this temple and do things this way, and I go to that temple and do things that way. The form is not important as long as there's only one God. For me, the Temple Fair is like a kind of fair where we can go shopping.

Fatima said:

> In Pakistan we also have something similar. We have a carnival where we pray and eat together. The children get juice and candies. We prepare a lot of food and give a small plate to each household of the neighbourhood. Everybody does this. So it's just the same [as the Temple Fair].
> [...]
> When we fast, we look at the moon and decide the date. You also look at the moon to work out the Lunar calendar and there is a festival for the moon [*she referred to the Mid-Autumn Festival, but she didn't know the name*].
> [...]
> Chinese and Pakistanis have very similar ways to celebrate the festivals. You have dragons and we have henna patterns. We both beat the drums. You may

104 *Wai-chi Chee*

beat the drum sideways [*she mimed beating the drum from the two sides*] and we beat the drum this way [*she mimed beating the drum up and down*].

The women evidently emphasized the similarities between the Fair and Islamic festivals, and diminished the differences, as shown in Fatima's analogy of beating drums, and associating Ramadan with Mid-Autumn Festival, and more powerfully, in Mona's claim that 'there is only one God' and that 'the form is not important'. The social worker confirmed this view:

> They [the South Asians] know we have Dragon Boat Festival, Mid-Autumn Festival, Chinese New Year, etc. Tai Kok Tsui Temple Fair is just another Chinese festival. They don't think it's against their religion to join these festivals. They're not interested to know the details. They don't think it's important. The children know it isn't their religion, though they may not fully understand. But when you tell them what to do and what not to do, they will follow.

The above responses from the actors delineate a situation in which the differences between Islam and Chinese popular religion are submerged under a broader understanding of the universal ideal of religion as representations of common human good that calls for common acts. Far more emphasis is put on the community values of religious activities than the doctrine of religion itself.

The reincarnation of a traditional Fair

The downplaying of the religious elements of the Fair by the South Asian participants goes side by side with the promotion of the Fair by the organizers as a social and cultural activity, rather than a religious ritual. As I will explain, the organizers did so out of political concerns. It is noteworthy that Hong Kong, as a Special Administrative Region, reverted to Beijing Government on 1 July 1997 after 156 years of British colonial rule, and it now has a very different religious policy from the People's Republic of China (PRC). China is officially an atheist state. Communist Party members cannot be religious believers, or take part in religious activities. Although religious freedom is recognized by the Chinese constitution, it is limited to the five state-sanctioned religions: Buddhism, Daoism, Islam, Catholicism, and Protestant Christianity. The central government's strict supervision on religion may be linked to past uprisings of religious secret societies against governments (Naquin 1976; Ownby 1996; Perry 1980, 2002). Unlike the PRC state, the Hong Kong government does not exercise administrative control over religious bodies or activities. The religious policy in Hong Kong follows a laissez-faire philosophy of non-intervention as a legacy of British colonial rule (Kwong 2002). The colonial status also sheltered Hong Kong popular religion from the anti-superstition drive during Mao's leadership of China, when religious practices were eliminated, and temples and ancestral halls demolished (Chan *et al.* 1984). The significant variations in the way that Falun

Gong is treated best illustrate the differences in religion policy between China and Hong Kong. Falun Gong is outlawed in China as an evil cult, but remains legal in Hong Kong and this group is free to have information displays and public protests against the repression of its followers by the PRC.

Despite Hong Kong's autonomy of provision for religious freedom, given the heavy governmental involvement in the Fair, the subduing of religious elements is necessary for the organizers. As discussed above, officially recognized religions are organized on the basis of institutions kept under state sanction, and all else is feudal superstition (Cohen 1991). Chinese popular religion is not within the PRC's five government-approved religions, and is generally regarded by the Communist Party as *mixin* ('superstitions'). This is a major conflict that the organizers of the Tai Kok Tsui Temple Fair must resolve. To comply with the Chinese government's promotion of the expressive aspects of local religion as cultural heritage for tourism and cultural preservation (Liu 2003), the Fair is advocated as a cultural and social activity rather than a religious one

The history of the Fair is described as below on its official website:

> Hung Shing Temple, situated in Fuk Tsun St. Tai Kok Tsui, originally was a temple in Fuk Chuen Village which was located at the intersecting point of Boundary Street and Tai Kok Tsui Road. In 1928, as the Government developed the area, Fuk Chuen Village was to be cleared. The Hing Shing Temple was moved to the present site in Fuk Tsun Street which was named after the Fuk Chuen Village. Inside the Temple, there was the Bronze Bell of the year 1887 and the foundation stone of 1930. On the 13th day of the second month of the lunar calendar, people organize a series of activities to thank Hung Shing for bringing luck and safety to them for the year. It has become the traditional date of Hung Shing Festival.[13]

The impression given by this website is that the Tai Kok Tsui Temple Fair is equivalent to Hung Shing Festival and has a long history, but it is not accurate. In fact, the Fair did not exist before 2005. While Hung Shing Temple Fair has long been celebrated in rural areas, it was not celebrated in any urban area until the first Tai Kok Tsui Temple Fair in 2005. The Hung Shing Festival is on the 13th day of the second lunar month, but to maximize the number of visitors, Tai Kok Tsui Temple Fair is held every year on the closest Sunday. It seems that attracting visitors is more important than keeping the traditional date.

As mentioned, the birth of this Temple Fair is closely related to the initiative of the District Office to promote tourism and to boost the sluggish economy after the SARS epidemic. Apart from responding to Hong Kong's social situation, almost every year the Fair had a special theme with political concerns. For instance, the 2008 theme was to celebrate the Beijing Olympics, the 2009 theme was to celebrate the 60th anniversary of the PRC, the 2011 theme was to celebrate the 60th anniversary of the Mongkok Kai Fong Association, and the 2012 theme was to celebrate the 15th anniversary of Hong Kong's return to China. The Temple Fair gains enthusiastic support from the government. To quote some

106   *Wai-chi Chee*

examples: at the 2011 Fair, the opening ceremony was officiated by a number of local political elites[14]; five streets were closed to traffic for as long as twenty-four hours to facilitate the parade, booths and *puhn choi* feast; the Hong Kong Tourist Board helped promote the Fair and invited foreign tourists to visit the Fair and to enjoy the *puhn choi* feast.

Political dynamics were even more salient in the 2009 Fair which celebrated the 60th anniversary of the PRC. In his opening speech at this Fair, Leung Wah Sing, chairman of the Mongkok Kai Fong Association, said that the aim of the Temple Fair was to promote traditional Chinese cultures and art to local people and tourists, and to enhance the sense of belonging to the community. He then pronounced that the 2009 Fair had a special theme to celebrate the 60th anniversary of the founding of the PRC, and to cultivate love for the mother country. The Fair, he claimed, also aimed to promote tourism and to boost the local economy to relieve the devastating impacts of the financial tsunami; thirty booths were therefore provided free of charge to the unemployed to do business. It is worth noting that nothing about religion was mentioned in his speech. These political and social missions of the Fair were reinforced in different ways throughout the day. The strongest symbols included the rows of Chinese national flags leading the parade, and the sixty dancing lions (signifying the 60th anniversary of the PRC), eighteen of which danced on high poles (symbolizing the eighteen districts of Hong Kong).

The cultural ambassador of the 2009 Fair was Lee Shing Chak, a famous geomancer, or *feng shui* master in Hong Kong (See Freedman 1979). This is a tricky position because *feng shui* is potentially feudal superstition. This was resolved by further downplaying the religious elements. In introducing Lee, the masters of ceremony emphasized that he has a PhD in Astrophysics. In his speech at the Fair, Lee said that a temple fair should not be understood as only for religious worship; it is in fact a legacy of culture, art and history. He concluded that the Tai Kok Tsui Temple Fair should be seen not as anything superstitious but as a means to gather social forces to fight against adversity.

As discussed above, the transcendence of the boundary of religion is made possible at the Tai Kok Tsui Temple Fair because the elements of religion are downplayed by both the organizers and the participants. The organizers' publicizing of the Fair as a social and cultural activity, rather than a religious one, opened up an entrance for the South Asian participants, who widened the door by saying that the Fair is just a cultural and social activity similar to their festivals. And this has enabled the conspicuous appearance of the South Asians Muslims in the Fair.

'Hong Kong is my home, though I may have a different way of life'

There is one area where the organizers and the South Asian Muslims do not agree. The organizers think the Fair is a chance for the South Asians to understand Chinese culture, but as discussed above, this is not an important reason for them to join the fair. Nonetheless, such disparity does not pose a significant barrier to either side.

South Asian children performing a mini-dragon dance or Chinese kung fu is publicized boastfully by the official organizers of the Fair, in the masters of ceremony's introduction and in newspaper reports, as ethnic minority groups learning Chinese cultures, and as a manifestation of 'ethnic harmony'. To them, 'ethnic harmony' seems to mean others adapting to Hong Kong's way of life, or the guests behaving according to the host's rules. But the South Asian participants think Hong Kong *is* their home, whether they live the Hong Kong life or not. Fatima said:

> Last time when I went back to Pakistan, I said I wanted to go home. My parents said, 'You are at home'. Oh, then I realized when I said 'home' I meant Hong Kong. If I go back to Pakistan for two months, I'll miss Hong Kong. I don't think I can stay in Pakistan for more than two months.
> [...]
> Back then every time when I went back to Pakistan I bought everything to bring back here because at that time there were only one or two Pakistani shops in Hong Kong. But now there are many more shops. I can get everything I need.

As we were talking, Fatima's son, a primary student, came to meet her. She said to me:

> You can speak in Cantonese with him. He speaks Cantonese and English. My son doesn't speak Urdu, which is my language. I have four sons. They all speak Cantonese. Sometimes they speak Cantonese among themselves and I don't understand. I may be angry if they're fighting and I don't understand. But I'm glad that they speak Cantonese. It's important in Hong Kong.

Mona said:

> I stay in Sri Lanka no longer than one month before I want to come back.

Tania said:

> My three kids study in the same Catholic primary school. They're the only South Asians in the school. I think they should study in a Chinese school because they're going to stay here. I'm glad that they learn Chinese. The Principal is a very understanding woman. I talked to her and she allowed my girls to wear trousers with the uniform.

Studying in a Catholic school but remaining a Muslim and wearing the uniform in their way are just two of the many examples that the South Asians who participated in the Fair see Hong Kong as their home without feeling the urge to adapt totally to Hong Kong's way of life. While they think it is true that the Fair is a chance for them to understand Chinese cultures, they do not think it is necessary for them to fully understand or adapt to the cultures before they can call Hong Kong their home. As mentioned before, the social worker told me the South Asians are not interested to know the details of Chinese festivals. She added:

> We tell them about Dragon Boat Festival. They know it's about a story of a Chinese official but they don't care about the details. They don't remember why he jumped into the river, though they remember people threw dumplings into the water so that the fish wouldn't eat his body. We also teach them how to make dumplings. They like sweet dumplings and make dumplings with sweetened beans. They use a simple way to wrap the dumplings instead of the traditional Chinese way. They also modify the dumplings to suit their taste; for instance, they like fried dumplings though we Chinese seldom fry dumplings. We also tell the children about Chinese taboos; for example at the Hungry Ghost Festival, they see people performing rituals in the streets, and we tell them not to step over the offerings and not to take the fruit. They don't understand why but they will follow what we tell them.

The organizers think the Fair is a chance for the South Asians to understand and appreciate Chinese cultures, but the South Asians also think it is a chance for them to introduce their cultures to the Hong Kong Chinese. Huma said:

> It's a chance for us to introduce our cultures to everyone, for example our jewellery and henna. Painting henna is our tradition. We do it when we have weddings or festivals. It's our Pakistani custom.

While the organizers seem to be suggesting that this is a chance for the South Asians to learn and appreciate Chinese cultures so that they can integrate into the community more easily, the South Asian participants think that Hong Kong *is* their home and that they are contributing to the Fair as much as any other Hong Kong Chinese participant; it makes no difference whether they understand or practice Chinese cultures in Hong Kong people's way. To them, being Chinese is out of the question; they do not even seem to bother whether they are Hong Kong people or not. They identify themselves as Pakistanis, Sri Lankans or Nepalese living in Hong Kong, where they keep their own cultures, despite different degrees of localization.

Although the organizers and the South Asian participants may have different understandings of the participation, a meeting point is possible. Both agree it is important that residents in Hong Kong should contribute to it and one's religious or ethnic identity should not be a barrier to one's obligations and rights as a member of a community. The South Asian participants are aware that they live in the community and benefit from it, and they are glad to do something in return, despite their alternative cultural identity. As Tania said, 'Hong Kong is my home, though I may have a different way of life'.

Conclusion

Plüss (2006) and other scholars claim that Hong Kong is not so much a multicultural city as a Chinese city that demonstrates limited inclusion for diverse cultures. Similarly, Ku (2006) argues that it is an illusion that Hong Kong is a cosmopolitan 'global' city with little racial discrimination, and that the social exclusion of ethnic minorities has long been in existence, though often hidden. They may be right at the higher level analysis of state policies and social practices. But this chapter has offered a more actor-oriented view to the dynamics of pluralism, both religious and ethnic, in a religious event in this global city where relationships of an immigrant religious group and the dominant local Chinese are restructured and redefined in ways that make sense to both. This has come largely out of the realistic necessity that they need to get along with each other at a community level, given the fact that Yau Tsim Mong is the district with the highest proportion of South Asians. As discussed in this chapter, the reciprocal relationship between the South Asians and the Centre, the social circle of the South Asians and local Chinese at the community level, the pride of being able to contribute to society, and the porous religious boundaries have all contributed to the participation of South Asian Muslims in this Chinese Temple Fair.

Eck (1997) emphasizes that pluralism is not diversity alone, but is active engagement with diversity to create a common society. This chapter has shown a form of religious pluralism, in everyday life, which emphasizes participation and engagement rather than religious doctrines; one which looks for similarities rather than differences. In claiming public space and public time, these Muslims exhibit what Hecht (2007) terms active pluralism, but different to what Hecht predicts, this active pluralism does not result in confrontation. By participating actively in a local community fair, Muslim women show that they are members of the community and are contributing as much to it as any other local Hong Kong Chinese. The religious label attached to the Fair does not seem to constitute a barrier, as they make sense of their participation in their own ways and accord legitimacy to diversity in order for pluralism to exist (Peletz 2009). The actors are crucial in shaping the values of religions. Participants in this Temple Fair, South Asian Muslims and Chinese popular religion practitioners alike, act in the name of god to interpret pluralism to include each other. The values of religions, as articulated in their understanding, lie in the universal ideal of promoting human good that calls for common acts. It is an umbrella big enough to accommodate both Islam and Chinese popular religion.

Notes

1 Sichuan face-changing is an ancient dramatic art in Chinese Sichuan opera. The performer wears layers of painted masks, which he pulls off one after another in split seconds.
2 Puhn choi, literally 'basin dish', is a traditional banquet in some Chinese villages, where mixed food filling a large basin is shared (Watson 1987).
3 The South Asian women in Hong Kong usually stick to their traditional clothes not only in special events but in everyday life (Ku 2006).

110   *Wai-chi Chee*

4   Information Services Department, 'Hong Kong: The Facts (Religion and Custom)', in www.gov.hk/en/about/abouthk/factsheets/docs/religion.pdf. Accessed on 1 March 2011. The number of Muslims reported here does not include the migrant workers, a large number of whom are female Indonesian Muslims. When they are included, the total number is estimated to be 250,000.
5   The SARS outbreak of 2003 caused more than 300 deaths in Hong Kong. 'Yau Tsim Mong', the cluster of Yau Ma Tei, Tsim Sha Tsui and Mongkok, is one of the eighteen districts in Hong Kong. Tai Kok Tsui belongs to this district.
6   See www.tkttemplefair.org.hk/en/chairman/statement.html
7   The two main types of services are elderly service and community service. Community services include family service, baby-sitting service, civil education, youth service, employment service, continuing education, and services for women, new arrivals to Hong Kong and South Asians.
8   According to the 2006 Population By-census, Yau Tsim Mong is the district with the highest proportion of South Asians.
9   All names given to the South Asian informants in this paper are pseudonyms.
10   I found her analogy highly interesting because coincidently there is a very similar saying in Cantonese that 'there are long fingers and short fingers', meaning that there can be pros and cons.
11   The Comprehensive Social Security Assistance Scheme is administered by the Social Welfare Department of Hong Kong to provide a safety net for those who cannot support themselves financially; it is designed to bring their income up to a prescribed level to meet their basic needs. It is non-contributory but means-tested. See Social Welfare Department, Comprehensive Social Security Assistant Scheme, www.swd.gov.hk/en/index/site_pubsvc/page_socsecu/sub_comprehens/. Accessed on 3 October 2009.
12   *Zakat* is an Islamic obligation to donate a certain percentage of one's earning to help the poor. On top of *zakat*, a Muslim is encouraged to give more as voluntary charity.
13   www.tkttemplefair.org.hk/en/history/history.html
14   Guests of honor at the opening ceremony include representatives from Home Affairs Department, Liaison Office of the Central People's Government in Hong Kong SAR, National People's Congress, Yau Tsim Mong District Council, Home Affairs Bureau, Legislative Councilors, Police Force, Independent Commission Against Corruption, Leisure and Cultural Service Department, Kowloon Chamber of Commerce and Social Welfare Department.

References

Census and Statistics Department (2012) 'Nationality and ethnicity', in www.census2011.gov.hk/flash/dashboards/nationality-and-ethnicity-db-203-en/nationality-and-ethnicity-db-203-en.html. Accessed 8 May 2012.

Chan, A., Madsen, R. and Unger, J. (1984) *Chen Village: The Recent History of a Peasant Community in Mao's China*, Berkeley: University of California Press.

City University of Hong Kong and Unison Hong Kong (2003) 'Research Report on the Employment Situation of South Asian People in Hong Kong', Hong Kong: City University of Hong Kong, Department of Applied Social Studies, Working Group of the Social Integration Project for Ethnic Minority People in Hong Kong.

Cohen, M.L. (1991) 'Being Chinese: The Peripheralization of Traditional Identity', *Daedalus*, 120(2): 113–34.

Eck, D. (1997) *On Common Ground: World Religions in America* [Multimedia CD-ROM], New York: Columbia University Press.

Freedman, M. (1979) 'Chinese Geomancy: Some Observations in Hong Kong', in William

Skinner (selected and introduced), *The Study of Chinese Society: Essays by Maurice Freedman*, Stanford, CA: Stanford University Press.

Frost, S. (2004) 'Building Hong Kong: Nepalese Workers in Construction Section', *Journal of Contemporary Asia*, 34(3): 364–76.

Garces-Foley, K. (2007) 'New Opportunities and New Values: The Emergence of the Multicultural Church', *The ANNALS of the American Academy of Political and Social Science*, 612: 209–24.

Geoffroy, M. (2004) 'Theorizing Religion in the Global Age: A Typological Analysis', *International Journal of Politics, Culture and Society*, 18(1): 33–46.

Hecht, R.D. (2007) 'Active Versus Passive Pluralism: A Changing Style of Civil Religion?' *The ANNALS of the American Academy of Political and Social Science*, 612: 133–51.

Information Services Department (2011) 'Hong Kong: The Facts (Religion and Custom)', in www.gov.hk/en/about/abouthk/factsheets/docs/religion.pdf, 1 March 2011.

Ku, H. (2006) 'Body, Dress and Cultural Exclusion: Experiences of Pakistani Women in "Global" Hong Kong', *Asian Ethnicity*, 7(3): 286–302.

Ku, H., Chan, K., Chan, W. and Lee, W. (2003) 'A Research Report on the Life Experiences of Pakistanis in Hong Kong' (Vol. 7), Hong Kong: Centre for Social Policy Studies, Department of Applied Social Sciences, The Hong Kong Polytechnic University.

Ku, H., Chan, K., Sandhu, K.K. and Unison Hong Kong (2005) 'A Research Report on the Education of South Asian Ethnic Minority Groups in Hong Kong', Hong Kong: Centre for Social Policy Studies, Department of Applied Social Sciences, The Hong Kong Polytechnic University.

Ku, H., Chan, K. and Sandhu, K.K. (2006) 'A Research Report on the Employment of South Asian Ethnic Minority Groups in Hong Kong', Hong Kong: Centre for Social Policy Studies, Department of Applied Social Sciences, The Hong Kong Polytechnic University.

Ku, H., Chan, K., Lo, S. and Singh, T. (2010) *(Re)Understanding Multiracial Hong Kong: Eight Stories of South Asians in Hong Kong*, Hong Kong: Centre for Social Policy Studies, Department of Applied Social Science, The Hong Kong Polytechnic University.

Kwong, C. (2002) *The Public Role of Religion in Post-Colonial Hong Kong: An Historical Overview of Confucianism, Taoism, Buddhism and Christianity*, New York: Peter Lang.

Liu, T. (2003) 'A Nameless But Active Religion: An Anthropologist's View of Local Religion in Hong Kong and Macau', *The China Quarterly*, 174: 373–94.

Loper, K. (2004) 'Race and Equality: A Study of Ethnic Minorities in Hong Kong's Education System: Project Report and Analysis', Hong Kong: Centre for Comparative and Public Law, University of Hong Kong.

Marty, M.E. (2007) 'Pluralisms', *The ANNALS of the American Academy of Political and Social Science*, 612: 13–25.

Moore, K.M. (2007) 'Muslims in the United States: Pluralism under Exceptional Circumstances', *The ANNALS of the American Academy of Political and Social Science*, 612: 116–32.

Naquin, S. (1976) *Millenarian Rebellion in China: The Eight Trigrams Uprising of 1813*, New Haven, CT: Yale University Press.

Niebuhr, G. (2007) 'All Need Toleration: Some Observations about Recent Differences in the Experiences of Religious Minorities in the United States and Western Europe', *The ANNALS of the American Academy of Political and Social Science*, 612: 172–86.

112   *Wai-chi Chee*

Overmyer, D.L. (2003) 'Religion in China Today: Introduction', *The China Quarterly,* 174: 307–16.

Ownby, D. (1996) *Brotherhoods and Secret Societies in Early and Mid-Qing China: The Formation of a Tradition*, Stanford, CA: Stanford University Press.

Peletz, M. (2009) *Gender Pluralism: Southeast Asia since Early Modern Times*, New York: Routledge.

Perry, E.J. (1980) *Rebels and Revolutionaries in North China, 1845–1945*, Stanford, CA: Stanford University Press.

Perry, E.J. (2002) *Challenging the Mandate of Heaven: Social Protest and State Power in China*, Armonk, NY: M.E. Sharpe.

Plüss, C. (2006) 'Becoming Different while Becoming the Same: Reterritorializing Islamic Identities with Multi-Ethnic Practices in Hong Kong', *Ethnic and Racial Studies,* 29(4): 656–75.

Roof, W.C. (2007) 'Pluralism as a Culture: Religion and Civility in Southern California', *The ANNALS of the American Academy of Political and Social Science,* 612: 82–99.

Watson, J.L. (1987) 'From the Common Pot: Feasting with Equals in Chinese Society', *Anthropos,* 82: 389–401.

Williams, R.H. (2007) 'The Languages of the Public Sphere: Religious Pluralism, Institutional Logics, and Civil Society', *The ANNALS of the American Academy of Political and Social Science,* 612: 42–61.

7 Sweetness and light

The bright side of pluralism in a Rajasthan town[1]

Ann Grodzins Gold

The municipality of Jahazpur is the administrative seat of a sub-district (*tehsil*) in provincial Rajasthan. With numerous government offices, and a hospital, Jahazpur is a regional hub for services unavailable in villages. Jahazpur's bus stand and streets are crammed with shopping opportunities of every kind. Rural and town lives have long intersected commercially in these lively markets. Twenty-first-century Jahazpur culture exists in perpetual engagement with national and transnational flows of goods, images, jobs, news, money, and much more. It is networked both literally and figuratively. Yet Jahazpur is undeniably and self-consciously a 'provincial' place: *mofussil*, or – as local people are much more likely to say, using the English words – a 'backward area'.

I lived in Jahazpur from early August 2010 through the middle of June 2011. My fieldwork methods combined traditional participant observation with unstructured interviews. I worked in close association with Bhoju Ram Gujar, a government school headmaster with whom I have done collaborative ethnographic research since 1980; throughout the text I refer to him as Bhoju. Other real names are not disclosed here. Five sections follow. I first describe Jahazpur, a *qasba* or market town, and characterize its non-rural, non-urban nature. Next I introduce two useful definitions of, and approaches to, pluralism that will inform this chapter's third segment: an ethnographic account of six festivals. A fourth section briefly treats dramatic and traumatic recollected ruptures in Jahazpur's peaceful society. In closing, I offer some simple observations of everyday commonalities and mutually cordial recognitions among the town's distinct communities, suggesting that these provide habitual foundations for ordinary pluralism as the fabric of civic life.

Placing Jahazpur

Jahazpur is set between hills, as are many cities and villages in Rajasthan, a region long ruled by warring princes seeking geophysical advantages. Three important hilltop structures – two shrines and a fort – are easily visible from most parts of town and accessible by paths, stairways, and most recently two new roads. On one hill stands the revered tomb of Gaji Pir, a Muslim saint who was also a warrior. Malaji, a regional hero-god of the Hindu Mina community, is

114   *Ann Grodzins Gold*

housed on the other hilltop in a recently expanded temple. Spatially more imposing than either shrine, Jahazpur's fort, dating back at least to the fifteenth century,
is in ruins.

Jahazpur's legendary origins date back to an episode contained in the first book
of the ancient Hindu epic tale, the *Mahabharata*: the vengeful snake sacrifice of
King Janamejaya. In Jahazpur lore, this textual tale has been embellished with
several additional local narratives and moral messages quite absent in classical
versions. Knowledge of these founding tales, associated not only with the town's
ancient past but with its river's birth, unifies all residents quite remarkably. I
recorded the snake sacrifice story from men and women; priests, merchants and
labourers; eighty-year-olds and twenty-year-olds; Hindus, Muslims, and Jains;
literate and non-literate. Of course there were different degrees of textual references (such as the names of kings), but it is essentially a universally shared oral
tradition among all who live in Jahazpur.[2] The same persons were a lot vaguer and
far less in accord on more recent centuries. From snatches of published recorded
history, I have learned that Jahazpur at various periods was ruled by Mughals, by
Ranas of the great kingdom of Mewar, and for about a century by the small adjoining kingdom of Shahpura.[3] Thus the fort changed hands often. It has been utterly
deserted since around the time of India's Independence in 1947.

Jahazpur's market and residences were originally contained within a fully
walled area. Four imposing gates to the outside, still standing, were locked at
night and manned by watchmen. Today referred to as 'inside the. walls', this
limited area forms the core of Jahazpur *qasba*. Any expansion of the town,
whether residential or commercial, has necessarily taken place exterior to these
walls. *Qasba* has been roughly defined – both by dictionaries and people I interviewed – as a settlement 'larger than a village but smaller than a city'. With its
population just under 20,000 in 2001 and predicted to reach 25,000 in the new
2011 census, Jahazpur fits that bill. Yet the semantics of *qasba* engage more than
demography.[4] Not every small town of comparable size is appropriately referred
to as *qasba*. Most broadly speaking, those ineffable qualities evoking the desig-
nation *qasba* have to do with a deep history and rich cultural heritage.[5]

However provincial when compared to cities, a *qasba* is notably characterized
by a *non-rural* consciousness manifest in a preoccupation with trade or business
(versus agriculture), and these days with education. Most significantly in the
context of this volume, a number of persons when pressed to list the characteris-
tics of a *qasba* during both recorded interviews and casual conversations stated
first that one defining attribute was diversity: multiplicity of castes, if only
secondarily of religions. Mushirul Hasan in his literary and historical study of
qasba life in the eastern Uttar Pradesh region during the colonial era, particularly
celebrates *qasbati* pluralism. He writes that in North Indian *qasba* culture,
'Besides differences and distinctions there were also relationships and interactions . . . The stress is therefore on . . . religious plurality as the reference point for
harmonious living' (Hasan 2004: 27, 31).

Hasan translates from the memoir of Hosh Bilgrami, who looks back from
darker times:

Bright side of pluralism in a Rajasthan town   115

When the conch sounded in the temples in its notes...the Muslims heard the voice of unity and kinship. When the call for prayer (*azan*) sounded, the mellifluous voice entranced the Hindus to accept Allah's greatness. During Muharram, Hindus and Muslims walked shoulder to shoulder reciting elegies and dirges. Music did not provoke violence nor did the Pipal tree cause conflict.

(Bilgrami, cited in Hasan 2004: 127)

The plural nature of Jahazpur was one of the reasons I was drawn to study it: its many Hindu temples; its Muslim mosques and tombs of revered saints; its ancient and living Jain presence; its numerically strong Scheduled Caste and Scheduled Tribe populations.

As is the case throughout Rajasthan, Hindus are the majority in Jahazpur. However, inside the walls in the oldest part of town live a significantly higher percentage of Muslims. I have been regularly given estimates as high as 40 per cent. Jain families, here as elsewhere, are successful in business and influential in local politics. Although a full treatment lies well beyond my limited scope here, it is important to keep in mind that keen issues of pluralism versus prejudice arise within religious communities in Jahazpur as well as across them. The fissures and negotiations between upper caste Hindu, and disadvantaged groups such as former leatherworkers, butchers and sweepers, engage identity politics and notions of primordial difference as acutely as religion, or at times even more acutely.[6] Moreover, as I will show, the town and country divide among Hindus is another significant line of difference with theological as well as sociological ramifications.

Similar divides exist among Muslims. The majority of Jahazpur's Muslims are known as *deshvali*, understood as locals who accepted Islam during the Mughal period.[7] Many said this conversion took place during the time of Hazrat Khwaja Moinuddin Chisti, known as Garib Navaz, the beloved Sufi saint of Ajmer whom Hindus also revere. *Deshvali* Muslims, at least in most conversations with me and Bhoju, downplayed their differences from Hindus. They acknowledged shared roots, shared lineage names, and shared cultural traditions. Hindus, especially members of the bourgeoisie, reciprocated; they described *deshvalis* as 'like us' – solid citizens, landowners. Hindu othering, therefore, is directed at *pardeshi* (foreigner) Muslims, although many lineages in this internally highly diverse category have also lived in Jahazpur for generations. Some Hindus label *pardeshi* Muslims as rootless trouble-makers, an attitude with an evident class dimension as *pardeshis* are by and large poorer.

Yet another factor to acknowledge, although again beyond my scope here, is that individuals – no matter into what community they were born – possess many varieties of conviction. Besides those who are enthusiastically involved in the performance of public rituals on traditional festival days on which this chapter focuses, there are those who follow various gurus and paths, embracing quite disparate teachings. These might stress spiritual inner practices over extravagant ritual trappings, or adhere to reform traditions dedicated to social uplift. Both

116   *Ann Grodzins Gold*

types of groups may be notably integrated across caste boundaries and present egalitarian messages. Members of these groups might eschew some of the very activities that other Hindus most enjoy and value including the public displays that concern us here.

Approaches to pluralism

I have found it useful to combine two rather different definitions of pluralism which, while seeming to speak of all societies, not insignificantly both emerge from ethnographic and historical research in South and Southeast Asia. One economically elegant view is proposed by Michael Peletz who defines pluralism as, 'conditions or settings in which diversity is accorded legitimacy' (2009: 2).[8] The other is 'living together', which Shail Mayaram (2005, 2009) has explored extensively in the context of Ajmer, a large Rajasthan city not too far from Jahazpur. In Mayaram's words, living together comprises, 'shared imaginaries and grammars that are rooted in everyday perceptions of being in the world' (2009).

Jahazpur *performs* an innocent and idealized pluralism at national holidays, as is the case all over India. It can seem both corny and artificial, as when Jahazpur's school children dance together dressed up as imagined Christian, Sikh, Hindu and Muslim (even though the two former religions do not even figure in the local population) (see Figure 7.1). Yet I do not dismiss such performances. Like civil behaviour when it covers up deeper currents of distrust or dislike, I believe these enactments may help to diffuse hostility and affirm plural consciousness. In what follows I shall engage both performed and organic manifestations of plural society at work and at play in Jahazpur.

A focus on pluralism in the context of festivities could seem to highlight special rather than everyday relationships, but such events are too numerous to be considered exceptional or antistructural. Rather, I suggest viewing them as cultural performances – a term coined by pioneering urban anthropologist Milton Singer to describe bounded activities (such as concerts, recitals, rituals, parades) in which people deliberately enact their culture as they wish it to be perceived – in other words, self-consciously (Singer 1972). As does Chee Wai-chi in her contribution to this volume, I see town festivals as opportunities to enact membership in a local community in public spaces where religious identities may have more porous boundaries than they do at home.

Jahazpur's menu of cultural performances is quite extraordinary; I found it dazzling at the beginning and exhausting or even numbing after a few months. The festivals treated here I observed while still dazzled. My title intentionally bears the ironic edge that the phrase 'sweetness and light' usually carries in English – the subtext that *all* of human life cannot be conviviality. That is true in Jahazpur needless to say, as readily signed by visible police presence in the streets whenever large groups gather in celebration; by plenty of individual comments; by a few actual disturbances. Historically here as elsewhere, inter-community violence has indeed occasionally flared specifically during public celebrations.

Figure 7.1 India's pluralism performed by Jahazpur school children on Republic Day (photo by Ann Grodzins Gold)

Yet I hope to conclude that beautifying streets and shared sweets help to produce a feel-good version of reality that – however sugar-coated – matters. Looking at public religion performed in Jahazpur, following Mayaram's urged trajectory, I seek evidence of pluralism in practice, constructive rather than negative visions.

Public religiosity on the ground: An ethnographic tour of six festivals

Before plunging into the particulars of festival events, I address a broader context for my Jahazpur observations: the growth and proliferation of religious spectacles in India in recent decades. According to Meera Nanda's well-documented if unrepentantly polemical study, in the twenty-first century in India there are more public displays of religion than ever before (Nanda 2009). Nanda's focus in her recent book is solely on Hindu manifestations of this phenomenon, which she views with disapproval. Her general point on the efflorescence of public religion is perfectly true of Jahazpur: it was tempting (and I indeed succumbed at the beginning of my fieldwork) to focus energies and attention on nothing but these near constant serial displays. Nanda dubs all this, 'the rush hour of the gods' – a phrase she borrows from a 1967 work by Neil MacFarland about postwar Japan

118   *Ann Grodzins Gold*

(Nanda 2009: 63). However, based on my Jahazpur experience, I might question Nanda's claim that some forms of a politically backed Hinduism are inevitably the major perpetrators and beneficiaries of these phenomena. Where other South Asian religions coexist with Hinduism, as is the case in Jahazpur, they also have increased displays, and increased claims on public space. I would add that if – as Nanda also argues – these elaborate or even excessive displays may be in part a result of globalization (influenced by media and economic flows), they are also evidently rooted in local circumstances.

An old acquaintance of mine, who is among other things a successful speculator in the local real estate boom, lives in his ancestral village not far from Jahazpur. When I exclaimed over the gaudy, entrancing splendour of Krishna's birthday – Janamashtami, my first Jahazpur festival – his response was to tell me that Jahazpur's public displays were particularly gorgeous because of its large Muslim population. This, he said, inspired 'competition' between Hindus and Muslims. Each community works harder and spends more to create vivid spectacles. Others we questioned confirmed this more or less friendly rivalry understood to result in a public good (eye candy).

I take a limited time period, in 2010 – a literal slice of Jahazpur's public life – and describe six festivals that occurred within it:

1   **Janamashtami** (Birth Eighth): 2–3 September; Bhadra dark 8th (Hindu).
2   **Ganesh Chaturthi** (Ganesh Fourth): 10–11 September; Bhadra bright 4th (Hindu).
3   **Id al-Fitr** (Celebration of the End of Ramadan): 11 September (Muslim).
4   **Teja Dashmi** (Teja Tenth): 17 September; Bhadra bright 10th (Hindu).
5   **Jal Jhulani Gyaras** (Water Swing Eleventh):18 September; Bhadra bright 11th (Hindu).
6   **Anant Chaturdashi** (Endless Fourteenth): 22 September; Bhadra bright 14th (Jain).

The first two of these involved elaborate light decorations and *jhanki* or glimpsed divine scenes both inanimate and portrayed by living people; the last two had town-wide processions as their main feature. Id al-Fitr is a collective prayer gathering. Teja Tenth combined a county fair atmosphere with spirit possession and divination. Occasionally I find it helpful to draw on later events for comparative purposes.

All these festivals seem to be about nothing but religiosity in place. Festivals transform public places with lavish light displays, fabricated passageways, banners, arches, festoons of tinsel, and sound. Processions traverse places, temporarily claiming them with feet, music, flags and motor caravans. The Muslim holiday that falls within my selected time scope happens to be Id. While the *Idgah* is certainly a transformed space, it sits vacant for most of the year just waiting for Id's intense hours of collective prayer and community solidarity. It is a space set apart, while other festivals work their magic on everyday spaces. Scripturally chartered, Id is less flamboyant than other Muslim celebrations I

Bright side of pluralism in a Rajasthan town 119

observed later in the year: notably the 'Urs of Gaji Pir in November, and Muharram's two *taziya* processions in December and January.[9]

Some processions originated long ago in Jahazpur's colonial or princely pasts, while others are relatively new. Most tellingly, confirming Nanda, just about all of Jahazpur's public celebrations have become more elaborate in living memories. The delightfully emphatic Kamala told us that Jal Jhulani Gyaras (the most ambitious and widely attended of annual Hindu processions) had been going on 'since the creation of the universe' – a possible exaggeration. But we heard frequently that the number of 'chariots' (*bevan*), portable thrones for temple deities, had dramatically multiplied over the last few decades. One result which we observed in 2010 was that, on reaching the water reservoir, different deities were bathed at different points along the shore. Suspecting some kind of caste segregation, we asked many people about this. Everyone asserted that it was purely and simply the result of a traffic jam: all the images could no longer have their baths in one place. In part this increase in numbers is the result of more inclusive participation. Formerly excluded communities have joined, notably the 'Scheduled Caste' Khatik (former butchers) and Regars (former leatherworkers). Being the most recent to join the parade, their deities' respective chariots form the tail end of the procession, but it doesn't seem to matter to them. Once all the chariots are on the move they compose a glorious, colourful unified stream.

When we asked one of Jahazpur's senior Muslim gentlemen about change in Muslim festivals, he replied rather severely, 'There is no change at all. Islam is based on the Qur'an and what is written in it is what we are doing'. Implicit in this statement is a contrast to Hinduism: Muslim festival customs are consistent, even timeless, because Muslims have a book that guides them in all things. Nonetheless, he acknowledged that there were some variable factors such as a person's economic condition: 'if someone is rich, he is cooking nice food, if he is poor he cannot'. This conversation was specifically in reference to Id. Later in the year we learned from other interviews with other Muslims that Islamic celebrations associated with Jahazpur's two important *mazar* (tombs of saints) as well as Muharram's two processions, have by all accounts definitely changed and expanded over the last half century. Unlike Id, these events do not find their origin in the Qur'an.

Festivals are highly orchestrated but can nonetheless feel bewildering to a first-time outsider attendee. This awkward confessional extract from my field diary I tapped out in haste on the day when both Id al-Fitr and Ganesh Chaturthi were celebrated (although the *laddu* incident took place at Ganesh displays the night before):

> Beggars line the entrance [to the *Idgah*]; I gave them coins on my way out but Bhoju says you should do it on your way in, oh well . . . I took a [second] *laddu* last night when I was too full to eat it, which led to a problem of what to do with it. Often I do the wrong thing. Holidays are human.
>
> (fieldnotes, 11 September 2010)

120   *Ann Grodzins Gold*

Such failings I fear are typical for me, and serve as a cautionary commentary on the often bumbling outsider's point of view. Yet my glib rationalization, 'holidays are human', could be meaningful in a broader sense. These occasions give pleasure to casual spectators and meritorious stress to their organizers, from whom they demand intense commitments of time and resources. Festivals invoke divine presence while stimulating many kinds of very human activities. Critics of external religion frequently denounce them as pure show (*dikhavana*), an all too human penchant.

My descriptions of these festivals are based on my own sensory impressions. I also draw on knowledge gathered in interviews conducted either before or after, but never during, the events in question. I attend here almost exclusively to the sociological import of these six religious holidays, rather than to any deeper religious experiences they may provide. In keeping to the surface I do not intend to join those critics who deny true religious meaning to festivals, but merely to work within my own limits.[10] Another chapter in this volume – that by Angela Rudert on pluralism expressed through multiple media by a savvy female guru – plumbs some of the deeper ways spiritual teachings in India may find outer representations to demonstrate divine unity of religious paths.

Let us now walk through slightly less than three weeks of September 2010 in Jahazpur.

Janamashtami

> The glitter of the gods and the glitter of humans; it seems every woman has her most spangled outfit on for Janamashtami, and the little girls are resplendent. Even men seem to have some gold and silver threads in their shirts... Everything glitters for Lord Krishna.
>
> (fieldnotes)

Janamashtami celebrates Krishna's birth, in the prison where his evil uncle kept his birth-mother confined; and his miraculous escape to his foster home in bucolic Vrindavan. Baby Krishna is rocked in his cradle, and doorways to homes as well as temples are festooned with *bandarval*, the strings of leaves or ornaments that are used to celebrate human births as well.

Janamashtami was my first Jahazpur festival, and none that followed left me so stunned. It featured lavish light decorations at every Vaishnavite temple in town as well as school and political displays. I was awestruck by the way that coloured lights transformed the spaces I was just beginning to recognize as a daytime shopper, rendering them totally unfamiliar once again. From our suburban 'colony' of Santosh Nagar, a ten–twelve minute walk away from the *qasba*, many people strolled along in groups. Everyone happily answered the pleasant rhetorical question, 'where are you going?' with two words: *jhanki dekhna* (to see the *jhanki*). It gave me a simple sense of belonging to repeat this phrase.

Jhanki are scenes – whether constructed with cardboard or human bodies – depicting the divine play of Lord Krishna.[11] Most utterly charming were the beautiful children inside a school building who were costumed, made up and posed in scenes representing well-known exploits in Krishna's story (see Figure 7.2). Often the same scene was replicated multiple times to give more children a chance to participate.

Figure 7.2 Jhanki of Krishna the Butter Thief, Janamashtami (photo by Ann Grodzins Gold)

122 *Ann Grodzins Gold*

When Bhoju and I interviewed him a few weeks after the festival, the priest of the town's oldest Vaishnavite temple – Juna Char Bhuja or 'Ancient Four Arms' – asserted that 10,000 people had come to take *darshan* on Janamashtami. This is likely hyperbolic as that figure would be nearly half the population of Jahazpur. The priest also informed us that crowds did not cease pouring in until after midnight, and that he had passed out two and one-half *maun* of khir (milk-rice pudding) – that is, 100 kg.

Good-natured crowds moved at a good pace from one display to another, and although there was pressing in the tighter areas, there was never any pushing. When I lingered too long to capture a photograph I was gently but firmly advised to move along. The sole *jhanki* not surrounded by crowds was that set up by the BJP (Hindu nationalist political party) – and I couldn't help feeling pleased at its forlorn condition which seemed to testify to the local population's disinterest in divisive rhetoric.

Ganesh Chaturthi and Id

> People went all out for Janamashtami; this [Ganesh Chaturthi] seemed some-how another major effort that just didn't cut it; less crowds and less ardour put into the displays; still a nice Ganesh made of almonds and cashews . . . the news-paper says it [Id] is a festival of peace and love and so it felt . . . We said Id Mubarak hundreds of times. We clasped hands with many adults and children.
>
> (fieldnotes)

It was the night of 9 September when Muslim authorities in Delhi announced that Id would take place not on the tenth, as many had expected, but on the eleventh. Due to this unanticipated convergence of calendars, the Hindu festival of Ganesh Chaturthi and the Muslim celebration of Id al-Fitr, the end of the fasting month of Ramadan, would converge on the same day. Newspapers and television broad-casts made a great deal out of this simultaneity which had not happened in over a decade. Hindu and Muslim talking heads appeared alternately on the screen speaking benign platitudes. On the ground in Jahazpur, while we did not see a lot of interactions between the two groups, we did experience a general atmosphere of what appeared to be genuine mutual good will.

Ganesh Chaturthi is best known in Maharashtra where it involves annually constructed Ganesh images who reside in homes for a period of time and are grandly processed to be submerged in water on the climactic day. In Jahazpur what it involved, on the night of 10 September, was a slightly less lavish repeat of Janamashtami's displays – except that now it was the Ganesh shrines and temples, rather than the Vishnu and Krishna ones, that put up the lights and elab-orately adorned icons. There were over-abundant *laddus* (Ganesh's favourite food), and the scenes and sweets drew many from surrounding villages to admire beloved Ganeshji.

According to some elderly persons, Ganesh Chaturthi in Jahazpur used simply to be called *Danda Chauth* (Stick Fourth). Even today, little boys go around the

Bright side of pluralism in a Rajasthan town 123

market beating on the front steps of shops with their shiny painted wooden sticks – which were made by local lathe-working carpenters. They make a racket until shopkeepers give them money and send them off. The light displays at temples on the eve of the holiday are newer, although I have not been able to date their beginnings. This year several people with whom we spoke attributed high attendance to the abundant *laddus* offered for the taking as *prasad* (blessings). There was a gorgeous *badam-kaju* Ganesh – that is, Ganesh made entirely from almonds and cashews – with a neon Lakshmi by his side, uniting the key festival components of sweetness and light (see Figure 7.3). But in truth, when I conceived my title, I had in mind for sweetness the lovely milk-noodle pudding (*sevariyan*) that my Hindu research associate's Muslim friend's family served us on the day of Id.

Figure 7.3 Almond-Cashew Ganesh with neon Lakshmi, Ganesh Chaturthi (photo by Ann Grodzins Gold)

We went to the *Idgah* at 8:30 am; people were pouring in; the chairs were all taken, mostly by beautifully attired children. I was possibly the only adult female present as Muslim women in Jahazpur do not join in collective prayers, whether at *Idgah* or mosque. They were home preparing the festive foods. But it seemed as if every Muslim adult male in Jahazpur and its vicinity were present, to pray solemnly. Behind and to the side of the praying men, and paying them absolutely no attention, were children of all ages in their Id finery, playing and even eating (see Figure 7.4). Young children are not required to keep the Ramadan fast and there were snack sellers – a feature of almost every festival event in Jahazpur – just near the entrance to the grounds. The kids, unsupervised except by distracted older siblings, were having fun and evidently impatient for the prayers to close when even more fun could begin. The atmosphere was mellow. The police were there but seemed relaxed, their characteristic stance while on duty at festive events.

As the Id prayers closed, a number of Hindu political leaders arrived at the edge of the *Idgah*, where they stood and offered hearty *Id Mubarak* to Muslims as they left the ground. The mullahs (from Bangladesh I was told) were honoured by being mounted on rented horses led by Hindu owners. And for the rest of the day, Muslims welcomed Hindu as well as Muslim friends to their homes, overloading their plates with sweet milk puddings and salty chips.

Figure 7.4 Men pray, children play, at the *Idgah*, Id (photo by Bhoju Ram Gujar)

Teja Dashmi and Jal Jhulani Gyaras

Once again calendrical contiguity juxtaposes two events almost as disparate as Ganesh Chaturthi and Id, even though both are Hindu. This contiguity, however, is annual and both festivals have deep regional roots. Both were celebrated on a smaller scale in Ghatiyali, the Rajasthan village where I lived through almost two festival cycles in 1979–81. When Bhoju or I asked people to comment on the relation between Teja Dashmi and Jal Jhulani, few had much to say. Some asserted that the crowds who attended Tejaji's fair came mostly from the surrounding villages while Jal Jhulani was more attractive to Jahazpur town residents. However random their contiguity (upon which everyone insists) we can still view and contrast the tenth and eleventh of the bright half of Bhadrapad and thereby learn something more about pluralism within Hindu traditions.

Educated town persons insisted that Tejaji was a *lok devata* (folk deity) and therefore not *bhagvan* (God).[12] While they might make offerings to Tejaji, they ascribed him a definite lower rank in the scheme of things, which is both a cosmic scheme, and a sociological one. *Lok devata* may be petitioned for assistance with specific human problems in ways that it is not appropriate to petition *Bhagvan*. They are, moreover, accessible and able to give advice through divination and possession. Anthropologists have devoted considerable effort to analysing such distinctions in Hindu contexts.[13] Yet I could not help recalling the ways that, in my earlier research, I would hear village devotees collapse all 'divine hierarchy'. For those expressing pure devotion or *bhakti* to a caste or lineage deity, that being was simply and totally the Lord. Thus rural devotees worship regional folk-hero gods – such as Tejaji, Ramdevji, Pabuji and Dev Narayan, or one of the many mother goddesses – as supreme beings. The discourse of 'folk deity' versus 'God' strikes me as urban overlay, dismissive of rural devotional sensibilities. This theological debate becomes profoundly relevant to some contested moments in the history of Jahazpur's Jal Jhulani procession, as we will see.

On 16 September I went into town to see preparations for both Tejaji and Jal Jhulani. At the water reservoir where the gods would be bathed a whole team of Harijan women, on the payroll of the municipality, were cheerfully cleaning up.[14] Another crew made sure that the water itself was cleared of debris and choking plants. At the bus stand also, where the Tejaji fair would take place, the ground was nicely swept, the fruit-sellers had moved their stalls to the sides, and tinsel was strung overhead. The work and cost of cleaning, route marking, and basic decorations is assumed by Jahazpur's municipality for all public events – whether Hindu, Muslim, Jain or national.

Early in the day on the morning of the Tejaji fair, 17 September, we made a quick trip to the shrine, before the possession started and the crowds gathered. At this time I observed many middle- and upper-middle-class Jahazpur residents (identifiable by their clothes) coming to make their offerings, have *darshan* and take their leave. Later, in the afternoon, the crowds were indeed predominantly rural (see Figure 7.5). One of the main issues addressed at length by Tejaji's possessed priest had to do with a cow-shelter in a nearby village that had been

Figure 7.5 Crowd hands offerings for Tejaji into shrine, Teja Dashmi (photo by Ann Grodzins Gold)

raided by thieves who planned to sell the cows to butchers. According to the *bhav* (the priest possessed by an oracular divinity), a punishment of drought had been inflicted on the perpetrators' home area. The rural crowds listened with intense interest to all this, which would not have compelled *qasba* residents who visited in the morning. Thus an urban/rural division was enacted through timing more than patronage. Outside the shrine was another lively world of transactions; Tejaji's fair included a temporary market for clay pots and metal utensils.

On Saturday 18 September, Hindus in Jahazpur celebrated Jal Jhulani Gyaras, or Water Swing Eleventh, a regionally widespread event, but not everywhere as elaborate as it is here. One Brahmin explained the festival as a seasonal one: 'Now the month of Bhadra is almost at an end, and the water reservoir is full, and the crops are ripe, and for this reason, out of happiness, we take God for a bath'.

Jal Jhulani like Janamashtami is basically a Vaisnavite holiday – its mythological charter linked closely with Krishna's birth. The most common explanation of this link that we heard was that Jal Jhulani was Krishna's first bath, his *navan*, a ritual performed for human babies as well.

Every temple in town that believes its deity to be Vishnu or a form of Vishnu – thus the same temples that exhibited *jhanki* on Janamashtami – participates by carrying an image of their deity seated in an ornamented 'chariot' (*bevan*) to the water reservoir for a bath. While Jal Jhulani is celebrated all over Rajasthan in both villages and towns, Jahazpur's festival is famous – second-best in the district we were told. Thousands participate, and Jahazpur's own citizenry form the bulk of the crowd. The mood in the streets was mellow (see Figure 7.6). People told us that when the lead chariot passed through Mosque Gate, that would have been an opportunity for tension, but it was not. The police seemed at ease and even smiled. On Jal Jhulani, I felt that I could see beyond their uniforms to their own village origins; they know how to behave respectfully at a festival. There were several bands playing, and one of them was the Gaji Pir Band, which plays for both Hindu and Muslim events.

Figure 7.6 Hindu deities pass through 'Mosque Gate', Jal Jhulani (photo by Ann Grodzins Gold)

In conversations about Jal Jhulani, definitely Jahazpur's most complex and ambitious Hindu procession, we heard little about religious difference and far more about the establishment of a negotiated space-sharing among different caste communities. Altogether in 2010 there were 26 temples involved in the procession, and 23 chariots all told. Joining last and leaving first were two chariots belonging to Scheduled Caste communities: the Khatiks' Satya Narayan and the Regars' Ramdevji. I have written elsewhere of the Khatiks' struggle to build a Vishnu temple in the heart of Jahazpur in the 1980s (Gold n.d.). Once they achieved that, it was less difficult for them to join Jal Jhulani because their temple's deity was indisputably Vishnu. The Regars, however, had a greater struggle.

One Hindu merchant told us that about three years ago when the Regars first took out Ramdevji's chariot, 'the environment was very hot and there was a lot of tension'. A Regar lawyer had obtained legal permission to process Ramdevji. This, he stated, is after all a constitutional right. He continued, 'So you can take out your god, according to your dharmic feelings. So everyone stayed quiet; lots of police came. Their *bevan* came two minutes behind the others'.

Other high-caste Hindus stressed in interviews before the festival day that Ramdevji is *not* the Lord (*bhagvan*). They used the same 'folk deity' versus God distinction we heard in relation to Tejaji. These men said that the Regars had received permission to take out a chariot, but explicitly not one holding an image of Ramdevji. Their chariot should only carry a Salagramji – the smooth oval stone representative of Vishnu. To our amazement, when we looked into the Regar *bevan* in the midst of the festival's joyful tumult, there was Ramdevji himself in *murti* form. No one objected; perhaps no one noticed.

Linking Jal Jhulani Gyaras back to Janamashtami are the *bandarval* or garlands of auspicious leaves that are ordinarily hung on the door of homes to celebrate the birth of a child – especially a son. Many people hang these on Janamashtami to celebrate Krishna's birth; and take them down at Jal Jhulani, the day of baby Krishna's first bath. Like any sacred objects they must be cooled after they have served their ritual purposes, and hence they are thrown in the reservoir – that same reservoir that the municipality devoted so much energy to clearing of garbage before the festival. As night fell, the water was clotted with plastic bags which bewildered me until Bhoju told me that these bags contained all the newly discarded bandarval – too sacred to deposit in any ordinary trash.

Anant Chaturdashi

Jains are not in conflict with other communities. Numerically a tiny percentage of India's population, they follow a religion that is distinct yet not alien from its ancient Indic origins and present-day surroundings. Although there has been significant out-migration, many of the stores in Jahazpur's market still belong to Jain families. Few Jains are poor; some are very wealthy. Jains may be resented by other groups for their prosperity or for charging outrageously high interest rates on loans, but Hindus do not see them as different from themselves in the same way that they see Muslims as different (Gold 2013).

Given officially undated but massive archaeological evidence – many *Jain murtis* have emerged intact from Jahazpur ground – it is generally accepted that Jains were among the original settlers of this area. Thus, one Jain man told us, Jahazpur is an *atishay kshetra* – an abundant field: the kind of place where you don't need to bring images from elsewhere.[15] The Jain temple has in recent years made room for many intact emerged images of *tirthankaras* (a collective term for the twenty-four Jain teachers), producing a very powerful display. It was outside of this temple that the procession for Anant Chaturdashi began.

In Santosh Nagar, the neighbourhood where I lived, a Jain woman sits all day in her small open storefront. I got to know her through many brief street chats over many months. Although she would at times express distress over separation from her beloved Jain temple and community that was inflicted on her by living in the colony of Santosh Nagar, she was an enthusiastic participant in many Hindu practices. She regularly joined her neighbours in women's rituals dedicated to Hindu goddesses who protect families and children. She was also the one who reminded me repeatedly not to miss seeing the Jain's golden chariot in procession on Anant Chaturdashi – a festival in which she and her family were active participants.

As advised by our neighbour, we went to the temple in the afternoon. In the street there were already two bands, but not many people had gathered yet. The gilded chariot was already outside (see Figure 7.7). It held a picture of Mahavira – the twenty-fourth *tirthankara* and founder of Jainism – along with a small image of a seated ascetic. The Jain's golden chariot was not multi-coloured and ornate as were the Hindu chariots on Jal Jhulani, producing at once an image more austere and more indicative of wealth.

Figure 7.7 Jain chariot outside temple, Anant Chaturdashi (photo by Ann Grodzins Gold)

130 *Ann Grodzins Gold*

The procession, however, was anything but austere. It was long and loud! It left the temple around 3 pm, and moved very slowly through the market streets, making repeated halts for prolonged song and dance sessions. One of the singers with the band had a rhythm that reminded me of Elvis Presley. He was also holding a book which made me think he did not know the words by heart. I learned later that he was Hindu, not Jain, and participated out of *shauk* – a word that combines interest with passion.

Jain men and women were uniformly dressed, a collective decision they made before the festival. This of course serves to mark their distinct identities at this festival time in a visual fashion not customary for their community. Women of all ages joined in the dancing that followed the procession, which did not return to the temple until almost dusk. Some non-Jain onlookers in the market made offerings as the procession passed by their homes and shops. Only Jains (and Daniel and Bhoju and I) crowded on the temple roof for the subsequent *abisheka* – an elaborate ritual bathing of a small *tirthankara* image. We were told there would be lavish fast-breaking later at individuals' homes (although no one invited us).

Jains are a minority for whom neither living together nor legitimacy are issues. They may be reviled for sharp business practices, and I have heard them mocked for their worship of naked male figures, but their high economic status and their religion dedicated to the revered priorities of renunciation both contribute to Jains having no trouble claiming space in the public sphere. In the streets I was struck mostly by indifference on the part of non-Jains. In spite of the non-confrontational nature of this entire celebration, the police were on the job as usual, patrolling the procession route in groups of three or four.

Bitter with the sweet: Festival and *danga*

I would like to argue that sweet treats and pretty sights – the festival version of living together – consistently spread sweetness and light in public spaces. On festival days, as we have seen, even the police who are fundamentally mistrusted by one and all – appear to relax and to act like nice guys. Their perpetual presence is nonetheless a reminder that there are always other possible outcomes. Processions and festivals have historically been flashpoints for communal disturbances in India, and Jahazpur is no exception. I turn now to episodes of friction specifically between Hindus and Muslims; moments where the delicate fabric of 'Living Together' wore thin in Jahazpur.

Danga means 'riot' and is the term everyone uses here to speak of three painful moments of Hindu–Muslim friction viewed as blemishes on *qasba* history. Two of these so-called *danga* are specifically associated with festivals.[16] In this section we turn our attention from the bright to the dark side of public performative religiosity – consuming the bitter with the sweet.

We gathered many confused reports of dates and causes for *danga*. I am grateful to a local journalist for his help in organizing the multiple contradictory oral accounts into an orderly list. As I have been able to determine, there were two actual *danga* in the 1980s and one proto-*danga* in 1947 around the traumatic time

Bright side of pluralism in a Rajasthan town   131

of partition. In the 1980s the historical context was again a time of heightened national tension between religious communities due to the accelerating Ramjanambhumi movement.[17] The *danga* that took place in 1984 and 1989 featured destruction of property and police action: beating of perpetrators and enforcing of a curfew that was true punishment for everyone who lives here, especially shopkeepers. Hindu and Muslim alike, shopkeepers explicitly stated that even today the aftermath of these quarter-century old troubles continues to have a lingering impact on local business.

Highly condensed accounts follow; the first undoubtedly has the quality of legend rather than history: In 1947 the first ever Hindu–Muslim conflict occurred in Jahazpur. Apparently a British administrator had foolishly given official permission to Muslims to cut the branch of a pipal tree (sacred to Hindus) that was blocking the path of a *taziya* at Muharram. Although there was no actual fighting, this marked the first occasion when bitter enmity between the two religious communities was publicly, collectively experienced; when the spectre of violence (crashing all around the nation) loomed in Jahazpur's small *qasba*. The Minas – king's guards, soldiers, and outlaws as well as farmers who lived in the twelve surrounding villages – responded to a drumbeat alarm. They gathered *en masse* bearing any kind of makeshift weapon they could find. Muslims as a group fled temporarily to the hills and it all blew over without any actual fighting or destruction.

Most disturbing in the recollections we recorded of this event was the use of identity markers – as in this account by a prosperous old man from an artisan community who had witnessed it in his childhood: 'They [the armed Minas] announced that Hindus should not wear caps, but should tie turbans, so we know who is a Hindu; and no Hindu should cover his butt with pyjamas, he should wear a dhoti. Then we can tell who is Hindu and who is Muslim'. From these instructions we may surmise that the two communities in the 1940s did not necessarily distinguish themselves from one another in their dress; otherwise there would have been no need for such an announcement.

Almost forty years later, in 1984, a Muslim boy injured a Hindu boy in the course of a cricket game; both teams were mixed. Rumours spread and were distorted; disturbances followed, resulting in significant property damage and a curfew imposed on the town. In 1989 there were two confrontational events both involving annual festival processions: Hindus carrying bricks as part of the nationwide Ramjanambhumi movement tangled with a *taziya* procession; later Muslims threw stones at a Ramayana procession as it traversed their neighbourhood. Eventually stores were burned (but never within the main market) and again a severely enforced curfew was imposed. Many emphasized merciless police beatings both of perpetrators and innocent bystanders, including a well-known (and disliked) politician who happened to step out his front door at the wrong moment. This demonstrated effectively that the government would not tolerate communalism expressed in violence.

A series of minor episodes in 2001 involved damage to two of Jahazpur's peripheral Muslim shrines and a fire in the mosque of Pander, a nearby town. But

132 *Ann Grodzins Gold*

these were rarely named as *danga*. Nothing at all has happened since then, ten years ago; but sometimes the atmosphere gets tense. Local government exerts multiple pressures to ensure that Jahazpur remains *danga*-free. Today every procession must get permission from the police and has to go over their route and timings in advance, and submit it all in writing. They also are required to hold a pre-event peace meeting involving leaders from all communities and focused on maintaining civility and order. At every single festival, as we have seen, there is a quiet but alert and visible uniformed police presence.[18]

A route may change if any potential confrontation can thus be averted. In December 2010, for example, the Gayatri Parivar, a Hindu reform group, decided not to take their procession – which happened to fall on the same day as Muharram – to the major gathering place of Nau Chauk, although it was in their original route plan. That morning the *taziya* (brought out the night before) were at rest in Nau Chauk, awaiting their own parade later in the day. As it was expressed to us, the Gayatri Parivar did not wish to 'disturb the *taziya*'.

Jahazpur gets extra attention not just at festivals but at any potentially tense moment. In March 2011, police closed down the market where fans were gathered round many different stores' television sets to watch India play Pakistan in the World Cup semi-finals. Shortly before the end of the close match, police instructed all the viewers to hurry home, and the shopkeepers to lock up their stores. Some of Jahazpur's citizens were indignant, and I heard after the fact that a small victory parade had traversed the market in defiance of police orders, and without incident. By contrast, the final game in which India played (and defeated) Sri Lanka, was not nearly so rigorously policed.

Jahazpur's adult citizens from diverse communities express regret that their town has a reputation for *danga*. There were just a few truculent Hindus with whom we talked who seemed eager to keep the flame of communalism alive; there might be Muslims who feel the same way, but I did not have access to them. Those Muslims with whom I did speak, like most Hindus, emphasized mutual understandings and accommodations. Some explicitly attributed harmony to the saint Gaji Pir's blessings. Both Hindus and Muslims have asserted to Bhoju and me, using strikingly similar phrases, that whatever happened was never all that bad.

Here are three representative statements extracted from interviews about *danga* in Jahazpur:

An elderly Hindu man, formerly a produce gardener, lacking school education and struggling to make ends meet, put it very poignantly, telling us: 'In the past, Muslims and Hindus lived like brothers; they had affection [*prem bhav*] for one another, but now it isn't like that, a stone fell into this love'.

A college-educated Hindu Brahmin shopkeeper, energetic and vital, tried to dismiss the reverberations of Jahazpur's past disturbances, declaring almost defensively, 'So, it is true that there was a *danga*, but the people of Jahazpur did not beat one another! There was no murder, no knifes – still they call it *danga*! Nobody hit anyone. No one even slapped another person.'

This Brahmin's claims are echoed, in similar language but with more pious overtones, by a Deshvali Muslim man, around 60 years of age – a government

Bright side of pluralism in a Rajasthan town 133

servant with an eighth grade education who had dedicated his life to Gaji Pir. He told us:

> Jahazpur has had so many *danga*, but no one even slapped another person. Some think this is Gaji Pir's grace [*meherbani*]...There was no terrible destruction, just some stores and cabins were burned. But we have had so much ill fame [*badnam*] that the news even reached Delhi! Still no one even slapped another person....Not even a drop of blood was ever spilled!

As the first remembered trouble was in 1947 in the wake of partition, only the very elderly today are able to recollect a time of pure love preceding it. Although we could attribute this to a 'good old days' nostalgia, I would like to value the truth of collective memory – often evoked with a swell of feeling in voice and facial expression. Younger people in my experience are edgier, more suspicious, products of a more dangerous era. Nonetheless, the majority of Jahazpur citizens of all ages are habituated in multiple ways to a plural social universe; to shared commercial and residential spaces.

Ordinary pluralisms

In her recent study of pluralism in a Punjab town, Anna Bigelow makes a straightforward and pressing claim, writing that, 'Although it is essential to research places where conflict is endemic, it is equally important to see the day-to-day life of a place where tension and conflicts are managed productively' (2010: 239). I see Jahazpur as such a place and in closing I summarize some formal and informal ways of enacting and managing peaceful pluralisms observed over nearly a year's residence there. Constitutionally secular India's laws hold sway in Jahazpur, and we therefore find formal evidence of pluralism as granting legitimacy. The municipality, for example, cleans the streets and chalks the routes and pays for lights for all religious celebrations – whether Hindu, Jain, or Muslim – in public spaces. Alongside such evidence are those subtler forms of pluralism evoked by Shail Mayaram's questions:

> Are there shared imaginaries and grammars that are rooted in everyday perceptions of being in the world? What are the practices that we might see as making possible Living Together, enabling us to capture at least some of the fluidity and diversity of social formations we encounter in urban spaces?
> (Mayaram 2009: 9)

Let me point to a few such grammars and practices, both festival and everyday, as well as additional forms of granting legitimacy. Festivals reveal shared grammars – from the sparkling new clothes worn by children, to the omnipresent balloon-sellers and snack vendors, to the seeking of physical blessings by going under, respectively, the divine chariots at Jal Jhulani and the *taziya* during Muslim processions at Muharram (observed just a few months after the period of time documented in this chapter).

134　*Ann Grodzins Gold*

Outside of festival time we encounter many small examples of shared material worlds. In Hindu living rooms the TV is often located near framed pictures of deities; in Muslim living rooms it is located near framed pictures of fruits and flowers. Hindus keep basil plants on their roofs and worship them as the goddess. Muslims keep basil plants on their roofs because they are medicinally useful. We had one delightful interview with a deshvali Muslim comparing Hindu and Muslim wedding customs. Parts of weddings are the same, with modulations: e.g. the differently adorned grooms arrive on identically adorned horses. Parts are parallel: e.g. Muslims deliver the first wedding invitation to a Sufi pir's tomb while Hindus deliver it to Ganeshji, the god of beginnings. Parts of course significantly diverge: Muslim brides and grooms do not sit together until after their union has been sealed with a legally binding contract.

Hindu leaders scrupulously attend every Muslim event – both those scripturally chartered such as Id and those associated with local Muslim saints such as the two annual Urs festivals. This too is a form of granting legitimacy, even if it is equally blatant self-interested vote-seeking behaviour. The Ram Lila procession in 2010 (once a target for stone-throwing) was formally welcomed by one of the Muslim committees which – in a fashion completely similar to that of several diverse Hindu groups – erected a fancy archway. Their sign used distinctively Urdu words but was written in the common Indic script of *devanagari*.

Festival and everyday examples demonstrate a shared culture, a shared commercial world, a modulated, shared aesthetic. Even the shouting of different assertive slogans with different words but similar gestures and rhythms – which I have seen young men perform at both Hindu and Muslim events – reveals, however ironically, shared modes of asserting commitment to separate identities.

I suggest that these sharings all testify to an ongoing history of living together. During the three-day Muslim extravaganza celebrating the saint Gaji Pir, when his gorgeous coverlet (*chadar*) processes through Hindu neighbourhoods, Hindu women dart outside to deposit money in it. This is primarily a devotional expression, but in the language of this chapter, it testifies to granting legitimacy as well as shared grammars of religious expression. It was Bhoju, a Hindu, who took pains to capture this fleeting action with his camera (see Figure 7.8).

The omnipresence of police at Jahazpur festivals is due to the town's official classification as 'sensitive' (*sanvedanshil*): a place where trouble can happen. This is explicitly due to the high percentage of Muslims and the long shadow of the two *danga*, discussed earlier, that took place in the 1980s. Yet, as I have tried to demonstrate here in fair detail, celebrations in public space also provide both formal and informal indications of ordinary pluralisms. Such phenomena are deeply woven into Jahazpur *qasba* culture, and offer a vision of a diverse and peaceful community that is real. This does not mean that it is invulnerable to rupture.

As Jahazpur town becomes increasingly global, its pluralisms could be further undermined. As is well known, national and transnational Muslim and Hindu movements and politics deliberately seek to circumscribe identities, and to reject or eliminate plural world views. Such messages have certainly reached Jahazpur,

Figure 7.8 Hindu woman makes offering to Muslim saint, Gaji Pir (photo by Bhoju Ram Gujar)

but it does not appear to me, though my experience is limited, that they have taken deep root; not yet. I imagine this could be attributed to Jahazpur's rich cultural soil, characterized by a wholesome dense tangle of imaginations, practices, and interactions in which it is difficult for divisive forces to sprout and spread. For the time being, if public religiosity in Jahazpur may not be all sweetness and light, neither has it lapsed into bitterly divisive dogma and darkness.

Notes

1 I am very grateful for stimulating responses to oral versions of this chapter presented in Singapore, Syracuse, New York City and Oxford. Particular thanks go to Juliana Finucane, Chiara Formichi, Eli Gold, Vineeta Sinha and most of all to Jahazpur residents for sharing sweets and a great deal more. Bhoju Ram Gujar has been an indispensable fieldwork companion.
2 For an extensive discussion of this legend, see Gold (n.d.).
3 History books that mention Jahazpur, generally do so in passing – as the town was a pawn shuttled from one ruler to another, whether according to military defeat or princely largesse (see for example, Dangi 2002; Hooja 2006).

136 *Ann Grodzins Gold*

4 For the role of *qasbas* in eighteenth-century Kota, a former kingdom not far from Jahazpur, see Sethia (2003).
5 A responsive and kind audience at the Delhi School of Economics Sociological Research Colloquium enhanced my understandings of the semantics of *qasba*. For another perspective on *qasba* culture as 'peri-urban' see National Foundation of India (2011: 9).
6 For an insightful ethnography of both Hindu/Muslim and caste differences in the North Indian city of Kanpur, see Froystad (2005).
7 The *Rajasthani-Hindi-English Dictionary* defines *deshvali* as: 'those Muslims who had to pay the *jajiya* tax' which was a tax levied on non-Muslims living under Muslim government (Suthar and Gahlot 1995). The *Rajasthani Sabad Kos* glosses *deshvali* as, 'a caste of Rajputs who became Muslim' (Lalas 1967). Neither dictionary definition fully covers Jahazpur's *deshvali* usage, but taken together they at least point the way toward an understanding of *deshvali* Muslims as converts with known Hindu antecedents and residual genetic identity.
8 See also Varshney's similarly straightforward, 'Pluralism would indicate the coexistence of distinctive identities (A respects and lives peacefully with B)' (2002: 62). For an excellent historical and cultural overview of pluralism in India, see Madan (2003).
9 *Taziya* represent shrines dedicated to the martyrs Hasan and Husain who are mourned during Muharram. Although Jahazpur Muslims identify themselves as Sunni, Muharram is a major festival here.
10 While I have written this account independently, I attended all these events in the company of Bhoju Ram Gujar and Daniel Gold. For the interviews eliciting histories and exegesis Bhoju not only found persons willing to talk but usually asked the deeper questions.
11 For *jhanki* see Hein (1972).
12 See Singh (2011) for a recent and very stimulating discussion of Tejaji's worship in Rajasthan.
13 For one classic work, see Babb (1975).
14 Sweepers by caste perform their hereditary work, but are employed by the municipality in salaried positions to do so.
15 Why were the *murtis* in the ground? The common explanation was that some Jains had buried them to protect them from the iconoclastic emperor Aurangzeb; they then fled themselves and never returned.
16 Heightened emotions and crowds can make festivals fertile ground for unruliness and violence. There is considerable literature on festivals and communal disturbances (see for example, Freitag 1989).
17 This movement had to do with Hindu right-wing agitations against the Babri Masjid, a mosque built, according to the political claims of the Hindu right, atop the deity Rama's birthplace (Ramjanambhumi) in the town of Ayodhya. In the 1980s when Jahazpur's troubles took place, bricks intended to construct a new Ram temple were ceremonially processed from all over India. In 1993 a Hindu mob destroyed the mosque. The scholarly literature on all of this is vast; for one example, see Nandy *et al.* (1995).
18 The only time I saw police carrying weapons was at Muharram. I am not sure why this should be. For insights into the value of an institutionalized peace system, see Bigelow (2010).

References

Babb, L.A. (1975) *The Divine Hierarchy*, New York: Columbia University Press.
Bigelow, A. (2010) *Sharing the Sacred: Practicing Pluralism in Muslim North India*, New York: Oxford University Press.

Bright side of pluralism in a Rajasthan town   137

Dangi, S.M.S. (2002) *Shapura rajya ka itihas* [History of Shahpura kingdom], Shahpura: Shah Madansingh Manoharsingh Dangi Smriti Samsthan.

Freitag, S. (1989) *Collective Action and Community: Public Arenas and the Emergence of Communalism in North India*, Berkeley: University of California Press.

Froystad, K. (2005) *Blended Boundaries: Caste, Class, and Shifting Faces of 'Hinduness' in a North Indian City*, New Delhi: Oxford University Press.

Gold, A.G. (2013) 'Ainn-Bai's *sarvadharm yatra*: A Mix of Experiences', in Kassam, T. and Kent, E. (eds) *Lines in Water: Religious Boundaries in South Asia*, Syracuse, NY: Syracuse University Press (in press).

Gold, A.G. (n.d.) 'Carving Place: Foundational Narratives from a North Indian Market Town' in Waghorne, J. (ed.) *Place/No Place: Spatial Aspects of Urban Asian Religiosity*, manuscript submitted for publication.

Hasan, M. (2004) *From Pluralism to Separatism: Qasbas in Colonial Awadh*, New Delhi: Oxford University Press.

Hein, N. (1972) *The Miracle Plays of Mathura*, New Haven, CT: Yale University Press.

Hooja, R. (2006) *A History of Rajasthan*, New Delhi: Rupa and Company.

Lalas, S. (1967) *Rajasthani Sabad Kos*, Jodhpur: Rajasthani Shodh Sansthan.

Madan, T. N. (2003) 'Religions of India: Plurality and Pluralism', in *The Oxford India Companion to Sociology and Social Anthropology*, Delhi: Oxford University Press.

Mayaram, S. (2005) 'Living Together: Ajmer as a Paradigm for the (South) Asian City', in Hasan, M. and Roy, A. (eds), *Living Together Separately: Cultural India in History and Politics*, New Delhi: Oxford University Press.

Mayaram, S. (2009) 'Introduction: Rereading Global Cities: Topographies of an Alternative Cosmopolitanism in Asia', in Mayaram, S. (ed.) *The Other Global City*, New York: Routledge.

Nanda, M. (2009) *The God Market: How Globalization is Making India More Hindu*, Noida: Random House India.

Nandy, A.,Trivedy, S., Mayaram, S. and Yagnik, A. (1995) *Creating a Nationality: The Ramjanamabhumi Movement and Fear of the Self*, Delhi: Oxford University Press.

National Foundation of India (2011) *Svashasan ki disha mem racanatmak karya: chhote shahrom aur kasbai bastio ke jan-jivan me sudhar lana*, New Delhi: National Foundation of India.

Peletz, M. (2009) *Gender Pluralism: Southeast Asia Since Early Modern Times*, New York: Routledge.

Sethia, M.T. (2003) *Rajput Polity: Warriors, Peasants and Merchants (1700–1800)*, Jaipur: Rawat Publications.

Singer, M. (1972) *When a Great Tradition Modernizes*, New York: Praeger.

Singh, B. (2011) 'Agonistic Intimacy and Moral Aspiration in popular Hinduism: A Study in the Political Theology of the Neighbor', *American Ethnologist*, 38(3): 430–50.

Suthar, B.L. and S.S. Gahlot (1995) *Rajasthani-Hindi-English Dictionary*, Jodhpur: Rajasthani Sahitya Sansthan.

Varshney, A. (2002) *Ethnic Conflict and Civic Life: Hindus and Muslims in India*, New Haven, CT: Yale University Press.

8 Overcoming 'hierarchized conviviality' in the Manila metropolis

Religious pluralism and urbanization in the Philippines

Manuel Victor J. Sapitula

The increasing presence of Muslim communities in various urban neighbourhoods in Luzon and the Visayas has altered the religious geography of Philippine urban life, especially during recent decades. In a sense, the formation of Muslim communities in traditionally Christian environments all over the country has encouraged a trend toward diversification, a process that may be either welcomed or resisted by local stakeholders. In the case of Metro Manila, the presence of Moros (traditional Muslims from Mindanao) has contributed to the already diverse social and cultural landscape of the metropolis, which was a focal destination for migrants from several regions of the country. Besides 'primary communities' of Muslims established in Quiapo district in Manila and Maharlika Village in Taguig City during the 1960s, various 'secondary communities' of Moro settlers have arisen in various localities during the last two decades, accommodating new waves of migrants (Watanabe 2008).

Against the background of such increasing Muslim presence in the metropolis, this chapter looks into the processes pertaining to currently existing religious conviviality in Baclaran district, Parañaque City in Metro Manila. Despite its meagre size, Baclaran district has emerged in recent years as a prominent location for commercial activity and is thus densely populated during regular working hours. It is also the site of one of the largest Catholic shrines in the Philippines, the National Shrine of Our Mother of Perpetual Help (henceforth Perpetual Help shrine): the church building, expanded twice since 1932, has attracted a sizeable number of devotees; unofficial estimates locate devotees to be around 100,000 to 120,000 per week (Hechanova 1998). The weekly pilgrimage that started in 1948 with the inauguration of the 'Perpetual Novena' occasioned the economic expansion of surrounding areas around the church, as commercial establishments were started mostly by private business ventures, intending to tap a sizeable market. Since the 1990s, scores of Moros have likewise settled here in order to avail themselves of the opportunities for commerce and trade. Baclaran district has seen a significant increase of Muslim migrants from Mindanao, to the extent that it is one of the places in Metro Manila that has seen the formation of a secondary Muslim community (Watanabe 2007).

The increasing presence of Muslims within the perimeter of an established Catholic pilgrimage area is not unique to this locality, yet it poses issues about the nature of transformations of urban space and how this bears upon the emerging conviviality between diverse actors on the ground. In this light, the discussion of actually existing relationships in Baclaran district allows a reflection of the ways by which pluralism is lived and negotiated in urban space. A discussion of pluralism is particularly important as cities are potential sites of class and spatial polarization, especially with the influx of migrants from the suburbs or overseas (Sassen 1991). While this migration of Moro settlers from Mindanao resulted in the creation of 'hierarchized conviviality' (which is discussed substantially below), I will nevertheless demonstrate how the tendency toward polarization does not serve the interest of any of the actors, thus giving rise to pluralist thinking and practices on the ground.

The challenge of this paper is to locate specific ways by which Christians and Muslims in Metro Manila have made sense of each other's presence in the urban space, and the extent to which these notions have been identified, articulated and practised by actors on the ground. These meaning-making processes, though situated within specific historical junctures and socio-cultural formations in Baclaran district and in metropolitan Manila, are always redefined in the light of new experiences and the implementation of new social structures in the local and national arenas. In the task of understanding the interaction of 'Christians and Muslims', I recognize that significant internal variety is found among each camp in this particular field site, as well as in the Philippines and elsewhere; thus, a monolithic conception of either 'Christians' or 'Muslims' does not render service to the task of understanding the specific modes of encounter between them. This is especially relevant in the case of the Moros, who, although united by a common Islamic heritage that predates the arrival of Christianity, also organize themselves into thirteen ethno-linguistic groups with different cultural and socio-political heritage. There is thus a relevant distinction made between a 'Moro' who belongs to one of the thirteen ethno-linguistic groups just mentioned, and a *Balik-Islam*, a 'revert' to Islam from a non-Moro ethnic group (Angeles 2007). In this paper, however, I use 'Moro' and 'Muslim' interchangeably, insofar as either of these terms refers to the communities of settlers in Metro Manila and originating from various regions in Mindanao.

In the process of writing this chapter, I used field data from observations in Baclaran district from October 2009 to June 2010, and several subsequent shorter visits. After becoming familiar with the area nearest to the Perpetual Help shrine, I conducted semi-structured interviews and informal conversations with *barangay* (neighbourhood-based political unit) leaders in Baclaran, Muslim leaders in the area, the priests and the head of security forces at the Perpetual Help shrine, the merchants, and several Perpetual Help shrine devotees. I also found documents provided by the Parañaque City government helpful in providing a general perspective of the city's history and socio-economic profile. Lastly, published news write-ups from broadsheets (available online) provided me with the mass media representations of the events in Baclaran district, especially

140 Manuel Victor J. Sapitula

contentious issues pertaining to the urban management of places of worship and streets in the area. By Baclaran district, I here refer to the area presently within the jurisdiction of Barangay Baclaran (which is a political sub-unit of Parañaque City), as well as the immediately adjoining streets at its northern section, which used to be part of its territory and is still within the purview of the *barangay*'s bustling commercial life. This is relevant because the boundary that separates Barangay Baclaran from its neighbouring city was altered in the past, and a portion of the territory that is now considered to be part of Pasay City was once within the boundaries of the *barangay*.

Baclaran district through the lens of its churches, mosques and streetscape

Like any typical locality in the metropolis, Barangay Baclaran has acquired a degree of denominational diversity during the past decades: there is one Protestant church, two mosques and two Catholic churches in the locality, not including one *Iglesia ni Cristo*[1] chapel and another two mosques that lie close to the *barangay*'s boundary with adjoining Pasay City. In particular, the Perpetual Help shrine, owned by the Redemptorists (a Catholic religious congregation), is a prominent place of worship and is indisputably the largest religious structure in Baclaran district. The shrine houses a reputedly miraculous icon of the Virgin Mary, and is considered by many Filipino Catholics as a place of pilgrimage. In 1948, the Redemptorists introduced the 'Perpetual Novena', which attracted huge crowds of devotees every Wednesday, the designated day of devotion. The shrine was expanded twice in order to accommodate the increasing number of devotees, and the present church building was finished in 1958 – the same year this was declared by the Philippine Catholic hierarchy a 'National Shrine' (Hechanova 1998). The shrine sits in a network of arguably the busiest streets in the area, making the vicinities of the church compound a bustling commercial district in its own right. The immense popularity of devotional activities in the shrine signifi-cantly contributed to the growth of commercial activity in the district, although other factors have also played a role, for instance the increase in the number of buses plying along routes near the shrine, and the inauguration of the Light Rail Transit in 1984 and the Metro Rail Transit in 2000, which made travel to and from the shrine by public transportation easier.

The Masjid Rajah Sulayman Lumba Ranao (henceforth Masjid Sulayman) is one of the four mosques in the Baclaran district. The mosque sits in a portion of the reclamation area near Manila Bay almost across the Perpetual Help shrine; after some confusion regarding jurisdiction, the area where the mosque stands is now considered to be part of adjoining Pasay City. The community of mostly Maranaos and *Balik-Islam* has been occupying this place since 1990, when they were led there by Datu Guinar Mao, a Maranao *muballigh* (Muslim missionary), so that destitute Muslims living on the streets could fully practice their Islamic way of life (Watanabe 2007). The mosque was built in 1992, and in due course, as Muslims from other places transferred their residence here, the community significantly grew to around 300 families. Government authorities, however, have regarded their occupation of the land as illegal. The Philippine Reclamation Authority, the government entity that owns the land, had planned for the construction of an intermodal transport centre there. The swelling of the Muslim community has however stalled the project, pushing government authorities to favour the relocation of the residents and the mosque to another suitable location and thus allow the planned development.

While a sizeable number of residents accepted monetary compensation to facilitate their relocation, some of them rejected the terms of the government's offer and insisted on staying in the disputed property. These residents filed court petitions to prevent the demolition of their homes and the mosque. In 2007, the Pasay City Regional Trial Court junked the residents' petition, and police forces were deployed to dismantle the structures in the said property, sparing the mosque. Another demolition took place in 2009, and as in the previous occasion, the residents rebuilt their homes and refused to leave the premises. As of this writing, the mosque still stands and the community still resides in the disputed property, while a case on the ownership of the land is pending in the Philippine Supreme Court.

Baclaran district proper starts at the opposite side of Roxas Boulevard from the Masjid Sulayman, near the Perpetual Help shrine; as of 2009, the city government of Parañaque City recorded a total of 53 small- and medium-size commercial establishments in the area, the largest number compared to any other *barangay* in the city (Parañaque City Government 2009). Anecdotal evidence shows that commercial activity here dramatically increased within the last ten years, as vendors started conducting trade along sidewalks – and even along the main roads – especially on days leading to major public holidays (e.g. Christmas and Easter Holy Week). A considerable number of these vendors are Moro settlers, particularly from Maranao or Maguindanao ethnic groups: the entire Baclaran area, like other commercial districts in Metro Manila, is an attractive place for them to conduct trade because of the sizeable number of potential consumers. While some of the Moro settlers have invested in stalls (*puwesto*) that have matched established medium- and large-size businesses in the area, a considerable number have remained as street vendors due to lack of sufficient capital. In terms of regulating street vending, the *barangay* has shown the greatest leniency with regard to street vending. In contrast, the Metro Manila Development Authority (MMDA), being a national coordinating body with broad police powers, insists on an uncompromising application of the law regarding the clearing of streets from sidewalk vendors. Armed with a 2002 resolution, MMDA law enforcement forces conduct unannounced 'clearing operations' in Baclaran district and elsewhere, confiscating everything they can find along sidewalks to decongest the streets and roads. Somewhat in between these two extreme positions vis-à-vis street-vending is the city-level government, which fluctuates between tolerating sidewalk vending and banning it altogether for certain periods of time.

Especially during 2010, vending along the sidewalk and streets of Baclaran district has been a cause of concern on the part of the MMDA, the priests at the

142   *Manuel Victor J. Sapitula*

Perpetual Help shrine, and the general public. As a matter of the law, the Civil Code of the Philippines Art. 420 legislates that roads are considered 'public dominion', and in due course this was extended to include sidewalks. Clarifying this matter further, the Supreme Court stated that '[t]he occupation and use of private individuals of sidewalks and other public places devoted for public use constitute both public and private nuisances and nuisance *per se*' (cited in Padilla 1990: 59). As already noted, the MMDA is the staunchest defender of this Supreme Court ruling, and MMDA officials in the past have had pronounced clashes with local governments that tolerate or even endorse the use of sidewalks and streets for vending. For their part, the shrine authorities generally favour the orderly movement of traffic and pedestrians along streets adjacent to the church compound, and have thus called for the enactment of rules pertaining to the problems posed by sidewalk vending. The head of the shrine's security operations reiterated the necessity of doing this, as the shrine's security forces only have jurisdiction inside the church compound; the lack of effective regulation along the streets has led to an increase of petty crimes even within the shrine's premises.

The regulating and/or limiting of sidewalk vending is expectedly resented by the vendors, as it prevents them from engaging in trade, which often is their only source of livelihood. Thus, the 'clearing operations' resulted in violent confrontations between MMDA personnel and distraught vendors who resisted the confiscation of their wares. The periodic street raids cause deep resentment among Muslim settlers, as a number of them have been driven away from the streets, had their goods confiscated, and were prevented from going back to vending in the area. This is indicated in a letter by the residents' community leader, Abdelmanan Tanandato, to President Macapagal-Arroyo in 2007, wherein he requested that residents around Masjid Sulayman not be prevented from conducting trade in Baclaran district. In my talks with other Moro community leaders in the area, they mention that Muslims generally feel that they are treated as 'second class citizens' and thus cannot fully integrate into the community life of this district (The Urban Poor Associates 2007).

Examining the 'hierarchized conviviality' in Baclaran district

A closer look into the engagement of Moro settlers in everyday life in Baclaran district allows us to highlight two important points. The first is that, aside from the complex legal questions in the case of both the existence of the mosque and street vending, the dimension of class plays a prominent role. The Moro residents around Masjid Sulayman generally fit the category of *maralitang tagalungsod* (urban poor), and thus their fight for their right to decent housing and livelihood resonates with other urban poor's demands for the same in their respective communities. One instance worth mentioning is the allegation that basic services are being withheld from residents: in the June letter mentioned above, Tanandato complained to President Macapagal-Arroyo that basic services were not catered to the community, resulting in a steep rise in the numbers of those getting sick, especially among children. This is similar to other cases of basic services being

'Hierarchized conviviality' in Manila 143

withheld from urban poor communities in Metro Manila, as reported by residents in a number of occasions. Likewise, the response of the residents around Masjid Sulayman to threats of demolition and eviction have been organized and sustained, a feature that is also found among other urban poor communities (Berner 1997).

Aside from the class dimension, religion is an important factor here. Metro Manila, like much of the Philippines, is overwhelmingly Christian in terms of population: as of 2000, it has a total of 9,880,102 inhabitants, 89 per cent of whom are Roman Catholics, 2.9 per cent members of the indigenous church *Iglesia ni Cristo*, and 1.2 per cent mainline Protestants (National Statistics Office 2000). In the case of Baclaran district, the preponderance of the Christian presence is tied to the economic development of the area, linked to devotional activities at the Perpetual Help shrine. Particularly after 1948, Baclaran district underwent significant commercial expansion as the influx of devotees triggered the emergence of a pilgrimage-based economy. Using Vitor Ambrosio and Margarida Pereira's (2007) schematization of the urban development of places near shrines, Baclaran district may be said to have successfully passed incipient development as a pilgrimage town. The Muslims, in contrast, amount to only 0.59 per cent of Metro Manila residents in the same period (National Statistics Office 2000). There are indications that their presence is not welcomed or appreciated by existing communities: there were documented cases of Christian residents opposing attempts to construct mosques in areas near their residence, as they argued that it was illogical to build a mosque in a predominantly Christian area (Watanabe 2008). In the case of Baclaran district, residents believe that the mosque was targeted for demolition because it was an unwelcome sight in the area. In an interview with the Agence France-Presse (2008), Abdelmanan Tanandato remarked that 'if this [mosque were] a church, the government would not demolish it; because this is a mosque, the government will try to change the surroundings, because they don't want to see that the mosque has been erected in between two big churches'.[2]

The confluence of class and religious factors mentioned above serves to illustrate the persistence of 'hierarchized conviviality' in the Manila metropolis, a structure of urban social stratification resulting from processes of 'othering' identities and groups that do not conform to standards imposed by traditional elite forces. Since the Spanish conquest of Manila in 1574, a 'core elite' of Spanish citizens and members of religious orders came to the centre of urban colonial life. The combination of the notion of 'pure Spanish blood' and the superiority of Catholic Christianity made its way into the foundational discourse of Manila as a colonial city (Bernad 1974). With the demise of Spanish colonialism in the Philippines, the 'pure Spanish blood' faded away, with the rise of local Filipinos and Filipino-Chinese as the new 'core elites', but their origins from lowland upper-class families, high educational attainment, and nominal Christian affiliation, have basically remained the same.

As Manila and its surrounding territories increasingly became the hub of the political, commercial, educational and religious administration in the country, the

144 *Manuel Victor J. Sapitula*

gap between the highly urbanizing capital and the countryside further widened, thus paving the way for increasing labour-driven migration to the capital. Here it is particularly relevant to recall Manuel Caoili's (1999) discussion of the role of Manila as a 'primate city' and the dependent development of Third World economies. One clear example of this is the flocking of people from rural areas to cities: in the case of Metro Manila, in-migration from 1975 to 1980 comprise one-third of all inter-regional migrations across the country; the majority of the in-migrants are from other provinces in Luzon and the Visayas, aged 15 to 24, and they are mostly women (Abejo 1985). The high rate of migration to Metro Manila coincided with the increasing number of slum areas, which is an indication that a significant number of migrants were not adequately absorbed into the commercial life of the metropolis and remained at the periphery of urban life (Berner 1997). The 'beautification projects' pursued during the martial law years were likewise extremely inimical to the urban poor, whose houses were demolished, and residents were forced to relocate where there were no basic commodities and services (Berner 1997). This punitive measure has exacerbated the marginalization of urban poor communities from the burgeoning urban and middle-class lifestyle in the metropolis, leading to the growth of more prejudice against the urban poor among the middle class.

The existence of 'hierarchized conviviality' between Christians and Muslims is mostly traceable to the increasing migration of Moro settlers to Metro Manila during the late 1970s, a phenomenon that changed the religious landscape of the metropolis. The frequency of interaction between Christians and Muslims in Metro Manila has significantly increased during the last four decades. This phenomenon was initiated by higher levels of migration away from Mindanao, mostly due to the escalating armed conflict between Philippine government forces and Moro separatist groups. Rising numbers of migrants strained the spatial and economic resources in existing Muslim residential communities (i.e. Quiapo in Manila and Maharlika Village in Taguig), thus leading new settlers to establish Muslim communities in other parts of the metropolis. In these new locations, Moro settlers were closer to Christian residents, and vice versa; yet, the sense of separation experienced by Muslim communities in these larger neighbourhoods has led outsiders to exoticize Muslim communities, contrasting their lives with the 'normality' of city life (Naylor and Ryan 2002). In certain cases this exoticized view deters individuals from choosing a place of residence near a Muslim community: in a national survey done in 2005, more than half (57 per cent) of Metro Manila residents would rather pay higher rent to be further away from an identifiable Muslim community, despite the fact that their knowledge of Islam does not come from personal dealings with believers, but rather from mass media, friends and relatives (Human Development Network 2005). This exoticized view prevented interaction between traditional Christian residents and Muslims in their new communities, and while it may be said that the two groups 'lived side-by-side', they were not 'living together' in terms of the quantity and quality of their interpersonal and inter-group encounters.

The case of Baclaran district provides additional context to discuss the

'Hierarchized conviviality' in Manila   145

emergence of 'hierarchized conviviality', insofar as the process of 'othering' is mediated by the successful consolidation of a pilgrimage-based economy related to a Catholic shrine. Unlike other places in Metro Manila where traditional economic elites own a sizeable portion of land and property (among others, the Ayala family in Makati City, and the Ortigas family in Pasig City), the commercial establishments in Baclaran district are owned by different merchants, from individual entrepreneurs to merchant associations. Those who entered the district's commercial life in the 1990s tended to have the most established businesses, and in due course they were able to expand their investments by owning more stalls or venturing into other commercial endeavours in the area. In contrast, Muslim merchants are relatively new to this commercial environment, and while a number of them were able to settle successfully by investing in fixed stalls, the number of established merchants among Muslims is significantly smaller, with a large portion of Muslims remaining at the periphery of commercial life and resorting to street vending (Watanabe 2008). For the most part, street vendors are regarded negatively by stall-owners, who see them as competitors – except for those that have regular bulk orders alongside their retail shop business. On the part of devotees in the Perpetual Help shrine, the increase of commercial activities along the streets prevents their movement to and from the shrine; furthermore, the lack of effective regulation of commercial activity gives the impression that Baclaran district is generally not a safe place, although devotees perceive difficulties and perils as 'necessary sacrifices' and it does not deter them from visiting the shrine.

Thus, in the case of the merchants, we witness the formation of a new set of hierarchical relationships, where Moro migrants (especially the street vendors) are at the lowest rung, the least legally protected and, under existing arrangements, are the least likely to be integrated into the commercial life of the district. While devotees were not particularly organized along class lines, a new form of stratification among merchants was formed, largely based on the ownership of capital, the acquisition of secure places in commercial buildings, and the assurance of stability of trade activities. Thus, the diversification process, mainly due to the entry of Moro migrants and settlers, has not led to significant transformations of mercantile structures and relationships; and the non-integration of street vendors is a clear instance of 'hierarchized conviviality'.

Overcoming 'hierarchized conviviality': Reflections on fostering religious pluralism

In the previous section, I demonstrated the existence of 'hierarchized conviviality' in Baclaran district in terms of class- and religion-based manifestations, linking particular events in the district with cultural and political processes at the metropolitan and national levels. Its genesis lies in the increased migration of Moros from Mindanao to Metro Manila and the concomitant failure of social structures in the metropolis to incorporate a considerable number of the new entrants to the mainstream of urban life. The migration of Moro settlers to the

146 *Manuel Victor J. Sapitula*

capital likewise activated established stereotypes about Muslims among the majority Christian residents, the origins of which are not based on first-hand experience but on dynamics of 'cultures of distrust' sown during the Spanish and American colonial periods. The challenge, then, is to chart a course for pluralism to take root as a viable alternative to the culture of distrust that tends to perpetuate 'hierarchized conviviality', thus preventing the formation of mutually beneficial linkages among the parties concerned.

It is important to note that the pluralist alternative, which I deem necessary, is characterized by a process of engagement in which differences are not dismissed as insignificant, nor are these heightened as absolutes. Keeping in mind these real and substantial differences on the ground, Michael Peletz (2009) explains that pluralism involves granting legitimacy to diversity as well as the acceptance of the equal status of what is instead perceived as 'other'. Thus, different from various discourses about 'tolerance' where legitimacy is granted only within the boundaries established by the majority, pluralism is based on the possibility of actors to retain their differences; as Diana Eck (2003: 196) explains, 'pluralism is not syncretism, but is based on respect for differences'. This type of pluralism, which cannot be solely the product of adherence to legal formulations or imposed by external agents, resonates with what William Connolly (2008) refers to as 'deep pluralism', which might be less predictable and rigid but more capable of arousing the courage needed to promote authentic forms of freedom and to prevent violence.

Particularly related to this challenge of fostering 'deep pluralism' in the context of Baclaran district is confronting the 'hierarchized conviviality' between established merchants and street vendors, which, as demonstrated above, is also an issue between Christians (who are mostly the established merchants) and Moro settlers (who mostly remain sidewalk vendors). The lack of corrective measures to address this issue leads to increasing problems about the sedimentation of negative stereotypes, which, when combined with a 'siege mentality' among established merchants, further prevents the formation of pluralist sentiments.[3] In this regard, well-crafted policies that aim to promote social cohesion will invest significant resources in breaking the hierarchy between established merchants and sidewalk vendors so that all aspiring merchants can properly enter the commercial life of the district and be assured of legal support and protection. In this sense, one tends to doubt the effectiveness of the local governments' suggested strategy of solving the problem of sidewalk vending by legalizing the practice, either occasionally or permanently; besides the fact that it can be challenged as a violation of existing laws, the legalization of street vending itself does not address 'hierarchized conviviality', but actually further affirms it, albeit indirectly. The problem with affirming this present arrangement is that it ultimately does not encourage the formation of pluralist sentiments among the various actors.

These problems notwithstanding, however, pluralist sentiments do stand a chance of being cultivated among various actors on the ground. Among Christian merchants in Baclaran district, these emerging pluralist sentiments were particularly manifested when, during conversations, they chose to qualify their

'Hierarchized conviviality' in Manila   147

statements about Muslim settlers. Although voices were raised concerning the drastic increase of Moro street vendors, a number of Christian merchants think positively about Muslim merchants who decide to own legitimate stalls and businesses in the area. In fact, as established Christian merchants encountered their Muslim counterparts through business dealings, a number of the former expressed a notable change of views about the latter; they now think that what they initially heard about Muslims was mostly exaggerated and did not necessarily apply to all Muslims, regardless of circumstance. While these responses do not suggest that Christian merchants in Baclaran district do not subscribe to stereotypes about Muslims, these imply that they were willing to modify their stance if regular contacts with Muslims belie their initial assumptions about them. On the Muslim side, Moro settlers living around Masjid Sulayman have appealed to the influence of a Catholic prelate in finding a solution regarding the impending demolition of the mosque. In 2007, the residents approached Broderick Pabillo (Auxiliary Bishop of Manila) in order to hand him a letter addressed to President Macapagal-Arroyo airing their grievances; community leader Abdelmanan Tanandato explained in a separate letter that his group did not approach the Office of Muslim Affairs anymore, because this had already lent support for plans to demolish the mosque. Likewise, a Catholic priest known for his wide-ranging activism, visited the Muslim residents in 2009; the priest, when interviewed by the local media, lent his support for the Moro residents and opined that the mosque ought to be maintained as a symbol of Christian–Muslim understanding (Flores and Villanueva 2009).

What is particularly significant in these occurrences is the centrality of the local community in the formulation of solutions that address 'hierarchized conviviality' in their midst. In both instances mentioned above, there emerged a realization on the part of both Christian and Muslim actors in Baclaran district that fostering meaningful ties with the 'other' is more beneficial in the long run than operating on the basis of negative stereotypes that prevent the promotion of such ties. In this regard, implicit biases towards the 'other' are questioned and abandoned through the experiencing of everyday interactions, maintaining peace and order, fulfilling religious obligations and conducting commerce and trade. Thus, the cultivation of pluralist sentiments is attuned to the needs and realities of the local community, and the actors living in that social space are the ones who develop the necessary resources that enable them to 'grant legitimacy to the other'. Furthermore, the formation of inter-group bonds between Christians and Muslims in various areas of cooperation counteract 'flashpoints' that give rise to the thinking that minority groups are necessarily implicated with the persistence of social disorder (Sampson 2009).

It is likewise important for pluralist sentiments to take root that Muslim migrants are empowered to organize themselves and take an active part in the life of the community. In this regard, the Moro settlers have organized themselves into merchant or residential associations (mostly along ethnic lines) in order to promote their own interests and welfare. The Muslim merchants have organized commercial associations in the past, and they have coordinated with *barangay*

148   *Manuel Victor J. Sapitula*

authorities in the task of maintaining peace and order in the areas where Muslims are a majority. In the case of the residents around Masjid Sulayman, the Samahan ng mga Nagkakaisang Nademolis sa Roxas Blvd. Baclaran (Association of Evicted Residents in Roxas Blvd. Baclaran), a residential association formed by the settlers, has been active in presenting their cause in court, with government officials and media agencies. The association's recourse to the legal system provided brief respites from threats of demolition, especially in the Court of Appeals' 2007 ruling, which granted a 60-day temporary restraining order against the demolition of the mosque and the residents' homes.

Nevertheless, these manifestations of participation by Moro settlers into the economic and social life in Baclaran district are still fraught with limitations. Diana Eck (2007) argues that various groups are able to participate in the ordering of social life without shedding their distinctive identities; to this, I must add that the level of participation should rise beyond the need to protect one's community from external forces which are deemed unsympathetic or hostile. Especially in the case of the residents around Masjid Sulayman, the engagement with broader social processes is still at the level of defensive protectionism, as the threat of the mosque's demolition puts them in an attitude of distrust vis-à-vis social forces outside their community. The same can be said of sidewalk vendors, whose efforts toward self-organizing are still mainly against the backdrop of impending demolition of their stalls and confiscation of their wares. As of this writing, no identifiable Muslim participation has occurred in regular civic rituals like the town *fiesta* (the town's foundation feast day), although Muslim settlers in other areas of the country have actively taken part in local *fiestas,* just as immigrant Muslims in other parts of Asia participate in community affairs as a sign of integration with their host societies (see Wai-chi Chee's contribution to this volume, on South Asian Muslims in Hong Kong). The participation of various organizations in the town *fiesta* is a conspicuous manifestation of the community's acceptance and support, and the absence of Muslims in the city's civic commemorations is a glaring manifestation that they have not integrated fully into the city's civic space.

The move from defensive protectionism to more positive forms of engagement, which is a very significant challenge on the part of Muslim communities, opens opportunities for Muslim settlers here and elsewhere to craft new ways of expressing their sense of connection with the district, and their mosques, like churches, have the potential of becoming relevant civic spaces in the metropolis. 'Civic spaces' fulfil an important role in organizing communities, and are by nature inclusive spaces; in the past, religious edifices in the metropolis and its adjoining areas served as important civic spaces. One example is the Shrine of Mary, Queen of Peace (Our Lady of EDSA), a Catholic chapel built in commemoration of the 1986 EDSA Revolt, which became the rallying location for the protests that led to President Estrada's resignation from office in 2001. The Perpetual Help Shrine in Baclaran district also assumed the role of civic space during the martial law years, when political dissidents and conscientious objectors of the regime sought refuge in this church (Hechanova 1998). In

'Hierarchized conviviality' in Manila   149

Muslim-majority Malaysia, the National Mosque and Kampung Baru Mosque in Kuala Lumpur particularly stood out to become important sites of political participation and protest among Malaysians in the 1970s (Sirat and Abdullah 2008). As the Manila metropolis undergoes further diversification with the entrance of new settlers from all over the country, one expects the nearly absolute identification of religious civic spaces with Catholic places of worship, to give way to an emerging diversity of alternative religious spaces for engaging social life in the city. The mosques in Metro Manila fulfil an important role in this regard, insofar as it contributes to the Muslim communities' position on social issues of metropolitan and national proportions.

Concluding remarks

In this chapter, I demonstrated the existence of 'hierarchized conviviality' among merchants and residents in Baclaran district against the backdrop of class- and religious-based interests that inform actors on the ground. As a product of historical trajectories and forms of urban transformations, 'hierarchized conviviality' is a persistent feature of urban transition processes in Metro Manila – particularly in this contribution, I showed how the stratification between Christian and Muslim merchants and residents in Baclaran district were reinforced by contesting claims to urban space and the emergence of stereotypical thinking. However, these impending conflicts notwithstanding, local actors have found ways to engage with their perceived 'others' and thus began a process of cultivating pluralist thinking. Christian and Muslim merchants alike recognize the formation of cooperative ties as essential for their own commercial stakes in the district.

The significance of the Baclaran district case lies in its capacity to demonstrate the 'paradox' that Anthony Reid has observed in Southeast Asian societies – that of the persistence of religious diversity and pluralist sentiments against the backdrop of dominant religious orthodoxies (Reid and Gilsenan 2007). The Philippines is not exempted from this paradox, and it is especially in the discussion of Christian–Muslim relations in urban life that one comes across the complexities of this relationship, and the possibilities and pitfalls of this particular mode of encounter. In an article on the relationship between the Catholic Church and the state in Poland, Geneviève Zubrzycki (2010) introduces the concept of 'monocultural identity' to describe the conflation of religion and discourses of nationhood in public life; and yet, even in this near-total identification between Catholicism and 'Polishness', various spaces for contesting this conflation have emerged from time to time. In the case of the Philippines, despite the heavy identification of the public sphere with Catholic principles and traditions, 'neutral public spaces' are guaranteed by the constitutional provision on the separation of Church and State, and recently with the increasing recognition of the distinctness of the Muslim experience vis-à-vis Philippine nation-building. For instance, the Philippines enacted the Code of Muslim Personal Laws in 1977, thus recognizing the existence of 'plural legal regimes' in the country to account for Muslim sources of law and jurisprudence (Mastura 1994). Likewise, in recent

150   Manuel Victor J. Sapitula

peace talks between the Philippine government and the Moro Islamic Liberation Front, both sides highlight the need to correct historical distortions and the marginalization of Moros in Philippine public discourse.

Nevertheless, these promising trajectories talked about by Filipino and Moro elites on high-level encounters cannot be a substitute for the cultivation of pluralist sentiments in local communities, especially in places where Christians and Muslims find themselves living in increasingly close proximity. Ultimately, it is in the particularity of local communities, its resources and limitations, and its sense of determination, that actors either succeed or fail in crafting sustainable networks of trust. The repercussions of their successes or failures go beyond their borders and affect the integrity of supra-local efforts and arrangements. In the Baclaran district case, the solution to 'hierarchized conviviality' entails the reconfiguration of urban social space so that all stakeholders are assured of adequate residence and livelihood, equal legal protection and participation in the cultural enrichment of the district. Thus, fruitful coexistence, that is, one that goes beyond simply 'living side-by-side', between Christians and Muslims in Metro Manila – and elsewhere – depends upon the sincere and continuous attempts of both government and the public to address broader socio-economic issues that thwart trustful encounters, thus also preventing the full participation of all parties in the task of charting the community's future.

Notes

1 The *Iglesia ni Cristo* (Church of Christ) is an indigenous Christian denomination founded in the Philippines in 1914 by Felix Y. Manalo. The church combines a highly centralized bureaucratic organization, evangelistic preaching and extensive use of Philippine languages in propagating its doctrines. As of 2000, there are 285,587 (2.9 per cent) *Iglesia ni Cristo* members in Metro Manila, making it the largest single Christian denomination after the Catholic Church.
2 The two big churches referred to in the video clip are the National Shrine of Our Mother of Perpetual Help (built in 1932) and the Archdiocesan Shrine of Jesus, the Way, the Truth and the Life (built in 1999).
3 During informal interviews with a number of established merchants of Baclaran district, some of them expressed irritation at the perceived increasing 'domination' by 'Muslims', rather than street vendors *per se*. This way of thinking among established merchants betrays their concern that new waves of Moro migrants would endanger their business interests.

References

Abejo, S. (1985) 'Migration to and from the National Capital Region: 1975–1980', *Journal of Philippine Statistics,* 36(4): ix–xxii.

Agence France-Presse (2008) *Philippine Muslims in Search of a Homeland*, Manila, Online video. Available from www.youtube.com/user/AFP#p/search/8/UhJD956_Uv8 (accessed on 18 March 2011).

Ambrosio, V. and Pereira, M. (2007) 'Case 2: Christian/Catholic Pilgrimage – Studies and Analyses', In Raj, R. and Morpeth, N.D. (eds) *Religious Tourism and Pilgrimage Festivals Management: An International Perspective,* Wallingford, UK: CAB International.

'Hierarchized conviviality' in Manila 151

Angeles, V.S.M. (2007) 'Moros in the Media and Beyond: Representations of Philippine Muslims', *Contemporary Islam*, 4: 29–53.

Bernad, M.A. (1974) *The Western Community of Manila: A Profile*, Manila: National Historical Commission.

Berner, R. (1997) *Defending a Place in the City: Localities and the Struggle for Urban Land in Metro Manila*, Quezon City: Ateneo de Manila University Press.

Caoili, M.A. (1999) *The Origins of Metropolitan Manila: A Political and Social Analysis*, Diliman, Quezon City: University of the Philippines Press.

Connolly, W.E. (2008) 'Deep Pluralism', in Chambers, S.A. and Carver, T. (eds) *William E. Connolly: Democracy, Pluralism and Political Theory*, London: Routledge.

Eck, D.L. (2003) *Encountering God: A Spiritual Journey from Bozeman to Banaras*, Boston, MA: Beacon Press.

Eck, D.L. (2007) 'American Religious Pluralism: Civic and Theological Discourse', in Banchoff, T. (ed.) *Democracy and the New Religious Pluralism*, New York: Oxford University Press.

Flores, H. and Villanueva, R. (2009) 'Running Priest Joins Bid to Save Baclaran Mosque', *The Philippine Star* [online], 21 September. Available at www.philstar.com/article.aspx?articleid=507079 (accessed 10 March 2011).

Hechanova, L.G. (1998) *The Baclaran Story*, Quezon City: Claretian Publications.

Human Development Network (2005) *2005 Philippine Human Development Report: Peace, Human Security and Human Development in the Philippines*, 2nd edn. Quezon City: HDN Secretariat.

Mastura, M.O. (1994) 'Legal Pluralism in the Philippines', *Law & Society Review*, 28(3): 461–76.

National Statistics Office (2000) *2000 Census of Population and Housing: National Capital Region*, Manila: National Statistics Office.

Naylor, S. and Ryan, J.R. (2002) 'The Mosque in the Suburbs: Negotiating Religion and Ethnicity in South London', *Social & Cultural Geography*, 3(1): 39–59.

Padilla, A. (1990) *Civil Law, Civil Code Annotated: Civil Code of the Philippines*, Vol. 2, 6th edn. Manila: Padilla Press.

Parañaque City Government (2009) *Socio-Economic Profile*, Parañaque City: City Planning and Development Coordinator's Office.

Peletz, M.G. (2009) *Gender Pluralism: Southeast Asia since Early Modern Times*, New York: Routledge.

Reid, A. and Gilsenan, M. (eds) (2007) *Islamic Legitimacy in a Plural Asia*, New York: Routledge.

Sampson, R.J. (2009) 'Disparity and Diversity in the Contemporary City: Social (dis)order Revisited', *The British Journal of Sociology*, 60(1): 1–31.

Sassen, S. (1991) *The Global City: New York, London, Tokyo*, Princeton, NJ: Princeton University Press.

Sirat, M. and Abdullah, A.H. (2008) 'Mosques as a Type of Civic Space in Turbulent Times: A Case Study of Globalizing Kuala Lumpur', in Douglass, M., Ho, K.C. and Giok, L.O. (eds) *Globalization, the City and Civil Society in Pacific Asia: The Social Production of Civic Spaces*, London: Routledge.

The Urban Poor Associates (2007) 'Bishop Pabillo asked to help evicted Muslim families in Baclaran', *The Daily Urban Poor* [weblog post], 13 June. Available at http://urbanpoorassociates.blogspot.com/2007/06/bishop-pabillo-asked-to-help-evicted.html (Accessed 20 March 2011).

152   *Manuel Victor J. Sapitula*

Watanabe, A. (2007) 'The Formation of Migrant Muslim Communities in Metro Manila', *Kasarinlan: Philippine Journal of Third World Studies*, 22(2): 68–96.

Watanabe, A. (2008) *Migration and Mosques: The Evolution and Transformation of Muslim Communities in Manila, the Philippines* [Working Paper Series No. 37], Shiga, Japan: Afrasian Centre for Peace and Development Studies, Ryukoku University.

Zubrzycki, G. (2010) 'What is Religious Pluralism in a 'Monocultural' Society? Considerations from Post-communist Poland', in Bender, C. and Klassen, P.E. (eds) *After Pluralism: Reimagining Religious Engagement,* New York: Columbia University Press.

9 Actually existing religious pluralism in Kuala Lumpur

Yeoh Seng Guan

Malaysia is no stranger to mutating religious diversity and cultural pluralism. For centuries, given its strategic geopolitical position along the commercial trade routes between China and India (and beyond), an array of travellers to the peninsula – *inter alia* merchants, imperialists and missionaries – have left their imprints, both singular and hybrid, on belief systems, social practices and material cultures that make up the societal fabric of modern-day Malaysia. Together with its diverse and finely balanced Asian populace who are adherents of some of the major world religions – Buddhism, Christianity, Hinduism, Islam, Sikhism, and Daoism – the Malaysian Tourism Board was emboldened to make the claim of 'Malaysia [being] Truly Asia' not so long ago.

Notwithstanding the allure of magical religious pluralism and multiculturalism, it has been increasingly commonplace for many Malaysians to lament the deteriorating health of inter-ethnic and inter-faith relations in the public sphere over the past three decades in contrast to a nostalgic golden and cosmopolitan past (e.g. Lee 1988; Ahmad Fauzi 2000; Riddell 2005; Tan and Lee 2008). The specific reasons for this prognosis vary according to the different standpoints and emphases given by their respective interlocutors. Nevertheless, a common recurring trope that stands out can be characterized as an over-zealous and bureaucratic 'Islamization of Malaysian society' by a diverse and competing spectrum of local Islamic *dakwah* (missionary) groups and state agencies since the advent of Islamic revivalism in the 1970s.[1]

Moreover, this state-of-affairs is compounded by the durable legacy of the British colonial era crafted in the context of facilitating maximal capitalist resource extraction combined with a nationalist inflection characteristic of the postcolonial milieu. After securing political independence from Britain, and especially in the aftermath of the landmark Kuala Lumpur 'race' riots of May 1969, a master narrative of the putative constitutional 'supremacy' of Malays (*ketuanan Melayu*) vis-à-vis other Malaysian citizens has been entrenched in the national imaginary through the state ideological and repressive apparatus. In sum, a differential and racialized management of the plurality of migrants who flocked to the peninsula in search of a better life coupled with the challenge of nascent Malay ethno-nationalist groups has birthed a bifurcating religious landscape between Muslims and non-Muslims in the public sphere (Ackerman and Lee 1990 [1988]).

154 *Yeoh Seng Guan*

How has this trajectory played out in recent years in Kuala Lumpur, the globalizing capital city of Malaysia? Akin to other postcolonial cities in the Southeast Asian region, Kuala Lumpur can be viewed as a complex assemblage in motion; materially and symbolically folding, unfolding and refolding onto itself in multiple ways, through its multi-scalar entanglements with competing imaginaries and processes near and far. The heterogenetic urban swirl of city-ness, in part characterized by accentuated religious and cultural complexities, is vibrantly immanent in Kuala Lumpur (cf. Hannerz 1992). One of the central features of 'city-ness' (in Abdoumaliq Simone's terms) is the agency of 'crossroads' – where people 'take the opportunity to change each other around by virtue of being in that space, getting rid of the familiar ways of, and plans for, doing things and finding new possibilities by virtue of whatever is gathered there' (Simone 2010: 192).

This chapter situates some of these 'crossroads' in the religiously pluralist city-ness of contemporary Kuala Lumpur. I open with a recounting of an episode early in 2011 that generated both ire and bemusement among Malaysians. Then I proceed to delve into the key historical circumstances that have contributed to this particular intersection of varied emotional intensities construed in generic terms, finally situating how actually existing religious pluralism is materially articulated. This is pursued through a discussion of fieldwork data gathered from two different sites – one residential and the other commercial – in the city.

Love and sex in the city: The Valentine's Day affair

In the past few years, Islamic agencies at state and federal levels in Malaysia have been labouring to deter Muslims from celebrating Valentine's Day. The key reason offered is the event's alleged links to 'immoral' activities. In 2011, the anti-Valentine's Day campaign took on more fractious accents.

On 9 February, Parti Islam Se-Malaysia (PAS, the Islamic Party of Malaysia) Youth chief, Nasrudin Hasan Tantawi, was reported to have said that anti-vice campaigns on Valentine's Day in four states (Kedah, Kelantan, Penang and Selangor) controlled by the opposition coalition, the Pakatan Rakyat, would be conducted to ensure a 'sin-free' lifestyle.[2] This move was motivated in previous years by disturbing marketing gimmicks that promoted, among others, 'no panties day' as an expression of abiding female love for their partners, free hotel rooms for unmarried couples on Valentine's Day, and late night parties allowing the free mixing of men and women which inevitably leads to 'free sex'.[3]

His remarks quickly drew criticisms from a number of sources and sparked acrimonious (and amusing) debates among pseudonymous Malaysians in cyberspace. Leaders of his own party and from the opposition political coalition, Pakatan Rakyat, comprising secular-based parties like Democratic Action Party and Parti Keadilan Raykat (Justice Party) said Nasrudin had no *locus standi* to speak for the state governments under Pakatan Rakyat control.[4] By contrast, key politicians of Pakatan Rakyat's political nemesis, Barisan Nasional, took on a characteristic ominous persona, forewarning citizen-voters of the fragility of the former's syncretistic political ideology and the true colours of PAS which is to

Actually existing pluralism in Kuala Lumpur 155

turn Malaysia into a theocratic Islamic state when it comes into power despite recent assurances otherwise. Its 'moral policing' tendencies are clear indications of this unchanging aspiration.[5]

Nasrudin subsequently claimed that he was misquoted by the press as he was aware that the PAS Youth wing has no legal powers to conduct 'immorality checks' among Muslims. Nevertheless, he repeated his prognosis on the key causes of moral decline among Malay-Muslims in the country. This perspective was apparently shared by Islamic state agencies as both the Kuala Lumpur City and Selangor State Islamic Departments had similarly called for the ban of Muslims commemorating Valentine's Day a day after the Federal Department of Islamic Development (JAKIM) had launched their own anti-Valentine Day campaign, billed as 'Beware of Valentine's Day Trap'.[6]

In a scripted sermon read out on Friday prayers at various mosques throughout Kuala Lumpur and Selangor state on 11 February, Valentine's Day was characterized as essentially a Christian-inspired event and thus not religiously appropriate for a Muslim to participate. Moreover, it argued that many of those who celebrate it usually end up engaging in illicit sex. As evidence, the text cited that 257,411 unwanted pregnancies were reported between 2000 and 2008 as a result of the passions ignited on Valentine's Day. The sermon concluded by reminding Muslims that Jews and Christians would continue to deceive them, and would do everything possible to undermine their Islamic faith and Muslim personality. A seemingly innocuous activity like celebrating Valentine's Day is read inter-textually to be a conspiracy to weaken and dissipate Muslims and their faith.

Subsequently, on Valentine's Day, 'immorality' raids, code-named 'Ops Valentine', were carried out by the Islamic authorities at budget hotels, public parks, recreational lakes, beaches and other well-known dating spots. Close to 100 Muslim individuals were detained for *khalwat* (close proximity with the opposite sex) in Kuala Lumpur city and Selangor alone.[7] They were charged under the Syariah Criminal Offence Enactment 1995 which carries a fine of 3,000 MYR, a jail term of not more than 2 years, or both if found guilty. PAS Youth chief, Nasrudin, similarly reported of other kinds of 'successes' in their vigilante efforts. His counselling teams distributed around 3,000 leaflets to Muslim couples found in 'dark and quiet public spots'. Many were said to be 'receptive' and even thanked them for their timely interventions.[8]

The idiosyncratic interpretations of Valentine's Day by this assortment of Islamic agencies did not go uncontested. Two component political parties situated on opposite sides of the ideological divide – the Democratic Action Party (from Pakatan Raykat) and Gerakan (from Barisan Nasional) – marked their disagreement by playfully handing out carnations and chocolates to the public.[9] They contended that Valentine's Day is a non-religious and globally commercialized event that does not necessarily lead to 'immoral' activities. Similarly, but evoking a more serious register, the Christian Federation of Malaysia (CFM) and Council of Churches of Malaysia (CCM) took to heart the alleged Christian nature of the celebration.[10] In separate press statements, they made reference to one of the sources for Nasrudin's erroneous understanding of Valentine's Day – the National Fatwa Council ruling of 2005. The Council ruled that Valentine's Day 'had elements of Christianity that contradict Islam' and following it 'would destroy the faith and morals of the Muslim community'. A Muslim celebrating Valentine's Day was also read as opening herself to the charge of treachery, as several centuries earlier, this day was declared by Queen Isabella to be in commemoration of the victory of Christianity over Islam in Spain. Both the CFM and CCM contended that this inference was a factual error as Valentine's Day is presently a secular celebration taken over by the business world, and is no longer observed as a religious event by churches in Malaysia, or any other Christian denomination elsewhere in the world. It urged the National Fatwa Council to retract the ruling as it was 'hurtful' to Christians.[11]

They also identified a particular instalment of a Muslim program, *Halaqah*, aired two years earlier (February 2009) on Malaysian public television (TV9) as offensive to Christians. It featured a well-known motivational speaker on the television circuit, Ustazah Siti Nor Bahyah Mahamood, who opined that the immoral activities unleashed on Valentine's Day were firmly within the 'traditions of the Christian community'. Subsequent to the press statement, the producers of the program had issued a public apology for the slip-up. However, the video clip continues to be circulated virally in cyberspace.

Before the advent of the internet, expressions of 'conflict' by citizens, particularly along 'racial' and 'religious' lines, would have been downplayed or censored in the mainstream media as they are deemed to have the centrifugal power of unravelling the social cohesion of Malaysian society. Hitherto, this would not have been difficult to execute given the regime of strict censorship laws and media ownership patterns favouring the ruling government. Discursively, a typical mainstream news report would underscore the 'irresponsibility' of these actors and the necessity of swift punitive actions to pre-empt chaos. However, the rhizomatic capabilities of the internet have complicated attempts at centripetal control by the centre. Thus, while not exhaustive nor representative, the availability of a comments section in online news not only provides more visibility to the folds of everyday inter-faith relations but also possesses a reflexive and mobilizing function.

Talking points as expressed in a popular free online English daily – *The Malaysian Insider* – bear closer attention given its high readership.[12] One thread essentially rehearsed the contentions noted earlier. Against its detractors, readers pointed out that Valentine's Day has been anachronistically mis-recognized – Valentine's Day is not or no longer a 'Christian' religious activity, and hence allegations of conspiracy are mistaken. Another thread attempted to re-direct blame by illuminating and underscoring to the anonymous reading public the doctrinal differences between (Protestant) 'Christians' and 'Catholics', and that Valentine's Day is associated with the latter group.

A more robust discussion thread involving altercations, however, centred around the alienating tone of the Islamic proclamations in question. To comments that stated that non-Muslims should not be concerned about the *fatwa* (learned opinion) and subsequent religious policing activities since they apply only to Muslims, other readers contended in response that the key issue was rather the distasteful and bigoted views of religious leaders deployed to educate their constituency. This ran contrary not only to respectful etiquette in everyday relations but also against the government slogans of showcasing Malaysia as a model for religious tolerance and racial harmony through aspirational catchphrases like *Bangsa Malaysia* ('Malaysian Race') and more recently, the '1Malaysia' campaign introduced by the current premier of the country, Najib Abdul Razak, when he took office in 2009.

Other comments tried to steer the discussion onto a more 'political' plane, of which there were two trajectories. Apart from disregarding the right to privacy, one underscored the pettiness of moral policing activities when bigger issues like corruption and lack of democratic freedoms continue to beset the country. The Islamic authorities were advised to re-direct their energies in addressing societal level problems that cut across religious boundaries. Others lamented that moral policing activities are not only hypocritical but disproportionately target vulnerable young and working class Muslims. Wealthy and upwardly mobile Muslims who can afford to be in ensconced in expensive hotels and high-end entertainment outlets appear to be outside their field of action.

The second thread capitalized on the zealous Islamic initiatives of PAS in showing the deep ideological discord within Pakatan Rakyat, and hence their impotence in replacing the ruling Barisan Nasional government, which ostensibly adopts a secularist political agenda. Despite the comparative invisibility of their well-known ambition of forming a theocratic Islamic State in recent years, these readers suggested that this stance is a chameleon marketing ploy to lull non-Muslim voters into complacency. The Valentine's Day affair was thus an opportune episode bringing to light the incompatible ideological colours of strange political bedfellows.

Although the policing of Valentine's Day by the Islamic authorities unfolded spectrally across many states throughout the country, Kuala Lumpur was the site where these activities were the most intensive. It produced tangible results in the largest number of Muslims caught in allegedly compromising *khalwat* positions, and by implication an index of the moral state of the globalizing city as a whole.

Crossroad urbanisms and managing ethno-religious pluralism

Throughout the Southeast Asian region, the centrality of the urban environment in re-constituting and cultivating collective subjectivities not only for its local residents but, more broadly, as centripetal imaginaries of state power, civilizational progress, and patriotism is a recurring architectural motif running through the colonial and postcolonial milieu (e.g. Kusno 2000). In this regard, Kuala Lumpur's transformation from a frontier mining settlement in the early nineteenth century to the postcolonial capital city of Malaysia imbued with high symbolic and economic power requires an abbreviated and contextual re-telling.

158   *Yeoh Seng Guan*

From the beginning, its genesis and evolution was deeply entangled with the extractive enterprise begun in the late eighteenth century. As British administrative control of the peninsula grew and deepened, a new spatial geography of inland urban centres and pluralist ethno-religious landscapes manifesting the 'colonial-immigrant complex' (Lim 1978) appeared on the horizons. Tin mining and cash crop plantations were the primary economic impetus for devising a liberal immigrant policy to attract successive waves of labour from the impoverished regions of China, India, and Indonesia, and subsequently overlaying a spectrum of settlers who arrived decades and centuries earlier and who largely resided in more accessible coastal and riverine settlements. The servicing of British and local elite capitalist investments prompted the cultivation of an essentially racialized and segregationist governmentality to manage the plural and mobile demographic and ethno-religious populace. As Joel Kahn succinctly puts it:

> Governing Malaya's colonial subjects...involved various mechanisms aimed at immobilizing them, thus tying them to particular places – peasant villages, forest reserves, plantation belts, factory zones, urban bureaucratic centers – each constructed discursively as the preserve of a particular race. This was done, moreover, not just or even mainly to serve the interests of capital but to facilitate the disciplining of colonial subjects and, therefore, to the benefit of an emergent modern state.
>
> (Kahn 2006: 140)

Within this broad trajectory, the genealogy of old Kuala Lumpur resonates with many other urban settlements birthed in the colonial era. Originally established by the mid-1800s as a multi-ethnic trading post, it had grown to sufficient prominence that by 1880, the British authorities decided to transfer strategically the administrative capital of Selangor state from the ancient royal coastal settlement of Klang to upstream Kuala Lumpur.[13] Subsequently, it was chosen to be the capital of the Federated Malay States (1896) and of British Malaya (comprising the Straits Settlements, Unfederated Malay States and the Federated Malay States), and finally of independent Malaya (1957) following World War II.

From contemporary British eyewitness accounts, the ethnoscapes of early Kuala Lumpur were striated by homogeneous ethno-religious enclaves that mushroomed as a consequence of both planned and spontaneous initiatives (Gullick 2000). For instance, Chinese pioneers (of predominantly the Hakka and Hokkien dialect groups) were reported to have congregated largely to the east of the confluence of the Gombak and Klang rivers, eventually forming the spatial template of modern day 'Chinatown'. To the north of 'Chinatown', Java Street – known today as Jalan Tun Perak (Tun Perak Road) but transiting as Mountbatten Road first – was observed to mark the boundary between the 'Chinese' and 'Malay' quarter.[14] By comparison, both the localities of Sentul and Brickfields became working class districts largely peopled by South Asian migrants (*inter alia* Sinhalese, Tamils, and Punjabis) sourced from other parts of the British

Empire to work on the railways and in the city public works department. Similarly, a large piece of land reserved only for Malays, called *Kampung Baru* (literally, 'new village'), was also created near to the town centre as a resettlement scheme. In subsequent decades, some of these early 'enclaves' or 'districts' have pluralized in terms of ethnic mix or were erased to make way for up-market commercial and residential developments given its strategic locations. What has remained intact as incongruent and mute reminders of the ethno-religious pluralism of the early inhabitants in these spaces are their respective places of worship – temples, mosques and churches – some of which stand in close proximity to one another. They also catalogue the doctrinal, linguistic and geographical diversities within each religious tradition through the multiple places of worship of each faith within the same locality.

Despite having ruled for several decades, documented cases of large scale or decisive conversions of 'native Malays' into Christianity during British colonial rule are weak in evidence. Partly, this is due to the expediency of colonial rule. In keeping with its economic priorities and with emergent secularist political philosophies back in the metropolitan centre, the colonial administration was careful in the manner in which 'Malay religion and customs' would be intervened and re-configured. Anti-colonial uprisings animated by millenarian religious imageries elsewhere in the Empire (e.g. Sepoy Mutiny in India) were also politically and economically instructive. Through strategies similar to those used in British India (e.g. Cohn 1996; Dirks 2001), the administration eventually re-calibrated the juridical realms of 'religion' and 'the secular'. By codifying and bureaucratizing Islamic beliefs and practices which were plural and partially or unevenly embodied throughout the 'Malay peninsula', the British helped to 'promote a very visible Islamization of social and political life, including at least a partial implementation of *hudud* or Islamic criminal law by the state' (Kahn 2006: 86ff). Moreover, because of the perceived restrictions on working with 'Malays', Christian proselytization and humanitarian work by European and American missionaries hailing from an array of theological traditions were targeted mainly at the waves of non-Malay migrants living, working or coursing through key urban centres in the peninsula.[15]

As a consequence of the manner this particular 'crossroad' was historically traversed, and coupled with the intervention of Malay ethno-nationalist movements, the ethno-religious arithmetic and identity politics of modern-day Malaysia is strongly coded by an oppositional bifurcation of religious identities and emotional intensities – between 'Muslim' and 'non-Muslim' life-worlds. Arguably, these differentiated governmentalities were further entrenched by Mahathir Mohamad early in his premiership. In 1984, he announced his decision to 'Islamize the government machinery'. This was read by political commentators as a strategy to win over support of Malay-Muslims who were swayed by a plethora of grassroots-based Muslim *dakwah* groups and by the formidable religious credentials of Parti Islam Se-Malaysia. In response to anxieties voiced by coalition members of Barisan Nasional, the legal fraternity, and non-Muslims, he reasoned:

160   *Yeoh Seng Guan*

> What we mean by Islamization is the inculcation of Islamic values in govern-ment. Such an inculcation is not the same as the implementation of Islamic laws in the country. Islamic laws are for Muslims and meant for their personal laws. But the laws of the nation, although not Islamic-based, can be used as long as they do not come into conflict with Islamic principles.[16]
>
> (interview with Mahathir Mohamad, *Utusan Melayu*, 26–27 October 1984)

However, during the long Mahathir administration (1981–2003), a series of federal, state and local council level policies set in motion practices and interpre-tations that fomented another particular kind of 'crossroad' formation, that of the re-drawing and blurring of boundaries and disparate domains. His administration also lent support to the significant expansion of religious bureaucracies at state levels through the provision of large amounts of resources by the Department of Islamic Development (JAKIM).

As these initiatives grew in scope and intensity, non-Muslims increasingly perceived them as infringing their everyday (non-)religious practices and under-mining their secular constitutional rights as Malaysian citizens (e.g. Yeoh 2005a). For instance, apart from the setting up of a range of public Islamic institutions in banking, financing, judiciary, and higher education, other efforts putatively target-ing *haram* (not permissible) activities have seeped beyond the porous domains of Muslim sensibilities. This included calls to close down licensed pubs, karaoke centres, and gaming outlets; ban the sale of alcohol; impose Islamic dress-codes for non-Muslim women in public spaces; have separate queues for men and women in shopping complexes and other public spaces; and censor advertisements that depict women (Muslim and non-Muslim) in sexually provocative poses or revealing parts of their bodily *aurat* (modesty) to the anonymous public. By draw-ing meticulous attention to these *haram* activities, what is also implied is that urbane Muslims were not unfamiliar with them in the past. Nor did they feel that these personal moral choices should be of concern to Islamic authorities. Nevertheless, despite these feelings of ambivalence, many have remained silent in the face of more vocal Islamic *dakwah* groups or chosen more clandestine ways of expression for fear of being accused of 'insulting Islam'.

Addressing an array of temptations believed lurking in a morally pluralist and ambivalent urban environment has also extended to the young. Nationalized Christian mission schools throughout the country have been instructed to remove signs of Roman Catholic crucifixes and Protestant Christian crosses on buildings, uniforms, books and other paraphernalia in deference to Muslim sensitivities. Unlike secular 'civic courses' before, students are segregated respectively for their respective 'Islamic Studies' and 'Moral Studies' classes, a compulsory unit of study that has been extended up to tertiary level education. There have been reported cases (especially in the alternative media) of Muslim school principals punishing students for bringing non-*halal* food to school, promoting the separa-tion of eating utensils in the school canteen, and of Malay-Muslim school teachers making derogatory remarks about other religions or questioning the patriotism of non-Malays.[17]

Actually existing pluralism in Kuala Lumpur 161

In tandem with the expansion of the Islamic religious bureaucracy, several amendments to sharia criminal law at state levels strengthened considerably the legal powers of Islamic authorities for the moral surveillance, enforcement and punishment of adult Muslims who transgress against these disciplinary rulings (e.g. Peletz 2002; Hamayotsu 2003). Other subsequent enactments further allowed the automatic enforcement of *fatwas* issued by state *muftis* (religious officials) and the Fatwa Council without due legislative process in the state assembly. Of this train of legislative crossroads, arguably the most controversial was an amendment to Article 121 (1A) of the Federal Constitution in 1988. This removed the jurisdiction of the civil courts over Islamic matters, and effectively created two spheres of competing jurisdictions between the Civil and the Syariah courts. In recent years, this jurisdictional conundrum involving Malaysians who have made personal faith choices straddling both domains have resulted in court decisions that concede or defer to the authority of the sharia courts (e.g. Yeoh 2011). In 2001, shortly after the tragedy of '9/11' (September 11) in the US, when Premier Mahathir Mohamad made the claim that Malaysia was already a progressive Islamic state worthy of emulation by other Muslim countries, the Malaysian Consultative Council for Buddhism, Christianity, Hinduism and Sikhism (MCCBCHS)[18] issued a press statement that contended:

> Over the past twenty years, in the process of Islamization of our laws and regulations government bureaucracy has imposed rules and regulations which have infringed on the religious freedom of both Muslims and non-Muslims and the trend seems to be getting worse over the last few years ... [because of] greater polarization among our different communities along the lines of race and religion, [we] call on the government to set up Inter-Religious Councils at National and State levels to promote inter-religious understanding.[19]
> (Catholic Bishops Conference of Malaysia, 1 August 2002)

In the intervening years since the above press statement was issued, several other agonistic debates on the management of religious pluralism in the country have further widened and deepened the fault-lines. For instance, in 2005, the Malaysian Bar Council organized a conference to discuss a draft bill proposing the formation of a national inter-faith commission in light of issues involving several high profile legal cases. The conference was boycotted by a loose coalition of Muslim NGOs called the Allied Coordination Committee of Islamic NGOs who felt that the Bar Council had an ulterior agenda. It also characterized a memorandum submitted by the MCCBCHS to the National Human Rights Commission (Suhakam) suggesting that Muslim converts be allowed to revert back to their previous faiths if the original reason for their conversion no longer exists (e.g. failed mixed marriages) as 'anti-Islam'. Similarly, the youth wing of PAS denounced the formation of an inter-faith commission as they contended that it would usurp the power of Islamic authorities. Moreover, they deemed any public discussion of various Islamic issues like *murtad* (apostates) by non-Muslims as offensive and as an 'insult to Islam'.

162   Yeoh Seng Guan

In 2007, on the occasion of the fifteenth anniversary of Malaysian Independence (*Merdeka*), the Christian Federation of Malaysia issued a press statement which aptly characterizes how Christian leaders perceived the state of religious and cultural pluralism in the country:

> Today, after fifty years of nationhood, we realize that we cannot take unity-in-diversity for granted. What divides us has become more accentuated than what unites us. Signs of polarization along ethnic and religious lines, along with other forms of chauvinism, racism and superiority are eroding our national unity.
>
> In order to face these challenges, the CFM feels the necessity to reinforce the importance of the supremacy of the Constitution and the rule of law, which are restated in the basic tenets of the *Rukun Negara* (National Principles). Only by doing so can we safeguard our democratic life, enhance good governance, and sustain unity not adverse to religious and ethnic pluralism.[20]
>
> (Christian Federation of Malaysia National Day Message, 29 August 2007)

In light of the preceding, the Roman Catholic Church embarked on a bold and unprecedented course of action in March 2008. The Home Minister had earlier prohibited the publisher from using the word 'Allah' to refer to the Christian God in their weekly Catholic newspaper, *The Herald*. Although indigenous Christians in the East Malaysian states of Sabah and Sarawak had been using the term for decades – and for centuries in the case of Christians in the Middle East – without causing any furore, the reason given was that this linguistic practice would potentially confuse Malay-Muslims and undermine national security in the long run. *The Herald* filed a judicial review challenging the ban arguing that it was unconstitutional. Subsequently, when the High Court ruled in favour of *The Herald* in December 2009, the Home Minister appealed the decision and applied for a stay of execution. Despite its stringent track record on public gatherings, the Home Ministry allowed a permit for a public protest by Muslim groups. A number of state-supported mosques in Kuala Lumpur and Selangor further lobbied for 'Allah' to be reserved for Muslims and to protect its sanctity against illegitimate use. In the subsequent weeks, several churches, including a Sikh temple and the office of the lawyer representing *The Herald,* were vandalized. In retaliation, three mosques and two Muslim prayer rooms were desecrated.[21] Against the trend, there were also assuring signs of inter-religious solidarity as small groups of concerned Muslims and non-Muslims voluntarily organized themselves to stand guard in various places of worship in Kuala Lumpur. Several months later, this particular episode saw a symbolic closure of sorts when perpetrators of the first arson attack on the Metro Tabernacle Church (situated in Kuala Lumpur) were convicted, and the church compensated. However, to date, the more salient issue of the Home Ministry not withdrawing its legal appeal has remained outstanding and unresolved.

Actually existing religious pluralism and halalizing a world class city

In 2004, the Second Kuala Lumpur Draft Structure Plan was unveiled by City Hall with great fanfare. Its authors contended that a new plan superseding the 1984 version was needed because the socio-spatial mutation of the city in terms of population growth, infrastructural and property development in the last two decades had rendered its earlier plans and preconceptions of spatial governance obsolete. Among others, this included the construction of the extensive Multimedia Super Corridor, the hypermodern Kuala Lumpur International Airport, and a federal government administrative complex called Putrajaya inscribed with mimetic Middle-Eastern architectural motifs. Greater in-migration to the suburbs of Kuala Lumpur from around the country and a net out-migration from Kuala Lumpur to areas outside of the city had also confounded population distribution patterns envisaged in the original Structure Plan of 1984. While the old administrative city limits of Kuala Lumpur was kept intact, the fluid mobility of people, ideas and artifacts facilitated by transportation and technology to the surrounding localities also necessitated a more dynamic concept of an expansive and interconnected metropolitan region – the Kuala Lumpur and its conurbation.

The plan also highlighted the grand vision of morphing Kuala Lumpur into a second-tier 'World Class' city in the first instance, and positioning it further to become a premier 'Global City' in the indeterminate future. More than a decade earlier, in 1991, then-premier Mahathir Mohamad had unveiled a similar utopic and teleological project when he promulgated Wawasan 2020 ('Vision 2020'), a road map to transform the nation-state of Malaysia into a 'fully developed' country in three decades. Apart from the Kuala Lumpur International Airport and Putrajaya, the iconic 88-story Petronas Twin Towers, built with Islamic architectural motifs and which briefly held the position of the tallest building in the world when it was completed in the late 1990s, was the most important signature of this developmental thrust forward. They aptly showcased Mahathir's vision of elevating Malaysia onto the global stage based on a neo-liberal economic platform coupled with a modernist Sunni Islamic religious ethos (e.g. Wain 2009).

Salient in the technocratic and lofty 'from above' discourse of the 2004 Structure Plan are the distinguishing traits of what Michel de Certeau has characterized to be the erotics of knowledge production as embodied in omni-visual power. Typically, the city's complexity and opaque mobility is frozen and made readable as a crystal-clear text (de Certeau 1984: 94). Disciplinary and instrumentalist knowledge are strategically deployed to grid and enframe space for the purpose of predictability and stability, and hence help lubricate flows of capitalist and utopian agendas. I suggest a similar kind of imaginative horizon is being beckoned into existence by Islamic state agencies in the first instance but given immediacy and personal relevance by an array of Muslim adherents negotiating with intertwined histories and overlapping everyday spaces found in Kuala Lumpur. To a large extent, this has been necessitated and facilitated by significant demographic changes in Kuala Lumpur. From 1971 onwards, the rapid urbaniza-

164   *Yeoh Seng Guan*

tion of Malay-Muslims was set in motion by the watershed New Economic Policy which, upon its expiry in 1990, became re-designated as the New Development Policy. Among others, these policies envisioned the modernization of Malay-Muslims through affirmative action quotas in tertiary education, business and employment opportunities largely found in urban centres, with Kuala Lumpur and its sprawling suburbs being the chief gravitational destination.[22] The key motif was to dissolve the colonial legacy of a spatial duality between non-Malay urban dwellers and Malay rural *kampung* (village) residents.

The arrival of the first generation of rural Malay-Muslim migrants to Kuala Lumpur in the 1970s saw many of them contributing to the already significant spread of urban 'squatter colonies' by erecting their own houses without prior official approval in established Malay squatter *kampungs* or on unoccupied land because of inadequate affordable housing (e.g. Yeoh 2001). Periodic city censuses carried out among 'squatter colonies' from the 1970s up to the 1990s indicated that ethnic Malays were significantly overtaking the Chinese in terms of demographic make-up. Surveys also noted that many of these settlements were ethnically homogeneous as residents reproduced the familiar in terms of vernacular cultural practices and religious sensibilities – including varieties of 'folk Islam' – of their home villages onto the alien spaces of the city. In more mixed squatter settlements, everyday negotiations included boundary-crossing aspects but they were also strategically framed by the overarching ethno-political discursive and administrative grid of the state. As coping strategies, they range from respectful recognition of each other's presence to mutual avoidance of each other. However, political alliances at the local level have largely tended to be within rather than across ethno-religious groupings even though they might be living in close physical proximity with each other (e.g. Yeoh 2005b). Similarly, in the management of the 'squatter problem', local politicians have opportunistically alternated between pathological and patronage perspectives as they laboured to square national unity and city development discourses with the pragmatics of having to secure their votes during the periodic State and Federal elections. Over time, a range of infrastructural facilities (including mosques, but less so for places of worship of other religious traditions) have been incrementally provided for these settlements in return for these favours.

However, under a robust 'squatter free' agenda outlined in the 1984 Structure Plan and in keeping with the utopian vision of transforming Kuala Lumpur into a 'World Class City' before the turn of the new century, the spatiality and sociality of these ethno-religious spaces were unravelled and reconstituted in a different register. During this period, civil society groups have observed that compared to the past, the forced eviction of urban squatters was far more intense and unrelenting as commercially valuable land was re-appropriated for a range of infrastructural, commercial and residential projects. Most squatters, resigned to the changing realities of the times, had opted to be relocated to high-rise housing flats, usually following an ethnic-based redistributive formula.

The rapid material and symbolic transformation of Kuala Lumpur also demanded that a host of 'unsightly' and 'illegal' roadside shrines, temples and *suraus* found in these squatter settlements – mostly of popular Hindu and Chinese

Actually existing pluralism in Kuala Lumpur   165

religious provenances – be evicted and demolished. Not all, however, were provided with satisfactory alternative sites (in terms of adherence to religious geomancy) in comparison to Muslim *suraus* which were easier to reconstitute. On a broader scale, accompanying the significant increase in Malay-Muslim urban population has been a corresponding mushrooming of new mosques as well as the renovation of older ones across metropolitan Kuala Lumpur, especially in new commercial and residential areas. In comparison to an earlier milieu, most of these new mosques have adopted Middle-Eastern architectural motifs and are strikingly larger in size.

By comparison, a longstanding lament of non-Muslim religious groups has been that land for places of worship in new suburbs has not been readily made available. Various church denominations have thus resorted to renting conference halls in hotels, buying over shop houses and factory lots in order to conduct their worship services. When alternative sites were offered, compromises were sometimes imposed by the authorities and private developers. For instance, small Hindu temples in squatter settlements were required to merge with each other even though they have different patron gods/goddesses and founding genealogies. Equally significant, over the years, human rights groups have documented the brusque and arbitrary manner in which these demolitions and relocations were executed. These narratives of victimhood by ethno-religious minorities are especially salient in the metropolitan Kuala Lumpur area.[23]

Similarly, I suggest that the lived domestic spaces of Kuala Lumpur residents also figure significantly in shaping the contours of everyday religious pluralism. In my fieldwork with former Indian squatters now living in a high rise flat, what is apparent is that while the authorities have resolved the bane of affordable housing at a formal level, the architecture of these structures have nevertheless fomented undercurrents of resentment even as they also arguably offer new opportunities for cross ethno-religious solidarities. In comparison to landed squatter houses that allow for organic modifications, living in these structures is considered traumatic and oppressive. First, for inter-generational households extending to grandparents, the compactness of these two-bedroom flats is viewed as hardly conducive. Second, the design of the common areas does not allow the effective dispersal of an array of sounds and smells emanating from the units. Instead, they reverberate and circulate in the corridors of the building. Finally, the high density of residents coupled with the poor maintenance of these buildings effectively disfigure these structures into vertical 'slums' and places of unhealthy ferment.

Where formerly there was the comparative safety of ethno-religious homogeneity because of the distance afforded by segregated dwelling in the cluster of squatter settlements, these structures have blurred the sacred boundaries in quotidian ways. For instance, my Hindu-Indian informants usually use a hand bell during their daily domestic *pujas* (prayers). Although they are clearly audible to neighbouring units, the 'religious noises' that are produced are momentary and localized. By comparison, my informants feel that the amplified and reverberated sound of the *azan subuh* (call to prayer at dawn) issuing out of a *surau* school

166   *Yeoh Seng Guan*

located within the building is of a different scale. These wake-up calls are not relevant to them, and are seen as culturally insensitive. But because they fear causing ill-feelings to their Muslim neighbours and inviting possible retaliatory action from both local Muslim residents and entrepreneurial politicians who want to be seen as defending Islam against its detractors, they have not publicly sought any redress. Unaccustomed to a Muslim soundscape, the issue of 'religious noise' extends as well to middle-class and ethno-religiously mixed residential areas where new mosques with powerful loudspeakers allow for greater aural reach than before.

Even in commercial precincts which have been ethno-religiously pluralist for decades, the interplay between government policies, demographic changes, local-level entrepreneurial politics has sometimes led to reduced opportunities to be interpreted in a racialized manner. This was evident in one of the oldest and lucrative commercial enclaves in Kuala Lumpur – 'Little India/Masjid India' – where I conducted fieldwork between 2004 and 2006 (Yeoh 2009a). In the past, 'Little India/Masjid India' has had a far more varied and unregulated ethnoscape – Chinese, Punjabis, Malays, and Tamils – eking out a living. But in part prompted by the overarching policies discussed earlier and by more recent urban planning innovations, 'Little India/Masjid India' has been re-branded as a destination for a host of *halal* cuisine and goods, and for tourists to visit and gaze at the old 'Malay' quarter of Kuala Lumpur. Subsequently, long established non-Muslim businesses have also found it financially necessary to voluntarily re-locate or change their usual wares and services to cater to the Muslim clientele.

At the time of my fieldwork, the religious festivals of Hindu Deepavali and Muslim Hari Raya Puasa were in close temporal proximity, a calendrical cycle that recurs once every three decades. Street vendors who had been setting up temporary stalls along the spine of the enclave during their respective festivities for several years without any problems suddenly found themselves caught in a novel crossroad. The Kuala Lumpur City Hall had decided to allot Malay-Muslim traders with 78 per cent of the 556 bazaar lots. Disgruntled Indian-Hindu traders contended that they were more accustomed to at least 350 lots instead. To suggestions by City Hall that they shift to the Indian–Hindu enclave of Brickfields during this special period, the traders reiterated their desire of doing business in familiar places. When City Hall officials did not relent on their decision, the affected traders read this episode as yet another instance of their continued neglect and marginalization as working class Hindu-Indians.

To be sure, the large and growing population of both working and middle class Malay-Muslims has significantly altered the entrepreneurial networks of production and marketing, and consumption patterns in Kuala Lumpur. While Johan Fischer has characterized this shift as the 'halalization of consumption', trajectories of the constriction and broadening of religious pluralism are evident (Fischer 2008). For instance, in order to tap into this substantial niche market, many non-Muslim local and foreign businesses have modified their products and services to meet an array of *halal* specifications monitored by the relevant Islamic agency. In the process, they have learnt to be more familiar with Islamic sensibilities and sensitivities. Many others have also entered into innovative business ventures with Muslim entrepreneurs, adding yet another complexion to a longer genealogy of Sino-Malay business partnerships in the country (e.g. Chin 2010). Similarly, Malay-Muslim foodways have broadened with the rise of urbane and cosmopolitan Muslims in Kuala Lumpur. Many traditional Muslim food businesses (including street vendors) have taken to learning the cuisine of non-Muslims but substituting non-*halal* ingredients with alternatives.

Nevertheless, the push to overtly comply with *halal* requirements does not automatically translate to a bona-fide appreciation of everyday religious pluralism. In a number of reported cases, it is evident that the much-valued *halal* logo has taken on the auras of both a commodity fetish and an ambivalent signifier. In business establishments, the display of the *halal* logo does not necessarily guarantee the 'purity' of the item consumed. On the one hand, imitation logos can be purchased. On the other, the convoluted chains of production and distribution also allow for the possibility of multiple points of contamination en route. For some Muslims, this has necessitated the additional practice of 'purifying' these goods through efficacious rituals and prayers in order to disperse doubt.

Conclusion

By providing these selective anecdotes of religious disenfranchisement (real and perceived), I do not wish to paint an alarmist nor determinist picture of the health of inter-religious relations in modern day cosmopolitan Kuala Lumpur. Indeed, it says something about the good sense and goodwill of ordinary Malaysians that religious conviviality continues to be vibrant in spite of the many acts of un-conviviality by groups which claim to speak for their collective interests (e.g. Loh 2010). In everyday conversations and in my ongoing fieldwork, it appears that many working class Malay-Muslims are not aware of what has been done in their name. And if they are, they do not approve of how these authorities and vigilante groups offend the sensitivities of non-Muslims. Similarly, for the younger generation of well-educated (especially in foreign universities) and urbane middle-class Malay-Muslims well acquainted with the libertarian powers of new media, the propagandist slant of traditional mainstream media has had a weakening hold in buttressing a jaundiced view of Malaysian citizenry based on 'race' and 'religion'.

Their aspirations are echoed in an array of cosmopolitan Malay-Muslim public intellectuals and Muslim civil society groups well known for their stance in upholding democracy, social justice and human dignity across ethno-religious lines (e.g. Hooker and Noraini 2003). They counsel against over-zealousness in adopting a Wahhabi-style reformist version of Islamic governance to 'purify' supposedly syncretistic local Muslim popular practices. They find the recent spate of *fatwas* and the preoccupation of the Islamic authorities with moral policing rather disconcerting, idiosyncratically myopic and unflattering to the wider ecumenical concerns of their faith. However, they are not in the position of formal power. Neither are they given much media space by the government authorities

168   *Yeoh Seng Guan*

to challenge the dominant mind-set of the religious intelligentsia and open up the public sphere for healthy debates. Instead, what often prevail in the media – mainstream and alternative – are views that close down or ostracize the exploration of difference, whether along the intellectual or experiential planes.

In my brief account of actually existing religious pluralism in Kuala Lumpur, I have appropriated Abdoumaliq Simone's imagery of 'crossroads' to contemplate how the contingent present might be grasped. In this regard, a significant 'crossroad' that was traversed not long ago is the electoral voting patterns of the General Elections of 2008. An analysis of this particular line of flight suggests a discernible dilution, if not confounding, of ethnic identity markers in shaping political decisions among the younger generation of urban voters. This trend is expected to broaden and deepen as the traits of city-ness spread rhizomatically. For decades, the ruling coalition, Barisan Nasional, and their oppositional political nemeses, have opportunistically relied on this colonialist-derived formula to territorialize, manage and guide democracy in the country. The signs are that as this particular political fiction weakens, other kinds of ideological interpellation come to the fore. For now, the rallying and differentiating powers of 'religion' are still salient given its transcendental referents, long historical arc, and its powerful economy of affect. As my discussion of the Valentine's Day episode suggests – and it is one of many others over the last few years – zealous attempts to accentuate the putative danger of hybrid cultural forms in urbane Malaysia, while effective in the short term, may have the unintended doubling force of unravelling its own bifurcated logic and potentially fragment hegemonic positions. Whether this itself will automatically lead to a 'crossroad' that will substantively be more religiously convivial for the residents of Kuala Lumpur – by 'getting rid of the familiar ways of and plans for doing things and finding new possibilities by virtue of whatever is gathered there' (Simone 2010: 192) – is as yet vaguely discernible and largely unthinkable at this point in time.

Notes

1   A recent variant of this thesis is explained in terms of the 'over-sanctification' of Islam in Malaysian society, viz., a concern by religious authorities on the details of the everyday lives of Muslims (Lee 2010).
2   In the twelfth Federal and State Elections held on March 2008, the ruling coalition, Barisan Nasional (National Front), lost not only its two-thirds majority in Parliament but also five of the 13 states to the Pakatan Rakyat opposition coalition. In the Federal Territory of Kuala Lumpur, ten of the twelve seats were captured by Pakatan Rakyat. One of the states (Perak) later reverted back to Barisan Nasional because of defections. This 'political tsunami' was unprecedented since Malaysia gained its independence in 1957.
3   Other celebratory events identified as lending themselves easily to 'illicit sex' are the New Year's Eve and the *Merdeka* (Independence) public gatherings.
4   See 'Politicians say nay to V-Day "immorality checks"', *Malaysiakini*, 10 February 2011. Available at www.malaysiakini.com.ezproxy.lib.monash.edu.au/news/155699 and 'Those who demonise V-Day the real enemies', *The Star*, 15 February 2011.
5   See 'Chua: V-Day "policing" proof of Islamic state agenda', *Malaysiakini*, 10 February 2011. Available at www.malaysiakini.com.ezproxy.lib.monash.edu.au/

Actually existing pluralism in Kuala Lumpur   169

news/155715. See also 'It's all right to observe Valentine Day, says Khairy', *The Star*, 12 February 2011 and 'Azmin: Celebrate Valentine's Day but know your limits', *The Star*, 13 February 2011.

6 See 'Pakatan states plan Valentine's Day crackdown', *Malaysiakini*, 9 February 2011. Available at www.malaysiakini.com.ezproxy.lib.monash.edu.au/news/155576. See also 'Embattled PAS Youth said statement misunderstood', *Malaysiakini*, 10 February 2011. Available at www.malaysiakini.com.ezproxy.lib.monash.edu.au/news/155711

7 See '96 Muslims nabbed in Valentine clampdown', *Malaysiakini*, 15 February 2011 and '88 Muslims nabbed for khalwat', *The Star*, 15 February 2011.

8 See 'V-Day romps elude PAS' morality rounds', *Malaysiakini*, 15 February 2011. Available at www.malaysiakini.com.ezproxy.lib.monash.edu.au/news/156090.

9 See 'V-Day flowers from DAP, chocolates from Gerakan', *Malaysiakini*, 14 February 2011. Available at www.malaysiakini.com.ezproxy.lib.monash.edu.au/news/156044.

10 Formed in 1986, the Christian Federation of Malaysia is a coalition of three major groupings of different Christian traditions and persuasions – namely, the Roman Catholic Church, the Council of Churches of Malaysia, and the National Evangelical Christian Fellowship.

11 See 'V-Day: CCM "hurt" by assumptions made in *fatwa*', *Malaysiakini*, 11 February 2011. Available at www.malaysiakini.com.ezproxy.lib.monash.edu.au/news/155775.

12 www.themalaysianinsider.com/malaysia/article/no-love-in-kl-and-selangor/

13 Indicative of the invested nature of contemporary historical research in Malaysia, the foundational myth of Kuala Lumpur has been re-visited and contested in recent years. Contenders include entrepreneurial Bugis, Sumatran Mandailing royalty, and Chinese-Hakka tin miners.

14 In many cases, British and other foreigner accounts did not distinguish between the varieties of geographically specific sub-ethnic or even different ethnic groups residing in the towns and villages they encountered. Later, in the census categories, they became conveniently lumped together as 'Chinese', 'Malay', and 'Indian' for administrative purposes.

15 This was later formalized in the Federal Constitution as Articles 11 (1) and 11 (4) which, while guaranteeing the freedom of religion, also prohibit the propagation of any religion to Muslims. Under various state enactments, it is an offence to propagate religious doctrines other than Islam to Muslims. There are, however, no corresponding laws prohibiting the propagation of Islam to non-Muslims.

16 Interview with Mahathir Mohamad, *Utusan Melayu*, 26–27 October 1984, cited in Hussin Mutalib (1993: 30).

17 See the annual human rights reports published by the local civil society group, Suaram (http://suaram-blog.blogspot.com/).

18 The idea of an inter-faith council was first mooted in 1983 in response to official statements that Malaysia would be transformed into an Islamic theocratic state. The Council of Churches of Malaysia played in a key role in its formation.

19 See Press Statement, 'Declaration of the Freedom of Religion in Malaysia' by Catholic Bishops Conference of Malaysia, 1 August 2002.

20 See Press Statement, Christian Federation of Malaysia National Day Message: Fifteenth anniversary of Merdeka, 29 August 2007.

21 For more details, see Suaram (2011), the chapter on 'Freedom of Religion and Matters Pertaining Religion', in Malaysia Human Rights Report 2010 (Petaling Jaya: Suaram Komunikasi, 2011).

22 The 2000 census figures indicate that ethnic 'Chinese' is still the majority at 43 per cent of the Kuala Lumpur City population of about 1.4 million. However, the 'Bumiputera' (Malays and indigenous peoples) component of the city has substantially increased by 77 per cent over the past two decades to make up 38 per cent (Kuala Lumpur Structure Plan 2020: A World Class City, p. 4).

23 Through the viral powers of new media and amoebic re-tellings in temples, these

170   *Yeoh Seng Guan*

narratives arguably fuelled the political agitation of Hindus and Indians, which culminated in the unprecedented Hindraf (Hindu Action Front) mass civil protest rally of November 2007. The heavy-handed treatment of these protestors by the police authorities and the inaccurate reading of the mood of the times by the Indian political elite subsequently significantly influenced the results of the twelfth General Elections the following year (e.g. Yeoh 2009b). See Willford (2006) for a broader discussion of Tamil identity politics in Malaysia.

References

Ackerman, S. and Lee, R. (1990 [1988]) *Heaven in Transition: Non-Muslim Religious Innovation and Ethnic Identity in Malaysia,* Kuala Lumpur: Forum.

Ahmad Fauzi, A.H. (2000) 'Political Dimensions of Religious Conflict in Malaysia: State Responses to an Islamic Movement', *Indonesia and the Malay World*, 28(80): 3–65.

Chin, Y.W. (2010) 'Sino-Bumiputera Partnerships: Promoting Inter-ethnic Relations at Mid-level', in Loh, F.K.W. (ed.) *Building Bridges, Crossing Boundaries: Everyday Forms of Inter-ethnic Peace Building in Malaysia,* Kajang & Jakarta: Malaysian Social Science Association and Ford Foundation.

Cohn, B. (1996) *Colonialism and its Form of Knowledge: The British in India,* Princeton, NJ: Princeton University Press.

de Certeau, M. (1984) *The Practice of Everyday Life,* Berkeley: University of California Press.

Dirks, N. (2001) *Castes of Mind: Colonialism and the Making of Modern India,* Princeton and Oxford: Princeton University Press.

Fischer, J. (2008) *Proper Islamic Consumption: Shopping among the Malays in Modern Malaysia,* Copenhagen: Nordic Institute of Asian Studies.

Gullick, J.M. (2000) *A History of Kuala Lumpur, 1856–1939,* Kuala Lumpur: Malaysian Branch of the Royal Asiatic Society.

Hamayotsu, K. (2003) 'Politics of Syariah Reform: The Making of the State Religio-legal Apparatus', in Hooker, V. and Norani, O. (eds) *Malaysia: Islam, Society and Politics,* Singapore: Institute of Southeast Asian Studies.

Hannerz, U. (1992) *Cultural Complexity. Studies in the Social Organization of Meaning,* New York: Columbia University Press.

Hooker, V. and Norani, O. (eds) (2003) *Malaysia. Islam, Society and Politics*, Singapore: Institute of Southeast Asian Studies.

Kahn, J. (2006) *Other Malays: Nationalism and Cosmopolitanism in the Modern Malay World*, Singapore: National University of Singapore Press.

Kuala Lumpur Structure Plan 2020: A World Class City, Kuala Lumpur: City Hall.

Kusno, A. (2000) *Behind the Postcolonial: Architecture, Urban Space and Political Cultures in Indonesia,* New York: Routledge.

Lee, J. (2010) 'Oversanctification, Autonomy and Islam in Malaysia', *Totalitarian Movements and Political Religions*, 11(1): 25–43.

Lee, R. (1988) 'Patterns of Religious Tension in Malaysia', *Asian Survey*, 28(4): 400–18.

Lim, H.K. (1978) *The Evolution of the Urban System in Malaya,* Kuala Lumpur: Penerbit Universiti Malaya.

Loh, F.K.W. (2010) (ed.) *Building Bridges, Crossing Boundaries: Everyday Forms of Inter-ethnic Peace-building in Malaysia,* Kajang & Jakarta: Malaysian Social Science Association & Ford Foundation.

Hussin, M. (1993) *Islam in Malaysia: From Revivalism to Islamic State,* Singapore: Singapore University Press.

Peletz, M. (2002) *Islamic Modern: Religious Courts and Cultural Politics in Malaysia,* Princeton, NJ: Princeton University Press.

Riddell, P.G. (2005) 'Islamization, Civil Society and Religious Minorities in Malaysia', in Nathan, K.S. and Kamali, M.H. (eds), *Islam in Southeast Asia: Political, Social and Strategic Challenges for the 21st Century,* Singapore: Institute of Southeast Asian Studies.

Simone, A. (2010) *City Life from Jakarta to Dakar: Movements at the Crossroads,* New York and London: Routledge.

Suaram (2011) *Malaysia Human Rights Report 2010,* Petaling Jaya: Suaram Komunikasi.

Tan, N. and Lee, J. (2008) (eds) *Religion under Siege? Lina Joy, the Islamic State and Freedom of Faith,* Kuala Lumpur: Kinibooks.

Wain, B. (2009) *Malaysian Maverick: Mahathir Mohamad in Turbulent Times,* Basingstoke, UK: Palgrave Macmillan.

Willford, A. (2006) *Cage of Freedom: Tamil Identity and the Ethnic Fetish in Malaysia,* Ann Arbor: University of Michigan Press.

Yeoh, S.G. (2001) 'Creolised Utopias: Squatter Colonies and the Postcolonial City in Malaysia', *Sojourn: Journal of Social Issues in Southeast Asia*, 16(1): 102–24.

Yeoh, S.G. (2005a) 'Managing Sensitivities: Religious Pluralism, Civil Society and Inter-faith Relations in Malaysia', *The Round Table: The Commonwealth Journal of International Affairs*, 94(382): 629–40.

Yeoh, S.G. (2005b) 'House, Kampung and Taman: Spatial Hegemony and the Politics (and Poetics) of Space in Urban Malaysia', *Crossroads: An Interdisciplinary Journal of Southeast Asian Studies*, 17(2): 128–58.

Yeoh, S.G. (2009a) 'Limiting Cosmopolitanism: Street-life Little India, Kuala Lumpur,' in Mayaram, S. (ed.), *The Other Global City*, London and New York: Routledge.

Yeoh, S.G. (2009b) 'The Streets of Kuala Lumpur: City-space, "Race" and Civil Disobedience', in Butcher M. and Velayutham, S. (eds), *Dissent and Cultural Resistance in Asia's Cities,* London and New York: Routledge.

Yeoh, S.G. (2011) 'In Defence of the Secular?: Islamization, Christians and (New) Politics in Urbane Malaysia', *Asian Studies Review*, 35(1): 83–103.

Part III

Pluralism and individual identities

10 Cosmopolitan Islam and inclusive Chineseness

Chinese-style mosques in Indonesia

Hew Wai-Weng

As Khan (2008: 52) has pointed out, 'the mosque is Islam's most emblematic building, as well as, an expression of collective identity'. Through Chinese-style mosques, Chinese Muslim leaders in Indonesia declare that there can be a Chinese way of being Muslim and that converting to Islam does not mean giving up Chinese cultural traditions. After the collapse of Suharto's New Order regime (1965–98), at least five Chinese-style mosques have been built across Indonesia, reflecting the return of Chinese cultural symbols into public spaces, as well as the reassertion of tolerance of Indonesian Islam. Such mosques always adopt the architecture of mosques common in mainland China, yet these are also reconfigured within Indonesia's local contexts. This choice can be seen as a manifestation of ongoing negotiations between transnational imagination and local configuration aimed at creating a distinctive 'Indonesian Chinese Muslim' cultural expression.

As argued by Appadurai (1996) and Gupta and Ferguson (1992), identity formation in contemporary societies is not only situated within boundaries of a territorial space, but also configured across and in-between spaces. It is both informed by the interaction between locally specific practices of selfhood and the dynamics of global positioning (Friedman 1994). Studying the Pakistani Muslims in Manchester, UK, Werbner (2002) examines the complex and interconnected relations between transnational flows and local forces; and suggests that there are multiple transnational orientations within such local communities. In this contribution, I explore the spatial dynamics of Chinese Muslim identity practices through three dimensions. First, I investigate the transnational connection to Muslims in mainland China and in the Middle East; second, the translocal linkage of Chinese Muslims from different parts in Indonesia; third, the local adaption of their identities. To a certain extent, through Chinese-style mosques, Chinese Muslim leaders creatively express and claim their connections to the 'diasporic Chinese', 'Islamic *ummah*' and Indonesian society, to manifest their unique identity.

This chapter also discusses both the symbolic and operational dimensions of Chinese-style mosques in Indonesia, dedicating particular attention to the Cheng Hoo mosques in Surabaya and Palembang, and thus argue that such mosques are a form of ethno-religious expression, as well as a local cosmopolitan space.[1]

176   Hew Wai-Weng

Symbolically, Chinese-style mosques can be seen as a place for representation of a distinctive Chinese Muslim identity in Indonesia. It is an attempt to construct a distinctive image of Chinese Muslims, pursued by combining both Chinese and Islamic elements. This is arguably a form of intentional hybridity that emphasizes symbolic unity and promotes a fixed image of Chinese Muslims in Indonesia.[2] Given that Chinese Muslims are dispersed across the archipelago, the effort to replicate the Surabaya Cheng Hoo Mosque in other cities, to some extent, also helps to forge a translocal imagination of Chinese Muslim cultural identity in the country.[3]

Operationally, instead, Chinese-style mosques become spaces for contestation of multiple Chinese Muslim identities in Indonesia. In the mosque, Chinese Muslims from all walks of life negotiate themselves between not only Muslim and Chinese identities, but also diversified Islamic and Chinese traditions. This is arguably a form of everyday hybridization that emphasizes organic diversity and implies fluid identities among Chinese Muslims. Both inclusive architectural designs and socio-religious activities show the Cheng Hoo Mosque as both a sacred and social space shared by all ethnic and religious groups. For example, during a Ramadan night in 2008, while Muslims (both Chinese and non-Chinese) were performing their evening *taraweh* prayers (non-obligatory evening prayers which take place during the fasting month) at the mosque, non-Muslims (mostly Chinese) were practising *qigong* (Chinese breathing exercise) at the corridor of the Indonesian Chinese Muslim Association's (PITI, Persatuan Islam Tionghoa Indonesia) office in the mosque compound. The mosque, then, can be seen as a local cosmopolitan space where diverse cultures converge and mingle.[4]

Changing mosque architecture

Mosque architecture can take various forms, taking into account local building materials, climatic factors and craft skills, as well as major political and historical events, in which the mosque serves as an important visible representation of Muslim identity and values (Frishman and Khan, 2002: 14). The shape of old mosques in Indonesia and Malaysia has different forms when compared to mosques in the rest of the world. Most of the old mosques, such as those in Demak, Banten and Kudus do not have domes and minarets, but tiered roofs and are often equipped with a *bedug* (large drum inside the mosque to summon to prayer). These mosques mostly predate colonization and were highly influenced by local cultures (Malay, Javanese, Chinese) and religions (Buddhism and Hinduism), rather than being inspired by Middle Eastern architectural styles (Nasir 2004; Heuken 2003).

The first dome-shaped mosque in Indonesia dates from 1881, and it was built by the Dutch colonial government. It is the Baiturrahman Mosque of Banda Aceh. Over time, domes and minarets became the dominant features of mosques also in this part of the Muslim world. After independence, such mosques were regarded as a marker of progress and modernity, as shown by the Istiqlal Mosque in Jakarta, built between 1961 and 1978. Rising modernist and puritan Islam, as well

Islam and Chinese-style mosques in Indonesia 177

as financial support originating in the Middle East (especially Saudi Arabia) also led to the spread of 'pan-Islamic models' of mosques. At the same time, in order to promote the rather 'secular' state ideology, Pancasila,[5] and to suppress political Islam, the New Order regime promoted the establishment of traditional tiered-roof mosques through the Pancasila Muslim Charity Foundation (Yayasan Amal Bakti Muslim Pancasila), established in 1982 (O'Neill 1993). Instead of the traditional crescent and star, the ornament on the roof is a reproduction of the word 'Allah' in Arabic script within a five-sided frame, a visual expression of the supremacy of the Pancasila ideology.

After the fall of Suharto in 1998, domes and minarets regained their popularity. This change can be seen in the fate of the Bandung Great Mosque. In the 1950s, it received a dome which was then replaced in 1970 with a traditional roof. Between February 2001 and June 2003, the mosque once again underwent a transformation: the renovated mosque now has two small domes and one large one, and two 810-metre high minarets (Dijk 2009).

Although Middle-Eastern inspired mosque architecture is prevalent, other competing architectures are not absent in Indonesia. One of the contrasting forms is the multipurpose and hybrid-design mosque, such as the Grand Mosque of Central Java in Semarang, which was completed in 2006 (Wiryomartono 2009). It is not only a building for worship, but also a place for cultural, business and leisure activities. In terms of architecture, it is eclectic, adopting various styles, forms and decorative motifs, attempting to blend indigenous Javanese, European and Middle Eastern building traditions.

Another interesting phenomenon in post-1998 Indonesia is the establishment of Chinese-style mosques, which I will discuss in the following sections. These diverse mosque architectures also reflect the plurality of Islamic practices, as well as the ongoing debates about 'Arabization', modernization and localization of Islam in Indonesia.

Chinese-influenced mosques

Although Chinese-style mosques are commonly seen as a new phenomenon, Chinese involvement in building mosques and Chinese influence on mosque design has existed for a long time in Indonesia. For example, there is Chinese influence on the architecture of old mosques and tombs in Java, such as the tombs of Sunan Giri in Gresik, the design of the Cirebon palaces and the architecture of the Demak mosque in Central Java (Lombard and Salmon 2001; Al-Qurtuby 2003). Some mosques are also designed and built by Chinese Muslims, such as Kebun Jeruk Mosque in Jakarta and Sumenep Mosque in Madura.

These Chinese influences on Indonesian mosques had declined during Dutch colonial rule, as Chinese traditions and Islam were seen as incompatible and sometimes even conflicting. During the height of New Order period, conversion to Islam was seen as a marker of total assimilation, and the influence of Chinese culture on Islam was a taboo. Only during the late New Order, did Chinese Muslims begin to find a niche for expressing their identities. With the support of various Muslim organizations, Lautze Mosque was established in Jakarta by the Karem Oei Foundation, in 1994. As the mosque was originally a shop and residence-turned-prayer house, the Chinese influence on Lautze Mosque is rather modest and implicit, reflected in its red-colour entrance door and walls inside the mosque, as well as in multiple Chinese-style Arabic calligraphy artworks hanging on the wall. Mosque Lautze II in Bandung resembles the design of its predecessor. The first explicit and indeed trend-setting Chinese-designed mosque was the Cheng Hoo Mosque in Surabaya, followed by the homonymous one in Palembang.

Symbolic unity: Identity manifestation through the Cheng Hoo Mosque

Chinese Muslim leaders have strategically used the political openness of the post-New Order period to celebrate and promote their distinct identity, for example through the Cheng Hoo Mosque in Surabaya (see Figure 10.1). This was established by East Java PITI through its Muhammad Cheng Hoo Foundation (Yayasan Haji Muhammad Cheng Hoo Indonesia). Its construction began in 2001 and was completed one year later. The mosque architecture has been inspired by the *Niu Jie* (Ox Street) Mosque in Beijing, which has more than a thousand years of history. The modification to its architectural design has been pursued by Aziz Johan, a member of PITI from Bojonegoro, East Java, and supported by a technical team consisting of Chinese Muslim leaders from within PITI.

Figure 10.1 The Surabaya Cheng Hoo Mosque (photo by Hew Wai-Weng)

Willy Pangestu, one of the Chinese Muslim leaders, member of the mosque design team, explained to me that: 'We wanted to build a mosque that can vividly show Chinese character. We studied a few mosques in mainland China and we decided to use the historical Niu Jie Mosque in Beijing as our blueprint' (Interview, Willy Pangestu, 6 November 2008). Although there are some Chinese-influenced old mosques and prominent local Chinese Muslim figures in Indonesia, PITI did not draw on them in building their Surabaya mosque. Instead, PITI adopted China's mosque architecture and named the mosque after a famous Muslim admiral from mainland China, Cheng Ho, to manifest a distinguishing image of Chinese Muslims' cultural identity, and to emphasize the contribution of Cheng Ho in disseminating Islam in Java.

The temple-like design provoked some disagreement among Chinese Muslims in PITI. As Willy told me, some worried such a design might violate Islamic teachings, alienate local Muslims and promote exclusivity. There were also some concerns that the contribution of non-Muslims to the mosque might not be *halal* (permitted under Islamic law). However, with the endorsement of Muslim organizations and the local government, he managed to convince those opposed to that idea that Chinese-style mosques are not only acceptable under Islam, but actually desirable as a manifestation of cultural pluralism and religious tolerance. Indeed, since its establishment, the mosque has been regularly featured in various media outlets, visited by many prominent Muslims and listed as a site of religious tourism.

Arguably, there are at least two different, yet not contradictory, motivations behind the establishment of the Chinese-style mosque: the first one is ethnic empowerment (mostly promoted by businessmen and intellectuals), and the second is religious preaching (mostly promoted by religious teachers and preachers). Regarding ethnic empowerment, Cheng Hoo Mosque acknowledges the contribution of ethnic Chinese to spreading Islam, in the hope that 'anti-Chinese' sentiments among Muslims would be reduced. This notion is supported by some non-Muslim Chinese businessmen, as most of the funds for building the mosque came from them. Challenging the dominant discourse of 'assimilation through Islam' during the New Order period, they built a Chinese-style mosque to promote the idea of 'blending through Islam', suggesting that being a Muslim places the ethnic Chinese closer to non-Chinese Indonesians (the majority of whom are Muslims), but not at the expense of losing their Chinese cultural identity.

Meanwhile, many Chinese Muslim preachers and religious teachers supported the establishment of the Chinese-style mosque, but for different reasons. They believed that the strategic use of Chinese cultural symbols could show Islam as a universal religion and not a religion for 'indigenous' Indonesians only. In fact, most of the Indonesian Islamic organizations, including Nahdlatul Ulama (NU) and Muhammadiyah, endorse the establishment of Chinese-style mosques as a form to *dakwah* (preaching) to Chinese Indonesians. As stated by former chairman of NU East Java, Ali Maschan, 'the construction of Chinese-style mosques will help the development of the *dakwah* movement in Indonesia, especially among ethnic Chinese, who will potentially convert to Islam. Even though they

180   Hew Wai-Weng

do not convert to Islam, at least, the mosque will reduce their prejudice toward Islam' (Interview, Ali Maschan, 27 November 2008).

Mixing Chineseness and Islam

In this section, through a discussion of Cheng Hoo Mosque's architectural design, I argue that the mosque is both representational and aspirational, as it 'says' and 'declares' something, which hints at social interactions, ethnic identities and religious discourses in Indonesia. The architectural design of Cheng Hoo Mosque 'says' that Islam and 'Chineseness' can get along together, 'declares' that one can be an authentic Chinese and truly Indonesian, as well as 'promote' inclusive and tolerant Islam.

Indeed, Cheng Hoo Mosque, a mixing of Chinese, Islamic and Javanese cultures, is a clear statement that Chinese, Islamic and Indonesian identities are compatible. According to the mosque handbook (YHMCHI 2008), its outlook resembles the architecture of *klenteng* (Chinese temple) and is intended to display the Chineseness of Chinese Muslims in Indonesia, as well as 'to remind the Buddhist forefathers of ethnic Chinese'. Different from Chinese temples, the roof of the pagoda-like building is carved with the word 'Allah'. Decorations, such as animal-like ornaments were omitted because they might be seen as un-Islamic by many Muslims. The building is dominated by three colours: red, green and yellow. The green refers to the Islamic tradition; the dominant red represents Chinese cultural traditions, symbolising the spirits of luck, fortune and prosperity. To emphasize inclusiveness, the handbook about the mosque is published in four languages: Indonesian, English, Chinese and Arabic.

The main hall of the mosque is 11 x 9 metres large, with an eight-sided roof (*pat-kwa*). The length of 11 meters symbolizes the measurement of the Ka'ba (cubicle shrine within the Masjid al-Haram mosque complex in Mecca), demonstrating the commitment to the Islamic faith. The length of 9 meters represents the number of the *wali songo* (the nine Muslim saints that according to local beliefs Islamized Java), showing an appreciation of local Javanese traditions. Meanwhile, the design of an eight-sided roof (*pat-kwa*) not only characterises the philosophy of luck and prosperity shared by the ethnic Chinese, but also indicates Islam as a religion of peace. The usage of *pat-kwa* design suggests that the acceptance of Islamic and Javanese tradition does not necessarily mean the fading of Chinese cultural identity.

Through the interior design of Cheng Hoo Mosque, Chinese Muslim leaders intended to send a message that the Mosque belongs to all Muslim groups, and that this is a site of interaction between diverse Muslim organizations, especially NU and Muhammadiyah. By installing a *bedug* drum and a podium (a pulpit used by an imam or preacher to deliver a sermon), they appropriate both the traditions of NU and Muhammadiyah to show that the mosque is a prayer hall for all Muslims regardless of their religious affiliations. A *bedug* was therefore placed on the side of the mosque, which is common for NU followers, as well as Muslims in China. Meanwhile, the podium is specially designed to suit

Muhammadiyah practices, as its front is closed rather than open. Not only being inclusive of diverse Islamic groups, Cheng Hoo Mosque also tries to show that Islam is tolerant of other religions, namely Christianity. In the front of the main building, there is a space which is used by the imam to lead prayers and deliver sermons. According to the handbook of the mosque (YHMCHI 2008), this part of the mosque was constructed like a church's door (resembling a Romanesque arch), which means Islam acknowledges Jesus Christ as one of God's messengers, as well as, striving for peace and respecting other religions.

On the right side of the Mosque there is a relief of Muhammad Cheng Ho and his fleet, which illustrates his journey from China to Indonesia in the fifteenth and sixteenth century. The commemoration of Cheng Ho through the relief and the naming of the mosque have different meanings for different audiences. For Chinese Muslims, it delivers a message that being a Chinese Muslim has long precedent, as 600 years ago there was a Chinese admiral who was a pious Muslim. For non-Chinese Muslims, it promotes the contribution of Cheng Ho to the spread of Islam in Indonesia. For non-Muslim Chinese, it proves that being a Muslim does not mean discarding one's 'Chineseness'.

The strategic architectural design of the Cheng Hoo Mosque does not symbolize an existing ethno-religious reality, but rather seeks to bring a new reality into being. As I discussed elsewhere (Hew 2011), Chinese Muslim identities in Indonesia are fluid, and different individuals have different attitudes towards their religious practices and cultural orientations. Through the mosque, some Chinese Muslim leaders try to promote a distinctive Chinese Muslim identity through the co-existence of Islamic and Chinese identities. Indeed, the materiality and tangibility of the mosque makes Chinese Muslim cultural identity unequivocally 'real' and therefore essential in their identity construction. As the founder of the mosque, Bambang Sujanto says:

> The population of Chinese Muslims is small, diverse and scattered. As happened in the past, our identity will easily disappear or be assimilated into the Muslim majority. Thus, we need a physical space – a mosque that can project and uphold our identity. The structure of mosque could stand for long time, and sustain our uniqueness over a few generations. Converting to Islam does not mean giving up our Chinese cultural identity. There can be a Chinese way of being Muslim.
> (Interview, Bambang Sujanto, 27 November 2008)

The intentional mixing of Chinese, Islam and local cultural elements expressed by the architectural design, are also reflected in the activities of the mosque. As I observed during the *halal-bihalal* (mutual forgiving event) and sixth anniversary celebration of Cheng Hoo Mosque in October 2008, the strategic intercultural mixing can be seen from the food, entertainment program, prayers and invited guests. The event began with dinner that serves both *halal* Chinese and Indonesian dishes. Various entertainment programs, including Chinese traditional music performances, and traditional dances from Java and Southern Kalimantan

182   Hew Wai-Weng

were then staged. The *do'a* prayer for the event was recited by Gunawan Hidayat, a Chinese Muslim religious teacher, and then translated in both Indonesian and Mandarin. Interestingly, the Indonesian translation was read by Wang Zhan, a Hui Muslim student from China who was studying at the State Islamic Institute (IAIN, Institut Agama Islam Negeri) Surabaya; while the Mandarin translation was read by Dion Sultan, a Javanese Muslim who had pursued his undergraduate studies in mainland China.

Among the prominent invited guests of the celebration were former governor of East Java Muhammad Noer, leading Chinese entrepreneur Alim Markus, the chairman of the Surabaya Chinese Association (Paguyuban Tionghoa Surabaya) Lin Ou Yen, as well as many local religious scholars. The then chairman of NU, Hasyim Muzadi, was supposed to give a religious talk, but he was replaced by Muiziddin, a Chinese preacher. This shows the deliberate efforts of Chinese Muslim leaders to promote cultural diversity and religious inclusivity.

Transnational connections and local configurations of the Cheng Hoo Mosque

The monthly magazine of the East Java PITI, *Komunitas* ('Community'), creatively displays both the images of Niu Jie Mosque in Beijing and Cheng Hoo Mosque in Surabaya, on the cover of its 2008 Idul Fitri edition. Through the Cheng Hoo Mosque, Chinese Muslim leaders in Surabaya draw on both the architectural design of old mosques in China and the religious symbols of two major local Muslim organizations, NU and Muhammadiyah, to manifest their unique identity.

Chinese Muslims in Indonesia are mostly converts and ethnically different from Hui Muslim in China, thus there are no direct historical relations between them.[6] Although there might have been some Hui Muslims in Java during the fifteenth and sixteenth centuries, most of them had been assimilated. Most recent migrants are majority non-Muslim Han and almost all Chinese Muslim leaders in PITI are converted ethnic Hans. Furthermore, in terms of mosque styles, there is a tendency to 'Arabization' among Hui Muslims in Xi An, China, as shown by the shifting style of mosque architecture: some new mosques built by Hui communities now adopt Arabic style, while the traditional Chinese style has been questioned as not sufficiently 'Islamic' (Gillette 2000). Despite the difference between Hui and Han, and the diversity and changing of Hui Islamic expression in China, many PITI leaders still construct their own Islamic tradition through imagined linkages with Muslims in China by promoting the history of Cheng Ho and building a Chinese-style mosque, because Islam in China is seen as more culturally authentic and historically rooted, compared to Chinese Muslims in Indonesia.

By referencing Muslim tradition in China, which they see as having a longer history than Islam in Indonesia, Chinese Muslims in Indonesia claim their religious credentials and reappropriate their cultural identities – because being Muslim and Chinese at the same time is neither improper or new. As stated by one

Islam and Chinese-style mosques in Indonesia 183

of the mosque design team members, the adoption of mosque architecture in China is 'a means of showing that Islam is not a new religion for ethnic Chinese as perceived by many Chinese and Muslim Indonesians. In fact, Islam arrived in China earlier than in Indonesia'. (Interview, Willy Pangestu, 6 November 2008.) To some extent, Hui Muslim culture in China has become their Islamic 'imaginary homeland' (Rushdie 1992), in which they find inspiration for identity formation in their 'living homeland', Indonesia.

Some Chinese Muslim leaders are also keen to develop transnational Chinese Muslim networks, by paying visits to Hui Muslim communities in China and inviting Hui Muslim leaders to visit Indonesia. For many of them, the cultivation of ties with Muslims in China does not undermine their national belonging, but allows them to promote better relations between ethnic Chinese and non-Chinese in Indonesia through their cooperation with local Muslim organizations. For example, in 2008, with the support of the Surabaya Chinese Association, the Cheng Hoo Foundation organized a trip for local NU and Muhammadiyah Muslim leaders to visit Muslim organizations and observe Muslim life in mainland China. Among the places they visited were Huai Sheng Mosque in Guangdong, the hometown of Cheng Ho, a garden named after him in Yunnan, as well as Beijing University and Niu Jie Mosque in Beijing (Tjahjono 2008). Bambang Sujanto, who led the trip, believed the trip would not only deepen the Muslim leaders' understanding of Islam in China, but also improve the perception of local Muslims towards ethnic Chinese in Indonesia. He said,

> By witnessing Muslim life in China themselves, the religious leaders will acknowledge that Islam has long existed in China and that Islamic practices are still alive today. We hope they will share this information with their followers in religious classes or talks. This will improve the perception of ordinary local Muslims towards Chinese Indonesians. We are not all non-believers. We are not just 'economic animals'.
>
> (Interview, Bambang Sujanto, 27 November 2008)

It is quite clear that for many Chinese Muslim leaders in Indonesia, the strategic transnational connection with Muslims in mainland China is not a form of desire for return, or attachment, to mainland China, but an effort to manifest their identity and to redefine their minority position. The transnational linkage does not imply disloyalty or lack of patriotism, and sometimes it helps promoting better relations between Indonesia and China, as well as between local Muslims and ethnic Chinese. This transnational linkage is driven by local purposes and is not for shaping politics towards mainland China. Thus, it is not a form of 'long-distance nationalism' (Anderson, 1992). To a certain extent, the transnational imagination of Chinese Muslims is similar to the diasporic action of Pakistani Muslims in Britain (Werbner 2002: 130), in which 'buying in' to a diaspora today includes buying into local citizenship and fighting for citizenship rights. The cultivation of ties with Muslims in China also adds another scenario to transnational Muslim linkages, which are often seen as hostile to ethnic culture (Roy

2004) and linked to the Middle East (Mandaville 2001). Nevertheless, it is important to note that the transnational linkages of Chinese Muslims in Indonesia are not only limited to Muslims in China, but extend to Muslims in other parts of the world, such as those in Palestine, as well as to transnational Islamic movements, such as the Hizbut Tahrir Indonesia and the Muslim Brotherhood.

Their transnational linkages have been locally configured through Chinese Muslims' connections with media networks, government officers, military leaders, religious groups and Chinese organizations. PITI especially has established good relations with both NU and Muhammadiyah in Surabaya. Before the construction of the mosque, PITI leaders asked NU and Muhammadiyah leaders to endorse the mosque design. Despite some objections from the hard-line Muslim individuals, both NU and Muhammadiyah leaders supported the design.[7] NU and Muhammadiyah leaders and preachers have been frequently invited to give sermons during Friday prayers and Islamic study sessions at the mosque. As some PITI leaders told me, one reason why the first Chinese-style mosque was built in Surabaya is because East Java is the stronghold of NU, which generally has more flexible attitudes towards various cultural expressions of Islam. In terms of language, Indonesian is the main functional language in the mosque. Most of the preaching, religious study sessions and meetings are conducted in Indonesian. At the same time, Javanese, Mandarin and Hokkien are also spoken during interpersonal conversations.

The establishment of Cheng Hoo Mosque will not be a success without support from the non-Muslim Chinese too. Given that the mosque is situated in a majority non-Muslim neighbourhood, PITI consulted local residents and gained their support for the mosque. To ensure non-Muslim Chinese residents are not disturbed, the mosque does not use a loudspeaker when calling for the morning prayer (*azan subuh*). Besides, most of the donors to the mosque are non-Muslim Chinese, who contributed about 70 per cent of the total construction fee.[8] According to a plaque placed in the compound and listing the names of donors – with their respective contributions – these included several well-established Chinese-owned business groups, such as the Salim Group (with 200 million IDR, circa 20,000 USD), Maspion Group (100 million IDR, circa 10,000 USD) and Gudang Garam (100 million IDR). As some Chinese Muslim leaders have mentioned, the non-Muslim Chinese have supported the construction of Cheng Hoo Mosque because they acknowledged the role of PITI in protecting them from possible 'anti-Chinese' riots, as well as bridging the divide between Chinese and Muslims in Surabaya.

In short, Chinese Muslim leaders-cum-businessmen, and their well-connected networks, were crucial in the success of Cheng Hoo Mosque. On the one hand, they have business cooperations with non-Muslim Chinese businessmen. On the other hand, they have established close relations with Muslim organizations, especially NU, through religious affinity. Their relationship with NU goes beyond the religious domain, as some of them provide business training to NU members, while others are actively involved with the National Awakening Party (*Partai Kebangkitan Bangsa*), which is closely linked to NU. Besides a close relationship with local government officials and military leaders, PITI has a good media

Islam and Chinese-style mosques in Indonesia   185

network, especially through *Jawa Pos* and several local Chinese newspapers. Cheng Hoo Mosque thus also plays a role in promoting good relations between different groups of Indonesian society, including both Chinese and Muslims.

Translocal ethno-religious imaginations of Chinese-style mosques

Following the success of the Cheng Hoo Mosque in Surabaya, many Chinese Muslims in other parts of the country sought to replicate the Chinese-style mosque and, in some cases, adopted the Cheng Hoo name. Many PITI branches, from Sumatra to Sulawesi, from Java to Kalimantan, announced their intention to build Chinese-style mosques; yet by 2010 only the Palembang mosque had been completed. Chinese Muslim individuals have also established Chinese-style mosques in the compounds of their Islamic boarding schools. In Pandaan, near Pasuruan, East Java, even non-Chinese Muslims have built a mosque that resembles the architectural design of the Surabaya Cheng Hoo Mosque, with the intention of supporting social blending (*pembauran*) and promoting religious tourism (Muzakki 2009: 201).

The al-Islam Muhammad Cheng Hoo Mosque of Palembang, completed in August 2008, is the second Chinese-style mosque in Indonesia named after Admiral Cheng Ho (see Figure 10.2). Its construction was initiated by PITI South Sumatra, as its leaders visited theirs counterparts in Surabaya and were inspired by the architectural design of the mosque there. However, instead of mimicking the design of Niu Jie Mosque in Beijing, the Palembang mosque reappropriates the pan-Islamic features of mosque architecture with Chinese and Palembang-Malay cultural influences. The mosque shares similar aims as discussed for the Surabaya case, include uniting Chinese Muslims, preaching Islam, and showing that Islam and Chinese can co-exist harmoniously. The naming of the mosque after Cheng Ho was seen as 'setting history straight' (*pelurusan sejarah*), and commemorating the Chinese admiral who visited Palembang during the fifteenth century, thus contributing to the spread of Islam in Sumatra (PITI Palembang 2009).

Painted in green and red, this mosque combines Chinese, Palembang and pan-Islamic architectural features. It has a dome with a crescent and star, and two minarets which resemble the design of Chinese pagodas. Each minaret has five floors, adorned with the Palembang feature of a goat's horn, and reaching 17 meters in height, thus symbolising the five daily prayers with 17 *rakaat* (prostrations during prayer). According to the mosque hand-out (PITI Palembang 2009), its design reflects the similarities between Chinese and Palembang-Malay cultures. There it is also stated that the establishment of the Palembang Cheng Hoo Mosque is a response to the socio-cultural development of Islam among Chinese Muslims, resembling the cultural accumulation of Islamic practices among other Muslims in Indonesia, such as the combination of Minang culture and Javanese custom with Islamic teachings and traditions. It is indeed an important argument, as it is suggesting the imagination of 'Chinese Islam' as another form of ethno-religious identity in Indonesia, alongside 'Javanese Islam' and 'Minang Islam'.

Figure 10.2 The Palembang Cheng Hoo Mosque (photo by Hew Wai-Weng)

Given that Chinese Muslims are dispersed across the archipelago, PITI's efforts to replicate the Surabaya Cheng Hoo Mosque in Palembang and in other cities shows their attempts to forge a 'translocal' Chinese Muslim cultural identity. This is a rather new ethno-religious phenomenon, in contrast to other traditions such as 'Javanese Islam' and 'Bugis Islam', which are relatively based on geographically-bounded locations.[9] Given that Chinese Muslims from Medan to Makassar are extremely diverse, mosque architecture that adopts Chinese features can be seen as a symbolically unifying characteristic. Today as in the past (Hew 2011), the religious practices of Chinese Muslims across the archipelago are influenced by the localities in which they are situated and many of them are eventually culturally absorbed into the local Muslim majority. Therefore, the Chinese-style mosques do not reflect an existing ethno-religious reality, but rather are constructing a new imagination of translocal Chinese Muslim identity within Indonesia. PITI branches across the Indonesia, in Sumatra (Medan), Java (Semarang, Jakarta), Bali (Denpasar), Sulawesi (Makassar) and Kalimantan (Pontianak) intend to establish similar mosques, and the realization of their plans will decide how far this translocal imagination can go.

This 'translocality' of Chinese Muslim identities, on the one hand challenges 'ethnolocality' (Boellstorff 2002), which associates ethnicity with a specific region; on the other hand, it connects them to their 'imaginary homeland' in

China. Indonesian nationalism, generally speaking, allows different ethno-regional groups to imagine their claim to the nation, and to recognize each other as equal constituents of the nation. For example, one can simultaneously be both Javanese and Indonesian. This 'ethnolocality' is best exemplified in 'Beautiful Indonesia Miniature Park' (Taman Mini Indonesia Indah), which consists of different ethnic 'houses' representing, for example, Javanese traditions in Java, Balinese customs in Bali, Madurese culture in Madura and so on. Chinese Indonesians, who do not constitute a specific locality and could not claim aboriginality in any part of Indonesia, were denied a representation of their identity in the park during the New Order period.

In post-Suharto Indonesia, the Indonesian Chinese Clan Association (Paguyuban Sosial Marga Tionghoa Indonesia) is building the 'Chinese Indonesian Cultural Park' (Taman Budaya Tionghoa Indonesia) at Taman Mini to position ethnic Chinese as one of the many legitimatized ethnic groups. Instead of manifesting localized Chinese culture, such as *peranakan* traditions, the cultural park draws heavily on the designs of ancient buildings in mainland China (Kitamura 2007). To some extent, Chinese Clan Association is caught by the concept of 'ethnolocality', in which they can only claim their aboriginality and geographically bounded identity through linkages with their 'imaginary homeland' in mainland China. Chinese Muslims face the same dilemma. In order to build translocal connections among them and within the Indonesian nation-state, they have to refer to mosque architectures as featured in mainland China, to bind them together. However, their transnational linkages do not undermine their national belongings, as discussed above. Furthermore, their translocal imaginations are not socially exclusive, and are always locally grounded, as reflected in the adoption of Palembang culture in the Palembang Cheng Hoo Mosque and Javanese tradition in the Surabaya Cheng Hoo Mosque.

Besides PITI, individual Chinese Muslims such as Anton Medan and Iskandar Abdurrahman have also engaged in the construction of Chinese Muslim imaginations through building Chinese-style mosques. In the compound of his Islamic boarding school in Bogor, the gangster-turned-preacher Anton Medan has built Mosque Tan Kok Liong (after his own Chinese name) to resemble the architectural design of a Chinese palace during the Qing Dynasty. Meanwhile, Iskandar Abdurrahman, or Chang I Pao, a Muslim activist of mixed Chinese-Javanese heritage, is building an 'Arwana' mosque, which is an acronym for Arab, Jawa (Java) and China, as part of his Islamic school in Salatiga.

Not all Chinese Muslims share enthusiasm for building Chinese-style mosques. For example, Syafii Antonio, a prominent Chinese Muslim intellectual who is active in promoting Islamic economics, avoided a Chinese architectural design for the mosque in his Andalusia Islamic Centre near Jakarta, using instead a Moorish design from Spain. He said it was his attempt to 'revive' the famously tolerant period of Islamic civilization. Suggesting that there were already a number of Chinese-style mosques in Indonesia, he advocated this different style, hoping that his Islamic centre would be open to all Muslims, regardless of their ethnicity (Interview, Syafii Antonio, 11 January 2009).

188 Hew Wai-Weng

Operational diversity: Identity contestations in the Surabaya Cheng Hoo Mosque

In the preceding sections, I discussed Chinese-style mosques as forms of intentional hybridity that emphasize symbolic unity and promote a translocal imagination of Chinese Muslim identity. Despite promoting a fixed image of Chinese Muslims, I will here argue that Chinese-style mosques are also a space for contestation of diverse and multiple Chinese Muslim identities; for example, between Chinese-cultured and non-Chinese cultured; between first-generation converts and second-generation Muslims; between NU and Muhammadiyah followers; between upper and lower class, male and female, leaders and ordinary members, merchants and preachers, sharia-minded and secular-oriented. In the mosque, Chinese Muslims from all walks of life negotiate themselves between not only Islamic and Chinese identities, but also diversified Islamic and Chinese traditions in Indonesia. This is arguably a form of everyday hybridization that emphasizes organic diversity and implies fluid identities among Chinese Muslims. Here, I will provide a snapshot of diverse religiosities at the Surabaya Cheng Hoo Mosque.

During Idul Fitri 2008, after morning prayers at the Surabaya Cheng Hoo Mosque, Dr Fuad Amsyari, vice chairman of the advisory board for Indonesia's Ulama Council (MUI, Majelis Ulama Indonesia), gave a sermon in front of a thousand Muslims from various ethnic backgrounds. Ironically, although he was speaking in a mosque that promotes diversity and tolerance, his sermon emphasized the importance of sharia implementation, not only at the personal and family level, but also on the societal and state arenas. He also reiterated the 2005 MUI *fatwa* denouncing secularism, pluralism and liberalism. Meanwhile during the celebration of Maulid 2008 (birth of Prophet Muhammad), hardliner Habib Rizieq Shihab, leader of Islamic Defenders' Front (Front Pembela Islam) delivered a fiery religious speech in the Palembang Cheng Hoo Mosque. This occasional presence of conservative or hardliner preachers in Cheng Hoo mosques both reflects the neutrality of the mosque (in term of religious affiliation), and the diversity of religious practices there.

Most religious speeches and sermons in the mosque are rather moderate and tolerant, however. For example, during Idul Adha 2008, in his sermon, KH Abdurshomad Buchori, Chairman of MUI East Java, criticized both Islamic fundamentalism and terrorism in Indonesia and abroad. Meanwhile, during a talk before the breaking of fast in Ramadan, Syaukanie Ong, a Chinese preacher, urged the non-Chinese majority crowd to embrace cultural diversity and eliminate their negative stereotype of Chinese Indonesians. According to the Friday sermon schedule of the Surabaya Cheng Hoo Mosque, the invited preachers and religious teachers come from all religious backgrounds, including local leaders from NU and Muhammadiyah, lecturers from Islamic institutions and public universities, as well as, Chinese Muslim preachers. This is a conscious decision of mosque officers to get along with various groups in Indonesia.

The Surabaya Cheng Hoo Mosque is committed to the Pancasila state ideology

Islam and Chinese-style mosques in Indonesia   189

and is neutral in term of religious and political affiliations (YHMCHI 2007). Nonetheless, given that Surabaya is the stronghold of NU, it is not surprising that many Chinese Muslim leaders and businessmen at the mosque are associated to this group. Some of them have close relations with local *kiyai* to establish business networks and to ensure protection, while some favour NU because of its more flexible attitude towards religious practices. For middle-ranked leaders, religious teachers and ordinary members in PITI, their religious affiliations are more diverse. A few of them are members of Muhammadiyah and other Muslim organizations.

The differences of religious affiliations among members of the mosque community do not generate tensions or conflicts. The only major incident that I heard of, during my period of fieldwork, was the replacement of the mosque committee chairman, from a Muhammadiyah-inclined to an NU-affiliated *ustadh* (religious teacher). One of my informants reported that the relatively rigid and conservative *ustadh*, Burhadi, was not favoured by some Chinese Muslim leaders because he often criticized 'un-Islamic' practices, such as not wearing 'proper' Islamic dress in the compound of the mosque. Hariyono Ong, who trained in an NU Islamic boarding school instead, replaced Burhadi in early 2008, and is said to be more flexible in religious practices, as he also attended non-Muslim Chinese funeral ceremonies.

During fieldwork, both NU and Muhammadiyah-affiliated religious teachers active in the mosque maintained that they were tolerant of each other's activities (Interview, Hariyono Ong, 30 September 2008; Lukman Tjoe, 2 November 2008). Hariyono Ong, the imam of the mosque, organized Islamic studies and chanting (*zikr*) sessions, during Ramadan, every 10 days. The sessions began with NU-affiliated *kiyai* delivering religious speeches, followed by Hariyono leading the *zikr* before breaking the fast. Meanwhile Lukman Tjoe, a Surabaya PITI *ustadh*, organized weekly study sessions on Sunday morning (*pengajian minggu*), of which most speakers came from Muhammadiyah. There were also Islamic guidance classes for new converts every weekend, facilitated by *ustadh* Gunawan who did not have any strong affiliation. Apart from these different affiliations, a broad spectrum of religiosity and Islamic piety exists at the Cheng Hoo Mosque. At the opposite ends of the spectrum is a Chinese Muslim who admitted he still drinks beer and eats pork at home, as well as a Chinese woman who privately stated that she is a supporter of Abu Bakar Basyir, the former leader of the terrorist group Jemaah Islamiyah.

The Cheng Hoo Mosque as a discursive cosmopolitan space

Since its establishment, the Surabaya Cheng Hoo Mosque has been frequently featured in the media and has been visited by many prominent figures. What makes this mosque so exceptional? I would suggest that the significance of this Cheng Hoo Mosque has to be examined in the larger context of post-1998 Indonesia. After the 'anti-Chinese' riots of 1998, post-New Order governments abolished several laws discriminating against Chinese Indonesians, in attempt to portray Indonesia as an inclusive nation (Hoon 2008). The *reformasi* period was

190 *Hew Wai-Weng*

also marked by violent events, such the Maluku conflict between Christians and Muslims, terrorist attacks in Bali and Jakarta, and more recently the attacks against Ahmadiyah followers. At the same time, mainstream Muslim organizations, such as Muhammadiyah and NU, have continued to promote Islamic moderation and religious tolerance despite their internal factionalism (Hefner 2005; Robinson 2008).

Within such contexts, Cheng Hoo Mosque is welcomed by many Indonesians as a symbolic marker of the acceptance of Chinese culture, as well as a clear statement of the inclusivity of Indonesian Islam. Thus, it is no surprise that this mosque has been often covered by the media, in which it can be seen a form of a discursive cosmopolitanism, deployed to manifest cultural diversity and religious pluralism in contemporary Indonesia (e.g. Arifin 2010; Ghufron 2009; Dariyanto 2009). In other words, the inclusivity of Chinese-style mosques is the antidote to rising puritanism and to the radicalization of Islamic doctrines among some sections of Indonesia's Muslim society. Indeed, as I indicated earlier, to project the cosmopolitan image of Islam, Chinese Muslims leaders have quoted the Qur'an to show that Islam is a '*rahmatan lil'alamin*' (blessing for all), which emphasizes '*hablum minalloohi wa hablum minannaas*' (a good relationship with God and among humankind) (YHMCHI 2008). Now, based on personal interviews and articles, I discuss Muslim leaders' public discourses of the Cheng Hoo Mosque as one that promotes peaceful, vernacular and 'touristic' Islam.

First, this is a peaceful mosque. Syafiq Mughni, chairman of the East Java Muhammadiyah branch, does not see any problem with the establishment of a mosque that adopts a Chinese design, arguing that the Qur'an does not regulate mosque architecture (Interview, Syafiq Mughni, 18 September 2008). He welcomed the Chinese-style Mosque because it reflects the universality of Islam and it helps preaching Islam to non-Muslim Chinese. He also suggested that the usage of Cheng Ho for the name of the mosque is timely, as Indonesian Islam is facing challenges from terrorism abroad and fundamentalism at home. According to him, Indonesian Muslims should learn from the spirit of Cheng Ho, who emphasizes peace and inclusivity.

Second, it is a vernacular mosque. For Rubaidi, East Java NU secretary, the Cheng Hoo Mosque is a fine example of the fact that Islam does not hesitate to adopt ethnic cultural symbols, practices and rituals (Interview, Rubaidi, 15 November 2008). As a proponent of the 'indigenization' of Islam, he sees this mosque as a form of resistance against the 'Arabization' of mosque architecture. Instead of merely adopting pan-Islamic designs, he supports the diversity of mosque outlooks, which reflect various local and ethnic manifestations of Islam.

Third, the Cheng Hoo Mosque is a touristic mosque. Since its establishment, the mosque has been visited by many prominent national leaders, as well as local religious, military, business and political elites. The mosque is not only a place of worship, but also a tourist destination attracting Muslim and non-Muslims visitors from across the country and abroad, to the extent that Muslim organizations and Islamic schools organize tours to visit this 'exotic' mosque in Surabaya. Along with the recently built pan-Islamic-design al-Akbar Great Mosque and

Islam and Chinese-style mosques in Indonesia   191

historical Javanese-style Sunan Ampel Mosque, the Cheng Hoo Mosque has been promoted as one of the religious tourist destinations (*wisata religi*) by the Surabaya Tourism Board (2010).

The Cheng Hoo Mosque as a living cosmopolitan space

Having reviewed public discourses of this mosque as a cosmopolitan space, it is now important to look also at the sociological reality of its cosmopolitanism. By illustrating some examples of activities carried on at the Surabaya Cheng Hoo Mosque, I argue that this mosque somehow embraces 'everyday cosmopolitanism', as 'ordinary members of different ethno-religious and cultural grouping mix, mingle, intensely interact, and share in values and practices' (Bayat 2008: 5). It is a place where Chinese and non-Chinese, Muslims and non-Muslims, upper classes and lower classes, males and females converge; as well as a space where religious, social and economic activities co-exist. As the former imam of the mosque, Burhadi, said, 'We wish this mosque to be like a supermarket, fulfilling the aspirations of all people' (Harahap 2007).

The busiest time of the week is on Fridays, when hundreds of men of various ethnic backgrounds come to the mosque for *zhuhur* prayers. Sometimes, conversion testimonies are held after the prayers. The mosque can only accommodate about 200–300 people, so every Friday, a temporary shelter is set up to cater for another 1,000 people. With the exception of a few Chinese Muslim leaders, almost all Muslims who perform Friday prayers here are non-Chinese who are either working or residing nearby. Instead of travelling all the way to Cheng Hoo Mosque, most Chinese Muslims perform their prayers at the closest mosque. Indeed, location is more important than mosque architecture for them. Meanwhile, the busiest time of the year is the fasting month, Ramadan, when hundreds of Muslims, mostly non-Chinese Muslims, gather for praying and breaking their fast. Some came to the mosque because it is close to where they live, or work, and because the mosque provides free food, while others visited this mosque for its unique appearance. For the evening *taraweh* prayer, the mosque accommodates both NU and Muhammadiyah followers, as it organizes two versions, one with 11 *rakaat* and another one with 23 *rakaat*.

In addition, the mosque committee exercise their inclusivity through collaboration with other socio-religious groups. For instance, PITI has organized a mass *khitanan* (circumcision) at the mosque for poor Muslims in Surabaya in cooperation with al-Irsyad, an Arab Muslim organization. PITI also extended their cooperation with non-Muslim organizations, in activities such as donating goods for flood victims, with a Buddhist organization, *Tsu Chi*. Indeed, charity events are frequently held at the mosque. A few Chinese Muslim leaders see themselves as middle-men, facilitating the distribution of donations from better-off Chinese individuals and organizations to needy Muslims, given that some Muslims might worry that the donations may not be *halal,* and Chinese organizations often lack direct connections with Muslim organizations.

During one evening, the noise of a bouncing basketball and the sound of

192 Hew Wai-Weng

Islamic chanting run through the mosque compound. Inside the mosque, a few Muslims, mostly non-Chinese, recite the Qur'an, led by a Chinese Muslim *ustadh*. Outside, Muslim and non-Muslim youth play basketball. They stop for a while after the *azan*, so that Muslims can perform their prayers undisturbed. This illustrates that the mosque fulfils both the religious and social purposes of a place of worship (Mortada, 2003: 87), being a sacred place, as well as a social space for the gathering of Muslims and non-Muslims. The mosque compound hosts PITI's offices, multipurpose rooms, a kindergarten, a canteen, an acupuncture clinic and badminton courts. Mandarin classes, *qigong* practice and dancing courses are also held in the complex. Like other mosques, the Cheng Hoo Mosque does not lack economic activities. The mosque committee raises money from renting out the sports facilities and hosting wedding functions, which are often held at the mosque. Some Chinese Muslims conduct informal businesses on the premises, such as selling biscuits, slimming products and Islamic insurance. The mosque thus operates as a business network for Chinese Muslims involved in large-scale industries (banks, factories), as well as small and medium-size enterprises (restaurants, grocery shops).

Conclusion

I wish to conclude by discussing three sets of paradoxes in the study of the Cheng Hoo Mosque: transnational imaginations and local configurations; intentional hybridity and everyday hybridity; cultural particularism and grounded cosmopolitanism. First, through the Cheng Hoo mosques, these Chinese Muslim leaders construct their Islamic tradition by adopting a mosque design from China; yet they reconfigure it in local contexts. Their strategic transnational connection with Muslims in China is not a form of longing to return to the mainland, but an effort to manifest their identity and empower their social position in Indonesia. There are also efforts to build Chinese-style mosques in other cities, which might contribute to the emergence of a rather new translocal ethno-religious imagination within Indonesia. However, these translocal imaginations have been repeatedly grounded and influenced by surrounding local cultures.

Second, the mosque does not symbolize an existing ethno-religious reality but rather brings a new reality into being, reinventing traditions to promote a sense of shared experience that can unify Chinese Muslims. The strategic combination of Chinese architectural design and local Islamic traditions can be seen as a form of intentional mixing to emphasize the 'Chineseness' of a Muslim house of worship. This fixity of identity through mosques does not reflect the complexity of cultural interaction and identity adoption of Chinese Muslims. The everyday hybridity of Chinese Muslim identities can only be observed through their daily involvement and activities in the mosque, where they constantly cross boundaries, not only between Muslim and Chinese identities, but also within diversified Islamic and Chinese traditions. In other words, the mosque is both a representative place and a contested space, the former promoting the symbolic unity of Chinese Muslims, while the latter reflecting the diverse negotiations of their identities.

Islam and Chinese-style mosques in Indonesia 193

Third, the establishment of Chinese-style mosques could 'universalize' Islam to demonstrate its compatibility with Chinese culture, but at the same time might also 'essentialize' Indonesia's Chinese within a stereotypical image. Yet this cultural essentialism does not always imply exclusion (Kahn 2006: 166). Indeed, the Cheng Hoo Mosque is a prime example of the celebration of inclusive Chinese cultural expression. Although the mosque is built in a Chinese style and managed by Chinese Muslims, it is a multi-ethnic religious space allowing both Muslims and non-Muslims from different ethnic groups to interact with each other. In fact, most of the followers of the mosque are non-Chinese Muslims, while many Chinese converts attend mosques close to where they live. We may call it 'inclusive Chineseness', in which the practice of Chinese culture is no longer a sign of ethnic exclusivity but rather a common heritage shared by all, whilst one can have the freedom to abandon his or her Chineseness without much social pressure.

In addition, by appropriating features from both NU and Muhammadiyah traditions, as well as the external design of a Chinese temple and internal structure of a Romanic church, the mosque design shows Islam as a cosmopolitan religion that celebrates differences within and between religions. Avoiding the use of loudspeakers to broadcast morning *azan,* and the cooperation of activities with Chinese organizations, shows that assertion of Islamic identity does not affect relations with their non-Muslim counterparts. Islamic cosmopolitanism is not only found in Islamic texts, historical encounters and cultural syncretism with local traditions, but also in everyday life strategies of minority groups. The Cheng Hoo Mosque can be seen as a 'cosmopolitan [space] envisaged in marginality' (Bhabha 1996: 195) whereby minority Chinese Muslims empower themselves by playing a significant role, promoting ethnic and religious harmony. Its inclusive architectural design and social activities can be seen as a form of 'grounded' vernacular cosmopolitanism, in which there is no necessary contradiction between cosmopolitan sensibilities and identity assertion, and such cosmopolitan practices are 'rooted' in the experiences of particular ethno-religious groups (Kahn 2008; also Appiah 1998; Werbner 2002; Werbner 2006).

In short, to a certain extent, Cheng Hoo Mosque is a local, socio-religious space that embraces both inclusive Chineseness and cosmopolitan Islam. However, this inclusivity does not guarantee the decline of class differences, racial inequality and religious conservatism in the mosque. Such cosmopolitan practices are not new, and can be traced back to the interactions between Islam, Chinese traditions and local cultures in the pre-colonial and colonial periods.

Notes

1   Cheng Ho is the Hokkien pronunciation for Zheng He (as pronounced in Mandarin). Given that most Chinese in Java are Hokkien, Cheng Ho is more commonly used to refer to the prominent Chinese Muslim admiral. Cheng Ho is often spelled with one 'o'. However, the mosque in Surabaya is called 'Masjid Muhammad Cheng Hoo' (Muhammad Cheng Hoo Mosque), spelled with two 'o's. Here, I use 'Cheng Ho' to refer to the Chinese Muslim figure, while 'Cheng Hoo Mosque' refers to the Chinese-style mosque in Surabaya. Despite being highly contested, recently there has been a

194 *Hew Wai-Weng*

growing historical re-articulation in support of the role of Cheng Ho in early Islamization in Indonesia.

2 Here, I use 'hybridity' to describe and analyse cultural mixing in a broader sense. I use 'intentional hybridity' and 'organic hybridity' to distinguish hybridity as a symbolic strategy and as everyday practice. Organic hybridity refers to unconscious exchanges and everyday adaptation of cultures, meanwhile intentional hybridity is a conscious effort to create a double consciousness of one's identity (Werbner 1997).

3 I am aware that in many works, 'translocal' usually has 'transnational' connotation, which refers to the linkages, connections and imaginations between places, beyond the paradigm of nation states. However, for analytical purposes, in this chapter, I use such terms to imply different spatial relations when I discuss Chinese-style mosques in Indonesia. 'Transnational' refers to the connection with places outside of the Indonesian nation-state, such as mainland China and the Middle East. Meanwhile, 'translocal' refers to linkage between places within the Indonesian archipelago, such as Palembang in South Sumatra, Salatiga in Central Java and Pontianak in West Kalimantan.

4 The notion of cosmopolitanism, despite being highly contested, has been deployed by many scholars to examine, theorize and sometimes promote the ideal of people from different ethnicities and religions living together. In this research, I use religious cosmopolitanism in a broader sense, to indicate its openness to difference, inclusiveness to diversity and willingness to transform itself (Kahn 2006; Werbner 2008)

5 The five guiding principles of the Indonesian state are belief in God, humanitarianism, nationalism, democracy and social justice. For a more detailed discussion of this, see Carool Kersten and Julia Howell's contributions to this volume.

6 The difference between Hui and Han is problematic and contested, as discussed in Gillette (2000). Hui is not a homogenous group and has different meanings in different historical periods. Their identities are also expressed diversely in different local contexts in China. For further discussion of the complexity of Hui, see Gladney (1991).

7 Given that the Qur'an does not mention or regulate mosque architecture, there are less controversies or debates surrounding the Chinese style mosque, as compared to the celebration of Chinese New Year, as I have discussed elsewhere (Hew 2011).

8 According to the mosque handbook (YMHCHI 2008), the first phase of its construction cost 500 million IDR (circa 53,000 USD), collected through selling trilingual 'Saudara Baru/Juz Amma' ('New Convert/Selected Verses from Qur'anic texts'). Meanwhile the total construction fee was 3,300 million IDR (circa 350,000 USD) and most of it came from public donations.

9 It is important to note that such ethno-religious traditions are not static, as many of them have undergone various changes as the result of interactions with other cultures, as well as influences of various translocal and transnational flows. For accounts of the dynamics of Javanese Islam, see Beatty (1999) and Ricklefs (2008).

References

Al-Qurtuby, S. (2003) *Arus Cina-Islam-Jawa, Bongkar Sejarah atas Peranan Tionghoa dalam Penyebaran Agama di Nusantara Abad XV and XVI* [Chinese-Islam-Java Flow: Reveal the History of Chinese Role in Spreading Islam in Archipelago during 15th and 16th century], Yogyakarta: Inspeal Ahimsakarya Press.

Anderson, B. (1992) 'Long-Distance Nationalism: World Capitalism and the Rise of Identity Politics', in *The Wertheim Lecture 1992*, Amsterdam: Centre for Asian Studies.

Appadurai, A. (1996) *Modernity at Large: Cultural Dimension of Globalization*, Minneapolis, MN: University of Minnesota Press.

Appiah, K. A. (1998) 'Cosmopolitan Patriots', in Cheah, P. and Robbins, B. (eds) *Cosmopolitics: Thinking and Feeling Beyond the Nation*, Minneapolis: University of Minnesota Press.

Arifin, E. N. (2010) 'Chinese-style Mosque a Symbol of Indonesia's Diversity', *The Jakarta Globe*, 4 May.

Bayat, A. (2008) 'Everyday Cosmopolitanism', *ISIM (International Institute for the Study of Islam in the Modern World) Review*, 22: 5.

Beatty, A. (1999) *Varieties of Javanese Religion: An Anthropology Account*, Cambridge, UK: Cambridge University Press.

Bhabha, H. (1996) 'Unsatified: Notes on Vernacular Cosmopolitanism', in Garcia-Morena, L. and Pfeifer, P. C. (eds) *Text and Nation*, London: Camden House.

Boellstorff, T. (2002) Ethnolocality, *The Asia Pacific Journal of Anthropology*, 3(1): 24–48.

Dariyanto, E. (2009) 'Pagoda di Atap Masjid Cheng Hoo' [Pagoda on the Roof of Cheng Hoo Mosque], *Tempo*, 6 September.

Dijk, C. van (2009) 'National Pride and Foreign Influences: The Shape of Mosques in Southeast Asia', *Off the Edge*, August 2009.

Friedman, J. (1994) *Cultural Identity and Global Process*, London: Sage Publication.

Frishman, M. and Khan, H-U. (eds) (2002) *The Mosque: History, Architectural Development and Regional Diversity*, London: Thamas & Hudson Ltd.

Ghufron (2009) 'Masjid Cheng Hoo, Sarat Pesan Kedamaian' [Cheng Hoo Mosque: Message of Peace], *Republika*, 16 December.

Gillette, M. B. (2000) *Between Mecca and Beijing: Modernization and Consumption among Urban Chinese Muslim*, Stanford, CA: Stanford University Press.

Gladney, D. (1991) *Muslim Chinese: Ethnic Nationalism in the People's Republic*, Cambridge, MA: Council on East Asian Studies, Harvard University.

Gupta, A. and Fergusan, J. (1992) 'Beyond "Culture": Space, Identity, and the Politics of Difference', *Cultural Anthropology*, 7(1): 6–23.

Harahap, A. R. (2007) 'Masjid Cheng Hoo: Mengakomodasi Seluruh Golongan' [Cheng Hoo Mosque: Accomodate All Groups], *Kompas*, 29 September.

Hefner, R. W. (2005) 'Muslim Democrats and Islamist Violence in Post-Soeharto Indonesia', in Hefner, R. W. (ed.) *Remaking Muslim Politics: Pluralism, Contestation, Democratization*, Princeton, NJ: Princeton University Press.

Heuken, S. J. A. (2003) *Mesjid-mesjid Tua di Jakarta* [Old Mosques in Jakarta], Jakarta: Yayasan Cipta Loka Caraka.

Hew, W. W. (2011) 'Negotiating Ethnicity and Religiosity: Chinese Muslim Identities in Post-New Order Indonesia', PhD thesis, Canberra: The Australian National University.

Hoon, C. Y. (2008) *Chinese Identity in Post-Suharto Indonesia: Culture, Politics and Media*, Brighton, UK: Sussex Academic Press.

Kahn, J. S. (2006) *Other Malays:Nationalism and Cosmopolitanism in the Modern Malay World*, Singapore: Singapore University Press.

Kahn, J. S. (2008) 'Other Cosmopolitanisms in the Making of the Modern Malay World', in Werbner, P. (eds) *Anthropology and the New Cosmopolitanism: Rooted, Feminist and Vernacular Perspectives*, Oxford: Berg.

Khan, H. (2008) 'Contemporary Mosque Architecture', *ISIM Review*, 21: 51.

Kitamura, Y. (2007) 'Museum as Representation of Ethnicity: The Construction of Chinese Indonesian Ethnic Identity in Post-Suharto Indonesia', *Kyoto Review of Southeast Asia*, 8/9, Available from http://kyotoreviewsea.org/kitamuraeng.htm (accessed 15 Oct 2010).

Lombard, D. and Salmon, C. (2001) 'Islam and Chineseness', in Gordon, A. (ed.) *The*

196   Hew Wai-Weng

Propagation of Islam in the Indonesia-Malay Archipelago, Kuala Lumpur: Malaysian Sociological Research.

Mandaville, P. (2001) *Transnational Muslim Politics: Reimagining the Umma*, London and New York: Routledge.

Mortada, H. (2003) *Traditional Islamic Principles of Built Environment*, London and New York: Routledge Curzon.

Muzakki, A. (2009) 'Negotiating Identity: The Cheng Hoo Mosque and Ethnic Chinese Muslims in Post-Soeharto Indonesia', *Chinese Southern Diaspora Studies*, 3: 193–203.

Nasir, A. (2004) *Mosque Architecture in the Malay World* (Translated by Abdullah, O. S.), Bangi: Penerbit University Kebangsaan Malaysia (UKM Publisher).

O'Neill, H. (1993) 'Islamic Architecture under the New Order', in Hooker, V. and Dick, H. (eds) *Culture and Society in New Order Indonesia*, Melbourne: Oxford University Press.

PITI Palembang (2009) *Masjid Al-Islam Muhammad Cheng Ho* [Al-Islam Cheng Ho Mosque], Palembang.

Ricklefs, M. C. (2008) 'Religion, Politics and Social Dynamics in Java: Historical and Contemporary Rhymes', in Fealy, G. and White, S. (eds) *Expressing Islam: Religious Life and Politics in Indonesia*, Singapore: Institute of Southeast Asian Studies.

Robinson, K. (2008) 'Other Cosmopolitanisms in the Making of the Modern Malay World', in Werbner, P. (ed.) *Islamic Cosmopolitics, Human Rights and Anti-Violence Strategies in Indonesia*, Oxford, UK: Berg.

Roy, O. (2004) *Globalised Islam: The Search for a New Ummah*, London: Hurst & Co.

Rushdie, S. (1992) *Imaginary Homelands: Essays and Criticsim, 1981–1991,* London: Granta.

Surabaya Tourism Board (2010) 'Cheng Hoo Mosque: Islam, Java and Chinese Architecture', Surabaya Tourism Website, Online, Available from www.eastjava.com/tourism/surabaya/chenghoo-mosque.html (accessed August 2010).

Tjahjono (2008) 'Yayasan HM Cheng Hoo Indonesia Ke Kampung Halaman Cheng Hoo' [Visiting the Hometown of Cheng Hoo], *Komunitas*, September: 9–11.

Werbner, P. (1997) 'Introduction: The Dialectics of Cultural Hybridity', in Werbner, P. and Madood, T. (eds) *Debating Cultural Hybridity: Multi-Cultural Identities and the Politics of Anti-Racism*, London: Zed Books.

Werbner, P. (2002) 'The Place Which is Diaspora: Citizenship, Religion and Gender in the Making of Chaordic Transnationalism', *Journal of Ethnic and Migration Studies*, 28(1): 119–33.

Werbner, P. (2006) 'Vernacular Cosmopolitanism' [Special Issue "Problematising Global Knowledge"], *Theory, Culture and Society*, 2(3): 496–8.

Werbner, P. (2008) 'Introduction: Towards a New Cosmopolitan Anthropology', in Werbner, P. (ed.) *Anthropology and the New Cosmopolitanism: Rooted, Feminist and Vernacular Perspectives*, Oxford: Berg.

Wiryomartono, B. (2009) 'A Historical View of Mosque Architecture in Indonesia', *The Asia Pacific Journal of Anthropology*, 10(1): 33–45.

YHMCHI (Yayasan Haji Muhammad Cheng Hoo Indonesia) (2007) *Juz'Amma 4 bahasa: Tuntunan Bagi Saudara Baru* [Guidance for New Converts], Surabaya: YHMCHI.

YHMCHI (2008) *Sekilas Tentang Masjid Muhammad Cheng Hoo Indonesia* [About Cheng Hoo Mosque], Surabaya: YHMCHI.

11 Ramadan in the newsroom

Malaysiakini, *Tempo*, and the state in Indonesia and Malaysia

Janet Steele

Ramadan, 2010

In August 2010, I spent two weeks in Jakarta and Kuala Lumpur, doing fieldwork for a study of Islam and the values of journalism at *Tempo* magazine (Indonesia) and the online news site *Malaysiakini* (Malaysia). As it was the month of Ramadan and I was talking with Muslim journalists at both news organizations about their faith, it seemed obvious that I too should fast, at least in a modified way.

Jakarta, Indonesia

As I explained to my *Tempo* friends on the first day of Ramadan, I would be doing what I called 'a modified fast of solidarity', which meant that I would get up at the usual time (about 5:30), eat breakfast, and not eat again until it was time to break the fast at Magrib. I would not join in morning prayers.[1]

My friends at *Tempo* greeted this plan with enthusiasm. 'Why even get up at 5:30?' one asked. 'There's no reason to start until 6:00.' I felt an overwhelming sense of solidarity and support. It was easy to talk with *Tempo* journalists about their faith in this context, and about how it coloured their understanding of their work. As editor Bina Bektiati explained, in Indonesia, treating a guest with respect is a kind of *dakwah*, or outreach (lit. calling to Islam). The way they welcome me, the way they take the time to explain things, all of this is *dakwah*, she said. In her words, 'there is nothing better than being a guest'.

I have known Bina since I first started doing research at *Tempo* in 1999. At *Tempo*, Bina told me, almost everyone fasts, even the Christians, because it's healthy. 'Getting up early and having nothing but a light breakfast is good for you. You remember what it was like when you were young, the special foods, and deciding what you are going to have when you *buka puasa* [break the fast]', she said. 'And you get new clothes at Lebaran.'

Permission to use a desk at *Tempo* was swiftly granted. It had been a number of years since I'd done fieldwork at the office on Jl. Proklamasi, and it seemed that little had changed other than the desktop computers were older and it was hard to find a functioning mouse. The newsroom was quieter than usual. A small television was tuned to al-Jazeera, with the sound turned down.

As the minutes slowly crept by, journalists dropped by my desk, one by one, to say hello. Bina, who seemed to have taken on the job of looking after me, explained that when you fast, late in the afternoon your blood sugar starts to drop, and you have difficulty thinking. I said that this must be why my Indonesian was 'running out', which made everyone laugh. The consensus was that it takes about a week to adjust. After a week, they said, you can wake up for *sahur*, or the pre-dawn breakfast, have a glass of water, pray, and go back to sleep.

For some *Tempo* journalists, night turns into day during Ramadan, as it's easier to work after you've broken the fast (see Figure 11.1). Deputy executive editor Arif Zulkifli told me that some of the younger reporters stay in the office all night and take *sahur* there, thus drawing upon the time-honoured tradition of sleeping at *Tempo* (Steele 2005).

Figure 11.1 Arif Zulkifli, breaking the fast at *Tempo* (photo by Janet Steele)

At some point late in the afternoon, someone changed the channel to Metro TV. A wag pointed out that we should tune in to the Surabaya station because in East Java you can break the fast a few minutes earlier.

At about 6:15 pm, Bina handed an office boy two ornate Chinese cups and some tea from Cirebon, and asked him to prepare hot sugary tea to *buka* or open the fast. At 6:30 we broke the fast with the tea, along with green lentils cooked in coconut milk and palm sugar. During Ramadan at *Tempo*, the company provides a simple meal, and most journalists eat together in the office. On the night of 11 August, dinner consisted of rice, vegetable soup, a fried potato patty, shrimp crackers, bananas, and a salad of pickles. As the journalists sat and ate together, everyone agreed that food never tastes as good as it does when you *buka puasa* during Ramadan.

The second day of Ramadan at *Tempo* was much the same as the first, except that a small group of journalists decided to leave the office for dinner. Four of us walked down the eerily quiet Jl. Pramuka to a place called Abunawas that looked like something out of the Arabian nights, or the piously romantic film *Ayat Ayat Cinta* (Verses of Love, 2008, directed by Hanung Bramantyo). We broke the fast in a small carpeted room, sitting on the floor and eating from a cloth laid out with glasses of water, fruit cocktails, and a small dish of dates. Taufik, the expert on Middle Eastern food, did the ordering.

Taufik, who is a Shi'a, couldn't break the fast until it got dark – he's from a different *aliran*, or 'stream', as Bina explained. Taufik's ancestors had come to Indonesia from Yemen, but both Bina and Dede are Javanese. We talked about the differences between Indonesia and Malaysia, and on the way back to the office from the restaurant, Dede pointed out that now all of the women at *Tempo* except for Bina wear a headscarf.

Kuala Lumpur, Malaysia

When I arrived in Kuala Lumpur the following week, I expected that the rhythm of life would be much the same as it had been in Jakarta. My plan was to arrive at *Malaysiakini* at about 11:00 am, and leave at between 7:30 or 8:00 pm, after everyone had broken the fast. About one-third of the editorial staff is Muslim, and I assumed that I'd be spending most of my time with them.

There was far less evidence of fasting at *Malaysiakini* than there was at *Tempo*. Not all of the Muslim journalists were fasting, and although people didn't eat or drink in front of those who were, life otherwise seemed to go on pretty much as usual (see Figure 11.2). Many of my friends expressed surprise that I intended to fast.

During Ramadan there is a special *pasar* or market across the street from *Malaysiakini*'s office in Bangsar, and people went there late in the afternoon to buy special foods to break the fast. Some of the journalists bought food on their way home from reporting. I visited the market with reporter Hazlan Zakaria at 5:30, and then again about an hour later with editor Fauwaz Abdul Aziz. Fauwaz explained that the market is so lucrative that a lot of civil servants take leave

Figure 11.2 Hazlan Zakaria, breaking the fast at *Malaysiakini* (photo by Janet Steele)

during Ramadan and set up stalls. Hazlan said he knows a guy who makes so much money selling food during this one month that he doesn't have to work for the rest of the year (see Figures 11.3 and 11.4).

Fauwaz is the son of a diplomat, and he grew up overseas. A devout Muslim and degree candidate in the graduate program at the International Islamic University, his views on matters of Islam are frequently sought out by his colleagues. Fauwaz said that during Ramadan the shops – even those run by Muslims – are still open during the day, and serve non-Muslims. There is nothing in Islam, he said, that forbids a Muslim shopkeeper from earning a living during Ramadan. However if you are a Muslim and you are caught eating during daylight hours, you can be reported to the civil authorities. 'There will be raids', Vicknesan, who is Indian-Malaysian and was at the time one of *Malaysiakini*'s senior editors, later told me. 'Not on a very large scale, but they will be highly publicized. All the papers will carry news of the raid and I suppose even the charging in court' (Vicknesan, interview, 19 August 2010).

In Kuala Lumpur, Magrib occurred one hour later than in Jakarta, at 7:37 pm. At 7:30, about five of us met in the pantry, a small back room near the prayer room and the toilets. My friends carefully removed the foods from their red and pink plastic bags, and we broke the fast together. The food was more varied than in Indonesia – we had Indian naan, daal, and savoury mutton murtabak, as well as sweet drinks and cakes.

Figure 11.3 Pasar Ramadan, Bangsar (photo by Janet Steele)

Figure 11.4 Vendors, Pasar Ramadan, Bangsar (photo by Janet Steele)

202 *Janet Steele*

The second day at *Malaysiakini* went much as the first, with interviews at lunch and tea time and breaking the fast together in the pantry. Yet after a few days, I decided to stop. I sent a note to my Muslim friends explaining that it was interfering with my ability to work – and although I had learned a lot from my experiment, I believed it was time to end it.

Although what I wrote to my friends was true, it was only part of the truth. It was clear to me that my fasting had become disruptive. Whereas in Indonesia my friends at *Tempo* had embraced my interest in fasting, at *Malaysiakini* I felt that many of the Muslim journalists were at best baffled by my interest in joining in, and at worst somewhat offended. While at *Tempo*, the feeling was 'we believe that if you fast, you are honouring us'(Arif Zulkifli, interview, 4 January 2011), the sense I received from non-Muslims and Muslims alike at *Malaysiakini* was that Ramadan is for Muslims, and that a non-Muslim has no business fasting.

Why were my experiences in Malaysia so different from those in Indonesia? *Malaysiakini* and *Tempo*'s newsrooms are both demonstrably pluralist places, embracing diversity and explicitly standing for religious tolerance. Headquartered in the global cities of Kuala Lumpur and Jakarta, the two news organizations adhere to international norms of journalism while at the same time reflecting what I have called a local 'idiom' of Islam (Steele 2011: 534). Interviews with journalists at both news organizations suggest some reasons for the differences, but a deeper explanation may lie in the histories of the two neighbouring countries. In Malaysia, the state is involved in religious affairs to an extent that is unimaginable in Indonesia. This level of state involvement, in addition to the more recent politicization of Islam, has had profound implications for the ways that Muslims and non-Muslims interact even in otherwise pluralist spaces like *Tempo* and *Malaysiakini*.

Pluralist spaces: Religion and ethnicity

Eni Mulia, the program manager for PPMN (Perhimpunan Pengembangan Media Nusantara), the Indonesian Association for Media Development in Jakarta, had a simple explanation for the differences between Indonesia and Malaysia. 'In Indonesia, you can't tell a person's religion by his race', she said pointing out that in Indonesia there are Javanese Christians, and Balinese Hindus, both of whom are ethnic Malays. While there is merit in this argument, why should this difference affect two news organizations that are known for their independence and commitment to pluralism?

Malaysiakini was launched in November 1999, less than one year after the arrest of former deputy prime minister and leading opposition figure Anwar Ibrahim.[2] The news portal was the creation of Steven Gan and Premesh Chandran, two young journalists who got their start in print journalism at the Kuala Lumpur newspaper *The Sun*. Believing that political control had corrupted the values of good journalism in the mainstream media, they planned to bring independent news and in-depth analysis to the Internet.[3]

Malaysiakini's editorial desk has three news sections (English, Malay, and Chinese) and a Tamil section that is primarily responsible for translations. At the time of the March 2008 general elections, *Malaysiakini*'s editorial desk consisted of 29 people. On the print side, there were nine editors and twelve journalists. In addition there were five video journalists and editors, a senior graphic designer, a senior analyst, and an online librarian. The group was remarkably balanced between Malaysia's three ethnic groups, with 13 Chinese (45 per cent), six Indians (21 per cent) and ten Malays (34 per cent).[4] Among the seven senior editors and producers who attended the daily editorial meeting, the split was two Chinese, three Indians, and two Malays. Although there have been some resignations and realignment since 2008 – chief editor Kabilian, an Indian–Malaysian, left *Malaysiakini* at the end of 2009 and was replaced by Fathi, who is Malay – the effort to maintain a balance has been consistent.

What makes *Malaysiakini* different from other news organizations is not the diversity of the newsroom *per se*, but rather the effort to deal directly with 'sensitive' issues such as ethnicity, race, and religion, and to do so within an environment of mutual respect. As editor-in-chief Steven Gan said,

> I think it is very difficult for Malaysians to think outside their own ethnic identification.... [It's apparent] when you fill out a form, in everything that you do. I know that people will argue that we shouldn't emphasize race in our reports, but if we try to report in a way that race doesn't matter, that is dishonest. Even when we hire people we think about how we are going to attain a balance. It's a conscious effort.
>
> (interview, 24 March, 2008)

Sometimes covering topics as controversial as the New Economic Policy (which gives economic privileges to ethnic Malays) or the issue of religious apostasy makes even people at *Malaysiakini* feel uncomfortable. For example Gan described a conversation he once had with a Malay reporter who preferred not to write about issues related to Islam. Gan recalls having told him, 'Look, you are a journalist. There is no way out. You have to do these stories.'

At *Tempo*, by contrast, approximately 80 per cent of the journalists are Muslim (Diah Purnomowati, email correspondence, 8 April 2011). Established in 1971, *Tempo* is Indonesia's leading weekly news magazine. Today *Tempo* is known for its hard-hitting editorial leaders and journalistic independence, but the magazine did not always enjoy such freedoms. Under President Suharto's authoritarian regime, *Tempo*'s journalists developed a set of strategies designed to protect the magazine. But sometimes these strategies were not enough, and in 1994 *Tempo* was banned, ostensibly because of a cover story on the purchase of 39 used East German warships. Although the real reason they were forced to close remains unknown (the official document stated only that the story had 'disturbed national security while failing to safeguard the Pancasila press'), most analysts agree that the cover story embarrassed the regime by reporting on infighting.

With Suharto's fall in 1998, *Tempo* returned to publication with greater

204　*Janet Steele*

journalistic zeal than ever. Today, *Tempo* is known for its independence and willingness to question cherished cultural beliefs, be they religion, nationalism, or deference to authority. The magazine is a strong defender of pluralism and the rights of religious minorities; founding editor Goenawan Mohamad is well known for his sharp criticism of those fired by 'religious egoism' who seem to 'feel that they represent the voice of God and the voice of Islam, although it is not clear from where they received their mandate' (Steele 2006). Deputy executive editor Arif Zulkifli expressed these same pluralist values when he noted a controversy over a banner in Aceh that stated 'honour those who fast'. Arif said 'So the sign says that Islamic people want to be acknowledged, want to be honoured by non-Muslim people who don't fast. Why don't they make a banner that says "honour those who don't fast?" Now *they* are the minority' (interview, 4 January 2011).

Who has the authority to speak about Islam?

In Indonesia, I never encountered a Muslim journalist who was unwilling to talk about his or her view of religion and work. In Malaysia, on the other hand, a standard reply to my questions was something along the lines of 'I'm not the right person to ask' or, 'I don't feel that I have the authority to comment.' As Aidila Razak, a young independently minded *Malaysiakini* journalist who earned her undergraduate degree in Australia said wryly, in Malaysia 'there's a state that's the expert' (interview, 17 August 2010).

Yet how did the state come to be seen as the 'expert' on matters of religion in Malaysia? Historians and scholars of Islam point to the legacy of British colonialism, which strengthened and even institutionalized the relationship between Islam and the state. As Roff explains:

> Prior to the protectorate period, Islam in Malaya had not, in any effective sense, been a "state religion." There was a general awareness that all Malays were Muslims and that this distinguished them from, for example, Chinese or Siamese. To undergo conversion to Islam was in fact to masok Melayu, "become a Malay," but this identification of ethnic group with religion was of future rather than present significance. In the realm of religious belief, as in that of political organization, the Malay state as a rule lacked the resources necessary for centralization of authority.
>
> (Roff 1967: 67)

All of this changed with the arrival of the British. Although the British were technically only 'advisors' in Malaya, with sovereignty continuing to be vested in the Malay sultans, the treaty arrangements they made left the traditional rulers without power to declare war, levy taxes, own slaves, or basically to do '[any]thing that counted' (Yegar 1979: 91). Under the British, the sultans became ceremonial heads of state.

There was, however, one exception to this near-total control. Under the 1874 Pangkor Engagement with the State of Perak, which became a model for British control of all the Malay states, questions touching upon Malay religion and custom were 'explicitly excluded from compulsory Residential "advice"' (Roff 1967: 70). Denied substantive political authority, the sultans not surprisingly turned their attention to issues of faith. As Roff has argued, this preservation and strengthening of the traditional basis of authority of the sultans in the realm of 'Malay religion and custom', combined with the centralized administrative power of British rule, produced 'an authoritarian form of religious administration much beyond anything known to the peninsula before' (Roff 1967: 72).

One direct result of colonial rule was thus the concentration of religious authority in the hands of state officials who were dependent upon the sultans for their position and power. Emulating British administrative structures, the states created a system of Islamic courts and legal procedures, along with the bureaucracy that was necessary to run them. As Roff writes, 'many of these developments...may be seen as a desire to emulate Western administrative systems in a field the Malays felt to be peculiarly their own' (Roff 1967: 72).

Thus strengthened by the administrative machinery of the British, the Malay states were given extensive new powers for governing the practice of Islam. Laws passed after independence reinforced the arrangements of British colonial rule. Each state had an appointed religious council, which was empowered to regulate Muslim affairs. State departments of religion were given responsibility for managing day-to-day administration of Islamic matters, and the 'putative right to determine and convey what it meant to be a good and sufficient Muslim' (Roff 2009: 103).

Whether or not most Malaysians are aware of this history, they are acutely aware of the states' power to regulate Muslim affairs and to determine who is and who is not a good Muslim. In the words of Aidila Razak, 'the reason why people say "oh, I'm not an expert" goes back to the fact that there's one Islam and nothing else is accepted. So because of that it is sensitive, because you're so scared to say something wrong' (interview, 17 August 2010). Shufiyan Shukur, *Malaysiakini*'s senior video editor, agreed, saying that only the *ulama* are authorized to speak about religion. 'So I cannot say something because I am not an *ulama*. You have to be approved. If you think you have gone through a religious education in the top university in India or Cairo, if you are not approved by this council of *ulama* and religious department, you cannot even teach religion' (interview, 18 August 2010).

In Indonesia, the role of the state in matters of religion is significantly different (Hefner 1997). As Hooker asserts, the Dutch 'thoroughly misunderstood Islam', and saw it as a tightly organized hierarchical religion similar to Roman Catholicism (Hooker 2003: 12). They wanted to trade, profit, and maintain order, and were determined to put down resistance to colonial expansion, which was often done in the name of Islam. Benda has argued that in Indonesia, the Dutch were far more concerned with rebellion than they were with regulating Islam. 'These fears had helped to shape a policy of alliance with those elements in Indonesian society – particular the princes and *priyayi* on Java, and sultans, rajahs, and customary *adat*-chiefs on the other islands – who for political reasons of their own were known to be either lukewarm Muslims or outright enemies of

206   *Janet Steele*

Islamic "fanaticism"' (Benda 1958: 19). It wasn't until 1889, when Christiaan Snouck Hurgronje was appointed Advisor on Native and Arabian Affairs that the Dutch began to reassess this policy of suppression.

With a more realistic view of Islam in Indonesia, Snouck assuaged Dutch fears by distinguishing between Islam as a religious and as a political force. Arguing that the Dutch had nothing to fear from Islam as a religion, Snouck counselled in favour of toleration for Muslim religious life. For example he saw no reason to create barriers for those who wanted to go on the Mecca pilgrimage, which had been facilitated by the 1869 opening of the Suez Canal, arguing that such inter-ference would violate the spirit of personal liberty enshrined in the Dutch constitution. Yet at the same time, Snouck called for a policy of vigilance against 'all those trends that bear, or tend to bear, a political character' (Benda 1958: 24).

What Benda calls 'the determined application of the twin policies of tolerance and vigilance', was to 'go hand-in-hand with Dutch support for and encouragement of those social elements least under the sway of Islamic fanaticism, the *adat*-chiefs and rulers of the Outer Islands, and the *priyayi*-elite on Java' (Benda 1958: 24). In Snouck's view, modernization was the key to managing Islam in Indonesia. This would be attained primarily through education, and by making the *priyayi* elites active participants in Dutch culture and social life. This policy actually enjoyed limited success. As Hooker notes, Indonesian nationalists had little sympathy for the Muslim cause, seeing it as a threat to future independence. The Muslim position was 'peasant-based and out of sympathy with socialist and liberal ideologies' (Hooker 2003: 14). Although in the closing days of the Japanese occupation a coali-tion of Muslim organizations advocated a draft known as the Jakarta Charter that stipulated that 'enacting the Sharia was incumbent on all Muslim citizens', Soekarno's more pluralist view of the Constitution prevailed (Laffan 2003: 407).

Significantly, the Dutch classified the local population as natives, and thereby subject to *adat* or customary law. Although they established a *Priesterraad* or Priest Court for Muslims of Java and Madura in 1882 that was supposed to administer Islamic Law, its jurisdiction was limited to marriage, divorce, and inheritance. Basically advisors, they could not enforce their own decisions, and had to request enforcement from secular judges. Although this regulation was largely procedural and unrelated to the principles of sharia, Hooker concludes:

> The result was a highly formalized system, extremely bureaucratic in nature and with a limited jurisdiction. Even the judges (penghulu) had to take their oath of office in the form prescribed for judges of the civil courts. In short, the Syariah never obtained the status of a "Muslim personal law" as in the neighboring British possessions. On the contrary, the Syariah had no real place of its own in the colonial plural law system. Its existence was minimal, and even this was conditional on an acceptance by some *adat* to the limited extent just described. The Syariah was never an "equal" system. Indeed, in some sensitive areas of law quite basic principles of Muslim family law were directly overridden, causing considerable social turmoil.
>
> (Hooker 2003: 48)

Thus in the Dutch East Indies, both sharia judges and the rural *ulama* were isolated from elite centres of power, a situation that was to have profound implications for the role of Islam in post-colonial Indonesia. Whereas in British Malaya, state religious authorities were given power to punish 'Muhammadan offenses' such as public fast-breaking during Ramadan, gambling, and failure to attend Friday prayers, in the Indies, 'Islamic leadership wanted to divorce all spheres of Islamic life from Dutch control' (Yegar 1979: 264). As Yegar writes, 'more often than not, British intervention in religious matters had almost complete Malay consent, and, at times, actually responded to the wish or instance of the Malay rulers'. Thus in Malaya, Islamic teachers and judges were co-opted by the state, whereas in the Indies the *ulama* offered a counter-weight to state power and control.

Politicization of Islam

Nagata has called Malaysian Islam 'unavoidably political' (Nagata 2010: 27). Although the rights of different categories of citizens are enshrined in Article 3 of the Constitution, the official religion of Malaysia is Islam, and the state has the last word on matters of religion. Because Malays are Muslim by definition and thus required to adhere to sharia, in practice freedom of religion for Malays is limited to choices within Islam.

As we've seen, laws passed after independence reinforced the arrangements of British colonial rule, and empowered the Malay states to regulate Muslim affairs through appointed religious councils. This kind of power was not to go uncontested, and today Parti Islam Se-Malaysia, the political grouping that became the political party PAS, competes with the United Malays National Organization (UMNO) not only for the allegiance of the Malay majority but also for the not inconsiderable patronage that comes with control of these state institutions.

Moreover, because 'management of religion is less a question of theology than part of a drive to maintain political control of the Malays', political competition tends to centre on which party is more religiously correct and has the greater moral authority (Nagata 2010: 27). Faced with competition from PAS, which claims to promote Malay interests within the context of an Islamic state, UMNO both tightened and centralized its control, federalizing a number of Islamic institutions. 'These and similar measures, together with a tightening of prohibitory legislation affecting Muslims concerning, for example, public breaches of the Ramadan fast...served both to evidence government concern for acceptable Islamization and to emphasize its own zeal in Islamic causes' (Roff 2009: 107).

In Indonesia, by contrast, the state is secular and based on the ideology of Pancasila, which does not specify an official religion, and requires only belief in one God.[5] Unlike Malaysia, in which political discourse focuses on 'the definition and meaning of the Islamic state', in Indonesia the state is officially secular, and Islamist goals are advanced by political parties or organizations (Bertrand 2010: 48). Although under Suharto the Indonesian Ministry of Religious Affairs had certain powers to regulate religious affairs, most of these focused on issues

208 *Janet Steele*

pertaining to 'security'. As *Tempo*'s Arif Zulkifli noted, the history of the ministry was 'very connected with the uprising of 1965', and was always dominated by retired military. 'The Ministry of Religion monitored all religious sermons to prevent the emergence of Islamic extremist groups', he said. 'The Ministry of Religion was a tool of Suharto to control society...the paradigm was the paradigm of minimizing conflict, minimizing differences' (interview, 4 January 2011).

In practical terms, this control of all matters Islamic by the state has led to a situation in Malaysia in which ordinary Malays feel reluctant to speak about religious matters. As liberal groups such as Sisters in Islam discovered, there can be real legal consequences to questioning the state's interpretation of Islam (Anwar 2001).

Ramadan in the newsroom

How do the role of the state and the politicization of Islam in Malaysia affect the actual functioning of the newsroom? Clearly the differing ethnic and religious makeup of the two news organizations is significant, and the fact that Muslims dominate the newsroom at *Tempo* is related to the solicitousness shown to those who are not fasting. Yet, as Arif Zulkifli's observation about the Acehnese banner urging non-Muslims to 'honour the fast' suggests, such religious tolerance cannot be assumed.

At *Malaysiakini*, which is known for its agenda of human rights, freedom of expression, and ethnic and religious tolerance, Ramadan raised a number of difficulties, even in a space that is demonstrably pluralist in that all religious are afforded equal legitimacy.[6] It was clear that my decision to fast was problematic. As Vicknesan said,

> I think for most Malaysians [fasting at Ramadan] is a religious ritual. They don't see it as having a social purpose, it is purely religious. You're well aware that there are religious divides in the country. And so the thing is, why would I want to partake? I'm a Hindu. If a Muslim comes up to me and says, and you know about Thaipusam festival, it's a body piercing, I want to do it, I would be very surprised! Why would you want to do that?
>
> (interview, 19 August 2010)

As Vicknesan went on to suggest, perhaps the Muslims at *Malaysiakini* reacted the way they did because they were worried that I might be fasting 'without understanding the whole picture. Why would you want to do it if you're not ready to come into the religion?' he asked.

For non-Muslims, the picture was even more complicated. Again, in Vicknesan's view, 'it never occurs to a non-Muslim, why don't I join my Muslim colleagues for fasting this month? We don't do it ourselves, so I suppose we wonder why would anyone else want to do it?' *Malaysiakini* video editor Shufiyan Shukur said much the same thing. 'I think that for the Muslims, they think why put yourself through the torture that we have to undergo? And then for the non-Muslims, they are afraid that you will become a Muslim. [*Laughs.*] Which is a big deal' (interview, 18 August 2010).

Although it made them uncomfortable to say it, several non-Muslims at *Malaysiakini* noted that during Ramadan there was a clear division between the Muslims and the non-Muslims: 'they fast and we don't fast'. Or as Aidila Razak said, 'maybe at *Malaysiakini* to be Muslim is sometimes considered to be quite conservative, and it's not really the thing to do? To be conservative. It could be that. You don't want to make a fuss about it because then you pressure other people to do it.'

Ordinarily at *Malaysiakini* one doesn't wear one's religious identity on one's sleeve, but during Ramadan these distinctions are clear-cut. Again, quoting Aidila:

> I thought about it, because yesterday I was with [a Chinese colleague] at the sessions court. So he asked me if I was going back to the office because it was 5 something or 6, and I said yeah, or I didn't know if I should just go back because there would be traffic jam blah blah blah, and then he said no no, you shouldn't just go back, I can go back you shouldn't because you're fasting and I'm Chinese. It was really strange he said 'I'm Chinese', therefore I can go back. He could be Chinese-Muslim. It's just the first time he said that to me – that I'm Chinese and you're Malay.

Several non-Muslims at *Malaysiakini* commented on how Ramadan posed unique problems for journalists. Not only does everything slow down during the fasting month, especially in government offices, but there is a feeling of 'tension'. Video editor Indrani Kopal commented,

> [Chief editor] Steven is more grumpy during Ramadan, that would be one thing. If you are fasting, you don't perform as well as you do when you're not fasting, so if the news is fast, quick, can you equally perform? Malaysians have this bad habit during Ramadan, saying that everything slows down. The whole system slows down. People go back early, the office closes, you call up somebody, and they say he's outside. You walk up to a shop that normally closes at 5 and it is closed because they are fasting. A lot of organizations, especially the government offices, they go home at 2:00, and they don't come back. The reason is "I'm fasting". A lot of people take advantage of this.
>
> (interview, 18 August 2010)

Although other *Malaysiakini* journalists disagreed with these sentiments, saying that life went on pretty much as usual, the tensions were nevertheless evident. As Hazlan Zakaria, a thoughtful writer and journalist in his early 30s noted, Muslims in Malaysia have been encouraged by the government to fear non-Muslims, and vice-versa. 'Here, there is this feeling that the government is trying to orchestrate

210 *Janet Steele*

Muslims against non-Muslims and Malays against non-Malays, which is creating this kind of so-called invisible backlash' (interview, 16 August 2010).

As Kahn has argued, at the time of independence, a single view of 'Malayness' came to dominate Malaysia, and more cosmopolitan alternatives lost out (Kahn 2006). In the realm of religion, this has come to mean, as Aidila put it, that 'there is a right way and a wrong way to be a Muslim – and only one way to be right. And you're scared of the consequences of being wrong.'

Although '*Malaysiakini* is trying to present a pluralist alternative', Aidila said, 'the state is saying "you must fast"'. On the other hand, she hastened to add, 'It's still an individual choice' (interview, 17 August 2010). Yet how much of a choice is it, when there is also such 'tremendous social pressure' and even harassment? Moreover, it is not only the Muslims who are scared of the consequences of being wrong. A senior Malaysian journalist who asked not to be named told me, 'I'm willing to state my opinion, but I do not want to be named, because anything [I say about] about Islam can be misconstrued.'

Ramadan and 'everyday resistance' in Malaysia

Not all of the Muslims at *Malaysiakini* fast. Those who do not fast have their own reasons, including health concerns or an inability to work. Similar to what Arif Zulkifli described at *Tempo*, those who do fast are decidedly non-judgmental about their colleagues, pointing out that fasting should not continue if it interferes with one's ability to work.

Yet interestingly, several journalists at *Malaysiakini* and elsewhere expressed a different reason for refusing to fast, and it had more to do with the state than with issues of health or the ability to do one's work. If anything, what I observed resembled James Scott's definition of 'everyday resistance', the 'Brechtian forms of class struggle [that] require little or no coordination or planning... [and that] typically avoid any direct symbolic confrontation with authority or with elite norms' (Scott 1985: 29). In the case of Ramadan in the newsroom, these 'ordinary weapons' included buying food for those who weren't fasting, openly eating in front of others, and complaining about the hypocrisy of the state religious authorities.

Even at *Bernama*, the Malaysian national news agency, where all Muslim journalists will fast, there are Malays who resent the state's ability to decide who is and who is not a good Muslim.[7] For Tengku Noor Shamsiah, a senior business and economics journalist, whether you fast should be a private matter 'between you and God', although she points out that 'even at *Bernama*, if you don't put on a veil, a *tudong*, they will look at you like, "she's not pious"' (interview, 1 December 2010).

Malaysiakini's Shufiyan Shukur suggests that it is hypocrisy rather than religion that is the problem. If fasting during Ramadan is supposed to remind people of what it means to be poor and hungry, then why are there such huge feasts in hotels?

The thing is, does fasting make you a better person? And it is supposed to let you feel what it is like to be starving for so many hours in a day. But for those who are poor, who are starving, who are living in poverty, they don't have the luxury of at 7:30, here comes the *azan*, and wow, food is there! They don't have that. They are starving from morning to night, with maybe one or two meals a day for 365 days a year.

To the upper echelons of Malay society, this whole Ramadan is a big gig, a show. Because you know, every evening somewhere in the major hotels and restaurants of KL and everywhere in the country people [are] making plans to have a good meal, a good *buka puasa* with friends, family and relatives. It goes on all the time. So this is why the restaurants and the hotels, they put up big huge buffets. And those who earn below subsistence, they don't get that. So to me, the entire Ramadan thing is a big and complete failure.

(interview, 18 August 2010)

Conclusion

On 19 August 2010, a journalist named Deborah Loh wrote an article for the online publication *The Nut Graf* in which she addressed the problem of what she called 'reciprocity in understanding', which is perhaps a necessary condition for pluralism. Called 'Why Fast During Ramadan if Non-Muslim?' the article focused on two non-Muslims who fasted during the entire month of Ramadan. Both of these individuals said that they did it for 'solidarity', and to better understand their Muslim friends. Yet the writer claimed she found this reason to be baffling, writing:

And yet, just what does "showing solidarity" mean in our context where Muslims and Malay Malaysians are the majority? And where non-Muslims have to abide, not by choice but by decree, to various directives such as a ban on new non-Muslim clubs in schools and a ban on using the word "Allah" when it isn't exclusive to Islam?

Or where non-Muslims have no say in the unilateral conversion of children if one's spouse converts to Islam, and have to give up burial rights over a deceased Muslim family member's body? Why should solidarity be shown with the majority if such are the circumstances for the minority?

(Loh 2010)

If we define pluralism as according legitimacy to different ways of being in the world, then it is hard to say that Malaysia, a country in which one group is accorded special privileges by the constitution, is truly pluralist. Even in spaces such as *Malaysiakini* which are avowedly pluralist in character, the state ideology has ways of influencing the ways that people think about one another. Worse yet, the politicization of Islam and the manoeuvring by political parties and groupings to outdo one another in displays of piety have had insidious effects on how people interact on a daily basis.

212   *Janet Steele*

Several veteran Malaysian journalists in their late 40s and mid-50s remembered fondly a day in which 'race' and religion were less politicized, and there was more possibility for real friendship among people of different ethnicities. Tengku Noor Shamsiah contrasted this perhaps idealized past with her experiences at *Bernama* today, describing her Malay friends' reaction when one of their Chinese colleagues brought in a moon cake. 'Now they have this moon cake that is *halal*', she said. 'But they still have got this perception, mistrustful among themselves. So one of the friends said "oh, I don't eat that." But for me, if you give it to me, I will take it – whether I eat it or not. It goes to respecting people' (interview, 21 December 2010).

Malaysiakini's Steven Gan and Shufiyan Shukur used remarkably similar language to describe an earlier time in which Malays and Chinese would happily visit one another's homes. Shufiyan, who spent much of his youth in the UK and returned to Malaysia in the 1980s, recalled:

> Many years ago, I was invited to my friend's Chinese [new] year. Now I don't get invited anymore. Why? Because in '81 when I first came back, they would say, okay, Shuf, this is pork. This is okay, this is chicken. But the chicken would come from a Chinese grocer, in fact. But now even my friends are very concerned about it. If they were to invite me, it would have to be a special occasion when everything was *halal*, that kind of thing. Or they [would have to] take me to ... a special lunch somewhere in a restaurant that's *halal*. But it didn't use to be like that. There's a lot of change. It's change I don't like to see, but that's just the way it is.
>
> (interview, 18 August 2010)

Chief editor Steven Gan also described a kind of social interaction that is now gone, replaced by a superficial state-sponsored 'multi-culturalism.' In the old days, he said, race was not emphasized as much as it is today. Relationships were more natural, and 'we thought less of ourselves as Chinese or Malay or whatever it is'.

> It is different now. And it is impeding all sorts of relationships, even friendships. I live in a housing estate that is almost 95 per cent Malay, and the Chinese there are pushed more or less unconsciously into a ghetto, and also I think that there is among the Malays a greater consciousness of Islam. And that has also helped to increase the gap ... And the open houses – again the Chinese are unsure about inviting the Malays into their house because you do not know exactly whether things are *halal*, and you are not so confident about that, and Malays are also uneasy about going because they feel it may be impolite to reject certain things. So it is not natural. It becomes more difficult in that sense.
>
> (interview, 2 July 2009)

A comparison of the experience of Ramadan in the newsrooms of *Tempo* and *Malaysiakini* suggests that where the state dictates religious practices, pluralism suffers. Although there is not a tradition of state involvement in religious matters in Indonesia, there are, as *Tempo* editor Arif Zulkifi said, people who believe that the state should insure that Muslims fast. These are the same people who are angry that cafes in Jakarta's Kemang area remain open during Ramadan and serve beer. 'It's as if having these cafes open pollutes the holiness of Ramadan', Arif said, but 'according to me it's ridiculous'.

'Fasting is a form of worship that is very personal. The Qur'an itself says, fasting is for Me [*untukKu*]. Your ritual is for Me and not for someone else. It's not necessary to show it off', Arif said (interview, 4 January 2011).

In Malaysia, the power of the state has meant not only that ordinary Muslims have to fear being detained and humiliated if they don't fast, but also that they see themselves as lacking the authority to talk about religion. As Hazlan Zakaria said, 'you see in Malaysia, a religious leader cannot even give a sermon without authority from the district religious office. And that shows how much control our government has over what we can and cannot say.'

'In Indonesia they have got it right', he added, as 'religion is more of a universal concept rather than something we force down somebody's throat. We are getting scarily close to that' (interview, 6 August 2010).

Notes

1 In both Indonesia and Malaysia, Ramadan began on 11 August, and ended on 9 September 2010. I observed the first week of Ramadan at *Tempo* magazine in Jakarta, and the second week of Ramadan at *Malaysiakini* in Kuala Lumpur. All interviews at *Tempo* were conducted in Indonesian; all at *Malaysiakini* were in English. All translations from the Indonesian are my own.

2 *Malaysiakini* has received a significant amount of scholarly attention since it was established a decade ago (Chin 2003; George 2006; Nain 2002; Tong 2004).

3 I have argued elsewhere that *Malaysiakini* uses the norms of good journalism – covering both sides, providing documentary evidence, and giving voice to the voiceless – to legitimize alternative views of events, thus challenging the authoritarianism of the Barisan Nasional (Steele 2009).

4 Malay-Muslims make up 60 per cent, Chinese-Malaysians 24 per cent, and Indian-Malaysians 7 per cent of the population of Malaysia (Hefner 2008: 3–16).

5 For a more detailed discussion of this, see Carool Kersten's contribution to this volume.

6 Here I'm drawing upon Michael Peletz's definition of pluralism as 'social fields, cultural domains, and more encompassing systems in which two or more principles, categories, groups, sources of authority, or ways of being in the world are not only present, tolerated, and accommodated but also *accorded legitimacy* in a basic Weberian sense' (Peletz 2006: 310).

7 Interviews with Tengku Noor Shamsiah, December 1, 2010; Syed Khedher, December 22, 2010; Vicknesan, August 19, 2010.

References

Anwar, Z. (2001) 'What Islam, Whose Islam?', in Hefner, R. W. (ed.) *The Politics of Multiculturalism: Pluralism and Citizenship in Malaysia, Singapore, and Indonesia*, Honolulu: University of Hawaii Press.

214 *Janet Steele*

Benda, H. J. (1958) *The Crescent and the Rising Sun: Indonesian Islam under the Japanese Occupation, 1942–1945*, The Hague and Bandung: W. van Hoeve Ltd, distributed in the USA by the Institute of Pacific Relations, New York.

Bertrand, J. (2010) 'Political Islam and Democracy in the Majority Muslim Country of Indonesia', in Saravanamuttu, J. (ed.) *Islam and Politics in Southeast Asia*, New York: Routledge.

Chin, J. (2003) 'Malaysiakini and Its Impact on Journalism and Politics in Malaysia', in Ho, K. C., Kluver, R., and Yang, K. C. C. (ed.) *Asia.com: Asia Encounters the Internet*, London and New York: RoutledgeCurzon.

George, C. (2006) *Contentious Journalism and the Internet: Towards Democratic Discourse in Malaysia and Singapore,* Singapore: Singapore University Press.

Hefner, R. W. (1997) 'Introduction: Islam in an Era of Nation-States: Politics and Religious Renewal in Muslim Southeast Asia', in Hefner (ed.) *Islam in an Era of Nation States: Politics and Religious Revival in Muslim Southeast Asia,* Honolulu: The University of Hawaii Press.

Hefner, R. W. (2008) 'Introduction: Civic Platforms or Radical Springboards?', in Hefner, R. W. and Horvatich, P. (eds) *Muslim Professional Associations and Politics in Southeast Asia*, Seattle, WA: National Bureau of Asian Research.

Hooker, M. B. (2003) *Notes on Indonesian Islam: Social Change through Fatwa*, Sydney: Allen and Unwin; Honolulu: University of Hawai'i Press.

Kahn, J. S. (2006) *Other Malays: Nationalism and Cosmopolitanism in the Modern Malay World*, Honolulu: Asian Studies Association of Australia, with University of Hawai'i Press.

Laffan, M. (2003) 'The Tangled Roots of Islamist Activism in Southeast Asia', *Cambridge Review of International Affairs,* 16: 397–414.

Loh, D. (2010) 'Why Fast During Ramadan if One is Non-Muslim?', *The Nut Graph*, Available from www.thenutgraph.com/why-fast-during-ramadan-if-one-is-non-muslim/ (accessed April 10, 2012).

Nagata, J. (2010) 'Authority and Democracy in Malaysian and Indonesian Islamic Movements', in Saravanamuttu, J. (ed.) *Islam and Politics in Southeast Asia*, New York: Routledge.

Nain, Z. (2002) 'The Media and Malaysia's *Reformasi* Movement', in Heng, R. H. K. (ed.) *Media Fortunes Changing Times: Asean States in Transition*, Singapore: Institute for Southeast Asian Studies.

Peletz, M. (2006) 'Transgenderism and Gender Pluralism in Southeast Asia since Early Modern Times', *Current Anthropology,* 47: 309–40.

Roff, W. R. (1967) *The Origins of Malay Nationalism,* New Haven, CT, and London: Yale University Press.

Roff, W. R. (2009) *Studies on Islam and Society in Southeast Asia*, Singapore: NUS Press.

Scott, J. C. (1985) *Weapons of the Weak: Everyday Forms of Peasant Resistance*, New Haven, CT: Yale University Press.

Steele, J. (2005) *Wars Within: The Story of an Independent Magazine in Soeharto's Indonesia,* Jakarta and Singapore: Equinox Publishing and ISEAS.

Steele, J. (2006) 'The Triumph of Moderation', *Foreign Policy*, Available from www.foreignpolicy.com/articles/2006/01/04/the_triumph_of_moderation (accessed 26 November 2012).

Steele, J. (2009) 'Professionalism Online: How *Malaysiakini* Challenges Authoritarianism', *International Journal of Press/Politics,* 14: 91–111.

Steele, J. (2011) 'Justice and Journalism: Islam and Journalistic Values in Indonesia and Malaysia', *Journalism,* 12: 533–49.

Tong, Y. S. (2004) 'Malaysiakini: Treading a Tightrope of Political Pressure and Market Factors', in Gan, S., Gomez, J. and Johannen, U. (eds) *Asian Cyberactivism: Freedom of Expression and Media Censorship,* Bangkok: Friedrich Naumann Foundation.

Yegar, M. (1979) *Islam and Islamic Institutions in British Malaya, 1874–1941*, Jerusalem: The Magnes Press, The Hebrew University.

12 Pluralist currents and counter-currents in the Indonesian mass media

The case of Anand Krishna

Julia Day Howell

This chapter examines the mass media, both print and electronic, as sites for the contestation of religious pluralism in Indonesia since the restoration of effective democracy in 1998. The *Reformasi* period (as the following decade came to be known) can be seen as one of destabilization and dispute over divergent notions of religiosity as properly communalist or autonomous, with the scales tipping towards the communalist since the Indonesian Council of Ulama (Majelis Ulama Indonesia or MUI) pronounced a series of *fatwa* against pluralism and liberalism in religion in 2005.

This shift is examined by following the trajectory of one movement, that built around the popular writer and eclectic spiritual development figure Anand Krishna.[1] In the first years of *Reformasi*, Krishna's easy-reading books on spirituality in many different religions crowded out other personal development and general religion books in big city stores. Through his books, and through his public appearances, many people were drawn to the spiritual development courses offered at his centres. Around the large open halls at the centres where he held his stress management and spiritual cleansing workshops (with titles like 'Seni Memperdaya Diri [The Art of Self Empowerment], 1 & 2' and 'Neo-Zen Reiki'), he provided prayer spaces appropriately appointed for people of all Indonesia's recognized religions. There were also niches for the symbols and pictures of the principal figures of other traditions. Workshop participants joined in short prayers from several of the major religions at the beginning of their sessions, but were encouraged to maintain their commitment to their professed religion, as shown on their identity cards.

Krishna himself did not nominate a religious affiliation on his identity card, and his life story traverses several religious traditions. Born in Surakarta, Central Java, in 1956 to parents of Indian descent, he received a Hindu upbringing, but his father also introduced him to the poetry of the famous Sindhi Sufi master Shah Abdul Latief, forming the basis of his abiding deep appreciation of Islam's devotional and mystical heritage. For his primary and secondary school education Krishna was sent to Lucknow, India. There he met and followed the remarkable Sufi teacher Sheikh Baba, who made his living on the streets selling ice blocks. Years later, after doing university studies and becoming a successful businessman in the Jakarta garment trade, Krishna was diagnosed with terminal leukaemia.

Setting aside his worldly affairs, he once more returned to India looking for direction in his extremity. Venturing into the Himalayas, he encountered a figure he described as a Tibetan lama, with whose inspiration he experienced a miraculous cure and determined thereafter to dedicate himself to spiritual cultivation and teaching. However, as has long been common in India, and is now a familiar feature of Western spiritual seeking, his path was not exclusively bounded by one religion. He remained deeply engaged with the Hindu traditions, Sufism and Buddhism, and formed close associations with the Hindu-derived Rajneesh (Osho) movement as well as with Sai Baba, famous for attracting not only Hindu aspirants but Christian and other seekers as well.[2]

On Krishna's return to Jakarta after his life-changing illness, a circle of cosmopolitan urbanites, both expatriates and locals, formed around him, discussing the short reflections he started to write on spirituality in the world's religions. With their encouragement, he pulled these together into popular books of 'appreciation' of the various religions. The success of the books launched him as a best-selling author. To reach a wider public directly and offer practical guidance in personal spiritual development, he then opened the Anand Ashram Centre in Sunter (north Jakarta) in 1991, offering on a commercial basis graded evening classes in the spiritual exercises (*olah rohani*) he had found beneficial.

By the turn of the century, Krishna had become one of Indonesia's most visible proponents of autonomous religiosity.[3] His centres, now located not just in Jakarta but also in Ciawi (in the hill country beyond Jakarta), Yogyakarta (servicing also Solo and Semarang in Central Java), Denpasar and Singaraja in Bali, and Lampung (Sumatra),[4] teach the several hundred meditation (*meditasi*) techniques Krishna has developed over the years and methods of 'emotional cleansing' drawn from several spiritual traditions, undergirded by popular psychology.

In an earlier publication (Howell 2005), I documented that early phase of Anand Krishna's career as a spiritual teacher, showing how he was able to offer his self-styled 'universalist' teachings without state interference, and attract appreciation from leading Muslim public intellectuals. He also received much free publicity in the glossy magazines that covered trends in health and personal development. I presented his movement as one case alongside two other groups that catered for relatively autonomous middle-class Indonesian seekers: the Brahma Kumaris (BK) and Salamullah. Jakarta branches of the Brahma Kumaris World Spiritual University were patronized by Muslims, Christians and Buddhists as well as by Hindus, who all tried out the BK's Raja Yoga meditation as an aid to their spiritual lives within one or another of the official Indonesian religions.[5] Salamullah, originally an informal Islamic prayer gathering around the retired television personality and spiritual healer Lia Aminuddin, became the platform for the emergence of a new 'perennialist' faith, as she channelled the Angel Gabriel.

The untrammelled operation of Anand Krishna centres, the BKs and Lia Aminuddin's Eden Community (Kaum Eden), together with the growing acceptance of previously marginalized Sufi orders, the formation of novel Sufi litany groups by laypeople, and the good business being done by commercial spiritual

218 *Julia Day Howell*

healers like reiki therapists and tai chi teachers outside the framework of any religion (Howell 2001, 2007), all seemed to indicate a softening of the deposed Suharto New Order's policy of restricting religious practice to the confines of one of five recognized religions. At that time, Krishna did not think the authorities were interested any more in investigating groups like his multi-faith centre.

I characterized the New Order regulatory policy still in operation in the late 1990s as 'delimited pluralism', noting that it was based on a Presidential Decision (No. 1, 1965) enunciated by former President Sukarno relatively late in the life of the Republic (nearly two decades after the declaration of Independence), just months before he was deposed by the New Order's leader, General, and then President, Suharto. In previous decades there was no legal clarity on what a person might claim to be his or her form of 'belief in One Almighty God' (*keTuhanan Yang Maha Esa*, one of the five principles, or Pancasila, enshrined in the Preamble to the 1945 Constitution by Sukarno[6]), or what kind of religion (*agama*) would be deserving of the protection and support of the state as mandated by the Constitution. Studying several religions was then common, as in the Theosophy Movement; so also was mixing and matching of traditions, most notably in the numerous *kebatinan* (mystical) groups, which often combined the iconography and theologies of Islam, Christianity and local Hindu and Buddhist heritages. Several *kebatinan* groups even strove for recognition as religions (*agama*).[7]

Jumping forward again to the early days of *Reformasi*, I read there among the middle- and upper-classes the signs of a new acceptance of unrestricted pluralism, accommodating more autonomous modes of religiosity (if not flagrantly eclectic amalgams of the major religions and local traditions such as were common in the early days of the Republic). I noted, however, that many factors, including changes in the political and economic climate of the country, could reverse that incipient change (Howell 2005: 490).

What in retrospect appears to me as a turning point (and to others as a dramatic intensification of the influence of religious conservatives in government and civil society) occurred within months of the appearance of that article, in fact just before the hard copies came out. I take that turning point to be the Indonesian Council of Ulamas' (Majelis Ulama Indonesia, MUI) pronouncement on 29 July 2005 of eleven *fatwa*. They were unprecedented in number on one occasion, but more importantly of unprecedented significance. The national board of this semi-governmental, notionally representative body published its determination that pluralism, secularism and liberalism (in religion) were undesirable and that Lia Aminuddin's movement (Salamullah) and the Ahmadiyah (an Indian interpretation of Islam, in Indonesia since 1925) were deviant. Although commentators have pointed out that the meanings of the words 'pluralism' and 'secularism' for the MUI authors of those *fatwa* were not what social scientists and most of Indonesia's secularly educated elites would associate with the terms (e.g. 'MUI's *Fatwa*...' 2005), nonetheless, on the face of it, this newly visible body was condemning the positive valuation placed on religious plurality in the Pancasila and the Constitution. The MUI *fatwa* also could be read as suggesting that an indulgent attitude towards religious diversity was promoting the erosion of proper religion ('secularism' in MUI's idiosyncratic sense). Moreover this juridical attack, apparently against even delimited religious pluralism, was followed by mob violence against Salamullah, Ahmadiyah and a number of other Muslim-founded groups or gatherings with unusual practices. Vigilante groups, most notably the Islamic Defenders Front (Front Pembela Islam), appeared to be orchestrating these attacks.

The frequency of such attacks, both against marginal Muslim groups and practices and against Christian churches, has increased since 2005 (Suaedy 2010).[8] Moreover, Suaedy, presently director of the Wahid Institute (which systematically collects data on infringements of religious freedom in Indonesia), has documented a pattern of indirect social control of religious expression effected by communalists. The pattern is as follows: an unusual form of religious expression attracts public attention; parties with a range of personal, political and/or ideological interests rally to have MUI, the Department of Religion's Religious Research Bureau (Litbang Agama) and/or the research office of PAKEM (a branch of the Justice Department charged with surveillance of minor religious groups) determine that the group is 'deviant'; then (or before that) vigilante groups mob these 'deviant' establishments; the police fail to intervene effectively, purporting that they are unable to do so; some of the attacked group are taken into custody, since they represent a threat to public order; the principals of the group are charged with 'blasphemy', as their 'deviance' constitutes a misuse of true religion; and finally the accused are tried and then jailed. The length of the sentence depends on how visible and vocal the vigilantes have been at the trial.

Suaedy, like other observers of the Islamic Defenders Front (e.g. Jahroni 2008; Wilson 2006, 2008), points out the way this pattern of interaction between non-government civil society actors, a semi-governmental body, and the bureaucratic arms of government apparently influence the actions (or lack of action) of elected representatives in government (often criticized for not intervening in the unfolding of such scenarios) and the judiciary. It is also apparent that the media play an important role in multiplying the effect of intimidation practised by the vigilante groups: the mobs they organize and the injuries incurred by victims make good news features; and their demonstrations, outside the court and in, can also be highly newsworthy. The media coverage contributes to the perpetuation, and perhaps intensification, of a vicious cycle of casting religious difference as socially dangerous and in creating acceptance for more and more restriction.

The post-2005 trajectory of Anand Krishna's movement can be read as a particularly salient instance of the role of the media in driving the kind of cycle described above. The media may well have amplified Krishna's exposure to attacks from religious conservatives because Krishna's career as a spiritual figure has been built in large part through the media. Not only has he published over 140 books carried in major bookshops across the country, but he has appeared frequently on national television and regional talk shows and radio programs. He has also made his own television programs: the 13 episode series called *Building Indonesia Anew with Anand Krishna*. It was aired on the Q and Swara television channels, and went into a second season. On those programs he was able to host

220   *Julia Day Howell*

quite a number of prominent people, including the late K.H. Abdurrahman Wahid (Indonesia's fourth president and most visibly resolute defender of full religious freedom); Bali Governor I Made Mangku Pastika, who became internationally famous as commissioner of police in the aftermath of the 2002 Bali bombings; the Sultan of Yogyakarta; an Australian ambassador to Indonesia; several members of the Indonesian Parliament; and a number of entertainers and other well-known people. In recent years he also became a regular contributor to widely read papers like the *Jakarta Post* and *Bali Times*. Therein he wrote on a wide range of social issues, from religious pluralism and the need to protect national integration, to shady development deals, and the need for environmental protection and for measures to restrict the alienation of agricultural land through long-term leases granted to Middle Eastern investors.

The following section shows that the trajectory of Anand Krishna's movement since 2005 has been shaped by the growing clout of communalist religious pressure groups in Indonesia. Further, I argue that the prosecution of a legal case against him starting in 2010 strongly resembles the pattern of marginalization of novel religious expressions identified by Suaedy (2010).

To develop this case, I start by documenting the changes in Anand Krishna's movement since 2005. It was then that he shifted his energies to creating forums promoting national unity and let his commercial spiritual development business in the Anand Ashram centres slip somewhat into the background. He turned over the teaching of his courses to Ashram regulars already trained in his techniques, and began devoting most of his time to what he hoped could be embraced as a common cause for all Indonesians, namely, fully egalitarian ethnic and religious relations in the original spirit of the Pancasila and its promulgator, Bung Karno ('Brother Sukarno', Indonesia's first president).

Where not otherwise indicated in the text, my report on the activities and claims of Krishna and his close associates in the Anand Ashram Foundation is based on interviews with him, with the director of the foundation Maya Safira Muchtar and with Krishna's son, Prashant Gangtani, in Jakarta in February and May 2011, and on correspondence with them from March 2010 through December 2011. Background material on Krishna's movement since 2005 comes from occasional short visits I made to the Anand Ashram centres in Jakarta, Ciawi, Yogyakarta and Denpasar, and to the L'Ayurveda Spa (owned by associates of the Anand Ashram Foundation) between 2005 and 2011.

Post 2005 adaptations to increasing communalist pressures

The television series *Building Indonesia Anew with Anand Krishna*, featuring as it did several champions of egalitarian, untrammelled religious pluralism and moderate Islam (most notably President Abdurrahman Wahid and the Sultan of Yogyakarta), helped carry forward Krishna's new 2005-plus agenda. But the major step in advancing the new program was the formation on 11 April 2005 of his National Integration Movement or NIM, known in Indonesian as the Gerakan Integrasi Nasional.

There was a substantial overlap between the office holders of NIM and his Anand Ashram Foundation, which serves as a coordinating body for the Anand Ashram centres and other initiatives developed by Krishna. Nonetheless, the office bearers were able to involve an impressive array of public figures in their massive launch of NIM's concept at a seminar attended by more than a thousand people on 1 September 2005. The seminar, held in Jakarta at the National Defence Institute (Lemhanas), was addressed by several luminaries, including the Defence Minister; former President Abdurrahman Wahid; the governor of Lemhanas, Mulyadi; and the Governor of Jakarta. It was called *Symposium Kebangsaan* (Nationalism Symposium) with the English subtitle 'For You, *Ibu Pertiwi*' ('For You, Mother Earth' [identified here with a figure from Javanese mythology]). The symposium addressed the core concerns of the NIM, namely to 'respond to threats to the unity of the nation, particularly those caused by disturbances in the name of religion and ethnicity'.

If that august assemblage had a serious, even ominous tone, the main activities of the NIM did not. These were the *Pesta Rakyat*, or People's Festivals, held every two weeks from 2006 to 2010 and in principle, if not actuality, ongoing. Everyone was invited: men, women, parents, children, grandparents and teens, all regardless of their religion or ethnic group. The 'festivals' were held where people of all sorts felt comfortable gathering, and where there was considerable visibility for NIM activities. The main *Pesta Rakyat* were held in Jakarta in the field in front of the National Monument (MONAS). NIM organizers claimed regular attendances of 5,000 people. Other festivals were held at the famous ancient Hindu and Buddhist monuments in central Java, Prambanan and Borobudur, as well as at big malls and in centrally located open spaces in Semarang and other cities.

The feature activity at the People's Festivals was designed to be as socially inclusive as possible: a laugh-in, called *Olahraga Tertawa* (Laughing Exercise). It was advertised with cartoon figures and the slogan: 'One minute of laughing is worth twenty minutes of light exercise!' Brochures explained its value as a holistic health practice to relieve stress, massage the heart and lungs, improve the flow of blood and make people happy. Other People's Festival activities included singing songs like *Aku Bangga Jadi Orang Indonesia* (I'm Proud to be an Indonesian) and *We Are One Family* (English title, Indonesian verses), and little impromptu dramas about picking up trash, not using plastic bottles, buying domestic products and other practices of civility. The NIM players would reach out in the middle of performances to draw in members of the crowd to take part in the dramas.

The People's Festivals show Krishna's gift for dramatizing in a popular style complex and sensitive ideas. That gift was already evident in different ways in his early writings and in the design of his spiritual development centres' curricula since the 1990s. But the festivals also called upon the creative energies of many young people, who predominated in the NIM and Anand Ashram regional centres in central Java and Bali since the NIM started. Considerable artistic work, as well as organizing, went into the festivals, and the young people's talents at clowning

222 Julia Day Howell

in the laugh-ins and acting out little plots in the educational dramas were important to the viability of the program. They were also the ones who introduced interested people to Krishna's books on NIM themes after the fun activities at the People's Festivals were over.

The talents of the NIM activists in organizing attractive public events with a serious message played a part in a particularly fateful celebration that they helped organize in cooperation with a major coalition of pluralist groups, the AKKBB (Aliansi Kebangsaan untuk Kebebasan Beragama dan Berkeyakinan, or National Alliance for Freedom of Religion and Faith). That was a celebration of pluralism, held on 1 June 2008 at the National Monument, Jakarta. The Alliance included human rights-oriented NGOs, both secular (like the Jakarta Legal Aid Institute and the Indonesian Legal Aid Foundation) and those associated with the Muslim community (like the Wahid Institute, named after former President Abdurrahman Wahid; the Maarif Foundation; and the International Centre for Islam and Pluralism [ICIP]), as well as a number of Christian groups. It was supported individually by prominent Muslim public intellectuals like Dawam Rahardjo, founder of the prominent Institute for Religious and Philosophical Studies (LSAF); Syafii Anwar, director of the ICIP; Professor Siti Musda Mulia, Chairperson of the Institute for the Study of Religion and Gender (LKAJ) and Secretary General of the Indonesian Conference on Religion and Peace; Ahmad Syafii Maarif, former chairman of Muhammadiyah (the second largest Muslim organization in Indonesia) and executive director of the Maarif Foundation; and the high-profile founder of the Liberal Muslim Network, Ulil Abshar Abdalla. At the time, the AKKBB was particularly concerned to demonstrate support for the Ahmadi community, which had suffered numerous serious violent attacks driven by the Islamic Defenders Front following the MUI *fatwa* on religious deviance in 2005. The concept behind the 1 June 2008 event, crafted with major input from Anand Krishna's NIM, was to celebrate the birthday of the Pancasila as an emblem of pluralism and to do that with an event themed as a kind of festival or party (taking off from the idea of the *Pesta Rakyat*), followed by a walk to the Hotel Indonesia fountain. The AKKBB organizers hoped that pitching the gathering as a celebration would not be as provocative to hardliners as something advertised as a demonstration. Accordingly, they encouraged people to bring their families, including young children (see Australian Broadcasting Corporation 2008).

At the event, the Islamic Defenders Front and other vigilantes did attack. Incensed with the idea that Ahmadis were in the crowd and their cause was being taken up by the festival-goers, Riziek Shihab of Front Pembela Islam, and Munarman, leader of a related group, the Islam Troop Command (Komando Laskar Islam), led the attack. They stormed the assembling men, women and children with staves, stones and hot sand. Between 70 and 80 people associated with the Alliance were beaten; nine required hospitalization (see David 2008; 'Hardliners Ambush...' 2008; 'Two Witnesses Testify...' 2008). According to one of the NIM people there on the day (Personal communication, Jakarta, February 2011), 'scores' of NIM people were among the injured and their testimony was important in convicting the Islamic Defenders Front assailants.[9]

Krishna and NIM activists also worked with the National Alliance for Freedom of Religion and Faith in developing a plan to at last challenge the 1965 Presidential Decision No. 1 (PenPres1, 1965). That was the directive which formed the basis for the delimited pluralism policy of the New Order; it not only named for the first time the religions to be supported and protected by the state, but included a section on 'the prevention of misuse or blasphemation of religion'. Importantly, that Presidential Decision, which had the effect of law, contained sections outlawing the 'insulting' and 'false use' of religion (the 'blasphemy' laws used against marginal religious groups and activities), as well as forbidding the 'interpretation' (meaning the free or non-standard interpretation) of one of the official religions. The challenge was to be made through a formal legal procedure: a request to the Constitutional Court for a judicial review of PenPres1, 1965. Technically the Alliance could not put the formal request forward, so this was finally done in November 2009 by former President Abdurrahman Wahid.[10] Three hundred community leaders signed the document (Platzdasch 2009). Members of the Alliance, in their private capacities, would be called before the Court in support of the request. Krishna expected to be one of them.

However, fate intervened. On 12 February of the new year (2010), just when the hearings on the Request for the Judicial Review of PenPres1, 1965 were about to be heard, Anand Krishna was reported to the National Commission for Women (Komnas Perempuan) by two former Ashram regulars, Tara Pradibta Laksmi (19 years old) and Sumidah (a woman in her 30s). They claimed that Krishna had sexually harassed them: hugging, kissing and intimately touching them while they were 'hypnotized' by his 'indoctrination'. The offence allegedly took place repeatedly, up to three times a day almost every day in April and June of 2009, at an alternative healing clinic, L'Ayurveda, owned by senior Ashram office holders.[11] The case was presented to the Jakarta city police three days later, by Tara Pradibta only. Lawyers for the plaintiffs called for Krishna to be charged under Article 290 of the Criminal Code, read in conjunction with Articles 294 and 64, which make it an offense to commit obscene acts with someone unconscious or helpless and to indecently deal with a person in one's care. A conviction would carry a maximum sentence of seven years.

Pluralism and prosecution on criminal charges

From the time harassment charges were laid, Krishna was unable to participate in the Alliance or in the movement to support the request for a judicial review of the blasphemy law in the High Court. The People's Festivals at the National Monument were called off in the face of threats from Islamic vigilantes. The Chief of Police Criminal Investigations, Ito Sumardi, asked the Anand Ashram Foundation not to hold the festivals because they were being closely watched by 'radicals' who said that Krishna was spreading 'occultism' (*klinik*). The *Jakarta Post* also cancelled Krishna's bi-weekly column of commentary on social issues, which had been running for two years. As the case unfolded, not just Krishna's personal behaviour came under attack, but his teachings.

224   *Julia Day Howell*

Almost immediately after the sexual harassment case was taken to the police, and before they had begun to investigate it or interrogate the accused, the story exploded on television. It was carried at first by TV1, then by Trans 7's i-gossip and other channels. It was explored not only in news items but in talk show programs and commentaries. According to the accused (which later came to include Ashram Director Maya Safira Muchtar, who supposedly procured for Krishna)[12] and a humorous send-up of the media coverage in an e-mail posted on the Liberal Islam Network list ('Dozens of Former Students...' 2010), the television coverage was seriously unbalanced, not only in slant but in time given to the accuser and accused. TV1 aired a barrage of clips of Tara Pradibta making highly explicit accusations several times a day for as long as 20 minutes at a time, and gave Krishna only a few minutes out of a day to give his version of the story. On one occasion Maya Muchtar waited in the TV green room without being called while the show presenters said they couldn't locate her. The story died down at the end of February 2010, but was back on air for a short period after 42 former students claimed that they also had been sexually harassed by Krishna.

On 15 March 2010, Krishna was called by the police for questioning for the first time as a 'witness', and then on 3 April as a 'suspect'. And the questioning turned rough. According to Krishna (who is a diabetic with blood pressure problems) and his legal advisor Astro P. Girsang, the interrogation went on for 11 hours without a meal or reasonable toilet breaks. Most of the questioning was aimed at his teachings. At 9 pm he suffered severe chest pains, and a half hour later, as he was being taken out of the station, he collapsed. At a police hospital to which he was delivered, he was seen by a doctor who gave him sleeping pills; after that he slept for two days. When he awoke, the doctors determined that he had had a heart attack. He was bedridden for some months and thereafter has had an ongoing heightened risk of stroke.

The case first came to trial on 25 August of that year (2010) and stretched over 15 months, interrupted nearly a year into the trial, on 8 June 2011, by the telling dismissal of the initial presiding judge, Hari Sasangka. The dismissal came shortly after Krishna's lawyers filed evidence with the Judicial Commission that the judge was conducting an affair with one of the young female witnesses for the prosecution ('Krishna's Lawyer Applauds...' 2011). Much of the judge's questioning, and that of the prosecuting attorneys, concerned Krishna's teachings, pressing him and witnesses for the defence on Krishna's alleged 'syncretism' and insinuating a hidden agenda in his activities to convert people away from Islam. Thus Mrs Norma Selamat, a Muslim accountant who once accompanied Krishna, her husband and others on a trip to India, reported feeling that the prosecuting attorneys were forcing her to say that Krishna was trying to 'Hinduize' her during the trip. Another witness for the defence, a 19-year-old student who had participated in Ashram activities, was asked during the trial whom she 'idolized'. When she replied, 'Mahatma Gandhi', the prosecutor commented, 'but you are a Muslim!', again implying that Krishna had pressured her to convert.[13]

The new presiding judge, Albertina Ho, celebrated for her probity and vigorous examination of previous human rights cases (cf. Angkasa 2011) finally acquitted Krishna of all charges on 22 November 2011 ('Anand Krishna Acquitted...' 2011). The grounds for dismissal of first presiding judge Hari Sasangka (that he had been repeatedly observed in compromising circumstances with a young female witness for the plaintiff), taken together with the heavy emphasis of his and the prosecuting attorneys' questioning on Krishna's teachings, and the finding of not guilty by the court under judge Albertina Ho, all strongly suggest that Judge Sasangka was, as Krishna and his lawyers claimed, biased against him. Moreover, the construction and prosecution of the case by the plaintiff's lawyers reveal numerous anomalies that are suggestive of a fabricated case. Early in the trial, the defence presented the police medical report on a physical examination of the plaintiff (Tara Pradibta), showing that she was still a virgin at the time of the trial. Further, none of the witnesses for the plaintiff reported seeing her sexually molested, only that they saw Tara Pradibta and Krishna go together into parts of a building where they could not be observed, whereas witnesses for the defence testified that there were no such private spaces at the therapy business where the offenses were supposed to have occurred (cf. Roy, Dianswara and Hakim 2011a). Witnesses for the accused, who according to the plaintiff saw the purportedly numerous assaults, denied that they had actually seen any. There were also discrepancies between the time and place of the alleged assaults and Krishna's actual presence, according to diarized appointments and witnesses to his presence elsewhere.

Not only were there problems with the evidence of the supposed sexual violation, but Tara Pradibta's account of the circumstances which prompted her to come forward with her complaint raised questions pursued by the defence. Paradoxically, while Tara Pradibta's lawyers charged that Krishna had 'brainwashed' her by 'indoctrinating' her to do whatever he, as her 'guru', wished, thereby 'hypnotizing' her and 'paralyzing her psychologically' ('The Trial of Anand...' 2011), Tara Pradibta testified that she first became aware of the offence when she underwent an exceptionally intensive hypnotherapy treatment by a psychologist appointed by her family. Tara Pradibta's family had removed her precipitously from her previous social contacts (including those with friends from the Anand Ashram Foundation) despite her protests, and required her to undergo four months of treatment with the psychologist Dewi Pratomo in strict isolation. Pratomo, who presented herself as a hypnotherapist, used a regime of hypnotherapy to cure Tara Pradibta of what she (Pratomo) identified as severe withdrawal (Susanto and Al-Yamani 2010). It was after several weeks of Pratomo's hypnotherapy that Tara Pradibta recalled the sexual violation supposedly perpetrated by Krishna in the preceding months.

Krishna protested, in his testimony and in the media, that he does not put himself forward as a guru (though he said he couldn't stop people from regarding him as such),[14] does not practise hypnosis or use the mind's power of suggestion except as a tool people can use themselves for self-empowerment (as in affirmations), and had not been teaching classes of spiritual exercises himself for over five years (cf. Roy, Dianswara and Hakim 2011a, 2011b). At the trial, his lawyers presented arguments to the effect that 'repressed memory syndrome'[15] has been

226 *Julia Day Howell*

discredited by professional bodies in the US and is not acceptable as evidence in almost all states there. They called in nationally eminent psychologists to debunk the practice.

Despite that, presiding judge Hari Sasangka did not set aside Tara Pradibta's accusation against Krishna. To the contrary, he allowed 'expert witness' to be provided for the plaintiff by Dewi Pratomo who, Krishna's lawyers insisted, as Tara Pradibta's treating psychologist could not be disinterested (Roy *et al.* 2011a). Moreover, Pratomo's expertise was open to question, since her qualifications from the Jakarta-based Hypnotherapy Motivation Institute had been completed only recently by distance education. Expert witnesses for the defence, leading psychologist and expert on altered state experiences Professor Dr Luh Ketut Suryani and hypnotherapy specialist Adi W. Gunawan, both challenged the professionalism of using such a large number of treatments (45) over just three months ('The Trial of Anand...' 2011). They testified that such a procedure could actually implant false memories, and not actually heal the client.

Then on 9 March 2011, seven months into the trial, before presentation of all the evidence had been completed, before summations, and before the pronouncement of a verdict, then presiding judge Hari Sesanka ordered Krishna jailed on the grounds that as long as he was free there was danger he would 'reoffend' (Andriyanto 2011). The jailing caused consternation, not only among the Anand Ashram community but among the legal fraternity. Eminent human rights lawyer and Presidential advisor Adnan Buyung Nasution publically decried the jailing of a person not yet convicted of an offence on the grounds that he might offend again (interview with Adnan Buyung Nasution, Jakarta, 12 May 2011; see also More 2011). Further, as Krishna had punctually attended all previous hearings, there were no grounds for suspecting that he would abscond.

In desperation, seeing his hopes of a fair trial fading, Krishna commenced a hunger strike in protest against the jailing and against what he held it represented: baseless slurs on his character and unfair treatment by the judge. Krishna persisted with his fast to the point where he had to be hospitalized on 17 March, and yet continued his fast in hospital. As his condition became increasingly parlous, a stream of prominent people began publicly to voice their concerns over his condition and irregularities in the trial. They included Gus Nuril (General Chairman of Justice and Religious Freedom Rights Forum), Djohan Effendy (former Secretary of State), A.S. Hikam (former Minister of Research and Technology), Poppy Dharsono (MP from Central Java), Franz Magnis-Suseno (leading Catholic Theologian and human rights spokesperson), Ida Pedanda Sebali Tianyar Anbawa (head of the Balinese Hindu Sabha Pandita Parisada) and actress Ayu Dyah Pasha. Significantly, their outcries and visits to his hospital bedside attracted major press coverage, and dramatic photos appeared in major newspapers of a desperately weak Krishna hardly able to lift his head to receive these notable visitors (e.g. 'A.S. Hikam Prihatin...' 2011; 'Franz Magnis Suseno Kecewa...' 2011). Leading columnist and social critic Julia Suryakusuma (2011) also devoted one of her weekly *Jakarta Post* essays to Krishna's judicial 'persecution'. After 49 days of fasting, when hopes for his life were fading, Krishna's

Indonesian mass media: Anand Krishna   227

family was able to prevail upon the judge to release him from hospital detention to their care (Santosa 2011; Victoria 2011).

After Krishna recovered, his trial continued under presiding Judge Hari Sasangka until that judge's removal from the Jakarta court to a remote post in Ambon. As noted, the new presiding judge, Albertina Ho, acquitted him after re-examining evidence presented earlier, and questioning more deeply a number of the witnesses.

Media opportunities for shaping attitudes toward religious pluralism

Krishna and his circle believe that figures hostile to his universalist spirituality, allied with individuals who had a personal interest in creating a scandal, orchestrated the prosecution of the sexual violation case against him. He also feared that blasphemy charges would be added to the sexual harassment charges, since his teaching were being described as deviant and blasphemous in the press. He, his son and Ashram supporters claimed that threats were personally delivered to him by an Islamic 'fundamentalist group' in a series of visits to his home from February to August 2010 (Roy *et al.* 2011a: 10; interviews at the Anand Ashram, Sunter, May 2011). Whatever happened in private, there is much to show that certain Islamists took advantage of the airing of the sexual violation accusations against him to publicly discredit his teachings along with his character.[16]

The public discrediting of Anand Krishna began on 13 February 2010, just a day after Tara Pradibta and Sumidah took their complaints about sexual interference by Krishna to the National Commission for Women, and before they went to the police. That day *Sabili*, an Islamist newspaper, carried an article entitled 'Kasus Anand Krishna: Dari Pelecehan Agama Hingga Pelecehan Seksual' ('The Anand Krishna Case: From the Violation of Religion to Sexual Violation') ('Kasus Anand...' 2010). The article reported on J. Amin Djamaluddin, an official on MUI's national board, saying that Krishna taught '*sinkretisme*' and debased the concept of God, in effect blaspheming (a criminal offense). On 17 February, *VivaNews* carried accusations that Krishna tried to persuade Muslims not to do their daily prayers and that he taught the way to God was only by sex (Kristanti and Nurlaila 2010).[17] On the TV talk shows that ran the scandal that February, Tara Pradibta's friends also described Krishna's teachings as 'religious syncretism' that offends against blasphemy laws. While a part of both the Muslim and Christian communities already held this view, it is certainly the case that the sexual harassment case provided the opportunity for unprecedented public attention to be given to it.

Other opponents of Krishna's teachings weighed in after these first salvos. On 24 February, on Trans7's i-gossip program, communalist lay preacher Habib Abdurrahman Assegaf discussed how he distrusted the 'brainwashing' that goes on in 'cults' like Krishna's. The next day Tara Pradibta's lawyer Agung Muttauch stated in a *Tempo* article that the 'sexual harassment [case] was only one entry gate to more serious issues. This is [going to become] religious blasphemy' (*TempoInteraktif* 2010).

228   *Julia Day Howell*

Then on 8 March 2010, Abrory Abdul Jabrar, a one-time participant in Ashram activities, started publishing articles setting out the 'blasphemous' teachings he had found in Krishna's books and accusing him of indoctrinating his students (e.g. 'Murid Harus Rela...' 2010). Abrory featured prominently in Krishna's trial as a witness for the prosecution and contributed items on the case to the Islamist media. The second chief judge, Albertina Ho, questioned his testimony closely, revealing what appeared to be his conspiratorial role: he advertised, via a web registration site, for others harassed by Krishna to come forward, and hosted meetings of witnesses at which, apparently, strategies for presenting testimonies were formulated ('Membongkar Rekayasa...' 2011; see also Roy *et al.* 2011a: 10).

In the same month (March 2010), the Ashram Foundation learned that Professor Utang Ranuwijaya, a member of the MUI *fatwa* committee instrumental in framing a *fatwa* against yoga, had begun collecting data to pronounce against Anand Ashram teachings and practices. In April, *Detik* carried news that Krishna's alleged victims were urging police to close down Krishna's centres. Then on 16 September 2010, members of the Islamic Defenders Front made an appearance *en masse* at Krishna's trial (Ratya 2010).

Conclusion

Given Suaedy's (2010) findings that sentencing outcomes in trials of non-mainstream religious figures are correlated with the amount of conservative outcry against them, Krishna had reason to fear that he would not be treated impartially. And evidently he was not; that is, not until the first chief judge, Hari Sasangka, was dismissed for egregious violation of legal ethics, and was replaced by Albertina Ho. However, if the media coverage achieved by Muslim communalists helped sustain biased prosecution of fabricated charges under the first chief judge, it is also likely that the media attention eventually captured by nationally prominent champions of the rule of law and religious freedom was crucial to the more careful handling of Krishna's case subsequent to the dismissal of the first chief judge. Those champions came forward in Krishna's defence after he was jailed and undertook his hunger strike, influencing the choice of a replacement judge of the stature of Ho. Krishna's high media profile in the years preceding the allegations made him particularly vulnerable to sensational reportage following on the allegations, but the high profile of those who eventually spoke up for justice in his trial also must have had a bearing on the appointment of a judge of Ho's reputation. Further, that support would have changed the odds against acquittal, which, as Suaedy has shown, in cases such as this involving suggestions of religious deviance have consistently gone against the accused. This too demonstrates the importance of the media as sites for the contestation of religious pluralism.

The role of the media in the Anand Krishna case lends weight to the view that we must consider more than just specific laws on religion–state relations and the electoral contestation that may change them when assessing the scope for religious diversity in Asia and elsewhere. Looking beyond the forms of procedural democracy, one must also attend to the effective protection of free religious expression evident in the deployment of police protection, the prevalence of pecuniary corruption in the courts and public administration, and the susceptibility of the courts to ideological pressures, including those fanned in the mass media.

In this case it is also evident that the now intensely globalized electronic mass media, along with the increasingly internationalized educational, work and leisure experiences of middle- and upper-class Asians, are shaping the discourses through which forms of religious influence are challenged, and guilt and innocence disputed. At issue in Krishna's trial was not simply the occurrence of a sexual act but its perpetration on one whose will had been disabled by their being made 'unconscious' or 'helpless'. Without witnesses of the violation, the alleged victim's own testimony about what happened while she was allegedly helpless was crucial but problematic. The imported constructs of 'brainwashing' (*cuci otak*) and 'repressed memory syndrome', and a particular practice of hypnotherapy to recover 'lost' memories, came into play as the means by which the prosecution could show how the alleged victim's knowledge of her violation could be recovered. The defence lawyers then attempted to discredit those constructs citing locally less well known American court cases in which the concepts of brainwashing and repressed memory syndrome have been discredited.

It is noteworthy, however, that the grounds for Krishna's acquittal did not specifically discredit either the notion of brainwashing or repressed memory syndrome. A link between the now widely-circulating notion of dangerous 'cults' (*kultus*) and 'brainwashing' (*cuci otak*) may well have been reinforced in the popular imagination through media coverage of this case.

We have yet to consider what the outcome of Anand Krishna's case betokens for the free expression of religion in Indonesia. It is certainly a victory for justice in the legal system[18], and therefore for human rights in Indonesia, but it is questionable whether others with fewer social assets could expect a similar reversal of bias. His was, after all, but one among many cases prosecuted against supposed religious deviants and minorities. Almost all of these cases have concluded with convictions. Also, vigilante violence against minorities still meets no or minimal police restraint and, when punished, typically attracts only modest sentences. Moreover, there remains considerable public pressure to maintain quite strict delimited pluralism. Yet this particularly prominent promoter of universalist spirituality *is* now free to continue with both his teaching and his advocacy of greater freedom of religion. And there is still considerable appreciation among cosmopolitan middle- and upper-class Indonesians for spirituality not rigidly circumscribed by legalism. One indication of this is the healthy market for spiritually based personal development programs, especially, of late, for those with a practical orientation towards worldly success. Numerous commercial programs, whether generically spiritual or 'spiritual' with a modest Islamic colouration, like the highly profitable ESQ training (Howell 2012; Rudnyckyj 2010) and smaller provincial spiritual training centres like Bioenergi and Bhakti Nusantara (Muttaqin 2012) do good business, even attracting people of diverse religious

230   *Julia Day Howell*

affiliations to programs with heavy Islamic colouration. A number of Krishna's more recent books, too, have been in this spirituality-for-success genre (with titles like *The Hanuman Factor: Life Lessons for Spiritual CEO, Youth Challenges and Empowerment,* and *Total Success*[19]), in contrast to the 'appreciation'-of-other-religions genre that he developed earlier in his career as a spiritual teacher. In the present climate, moving further in the direction of the more practical spiritual books and courses could be an attractive option.

As for activism, Krishna has announced that for now, just freed from prosecution, he is only focusing on personal renewal. Still, we can ask whether his kind of universalist spirituality can be made more secure legally. He was part of the National Alliance for Freedom of Religion and Faith which challenged delimited pluralism via their request for a judicial review of PenPres 1, 1965. In making that challenge, the Alliance sought also the removal of the statutes against blasphemy and the 'free' interpretation of religion contained in that body of law. The movement drawn together in the Alliance is not dead, but the Alliance itself is moribund and there is little if any expectation that under the present government sufficient political support can be garnered to justify attempting another request for the legislation to be reviewed.

Notes

1   The full legal name of Anand Krishna is Krishna Kumar Tolaram Gangtani. He has used the name Anand Krishna since he turned to the promotion of spirituality following his recovery from cancer in 1991.

2   See Krishna's (2003) autobiography, *Soul Quest,* and the biographical note, 'Get to Know Him' on the Anand Ashram Foundation website (http://id.anandkrishna.org/?page_id=2). It is worth noting that in the early years of his adult life before his illness, Krishna had already been active in Sai Baba groups in Indonesia. He saw Sai Baba as a figure carrying the resonance of the great figures in all the major religions, and so as an inspiration for Indonesian religious tolerance (Personal communication, June 2012).

3   Building on my earlier work on personal autonomy in Sufi religiosity (Howell 2008) and on Asef Bayat's (2007) notion of 'active piety' in Egypt and Iran, I here place Krishna and others at one end of a spectrum of Indonesian religiosity that represents the degree of personal responsibility people assume for evaluating different sources of religious authority and the consequent autonomy they assert or deny (for themselves and others) in making choices among the possible ways of adhering to their religion. As in my analysis of contemporary Sufism in Indonesia (Howell 2008), I imply a contrast between highly autonomous religiosity and relatively constricted religious autonomy. Further, in this chapter I use the term 'communalist' (as in my 2010 analysis of the celebrity preacher Arifin Islam) to characterize those more constrained forms of religious autonomy in which advocates of an Islamic state or caliphate assert the necessity for community control over the religious practice and behaviour of believers. In what follows, 'communalist' overlaps with common usages of the term 'Islamist' to designate Muslims seeking state control of religious behaviour, but emphasizes the contemporary context of religious and political mobilization in which a degree of personal autonomy is the first step in activation of the communalist or Islamist agenda.

4   The centres are now coordinated through a body called the Anand Krishna Centres for Holistic Health and Meditation [English original], under the umbrella of the Anand Ashram Foundation.

Indonesian mass media: Anand Krishna 231

5 The 'official religions' referred to here are those specified in Presidential Decision No. 1, 1965, as religions deserving protection and support from the Indonesian government. The decision, that had the force of law, recognized that those traditions embody the *keTuhanan Yang Maha Esa* (Godliness; belief in One Almighty God) mentioned as one of the five fundamental values (Pancasila) of the nation in the Preamble to the 1945 Constitution (see note 6 below). The named religions were Islam, Protestantism, Catholicism, Hinduism, Buddhism and Confucianism. Confucianism was suppressed under the Suharto Government (1968–98).

6 The Pancasila included as its first principle of '*keTuhanan Yang Maha Esa*' along with four other principles: just and civilized humanity, unity of the nation, democracy, and social justice. Sukarno proposed the Pancasila to resolve tensions between those who wanted to found Indonesia as an Islamic state and those who did not, including Balinese and Christian minorities as well as Muslims concerned to safeguard the variety of Muslim visions for Islamic practice in society. Sukarno was himself a Muslim of Muslim Javanese descent on his father's side, but his mother was Balinese. From both his mother's culture and the Hindu elements in Javanese drama and literature he derived a deep appreciation for Indonesia's ancient Hindu and Buddhist heritages. He famously used Indic philosophical notions of multiplicity resolved in a higher unity to forge rhetorical devices like the Pancasila to inspire the resolution of the cultural differences that threatened to shatter the ethnically and religiously diverse new nation of Indonesia.

7 Eclectic groups with a new revelation, both those claiming to be a religion in their own right (*agama baru* or 'new religions') and others that held back from such claims, were explicitly targeted by Presidential Decision No. 1, 1965. In that decision President Sukarno determined that such groups should 'return to their origins [in the recognized world religions]', and in effect made them illegal.

8 Other sources also call attention to a decline in protection for religious freedom in Indonesia. See also Asian Human Rights Commission (2011), Australian Broadcasting Corporation (2008) and several reports by the International Crisis Group.

9 The two served 9 months of 18-month jail sentences; they were released in July 2009 for 'good behaviour'.

10 For an analysis of the decision of the court, see Bagir, Usman and Naipospos (2010).

11 Later, under a new presiding judge, the plaintiff changed her testimony, claiming the sexual relations occurred only six times, but at three different locations (More and Ebo 2011).

12 While that accusation was aired in the media, no charges were actually pressed against Maya Muchtar.

13 Interview in May 2011 with Mr and Mrs Slamet and others present at the trial.

14 Certainly Krishna does not claim to be a 'guru' in any sense other than an ordinary teacher (see Roy *et al.* 2011b). The word 'guru' is, in fact, an ordinary Indonesian word for teacher, but in the context of this case the word guru has carried associations with mysteriously powerful leaders of 'cults'. And the business format of his teaching (large public classes that people pay to attend) is quite different from the tutelary format of either Hindu gurus of the past or Sufi *sheikhs*. In the Bali Anand Ashram the chair reserved for him at the centre of the meeting hall is evocative of the guru's chair in some Hindu sects. Nonetheless, in the predominantly Hindu context of the centre there, the associations attached to a spiritual guru are probably less sensational than non-Hindu Indonesians might expect.

15 That is, the 'recovery' of previously non-existent 'memories' through unintended suggestion under hypnosis.

16 Islamists were not the only ones to be publicly critical of Krishna. Professor Azyumardi Azra, a prominent Muslim moderate, voiced concern in the press over cult-like developments around spiritual teachers, which he considered unhealthy. Mutual friends of Krishna in private claimed that progressive circles were divided

232   *Julia Day Howell*

over the case, with some giving the benefit of the doubt to the women who claimed to have been harassed, and others withholding judgment on the grounds that religious and spiritual teachers of all stripes are likely to be subject to romantic fantasies (Confidential personal communications, Jakarta, May 2011). Probably Krishna's California-style interpersonal warmth struck some people who were otherwise sympathetic with him and his championship of religious pluralism as nonetheless uncomfortably out of line with local social conventions.

17   As reported in *VivaNews*, a former Anand Ashram course participant from 1998 to 2003, Titi [no other name given], claimed that Krishna gave special classes on spirituality and sex to seven couples, and that according to them (Titi did not participate) he taught that women needed to approach God through their guru, while men needed to do so with a partner chosen by the guru. Further, Krishna, she said, was acting as their guru and identified himself with the Hindu god Krishna, with whom, in the story he supposedly told, 156 women had amorous relations. Krishna denied Titi's accusations, insisted he does not put himself forward as a 'guru' (though some may regard him as such), and pointed out that he has no private classes or initiations (Widjaya and Saraswati 2010). Roy *et al.* (2011b) and the Ashram Centre administrators in Jakarta, Yogyakarta and Bali with whom I have spoken support Krishna's denials. Looking at what he has actually written, we find that sexuality is not a prominent theme. Among the over 140 books Krishna has authored, there are just three titles relating to sexuality and spirituality (Krishna 2001, 2005 [1998] and 2006). They presume a morally sound marital context for the practices described and do not subsume the spiritual to the sexual. Note that some Muslim preachers, like celebrity televangelist Arifin Ilham, also promote sexual fulfilment as one benefit of religious piety. In general, mass media religious proselytization in twenty-first century Indonesia (as elsewhere) heavily emphasizes the practical benefits of piety, both for businesses and for personal development and 'success' (see concluding remarks and Howell 2008). Improved sexual relationships are just one kind of improvement in everyday life that consumers of religious books, programming and courses look for and for which they are prepared to pay.

18   In mid-2012, after this chapter was finalised, Indonesia's High Court unexpectedly acted on an appeal by the prosecutor for the case against Krishna. On 3 August 2012 a spokesperson for the High Court announced that it had overturned Krishna's earlier full acquittal by the South Jakarta District Court and stated that the High Court had sentenced him to two years and six months in jail. The dramatic reversal occasioned protests by Krishna's community and by civil society activists concerned with religious freedom. Efforts on behalf of Krishna included an academic forum held at Gadjah Mada University in Yogyakarta on 18 October 2012 where professors of criminal law challenged the legal basis of the High Court's decision and recommended that the reversal of Krishna's acquittal be put before the International Court of Justice in The Hague. On February 16, 2013, Krishna was arrested and jailed. As this chapter goes to print, Krishna is still in jail.

19   The latter two have English titles but Indonesian language texts.

References

'Anand Krishna Acquitted of Sex Abuse Charges' (2011) *Jakarta Post*, 23 November. Online. Available from www.thejakartapost.com/news/2011/11/23/anand-krishna-acquitted-sex-abuse-charges.html (accessed 30 November 2011).

Andriyanto, H. (2011) 'Spiritual Guru Anand Krishna Ordered Detained During Sex Abuse Trial', *The Jakarta Globe*, 9 March. Online. Available from www.thejakartaglobe.com/home/spiritual-guru-and-ordered-detained-during-sex-abuse-trial/427796 (accessed 15 April 2011).

Indonesian mass media: Anand Krishna   233

Angkasa, N. (2011) 'Srikandi Penegak Hukum', *Kompasiana*, 24 October. Online. Available from http://hukum.kompasiana.com/2011/10/24/srikandi-penegak-hukum/?mid=50 (accessed 24 October 2011).

'A.S. Hikam Prihatin dan Bangga Kepada Anand Krishna' (2011) *Citra Indonesia*, 15 April. Online. Available from www.citraindonesia.com/as-hikam-prihatin-dan-bangga-kepada-anand-krishna/ (accessed 24 April 2011).

Asian Human Rights Commission. (2011) 'Indonesia: Human Rights in 2011 – The Decay of Pancasila and Constitutional Protections'. Online. Available from www.humanrights.asia/resources/hrreport/2011/AHRC-SPR-006-2011/view (accessed 3 January 2012).

Australian Broadcasting Corporation (2008) 'Indonesia, the Ahmadiyah and Radical Islam', *Religion Report*, Radio National. Online. Available from www.abc.net.au/radionational/programs/religionreport/indonesia-the-ahmadiyya-and-radical-islam/3258614 (accessed 3 March 2012).

Bagir, Z.A., Usman, H. and Naipospos, B.T. (2010) *Putusan tentang Pencegahan terhadap Undang Undang Dasar 1945 di Mahkamah Konstitusi*, Jakarta: Setara Institute.

Bayat, A. (2007) *Making Islam Democratic*, Stanford, CA: Stanford University Press.

David [no second name] (2008) 'FPI & Aliansi Kebangsaan untuk Kebebasan Beragama', Indonesia Matters. Online posting. Available from www.indonesiamatters.com/1797/aliansi-kebangsaan/ (accessed 6 October 2010).

'Dozens of Former Students to Fight Against Anand' (2010) *Jakarta Post*, 16 March. Online. Available from http://thejakartapost.com/news/2010/03/16/dozens-former-students-fight-against-anand-report.html (accessed 20 March 2010).

'Franz Magnis Suseno Kecewa' (2011) *Tribune News*, 17 April. Online. Available from http://tribunenews.com/2011/04/17franz-magnis-suseno-kecewa-pengadilan-anand-krishna (accessed 30 April 2011).

'Hard-liners Ambush Monas Rally' (2008) *Jakarta Post*, 2 June. Online. Available from www.thejakartapost.com/news/2008/06/02/hardliners-ambush-monas-rally.html (accessed 12 December 2010).

Howell, J.D. (2001) 'Sufism and the Indonesian Islamic Revival', *Journal of Asian Studies* 60(3): 701–29.

Howell, J.D. (2005) 'Muslims, the New Age and Marginal Religions in Indonesia: Changing Meanings of Religious Pluralism', *Social Compass*, 52(4): 473–93.

Howell, J.D. (2007) 'Modernity and the Borderlands of Islamic Spirituality in Indonesia's New Sufi Networks', in van Bruinessen, M. and Howell, J.D. (eds) *Sufism and the 'Modern' in Islam*, London: IB Tauris.

Howell, J.D. (2008) 'Modulations of Active Piety: Professors and Televangelists as Promoters of Indonesian "Sufisme"', in Fealy, G. and White, S. (eds) *Expressing Islam: Religious Life and Politics in Indonesia*, Singapore: ISEAS Press.

Howell, J.D. (2010) 'Indonesia's Salafist Sufis', *Modern Asian Studies*, 44(5): 1029–51.

Jahroni, J. (2008) *Defending the Majesty of Islam: Indonesia's Front Pembela Islam, 1998–2003*, Bangkok: Silkworm Books.

'Kasus Anand Krishna: Dari Pelecehan Agama Hingga Pelecehan Seksual' (2010) *Sabili*, 13 February. Online. Available from http://sabili.co.id/index.php?view+article&catid=82%Ainkit&id=1389%3Akasus-anand-krishna-dari-pelecehan-agama-hingga-pelecehan-seksual (accessed 30 March 2010).

Krishna, A. (2001) *Tantra Yoga*, Jakarta: Gramedia Pustaka Utama.

Krishna, A. (2003) *Soul Quest, Journey from Death to Immortality*, Jakarta: Gramedia.

Krishna, A. (2005 [1998]) *Jalan Kesempurnaan Melalui Kamasutra, Kenikmatan Seks, Kesujukan Cinta dan Kesadaran Kasih*, Jakarta: SUN.

234 Julia Day Howell

Krishna, A. (2006) *Sexual Quotient, Melampui Kamasutra, Memasuki Tantra*, Jakarta: One Earth Media.

'Krishna's Lawyer Applauds Judge Change' (2011) *Jakarta Post*, 9 June. Online. Available from www.thejakartapost.com/news/2011/06/09/krishnas-lawyer-applauds-judge-change.html (accessed 15 June 2011).

Kristanti, E.Y. and Nurlaila, A. (2010) 'Bertemu Tuhan Melalui Sex', *VivaNews*, 15 February. Online. Available from http://nasional.vivanews.com/news/read/129504-anand_ajaran_menuju_tuhan_melalui_seks (accessed 26 October 2011).

'Membongkar Rekayasa Kasus Anand Krishna – Saksi Abrory Djabbar' (2011) Online videos. Available from www.youtube.com/watch?v=A-kr2imrT0Y and www.youtube.com/watch?v=qCmh-mbqW3I (accessed 30 November 2011).

More, I. (2011) 'Adnan Buyung: Tindakan Hakim Ceroboh', *Kompas*, 24 March. [Online]. Available from http://megapolitan.kompas.com/read/2011/03/24/19493151/Adnan.Buyung.Tindakan.Hakim.Ceroboh (accessed 29 March 2011).

More, I. and Ebo, A.G.A. (2011) 'Gosip Dijadikan Fakta Dipersidangan?', *Kompas*, 26 October. Online. Available from http://nasional.kompas.com/read/2011/10/26/16475091/Gosip.Dijadikan.Fakta.Dipersidangan (accessed 27 October 2011).

'MUI's *fatwa* encourage use of violence' (2005) *Jakarta Post*, 1 August. Online. Available from www.thejakartapost.com/print/125713 (accessed 13 December 2010).

'Murid Harus Rela Diapakan Saja oleh Guru' (2010) *Kompas*, 3 August. Online. Available from http://lipsus.kompas.com/topikpilihan/read/2010/03/08/09053494/Murid.Harus.Rela.Diapakan.Saja.oleh.Guru (accessed 20 March 2010).

Muttaqin, A. (2012) 'Hybrid Spirituality and Religious Efficacy in Yogyakarta Spiritual Centres', unpublished thesis, University of Western Sydney.

Platzdasch, B. (2009) 'Opinion Asia'. Online. Available from http://opinionasia.com.article.print.742 (accessed 20 September 2010).

Ratya, M.P. (2010) 'Sambangi PN Jaksel, FPI Minta Anand Krishna Dihukum Berat', *Detik News*, 16 September. Online. Available from www.detiknews.com/read/2010/09/16/112254/1441587/10/sambangi-pn-jaksel-fpi-minta-anand-krishna-dihukum-berat (accessed 20 September 2010).

Roy, S., Dianswara, M. and Hakim, N. (2011a) 'Bebaskan Anand demi Keadilan', TIRO, *Majalah Bisnis dan Hukum*, February, pp. 8–11.

Roy, S., Dianswara, M. and Hakim, N. (2011b) 'Lebih Dekat dengan Yayasan Anand Ashram', TIRO, *Majalah Bisnis dan Hukum*, February, pp. 12–15.

Rudnyckyj, D. (2010) *Spiritual Economies: Islam, Globalization, and the Afterlife of Development*, Ithaca, NY: Cornell University Press.

Santosa, T. (2011) 'Sepuluh Doktor Minta Krishna Dibebaskan', *Rakyat Merdeka Online*, 19 April. Online. Available from www.rakyatmerdekaonline.com/news.php?id=24622 (accessed 21 May 2011).

Suaedy, A. (2010) 'Religious Freedom and Violence in Indonesia', in Atsushi, O., Masaaki, O. and Suaedy, A. (eds) *Islam in Contention: Rethinking Islam and State in Indonesia,* Jakarta: Wahid Institute; Kyoto: Center for Southeast Asian Studies; and Taipei: Center for Asia Pacific Area Studies (Academia Sinica).

Suryakusuma, J. (2011) 'When Persecution Becomes Prosecution', *Jakarta Post*, 21 April. Online. Available from www.thejakartapost.com/news/2011/04/21/view-point-when-presecution-becomes-persecution.html (accessed 22 April 2011).

Susanto, H. and Al-Yamani, Z. (2010) 'Saat Diobati, Tara Seperti Zombi', Wawancara Psikiator Hipnoterapis Dr Dewi Yogo Pratomo. *VivaNews*, 19 February. Online. Available from www.sorot.vivanews.com/news/read/130992-saat-diobati-tara-seperti-zombi (accessed 3 May 2010).

TempoInteraktif (2010) 'Anand Krishna Dituding Sebarkan Ajaran Sesat', 25 February. Online. Available from www.tempointeraktif.com/hg/kriminal/2010/02/25/brk,20100225-228390,id.html (accessed 3 May 2010).

'The Trial of Anand Krishna Enters a New Phase' (2011) *Antara News*, Bali Bureau, 22 May. Online. Available from http://bali.antaranews.com/berita/11100/the-trial-of-anand-krishna-enters-a-new-phase (accessed 23 May 2011).

'Two Witnesses Testify in FPI leader's Monas Trial' (2008) *Jakarta Post*, 2 September. Online. Available from www.thejakartapost.com/news/2008/09/02/two-witnesses-testify-fpi-leader039s-monas-trial.html (accessed 11 December 2010).

Victoria, W. (2011) 'Anand Krishna Achirnya Dirumahkan', *Rakyat Merdeka Online*, 27 April. Online. Available from www.rakyatmerdekaonline.com/news.php?id=25463 (accessed 21 May 2011).

Widjaya, I. and Saraswati, W. (2010) 'Anand Krishna: Saya Juga Bukan Dewa', *VivaNews*, 15 February. Online. Available from http://us.nasional.vivanews.com/news/read/129395-_saya_juga_bukan_dewa_ (accessed 3 May 2010).

Wilson, I.D. (2006) 'The Changing Contours of Organised Violence in Post New Order Indonesia', *Critical Asian Studies*, 38(2): 265–97.

Wilson, I.D. (2008) 'As Long as It's *Halal*. Islamic *Preman* in Jakarta', in Fealy, G. and White, S. (eds) *Expressing Islam*, Singapore: ISEAS Press.

13   A Sufi, Sikh, Hindu, Buddhist, TV Guru

Anandmurti Gurumaa

Angela Rudert

In Spring 2008 in the Sonepat district of Haryana, an attractive 42-year-old, female spiritual teacher and TV personality known as Anandmurti Gurumaa (also known simply as Gurumaa) sat regally upon an elaborate stage created for the dual celebratory events of her birthday (8 April) and her *sannyas diwas* (11 April), the anniversary day of her renunciation, signified here by a name most commonly associated with 'Hindu' ascetism.[1] Gurumaa's senior-most disciple created the stage for her, which had a different incarnation for each of the two evening events. The architectural structure remained the same. On the night of Gurumaa's birthday, when various classical Indian musicians performed for her and 3,000 or so guests sitting in the audience, the spaces on the stage's backdrop were fitted with Hindu symbols; Lord Krishna dominated centre stage playing his flute, flanked by arches on either side with the large Sanskrit syllable, AUM. On the night of Gurumaa's *sannyas diwas*, when *quawali* singers performed for an even larger crowd at what one might presume would be a 'Hindu' celebration, the Krishna and AUM decorations were replaced with screens created to look like Mughal geometric latticework. As the stage was being disassembled the following day, I noted to one of Gurumaa's senior-most disciples that the naked base structure strangely resembled a mosque, mandir and gurdwara. She replied, 'Yes, and it also looks like none of them!'

At this time, I had been residing for over two months as a scholar in Gurumaa Ashram, and I had been observing Gurumaa both in the field and through her media long enough to know that the 'spirituality' she teaches draws from multiple religious traditions.[2] Well before I entered the research field in India, I knew that Gurumaa had been born a Sikh, educated in a Catholic convent school, found her enlightenment in Vrindavan, the famous site of Lord Krishna's amorous play among the *gopis*, and that she sometimes referred to herself as a Buddha and sometimes as a Sufi.[3] But up until the very end of my first fieldwork stint in her ashram, I had been caught in the scholarly game of classification, trying to pinpoint this woman.

Finally, I addressed a formal query to Gurumaa, which caused her to laugh at me publicly. I should have known better. In fact, I had already given up identifying her strongly with one or another religious tradition; she told me face to face very early during my tenure in her ashram that she refused any such identification with an 'ism'. Regardless, my analytical training prevailed and I still wanted to know how she saw herself, or perhaps more importantly, how her followers – who themselves, I presumed, may have more difficulty transcending particular religious identities – would identify their master if they absolutely had to check one box. Would she be identified with any one religion or creed? Would she be considered, rather, a New Age guru? A meditation guru? A feminist guru? A TV Guru? Her boisterous laugh turned gentle as she responded to my ridiculous question, 'You are not going to be able to put me in any box; I'll keep you guessing!'

Anandmurti Gurumaa is a multi-talented, multi-lingual teacher of meditation and 'spirituality' situated at the intersection of Hindu, Buddhist, Sufi and Sikh mystical traditions. This young Amritsar-born female guru's discourses and musical compositions aired to satellite television and Internet audiences address the global fusion of linguistic, cultural and religious sensibilities encountered by her (mostly) urban disciples. Like the amorphous stage elaborately decorated to look like a temple one night and a mosque on another, Gurumaa too (having since dropped her ochre *sannyas* attire) adorns the physical body in different ways at different times, modelling idiosyncratic sartorial styles of religiosity and beauty that may look somewhat akin to Hindu or Muslim or Sikh styles and yet also like none of them.

This chapter examines the style of pluralism modelled by Gurumaa to her ever-expanding audience, exploring the notion that she draws from many classifiable 'isms', and yet remains difficult to place in any one of them. She is a little bit of everything rolled into one, or as one Indian American disciple explained, she's an 'all-in-one guru'. In both India and abroad, Gurumaa appeals to an educated class of urbanites who think of traditional 'religion' as a limiting boundary in a globalizing world of 'spiritual' possibilities. Regardless, Gurumaa's appeal to these followers lies precisely in her ability to acknowledge tradition in an intelligent way – especially the heritage of Indian spiritual expertise – while at the same time to make innovations (as she put it to me) pertinent to 'a new audience in a new time'. Thus, while Gurumaa models pluralism, it is naturally pluralism limited to some degree by the particularities of her physically manifest form and the audience attracted to the form. This essay suggests that we look at pluralism as it is mapped onto the body of a particular yet 'global' person as a somewhat parallel process to that pluralism mapped onto a particular and local yet 'global' city. As we do so, we might ask, 'Do we find similar limitations to that pluralism?'

What I refer to in this essay as the 'pluralism' embodied by Gurumaa loosely ties together disparate yet related notions that scholars have labelled variously: hybrid religious identity, religious plurality, religious syncretism or religious liminality (Das 1999; Madan 2003; Mayaram 2004; Oberoi 1994). This pluralism is held in contrast to the more politicized conceptions of pluralism as a virtue of civil society. Even as the boundaries of civil society expand from local to global proportions, pluralism as a political reality remains rooted in particular settings. This essay offers the idea that the more ephemeral pluralism embodied by individuals such as Gurumaa who seemingly move freely between cities, cultures and nation states – even religious identities – is likewise rooted in particularities, even while it evokes universality.

238   *Angela Rudert*

Following Mayaram, this essay takes as its starting point the understanding that within the theologies of many 'World Religions' (or 'isms' according to Gurumaa) the 'syncretic' is 'constitutive' (Mayaram 2004: 30). Thus, I offer the narrative of Gurumaa's pluralism from the perspective that the syncretic and liminal can and do exist within mainstream traditions themselves, are often inherent to them, and have sometimes been essential to their origins.[4] Such a perspective is one way to approach the scholarly 'problem' of contemporary mystics like Gurumaa who refuse to be labelled. Such a perspective also allows us to examine the insider's view held by many of Gurumaa's devotees – that her profound state of Self-realization places her above bounded categories we use to make sense of our world. Additionally, this perspective of inherent plurality, especially in Indic religiosity, allows us to see 'religion' and 'tradition' as bounded entities that nonetheless already hold within themselves the tension of continuity and change. The Sikh religious tradition, into which Gurumaa was born, provides an excellent example of inherent plurality as well as the tension of continuity and change within a tradition, or 'ism'.[5] In the case of Gurumaa, we might ask, what does it mean that this New Age TV guru's affinities lie with founders and luminaries from multiple traditions? Or, that she is equally comfortable giving commentary on textual sources considered 'Hindu' such as *Bhagavad Gita* as she is offering exegesis on the Sikh *Adi Granth*? What does it mean that Gurumaa's style of dress, singing, speaking, as well as spiritual practices she prescribes for her disciples are all somewhat of an eclectic mix of Sufi, Sikh, Hindu and Buddhist?

Gurumaa often speaks against religious boundaries and this essay will note some of these instances. The rhetoric of expansive spirituality as opposed to bounded, restricted, religion itself is nothing new, either in the case of Gurumaa's speech, or to that of other global Indian gurus of the twentieth and twenty-first centuries, or even to Indian gurus and holy men of centuries (and ages) past. Indeed, Gurumaa's own words on this subject, in a sense, follow an Indian 'tradition' of resistance to bounded religiosity during periods of complex intercultural exchange.[6] Herein, the primary concern lies in how Gurumaa fashions a certain type of pluralism through her very body. Rather, to employ language closer to the traditions from which she draws, through 'the body', or the physical frame in its entirety, even in its particularity: in a larger sense, her physical form (*rupa*). It has been common practice in India for Self-realized gurus to reflexively refer to themselves in the third person as 'this body'. Referring to one's own person as 'this body' not only 'others' the body, but it also specifically indicates one's present and particularly manifest form of this lifetime; it would be different in another and another and another. Moreover, the guru's *rupa* is a teaching in and of itself to the seeker on the path of guru-devotion (*guru-bhakti*).

As a place of pluralism, let us expand our understanding of Anandmurti Gurumaa's body to include the mind/body complex and the particularities of this human form. Therefore, personal narrative and biographical complexities are part of Gurumaa's *rupa*. It is significant that she was born into a particular female body at a particular place in a particular time and that she encountered various particular religious traditions in the ways that she did. All of these vectors come together as part of her physically manifest form. And that *rupa*, in its fullness, includes the voice, the beauty, the humour, the history, the pluralism, and the loyalties to Indic religiosities. And it is that embodiment which attracts a particular audience of people to the teachings and to the spiritual journey. That form, in its expansiveness, also has its own limitations. As the body becomes in a sense global and reflects a certain type of pluralism, it nonetheless remains a body situated in a particular place and time and gendered form.

The guru's *rupa*

In 2006, in a public speech in London (now made available to a larger audience on DVD) Gurumaa sings the Punjabi verse of Sultan Bahu, a seventeenth century Sufi *faqir*, who was revered by Sikh and Hindu Punjabis as well as Muslims: 'The master [*murshid*] is the gate of the Ka'ba where the lovers go to offer their salutations... Why go to Mecca and Medina when the *hajj* is happening in my own home?'.[7] After singing these lyrics, Gurumaa tells her audience that Bulleh Shah, another Punjabi Sufi from the following century, perfectly lived these words of Sultan Bahu, and she illustrates this with a tale of Bulleh Shah preparing his family for making the *hajj*.[8] To the great surprise of those in Bulleh's circle he took them not to Mecca, but nearby, to his master's home. Upon arrival Bulleh circumambulated his master ten times saying, 'See, I have done ten *hajj*!' After telling this story, Gurumaa asks her audience, 'So, who is a truly religious person?' and answers her own question:

> It is not the one who goes for pilgrimages. It's not the one who goes for *hajj*, not the one who goes to Harmandir Sahib, it's not the one who goes to Kashi... It's not the one who goes to synagogue, but it is the one who goes and visits the inner shrine of his own heart. Any *fool* can go to a temple![9]
>
> (*Amrit Varsha*, discourse in London, 30 April 2006)

Gurumaa half-jokingly explains that nowadays no one has to leave the comfort of the UK to go to places of pilgrimage anyway; they can just send someone else and receive part of the merit for their ritual. Well, if you are Hindu, she muses, then you would receive full credit since this practice of having someone else do your ritual for you has been in existence for centuries.

With her story of the master as the door to the Ka'ba, and circumambulation of the master as *hajj*, Gurumaa illustrates the notion of the human spiritual master as the personification or perfect manifestation of Divine Love. According to this view, in recognizing a door to divinity in the human form of the guru (or in this case, Sufi *pir*), and entering that door through devotion to the teacher, the devotee realizes that the same love exists within one's own body, one's own temple. Over and again, Gurumaa explains to her audience, 'The body is the temple of God. If you want to find God, just go within'. In this, she is not saying anything new, nor is she offering an idea unique to Indian spirituality. From within numerous traditions, teachers and scriptural teachings have idealized

240   *Angela Rudert*

mystic union over and above the ritualized performance of religion. Indeed to make this clearer to me, Gurumaa emphasized Jesus' teaching that the kingdom of God exists within the heart and is available to all. In sharing this ideal with her UK audience – made up of (mostly non-Muslim) Indian heritage listeners – through Sufi song, Gurumaa offers a sense of the universality within mystic spiritual paths, while at the same time, she pays homage to a much beloved Punjabi language poet-saint.

So why make a pilgrimage to those external places, Gurumaa asks, when you could be making the pilgrimage to the inner shrine of your own heart? In the context of north Indian spirituality, one common way to access this 'inner shrine' is through devotion and surrender to a master who embodies mystic union. The name Anandmurti Gurumaa itself tells us that in addition to being a 'Master mother' (*Guru-Maa*), devotees find this woman to be an 'idol', or perfect manifestation (*murti*) of 'bliss' (*anand*). As perfect manifestation, the guru's body as shrine exemplifies the expression of the divinity existing within the human form in a way perhaps more tangible to the devotee than does the external shrine to which he might make pilgrimage. In the example of Bulleh Shah, who rouses his entire family for the *hajj*, the master's body serves as both the paradigm of divine union and the place of pilgrimage, thus for the seeker (or at least for those in Bulleh's circle) God becomes more accessible at multiple levels. Even if the disciple does not circumambulate the master's form or even see the master as a doorway to divinity, she may nonetheless see the guru – in word and as well as in form – as a hub in a vast network in the global conversation on religion and spirituality. Many in Gurumaa's audience learn much of what they know about other people's religion from Gurumaa. Some amongst them shared with me their appreciation for what they understood to be her vast knowledge of 'all religions'.

Gurumaa was born in Amritsar, Punjab in 1966 to 'hair-keeping' (*kesdhari*) Sikh parents, and was known in childhood by the name Gurpreet. Devotees of Gurumaa have described their guru's parents as having been 'devout' and 'pure-hearted' and have qualified their Sikhism as being 'open-minded' and 'spiritual'. Asked for elucidation of these descriptions, informants explained that during her childhood Gurumaa's parents were devout and observed Sikh traditions, but also celebrated and honoured other religious traditions as well. While wearing the bodily signs of their Sikh faith by keeping their hair uncut, they were also known to have been 'saint lovers'. I heard the English expression 'saint lover' used in many instances in the ethnographic context to depict someone for whom the love of being with saints trumped any particular tradition from which that saint might come. Therefore, Gurumaa's parents (particularly her mother) were saint lovers, because they welcomed into their home 'saints' (quite fluidly defined here as holy people, lovers of God) from various traditions.[10] When I visited Gurumaa's Amritsar family home in 2009, just over four decades after her birth, I noticed not only pictures of Guru Nanak and Guru Govind Singh hanging on the walls of the home but also pictures of Radha and Krishna, and interestingly, familiar photographs of Anandmurti Gurumaa that I had seen sold in Gurumaa Ashram for devotional purposes (*darshan*).

Gurpreet willingly became her mother's regular sidekick, attending the gatherings (*satsang*) of a local teacher, who an Amritsar local described to me as Gurumaa's *gyan guru*, a teacher valued specifically for his scriptural knowledge.[11] Maharaj ji, as Gurumaa herself refers to him in stories, was a *gyani* in the little discussed *Nirmala Sant* tradition, an ascetic-leaning, syncretistic order within the larger more outwardly householder-oriented Sikh religion.[12] Maharaj ji had been the student of an internationally known guru of Ambala, Haryana, named Sant Dalel Singh, who would later become Gurumaa's *Gurudev* (divine teacher) as well as the guru who would bless the ochre clothes that she wore for many years as a sign of her renunciation (*sannyas*).[13]

Stories have it, that seers who came to Gurpreet's home to accept her mother's loving service (*seva*) as they passed through town, were awed by this girl child's spiritual aptitude. Gurpreet's parents chose to offer her English medium education in a local convent school, where she reputedly impressed her missionary teachers too with her scope of religious knowledge – to the point where they wished to convert her and put her to work in Catholic missions. Alas, her parents refused to give her up.[14] However, this early event foreshadows a similar told event when Sikhs and Hindus in Kanpur would argue over Gurumaa, each wishing she would choose to promote one religious tradition or the other, rather than speak one night in a gurdwara and the next in a mandir (Gurumaa 2010: 35–7). I heard another story later from devotees who explained to me that a famous Sikh TV *gyani* had similarly tried to convince Gurumaa to speak solely for the Sikhs, promising name and fame, but that she refused any such alignment with an 'ism'.

In her late teens, Gurpreet left home alone on a north Indian pilgrimage for a number of years. This journey included visits to pilgrimage sites of various traditions, but its main objective, as Gurumaa explained during an interview to Swedish scholar Marie-Thérèse Charpentier, was to commune with and seek companionship with 'like-minded' people, 'and [she] was therefore always roaming about in religious congregations where various sages, sadhus, and mahatmas – "those hidden friends who have tasted the nectar were sitting"' (Charpentier 2010: 79).[15] This affinity that Gurumaa feels with 'like-minded' souls plays out today in the friendships she maintains with Buddhist leaders as well as Sikh *gyanis*, Hindu yogis and Turkish Sufis, people who have likewise 'tasted the nectar' and thereby demonstrates a certain pluralistic theology in which mystical union or spiritual attainment and cultivation of oneself trumps religious difference.[16]

Returning to Amritsar, Gurpreet, at this time wearing all white, accepted the name Swami ji from the small but growing crowd of Hindus and Sikhs (occasionally joined by Muslims and Christians) who would participate in gatherings (*satsang*) she offered, sometimes in homes and sometimes in gurdwaras. In the songs she sang and the teachings she gave, she offered a taste of her own eclectic devotion (*bhakti*). This pluralistic devotion was grounded not only in the teachings from the Sikh holy book, *Adi Granth* (being itself somewhat pluralistic given that it includes Word – *shabad* – from the early Sikh gurus as well as from select Hindu and Sufi poet-saints), but also in a wider corpus of songs and stories including those of Punjabi Sufis and north Indian *sants*.[17] Partial it seems to the *sant* tradition of her region, Gurumaa's early-recorded repertoire includes not only songs of Nanak, Kabir and Ravidas (all also in the *Adi Granth*), but also songs of Paltu and Sahajobai, usually classified as Hindu, and songs of Sultan Bahu and Bulleh Shah, both Muslim Sufis. Additionally, it seems that anything she encountered and found personally inspiring she included in her personal canon of inspiration and shared with her audience, such as the Vedantic verses attributed to Adishankara. Many years later, in her early forties, she would add Jalaluddin Rumi to the list of poet singers whose verses she would put to music and whose stories she would tell.[18] Gurumaa's translation of Rumi's Persian verses into her own audience's language, Hindi, parallel's Nanak's translation of Kabir's songs into Punjabi for his own listening audience.[19]

Gurumaa's discourses have always included stories from traditions outside of those most familiar to her audience, even beyond Hindu, Sikh and Muslim. Thus she weaves into her teachings the tales of Zen masters, narratives from Buddhist sutras and Christian gospels as well as the stories of Vedic rishis and vernacular poet-singers from all over the Indian subcontinent, if mostly from north India.[20] Hers seems to be an ever-expanding repertoire of song and story. It is not as if her audience has not been introduced before to figures like Buddha or Shankara or Jesus or Nanak or Kabir, but they may not have heard about all of these figures from one source, from one hub. By introducing personalities (who themselves are often religiously hybrid) from multiple traditions into the conversation, Gurumaa performs a type of pluralism not so unlike that of her *sant* and Sikh guru predecessors in north India. As Gurumaa explained to her audience in Florida in 2008, Guru Nanak introduced his Punjabi fellows to Kabir. He shared Kabir's verses, with which he had felt affinity, in a way that they could understand, and in doing so 'he made a linguistic and cultural translation' for his audience.[21] Gurumaa offers a similar service today as she introduces to Hindi speakers – and to her Hindu listeners – Guru Nanak's verses, singing them in the original Punjabi, but translating and explaining their significance in Hindi (and sometimes in English).

Similarly, as she continues to expand her own canon, Gurumaa introduces not only verses and stories but also spiritual practices from various traditions to her listeners. My Amritsar storyteller, born a Sikh, told me she never would have known the beauty of the practice of *zikr* had it not been for Gurumaa introducing her to it. She knew of the practice, but only tried it and understood its devotional potency as well as its similarities to the Sikh practice of repetition of the name of God (*nam jap*) because of Gurumaa. Gurumaa sometimes urges her listeners to try to substitute other names of the 'Almighty' besides the ones they are most accustomed to.

Little is known of Gurumaa's short history with her guru, Sant Dalel Singh, the Nirmala *sant* whose almost life-size portrait hangs just above the head of Lord Shiva's *murti* in the ashram temple.[22] When I asked about her relationship with her guru, Gurumaa explained to me that she probably spent less than six hours total in his presence. She further explained that when he gave her *sannyas*, this act was far from any rituals I might associate with the formalized taking of *sannyas*.[23] This Sikh 'guru' of the Nirmala *sant* order did not initiate his disciples into renunciation, often referred to as 'giving *sannyas*', though people did come to live an ascetic lifestyle in his ashram.[24] One day Gurumaa (then known as Swamiji, wearing white) visited Dalel Singh's ashram carrying in her handbag the ochre clothes she intended to wear henceforth. At the opportune moment, she asked the *sant* to bless them for her *sannyas*.[25] His response was an affirmation, 'But you are already *brahmanishta* [established in Brahman, Supreme Consciousness]. What do you need the clothes for?' I just want them, she replied. So he took the clothes and then handed them back to her in a gesture she took as a blessing. The birthday of the Hindu Lord Ram was coming up in just a couple of days, so instead of putting the newly blessed clothes on right away, she and her long-time companion, known today as her 'right-hand man' and senior-most disciple, left by car for Haridwar and, on the bank of the Ganga, she dressed the body in the ochre robes for the first time.

Exactly how many years Gurumaa wore the ochre clothes blessed by Dalel Singh, I cannot say. It should be noted that the colour she chose is a colour worn commonly, not only by Hindu renouncers but also by Nirmala Sikhs, and Dalel Singh himself. Years later, even after she quit the robes, Gurumaa continued to wear the colour, albeit in fashionable saris and Punjabi suits (*salwar kamiz*). Understood by devotees to be empowered by her own self-freedom (*swatantrya*) and perhaps on some level also by her guru's words that she didn't need the robes, Gurumaa is a woman who has taken her *sannyas* 'forcefully' and 'in her very own style', as a full-time resident of Gurumaa Ashram once put it to me. Indeed, she took what she called her *sannyas* from a Nirmala Sikh, whom she regards as *gurudev*. Then she dressed herself for the first time in these clothes in a Hindu pilgrimage site. Years later, celebrating that event, the songs sung for her by performers were songs to Allah, and the stage upon which she sat resembled a mosque.

Body as place, body as stage

Through singing songs, through telling of stories, through acts of translation, and even through idiosyncratic adornment of the body, Gurumaa echoes her 'like-minded' friend Guru Nanak. After his three-day immersion in the Bein river, Nanak announced to those who would listen, 'There is no Hindu. There is no Muslim', and afterward incorporated sartorial styles from each of those traditions into his own dress. In her own way and for her own audience, Gurumaa has fashioned a mode of renunciation that we might call not Hindu, not Muslim, and not Sikh. At the same time, she does sometimes appear to be a little like each of these.

These days Gurumaa dresses according to her 'moods'.[26] She changes the colour and mode of her vestige when she feels like it. Sometimes she wears a sari, sometimes a Punjabi suit. Sometimes she wears a floor length knit sweater dress. She very often wears shades of orange, ochre, or saffron, and though fashionable, still reflecting through colour something of a Hindu vision of renunciation. She explained to me once that when she feels like a Sufi, she wears black, which left me wondering if she was feeling like a Punjabi housewife on those occasions

244   *Angela Rudert*

when she wore pink Salwar suits.[27] Gurumaa wears varying forehead marks, and most notably, one I find strikingly different from all others, a single long narrow vertical line directly down the length of her forehead. Once I took the opportunity to ask about these forehead marks: 'Are they symbolic of something? Or are they according to your mood?' (referring back to our earlier conversation). She answered, 'There is so much meaning in everything and yet everything is meaningless'. I refrained from asking questions about her appearance after that, realizing how petty these sounded to her.

Nonetheless, for two years, I kept noting in my fieldwork journal whatever colour and style of attire Gurumaa would wear at each and every event I attended or watched recordings of – until the day I watched the aforementioned London discourse from 2006. During this discourse, Gurumaa tells the story of a devotee who had demonstrated interest in the earrings she was wearing. She disparages this unnamed person for getting caught up in the external manifestation of beauty, though she jests, 'I *am* a beauty lover' and 'indeed, this body *is* a good one!' Gurumaa further asserts that she dresses herself with 'great intention' because it helps her to sort out her real listeners from those who will be concerned with what she is wearing. She likened these 'child-like' listeners to the sorts of narrow-minded followers of 'tradition' who would go to the gurdwara or to the mosque or to the temple or church to find God, when in actuality, God was right there within the shrine of their very hearts. Next she tells a humorous story about a Indian American woman in New York City who visited the most amazing museum in the world only to overlook rich historical and cultural artefacts from all over the globe and ask her guide, 'How do you get your marble floors so shiny?'

To the casual observer or listener, Gurumaa will not only look like a Hindu one day and like a Sikh the next, but will also sound like a Hindu one day and sound like a Sikh the next. One disciple explained: 'When Gurumaa talks on Sufism, she becomes a Sufi. When Gurumaa talks about Nanak, she becomes Nanak. When Gurumaa talks about Krishna, she becomes Krishna. She becomes everything for me!' But just about as soon as one might begin to classify Gurumaa as one of these, she will suddenly appear looking like and singing something quite different. For instance, a non-devotee scholar from Delhi happened upon Gurumaa's *Amrit Varsha* program on Sony TV and thought her expositions and singing of Kabir so true to tradition and linguistic style, that he took her to be a native Hindi speaker from Kabir's own region, Uttar Pradesh.[28] Gurumaa's television program *Amrit Varsha*, because it is produced directly from Gurumaa's discourses all over the globe, includes words spoken and songs sung to varying groups of immediate physical audiences in particular places. In its satellite television medium and now especially its Internet medium *Amrit Varsha* has a potentially limitless audience. Had my colleague watched Sony TV at any other time, he might have listened to one of Gurumaa's talks on Guru Nanak's *Jap ji Sahib* or listened to her sing the songs of Punjabi Sufi *faqirs* like Bulleh Shah or Baba Sheik Farid and tell the tales associated with their lives. Or he might have heard one of her US discourses given primarily in English. What would he have thought of her then?

What does it mean to wear one hat one day and another the next? Some do, and

A Sufi, Sikh, Hindu, Buddhist, TV Guru 245

will, get offended, as exemplified in the story Gurumaa tells of the mandir and gurdwara administrators who fought over the rights to host her discourses in Kanpur. Despite the fact that she always takes care to cover her head when singing from the *Adi Granth*, some Sikh listeners outside her fold have been greatly offended that she teaches the Sikh gurus' verses outside of the gurdwara and to Hindu audiences, feeling that she is taking what is theirs and Hinduizing it, claiming it for Hindus the way that the Indian constitution claims the indigenous traditions of Sikhism and Jainism as 'Hindu'. Gurumaa sometimes berates her own audience stating that some Sikh listeners will cringe when she asks them to sing along with her 'Shivoham' ('I am Shiva', refrain in Adishankara's *Atmashtakam*) or songs to Ram and Krishna and prefer instead that she chant Waheguru or sing solely Sikh verses. And she complains that her Hindu listeners are not open-minded enough to repeat the *zikr* of the Sufi 'Hu' or to practice remembrance of the name (*nam simran*) Waheguru. Gurumaa instead expands the meaning of the beloved and central Sikh practice of *nam simran* for her Sikh audience to include the chanting of any name of God, claiming regularly to all of her listeners that God doesn't speak only one language or reveal truth in only one language.

Gurumaa's stated intention in her multiplicity of offerings is to open minds and hearts. Some, however, might see Gurumaa's wearing of multiple hats and singing songs of various traditions as a way of marketing herself and her abundant audiovisual products to the largest possible audience. Indeed, one offended Sikh Internet critic – in a comment below one of her YouTube videos – likened Gurumaa to the infamous Ram-Rahim, a contemporary guru notorious for scandal as well as his attempts to appeal to both Muslims and Hindus with his dually linked moniker, seemingly borrowed from a Kabir song.[29] Crossing religious boundaries of cherished traditions, especially if conceived as doing so irreverently, can cause discomfort for many people. In a short conversation about my research project with a rickshaw driver in Delhi, I was quickly cautioned about gurus like Ram-Rahim after I had explained that the guru I was writing about was not Hindu, not Sikh, not Muslim, but a little of each. For writers of the YouTube comment as well as for my rickshaw driver (and no doubt for some others as well), multiply aligned spiritual teachers may not always be seen favourably or as pluralistic, but rather, to be 'strategically employ[ing]' syncretic modes (Mayaram 2004: 31).[30]

Possible critiques aside, for the singing of and adopting practices from multiple religious traditions, many spiritual seekers (*sadhaks*) in Gurumaa's circle have expressed to me that they now have greater appreciation for that which is outside of their inherited faith tradition 'because of Gurumaa'. My Amritsar storyteller told me that she loves 'tasting the nectar' that comes from doing meditation on the sound of 'Allah-hu' and that inspired by Gurumaa's breadth of knowledge she weekly sits with a local teacher who talks about the *Upanishads* and *Bhagavad Gita*. As the guru whose very form serves as the gate or the door for the disciple's own experience of the divine, Gurumaa offers her students a variety of inspirational sources, in hope that more students gain access. Some

246 *Angela Rudert*

listeners, like the lady at the museum awed by the shiny floors, or the child interested in Gurumaa's pretty earrings or the scholar concerned with classification and names, will get caught up in the motivations and meanings of religious accoutrements, and miss the real treasure housed within.

Gurumaa does wear the garb, and she does change it, and in my opinion, she does so precisely to keep us guessing, hence her unabashed amusement at my circumvent question regarding her identity. Describing herself to the seekers attending her Florida meditation retreat in 2008, Gurumaa states, 'I am not Hindu, Sikh, Muslim, Christian or Buddhist. I am just a baby. I am no one. Let me know after the retreat who you think I am'. Then she sang *Hare Krishna*. During the entire retreat whenever the audience awaited Gurumaa's arrival, they listened to her (then) recently released *Zikr: Call of a Sufi*, an album of intoxicating, droning calls to god as Allah, composed by Gurumaa and her flautist, Kanchman Babbar, after their journey to Turkey, undertaken to learn more about the medieval Sufi poet Rumi. In this American setting, I found Gurumaa's eclectic mix to be quite popular with most of those in her audience with whom I spoke, but I did meet one woman who left the venue quite disappointed and probably not to return, as she was an ardent devotee of Shiva and had come expecting songs to Shiva or talk of Shiva. It struck me some time later that this woman and her sentiments narrowly attuned to Shiva were precisely the sort of content worthy of a didactic story from Gurumaa on how our minds are trained by cultural and societal forces to remain bound and resist expansion. It would also be in full character for Gurumaa to note that even a life in America cannot offer the same expansive freedom as Self-realization.

Though refusing to be labelled or to check a box, Gurumaa dons the apparel, so to speak, of various traditions when she sings songs beloved of one or another group. But in constantly changing, from garb to garb, from singing Hindu *bhajan* to Sikh *gurbani*, from chanting Tantric or Vedic *mantra* to Sufi *zikr*, from decorating the stage (or temple) of her body according to her moods, she denies her regular listeners and observers the luxury of making tradition-bound truth claims, or as one devotee put it: Gurumaa helps them not to get 'stuck' in anything.

The message she gives in her changing is this: while the garb can be helpful, it can also become a hindrance to real freedom. Gurumaa is not the only contemporary guru who speaks of the limitations of religious boundaries to real freedom. This is not an uncommon message from contemporary Indian gurus, even those who seem very much Hindu. Another spiritual teacher quite familiar in the global context and who proved to be attractive to Euro-American seekers, Swami Muktananda (d. 1984) who established the Siddha Yoga tradition, expressed a similar notion, 'Who is a Hindu? Who is a Vaishnavite? Who is a Jain, a Buddhist, a Sufi or a Christian? If you are imprisoned in one of these false identities, how can you find the freedom of the Self?' (Muktananda 1999 [1980]: 31). There have also been New Age gurus who refused being labelled and who dressed to reflect a similar eclectic spirituality, such as Osho Rajneesh whose cross-religious vestige included Turkish caps and kurtas (Osho International Foundation 2000: 31).[31]

Though she sometimes appears like one or another type, Gurumaa identifies herself as not one and not the other, not Hindu and not Sikh (primarily), but also not anything. When there was crossover attendance between the mandir and gurdwara during Gurumaa's aforementioned visit to Kanpur, she explains, with turbaned Sikhs coming to the mandir and *tilaked* Hindus coming to the gurdwara, administrators from each demanded to know her religious identity. She answered, 'If you really want a reply, I am neither a Hindu nor a Sikh'. The religious administrators then suggested that she must be a Muslim out to make trouble for them both. She responds:

> If it comforts your heart, then know that I am not even a Muslim... In this entire world, more than 350 different religions are practiced. You may not even know the names of all of them. Even if you name all of them one by one and ask me if I belong to any of them, my answer will still be in the negative; I will still deny it... The only answer I have is that I am love; wherever I find the fragrance of love, that place is mine own [*sic*].
>
> (Gurumaa 2010: 37)

In the same printed book transcribed from discourses, Gurumaa retells the story in terms Hindu and Sikh, for whom Muslim would be 'other' to both, and in doing so addresses restrictive thinking to which some of her listeners who do ascribe to either of these two faith traditions might be prone. In addition to Gurumaa's words here, obviously parallel to Guru Nanak's famous statement noted earlier, she also echoes Kabir and other *sants* and Sufis who regularly criticized the orthodox representatives of Hindus and Muslims during their time. In Gurumaa's act of instructing the representatives from two faith traditions in Kanpur, she echoes the critique in the songs of the *sants* (and *faqirs* like Bulleh Shah) levelled against mullahs and Brahmins. Also in her statement, while Gurumaa negates religious belonging, she affirms certain theological aspects of it as well. She completes her conversation with administrators in Kanpur with an affirmation, 'In the same way, I am only "love"; wherever I find love, those people are mine and I belong to them. And so I am Hindu, a Muslim, a Sikh, a Buddhist, a Jew and a Jain; I am everything; I am all of these because I am none of these' (Gurumaa 2010: 37).

In my research prospectus, I proposed that in absence of lineage and institutional backing, an independent guru such as Gurumaa perhaps builds her lineage and her legitimacy by teaching the life and the words of great masters such as Buddha, Shankara, Kabir, Baba Sheik Farid, Guru Nanak, and Baba Bulleh Shah. Upon reading this proposal, Gurumaa addressed me the following day in a small public gathering to correct my apparent misunderstanding. She explained that the saints, *sants* and enlightened ones she refers to, sings of and teaches about are 'like-minded' individuals she 'feels affinity with'.[32] In Gurumaa's understanding, she does not have to stand on the shoulders of these giants in order to craft for herself a spiritual pedigree. But in referring to these masters, people are able to understand what she is saying. Gurumaa insisted that she must speak on the level of her audience and about that which they are able to relate because only a few

248 *Angela Rudert*

are ready to have a 'direct encounter' with her. And she further explained that because she is a woman, people are even less likely to take the truth 'directly' from her. Indeed, in order to do that, they not only have to put their gender bias aside, but must also be able to take that truth via all of her idiosyncrasy, and not be bothered by the fact that she's not a 'proper' Hindu or Sikh or Buddhist or Sufi, and to understand her as beyond categorization.

Gurumaa has taken her *sannyas* in her own way and she's teaching and implementing her innovations regardless of her gender and without institutional backing. The way that she does this resembles the way of a 'solitary *sant*'.[33] In similar fashion to a solitary *sant*, instead of a lineage, Gurumaa relates to a clan made up of 'like-minded' idiosyncratic seers whose songs she sings and whose stories she tells. Outside of a traditional religious boundary, as a member of a clan, Gurumaa exists beyond the boundaries of institutions, even such fluid institutions as *sannyas* or *gurudom*, while at the same time remains intimately connected to north Indian spirituality.

The centrality of the Indian-ness in Gurumaa's pluralistic spirituality, I learned through my direct encounters with Gurumaa. After Gurumaa laughed at me publicly and then told me she would keep me guessing, she delivered another line that has stuck with me: 'I'll be watching you'. I originally took this to mean she would be reading my work as she had the proposal, and of course, I have pondered the significance of doing ethnographic research on a fully responsive subject. In my later reflections, however, I have come to see that Gurumaa was also, always, watching me, and observing me, all the while that I observed her. Returning from my travels to her ashram, Gurumaa would often comment on my appearance, noting that I was looking and becoming 'more Indian' all the time, speaking better Hindi and wearing more Indian clothing.

In our most recent meeting in 2010 in New Jersey, Gurumaa made a comment about me, again in a small group, which was an affirmation of sorts in my mind and in the minds of those Indian Americans who surrounded us. She asked a question in Hindi to which I responded in Hindi. Gurumaa then announced, 'Angela is 40 per cent Hindustani [Indian]!' affirming a degree of Indian-ness which I had always felt myself, but also indicating a relative authenticity to this spiritually minded crowd for whom Indian-ness is the best. While Gurumaa is one who holds that you cannot put a patent on the Truth, that what she speaks today is a new version of the same Truth taught in earlier times, and in a great many places, she is also one who holds, speaks and exudes tremendous self-respect in her pluralistic, yet decidedly Indian spiritual heritage. She may have a bit of Turkish Sufism mixed in and little Zen Buddhism as well as other additions in her scriptural and inspirational canon from outside of India, and certainly strong respect and tolerance for other traditions, but I would be hard pressed to call her anything less than 90 per cent Indian! So while I enjoyed the fact that Gurumaa had in a sense figured out that on some level my longing to be in India was real and part of my own plural identity, I also have to ask myself, 'If I sized her up as 40 per cent American, how would she take it?'

Spiritual seekers and pluralism in Gurumaa's circle

Spiritual seekers (*sadhaks*) from around the world have been attracted to Gurumaa Ashram, the place which ardent devotees refer to as the 'Buddhafield', though thus far these spiritual aspirants have been predominantly of Indian heritage. When living there, I met seekers from various cities in India as well as non-resident Indian seekers from the UK, the US, Canada, and Australia. I met only a handful of seekers who were not of Indian origin. The vast majority of seekers who regularly frequented Gurumaa Ashram came from urban centres of north India, from Hindi and Punjabi linguistic regions, but they too, like Gurumaa, like me, and like most of us living in the world today, have their hearts connected to multiple places of belonging.[34]

Gurumaa's devotees answered my questions about their religious identities with varying interest. Most had little interest in talking about what they viewed as old or 'stale' traditions. Some devotees I recognized fairly obviously as belonging to traditions Hindu or Sikh by their names or by their dress, and many seemed perfectly comfortable living with these markers of their traditions while following their 'revolutionary master', who herself refuses categorization. Nonetheless many seekers I spoke with were drawn to Gurumaa because of the 'boundaryless' vision of spirituality that she verbalizes and embodies, even when their lives were grounded in one or another faith tradition. Because of the exposure offered to them by Gurumaa, they were interested in learning about the traditions outside of their inherited ones and many had incorporated meditation or chanting practices from other traditions into their regular spiritual discipline. However, I also found a great number of devotees who were ready to let go of what might best be understood as the 'attachments' to their inherited traditions even if not letting go of traditions themselves, and they expressed this in various ways.

A young Punjabi man living in Jaipur answered my question about his religious identity, 'I am nothing. I am spiritual'. A woman named Shelly* from Florida[35] who was born Sikh and married a Sikh responded, 'I like freedom! Let me do what I want to do. I'm just spiritual... I'm just a soul. Honestly, if I had to check a box... I'd pick Hindu.' This, she volunteered, is only because she adores Krishna and deems him 'the most absolutely interesting god!' Gurmeet*, from Delhi, wears the Sikh turban and sings Gurbani whenever he is not listening to Gurumaa's songs and teachings as he drives his cab or sits waiting for a customer's return. I asked Gurmeet once if he observed all the 'five Ks' of the Sikh tradition because I had never seen him carry the sword (*kirpan*). He responded, 'No I don't carry the *kirpan*. Well, I'm not a real Sikh. I just love Gurumaa. I'm nothing. I am a Sufi'.[36] A Facebook friend from north India who attended Gurumaa's Sufi Shivir posted this as his status: 'Knock, And He'll open the door / Vanish, And He'll make you shine like the sun / Fall, And He'll raise you to the heavens / Become nothing, And He'll turn you into everything – Rumi'.[37] Becoming 'nothing' in order to become everything seems to be something that really resonates with this student of Gurumaa who also posted these words, which he attributes to the man often understood as the father of yoga in

250   *Angela Rudert*

the west, Swami Vivekananda: 'FEEL like Christ and you will be a Christ; feel like Buddha and you will be a Buddha. It is feeling that is the life, the strength, the vitality, without which no amount of intellectual activity can reach God'.[38]

These few bold examples, I find indicative of a trend I see among Gurumaa's avid listeners and retreat participants who themselves ascribe to a boundary-less vision of the spiritual path that does not limit them to any one tradition, yet opens them to wisdom from each of them. Sometimes, like hers, their religious identities were somewhat confounding, looking like one thing and then another, and then not like either, sometimes labelled as 'nothing'.

I met a self-identifying Sikh family in the ashram who have spent years living back and forth between India and the US. Many years ago the father chose to cut his hair and even changed his name to end with the Sanskritized 'ra' suffix as opposed to the Punjabi 'er' suffix, choosing Ravindra* instead of Ravinder, the name given by his Sikh parents, because he enjoyed the 'a' ending sound. When living in the US, he changed the Pal in his name to Paul and he has not worn a turban for years. Dropping the more visible Sikh markers, nonetheless, Ravindra chants the *Mul Mantra* in his regular disciplined practice of mantra repetition (*mantra japa*). Gurumaa gave Ravindra this particular verse, also the first verse of Guru Nanak's *Jap ji Sahib*, which begins the Sikh holy book. Ravindra explained to me that Gurumaa often gives the *Mul Mantra* to her Sikh devotees because its meaning resonates deeply in their hearts. Ravindra's wife has never cut her hair and asks the same of their sons while they are in her charge. The sons are mini-turbaned teens attending a Sikh boarding school in India, an inclination that came first as a protection against the discrimination and potential violence their parents feared they would meet wearing turbans in the US after 9/11. Their mother insists that the boys first learn their own heritage well and then decide whether or not to keep their hair and other bodily signifiers of their faith. Like Gurumaa's mother, these parents, both self-ascribed 'saint-lovers', spend time with spiritual teachers from the syncretistic Sikh ascetic Nirmala and Udasi orders as well as with various Hindu *swamis* and *sadhus*, seeking, like Gurumaa herself once did, the company of 'like-minded' souls who have 'tasted the nectar'.

Shelly, in Florida, who prefers to call her path 'freedom', said this of her childhood in Kolkata:

> When I was a child, I was going to school, in a Christian school. Sang from Bible, played piano, spoke English. Came home every day and heard *Gurbani*. Mom was not conservative, but we always had *Guru Granth Sahib* at ceremonies. *Gurbani* was in my system! As I grew up, when I did something different, they [parents] would say, 'No, you're a Sikh.' Luckily we [her family, mainly she and her sister] met Gurumaa! Now when I'm in a mosque, I can enjoy. I read Quran. I *love* it. Read the Bible. I *love* it. But I'm not *stuck* in anything![39]

When I asked Shelly what she thought of Gurumaa's own religious identity, she replied, 'When you come on the planet, you take birth someplace. Gurumaa was

A Sufi, Sikh, Hindu, Buddhist, TV Guru 251

born a Sikh. Gurumaa would say. You *are* free. If you think you are the body, you are wrong. Go away!' [Speaker's own emphasis added]. Many of Gurumaa's disciples, I learned, are not so quick to check a box indicating their own religious or spiritual identity, even when they do wear a visible indicator of some faith tradition on their bodies. And some of them just might keep us guessing about their identities like Ravinder, also known as Ravindra, and Shelly with her '*Gurbani* in [her] system' and Lord Krishna in her heart.

As Gurumaa's devotees shared with me stories of their spiritual journeys and relationships to Gurumaa, they were also very keen to receive the same from me. I was a wonder to them: how in the world did this ordinary American woman get the karma to study saints? And more specifically, how did she manage to spend time with and have access to their beloved guru (and then to make her ashram trips with funding from her government)? As Gurumaa's devotees asked for my spiritual autobiography and I found myself in a position of having to narrate one, I recognized that I too did not want to be put into any box, even into that of a tradition that had brought meaning to my life – that I too was a rejecter of labels.

For many *sadhaks*, like Gurumaa herself, life is lived with one foot in one world (*loka*) and one foot in another, whether those *lokas* represent different religious traditions, nation states, or cultural ties. And even for those who live in mostly one small world, that world seems to be ever expanding to include the styles of other places. Even if travel to another *loka* is something one only dreams about, other places can be visited and experienced at some level through available technologies. Moreover, other *lokas* as well as other philosophies can be experienced at some level through encounters with the teacher whose own form they understand to be a gateway to the inner shrine of absolute intimacy and endless possibility.

Conclusion: 'Phir bhi dil hai Hindustani'

Vestments have long indicated religious belonging and have situated religious specialists in their traditions within India and in other parts of the world. Throughout her life and spiritual journey, Gurumaa has made her own choices and changes in her physical appearance following certain conventions in some cases (in her choices of white and then ochre), and breaking with convention in others. Furthermore, Gurumaa seems to watch others observing her with some level of bemusement.

Additionally, there are times that Gurumaa dresses the way people would have her dress. In a private conversation in Gurdaspur, Punjab, wearing toenail polish and earrings, but not adorned with the touch of mascara she would apply later, Gurumaa defended her self-styled modes of dress:

> Who says that masters need to dress badly? Sikhs are always very clean. Why can't masters have beautiful ashrams? Do you see any gods not looking nice? Look at Krishna with his peacock feather in his hair, wearing pink and green. [She explained that some people call her a revolutionary mystic and that

252   Angela Rudert

some call her glamorous.] Everything I wear people give to me. I dress as they like for me to. They want me to look like Durga, looking pretty in nice clothes and sometimes I wear those [nice clothes] and sometimes I want to wear cotton as I do today.[40]

(fieldnotes, 13 March 2008)

While she complies and dresses the way that people would like for her to dress, at least on some level – even just in playing the role of a woman, a north Indian one at that – she plays a certain role. She is, in part, who people want her to be: she has accepted names given to her at various times and she sometimes dresses as they would have her do it. Because of who she is and where she comes from she attracts certain people, at least initially. She lives in a female body that is ethnically Indian. She speaks Punjabi, Hindi and English. She has travelled much of the known world.

Gurumaa's desire to keep people guessing about her attire as well as her religious identity, however, implies a refusal on her part to be any single thing for her devotees, to fulfil their expectations of her or to indulge that which they would project onto her. Thus in exhibiting freedom through her body, she disallows those who listen to and watch her closely to become attached to any one idea of that freedom. She may be their 'idol of bliss' (*Anandmurti*), but she remains so in her very own way, in her own style.

Reflecting on my own 40 per cent Hindustani identity, I am reminded of the famous song from 1950s Indian cinema in which Raj Kapoor, playing Raju, 'a Chaplinesque Indian Everyman' sang (lip synced) the lyrics, offered here in Salman Rushdie's translation: 'Oh, my shoes are Japanese. These trousers English, if you please. On my head, red Russian hat – My heart's Indian for all that'.[41] Somewhat less comically than Raju, Gurumaa too reflects through her body a changing world of complex cultural exchange and encounter. As 'all-in-one guru', she is a bit the Indian everywoman, a twenty-first century Raju with a foot here and there and clothed with pieces from here and there. She maintains heart-connections with loved ones in multiple localities, and teaches truths from multiple traditions she has encountered, while 'for all that' (*phir bhi*) her heart (*dil*) remains Hindustani. Through words and through the body itself, Gurumaa speaks the language of her audience, an audience made up of people whose lives are often lived in multiple worlds of belonging.

Gurumaa, like many of the gurus of the twentieth century who brought yoga and meditation practices to America, and like the north Indian medieval poet *sants* who addressed the complex cultural interactions of their times, has her finger on the pulse of the way a great many people in our contemporary world feel today – at odds with the restrictions of inherited religious tradition in a world where spiritual possibilities seem endless. Her audience seems to hunger for knowledge from outside known boundaries even when they feel most comfortable within those traditions or feel somewhat beholden to them. From the particular place where she originates, from the particular place where she now stands, and among the particular audiences for whom her words resonate most greatly, Gurumaa addresses today's complex cultural encounter, and while doing so validates and affirms the heritage of Indian spiritual expertise as a whole. Those of fundamentalist viewpoints do and will find some of her words offensive. About this she expresses no regrets. As Gurumaa's known world continues to expand, as she begins to incorporate new registers into her spoken teachings, so too does her audience expand. She can sometimes look like a Hindu renouncer, sometimes look like a Sikh, sometimes look glamorous, glossy and New Age, but just listen to her a for a few minutes and you will hear quite clearly that her non-Hindu, non-Sikh, non-Muslim heart is indeed Hindustani.

Notes

1 I offer my appreciation to Anandmurti Gurumaa and many of her devotees who graciously participated in my study. My gratitude goes also to Ann Grodzins Gold, Marie-Thérèse Charpentier and Juliana Finucane for their early readings of this essay, as well as to Chiara Formichi. Financial support from FLAS and Fulbright-Hays enabled ethnographic fieldwork in India in 2008 and 2009. Harpreet Singh assisted in the translation of Sultan Bahu's Punjabi verse.

2 There is not space here to discuss 'spirituality' versus 'religion', though both words are problematic for scholars of religion. I will use spirituality in this essay in the way I heard it used in my fieldwork research context, as a vague indicator of boundary-less religiosity. Sometimes I heard the English gloss 'spirituality', even in Hindi conversation, but just as often, I heard the Hindi word *adhyatmik*, which literally means having to do with the supreme (*adhi*) spirit (*atma*). Gurumaa Ashram has recently been named Rishi Chaitanya Ashram. However, I retain the use of the name Gurumaa Ashram for English readability and because that was the name used while I conducted fieldwork.

3 This statement about Gurumaa having attained enlightenment in Vrindavan comes from multiple early (internal) sources: material published in an early version of the gurumaa.com website as well as in books published by Gurumaa Vani. Additionally, Gurumaa spoke of her enlightenment experience to scholar Marie-Thérèse Charpentier as having happened in Vrindavan (Charpentier 2010: 161). However, there is another story. In an effort to clear up confusion about her *sannyas diwas*, which some disciples were confusing with an 'enlightenment day', Gurumaa states in more recent internal web media that there is no particular day or time of enlightenment (see http://soulcurrymagazine.com/sc/sanyas-divas-enlightenment-day.html). Despite my conflicting sources, the story of Gurumaa's enlightenment as having happened in Vrindavan seems to be the prevailing narrative.

4 Having established the multivalence of the words 'Tradition, pluralism and identity' in her introductory essay to the volume by the same name, Das brings forth a question, '[I]s pluralism something external to tradition, or something internal to it?' (Das 1999: 9).

5 For a nuanced study of the pluralistic worldview from which the Sikh tradition emerged and that it continued to embrace during its early history, see Oberoi (1994), who writes, 'Asian religions did not stress singularization that was associated with the institutional framework of Christianity and the idea of heresy' (Oberoi 1994: 31–2). Mayaram (2004: 31) also mentions the 'so-called New Age Religion of the west' as producing syncretic combinations. See also Julia Howell's essay in this volume, for an example of a spiritual teacher who has embodied multiple ways of being.

6 For an argument that New Age gurus and their innovations follow a pattern of Indic boundary crossing, see Rudert (2010). For other arguments that complex intercultural

254 *Angela Rudert*

exchange can provide the setting for syncretic religiosity, see also Gold (1987) and Mayaram (2004).

7 Gurumaa sings the Punjabi verse in the London recording: 'Dar murshid da khana kaaba / Jithe Aashiq Sajde Karde Hoo…' A similar Sultan Bahu song can be found in Elias (1998: 110).

8 For more poetry in translation from both of these Punjabi Sufi poet-singers (both independently referred to as 'Rumi of Punjab') see also Mir (1995).

9 The word 'fool' in italics was emphatically stressed in the spoken words, thus italicized here. Harmandir Sahib is another name for the Golden Temple of the Sikhs in Amritsar. Kashi is one of three commonly used names for the city of Banaras (also Varanasi), pilgrimage place of the Hindus. *Hajj* is the name of the Muslim pilgrimage to Mecca and Medina.

10 It bears mentioning that the word 'saint' is not used without some complications in the Indian context. It is not an indigenous term and not a fully adequate translation for the Indic term *sant*. Saint in the specific sense implies a vetting process not utilized in the world of Indian *sants*. I found my conversation partners in fieldwork used the term with a more universal flavour to it, without any association with a particular tradition, institution or vetting system. The *sant* tradition, rather, implies some level of synchronicity as well as non-conformity. On the *sant* tradition of India, see Gold (1987) as well as Schomer and McLeod (1987).

11 This would mean, quite literally, the guru who gives gyan or knowledge (*jnana* Sanskrit*).* The word/spelling 'gyan' is a typical Punjabi transliteration and is pronounced gyaan. A *gyani* (also spelled *giani*) in the Sikh tradition refers to a teacher, or giver of gyan.

12 Oft-understudied groups like Nirmala and Udasi orders continue to thrive and serve within the larger Sikh population of north India. For an empirical study of the syncretism within Sikh tradition see Oberoi (1994).

13 For my Amritsar storyteller, 'gyan guru' became a way of distinguishing for me between Maharaj ji (gyan guru) and Sant Dalel Singh (Gurudev). In her mind, the relationship between Gurumaa and the first guru from childhood was a relationship of knowledge gyan. But the latter teacher, Dalel Singh, was the one with whom Gurumaa had the stronger heart connection. For some people (and arguably for Gurumaa) 'Gurudev' can be a formless divine teacher who lives in the heart, an 'inner guru', not necessarily manifest outwardly. Both of these explanations would be consistent with Gurumaa's teachings.

14 This story is a prevalent one in Gurumaa's internally published Internet and print media.

15 Inside quotations indicate where Charpentier quotes Gurumaa's words from their recorded interview.

16 The Karmapa, Tibetan Buddhist lama of the Kagyu lineage, visited Gurumaa Ashram in 2009 with a vibrantly colourful and devotional welcome. He is understood to be a special friend, and Gurumaa also meets him in Delhi and in Dharamsala when her schedule permits. I was present in 2008 when Gurumaa reconnected with some Buddhist nuns she had known from early years in her teaching career at the GPIW (Global Peace Initiative for Women) in Jaipur. Likewise, Gurumaa has shared her stories of spending time with Sufis in Turkey, where she did not know the language, but communicated with the help of translators and utilized the 'language of Love'.

17 *Shabad* comes from the Sanksrit word *shabd*, which refers to eternal word or voice as it has come through the human poet-saint. Therefore it can have the sense of (capitalized) Word, implying that the words are words revealed. For a helpful discussion of the various shades of meaning of 'revelation', see Singh (2000: 7–16). In the Sikh context, the Gurus' *shabad* is understood as expression of Truth 'heard' and Truth felt, articulated and understood through particular times and places through particular bodied agents. Singh discusses Sikh revelation in the context of specific, relevant

traditions of revelation, namely Vedic and Muslim, which both informed the early Sikh understandings of Guru Nanak as 'god's mouthpiece' (*gurmukh*).

18 Douglas Renfrew Brooks writes about the guru as 'living canon'. He also explains that guru-based traditions often do not follow sectarian philosophy, drawing rather from 'inclusive canons' (Brooks 1997: 286).

19 I sat in Gurumaa's listening audience at a meditation retreat held in Florida in 2008, when she noted Nanak's important act of translation of Kabir's verse.

20 Douglas Renfrew Brooks writes, 'gurus may cross doctrinal, historical, regional, linguistic, and social boundaries to make their points' (Brooks 1997: 286). When in Maharashtra, Gurumaa took special attention to tell me about Namdev and Jnaneshwar, two immensely popular medieval *bhakti* poets from that region. Gurumaa is always aware of her audiences' registers in various places. Like the *bhakti* poets before her (from Maharashtra as well as from her own region), she wants to speak in the language that people understand. Therefore, in Gujarat, Gurumaa sang *bhajans* in Gujarati for her devotees and in Bengal, she makes references to Ramakrishna and Vivekananda. When in Maharashtra, she is thinking about Namdev and Jnaneshwar. In order to be comprehensible to the largest number of people, she speaks in Hindi, the first or second language of the majority of her listeners.

21 Meditation Camp (*Shivir*), Melbourne, Florida. 25 January 2008.

22 The primary image (*murti*) in Gurumaa Ashram's small temple (*mandir*) is Lord Shiva as God of yoga (*Yogeshwara*) seated in lotus posture. It should also be noted here that in her octagonal shaped *mandir* there is also a small *Durga murti* inside as well as nearly life-sized images of Lord Buddha etched onto the outside of the mandir's eight-sided glass walls.

23 This explanation as well as the brief story that follows is my retelling of the story as Gurumaa told it to me in response to my question in a small ashram gathering.

24 I put the word 'guru' here in quotations because according to the Sikh tradition, immediately before his death, Guru Govind Singh established the holy book containing the songs of the first five Sikh gurus (*Adi Granth*) as the body of the guru, ending the human guru lineage in the mainstream Sikh tradition.

25 The opportune moment happened to be when the *sant*'s chief disciple had left the room. Gurumaa explained that Dalel Singh's chief disciple never seemed to like her and likewise, she has expressed her own concern over the way that the ashram has become sex-segregated since her master's death, presumably the chief disciple-*cum*-master's doing. Gurumaa's expression of disapproval to me for the way the ashram has turned out furthers an ongoing point she was making with me about masters and disciples, that disciples (with lesser minds) often just don't fully get their master's teachings. They can only comprehend as their limited capacities allow. In the rest of the story, Gurumaa quickly fled the ashram after having her renunciation clothes blessed, she explained, avoiding the scrutiny of the chief disciple who always felt threatened by her.

26 Private conversation in Gurumaa Ashram 10 February 2008.

27 Private conversation in Gurumaa Ashram 10 February 2008.

28 *Amrit Varsha* means 'rain of nectar', and is the name of Gurumaa's free public discourses given around the world. Her television show is created directly from these talks, what one clever journalist (referring to TV gurus generally, and Gurumaa included in the story) referred to as the 'spinoffs of [the gurus'] praxis'. See Renuka Narayanan (2002), 'Bhakti on Toast', *The Indian Express*, 18 August 2002.

29 See Charlotte Vaudeville's translation of Kabir's song in which the poet refers to the formless Lord as 'Allah-Rām' and 'Rahīm-Rām' in Vaudeville (1997: 217–8).

30 Ram-Rahim, a guru from whose ashram horrific scandal emerged in recent years, seemed to my rickshaw driver to be one 'strategically employ[ing]' syncretic modes. Some no doubt will say the same for Gurumaa, and she has often noted to me that 'conservatives' do not like 'renegade' or 'revolutionary' mystics. She also makes links

256 *Angela Rudert*

between what she says and does with those revolutionary mystics (often later taken to be the founders of world religions) whose deaths and/or persecution came from religious traditionalists who were afraid of their innovations.

31 Many critics would say that Osho is one who 'strategically employed' syncretic modes.

32 *Darshan* discourse, Gurumaa Ashram, recorded on 3 March 2008.

33 For this argument, I follow Daniel Gold's understanding of the 'solitary *sant*' in north Indian devotional traditions (Gold 1987). In Gurumaa's case, however, in contrast to the 'holy men' described by Gold, the solitary *sant* takes a feminine form (*rupa*).

34 Mayaram quotes Raimon Pannikar's introduction to the autobiography of the cross-dressed (Hindu-Christian) missionary, Abhishektananda, in which Pannikar asserts, 'To live at the meeting point of several traditions is the destiny of a large portion of the human race' (Mayaram 2004: 37).

35 Names that are followed by an asterisk have been changed.

36 This statement seems to me to come almost directly from a series of Gurumaa's talks on the topic 'What is a Sufi?' given to seekers on a meditation retreat called Sufi Shivir in her ashram in 2007. The aforementioned young man from Jaipur who also identified himself as 'nothing' had attended this retreat. Gurmeet had attended the shivir and then later read the transcripts published in Anandmurti Gurumaa's book called *Rumi Aur Mein*. The book is now also available in English translation, as *Rumi's Love Affair*. In the talks from Gurumaa's Sufi Shivir – echoed later in Gurmeet's words – Gurumaa gives multiple definitions for the term 'Sufi' and ultimately equates Sufi with love. She also says that a Sufi is 'nothing' because a Sufi is not this not that, and not concerned with identification as something, but concerned with Love, Divine Love. During this discourse, Gurumaa states that when a person feels he is 'something' or 'someone', he disables himself from becoming 'everything'. However, 'when he becomes nothing, then he becomes "everything". I am everything!' (Gurumaa 2010: 37).

37 Facebook post, 30 November 2011 12:08 pm (EST). https://www.facebook.com/profile.php?id=1396744561 (accessed 30 November 2011).

38 Facebook post, 23 November 2011, 1:56 pm (EST). https://www.facebook.com/profile.php?id=1396744561 (accessed 30 November 2011).

39 Telephone conversation, 14 September 2009. [Speaker's own emphasis added]. Gurbani refers to songs of the Sikh gurus from the *Adi Granth*. *Guru Granth Sahib* is another common name for the *Adi Granth*.

40 Paraphrased from a conversation that occurred on 13 March 2008, recorded the same day in field notes.

41 This apt phrase describing Raju, 'the Indian Everyman', comes from scholar Philip Lutgendorf's short summary of the film Sri 420, published on Lutgendorf's website, Phillip's Films: www.uiowa.edu/~incinema/shri420.html. *"Mera Joota hai Japani, mera pantaloon Inglistani, sir pe lal topi Rusi, phir bhi dil hai Hindustani"* are the lyrics translated by Rushdie (1991: 11).

References

Brooks, D.R. (1997) 'The Canons of Siddha Yoga: The Body of Scripture and the Form of the Guru', in Douglas, R.B., Durgananda, S., Muller-Ortega, P.E., Mahony, W. K., Bailly, C.R. and Sabharathnam, S.P. (eds) *Meditation Revolution: A History and Theology of the Siddha Yoga Lineage*, South Fallsburg, NY: Agama Press, Muktabodha Indological Research Institute.

Charpentier, M.-T. (2010) *Indian Female Gurus in Contemporary Hinduism: A Study of Central Aspects and Expressions of Their Religious Leadership*, Abo, Finland: Abo Akademi University Press.

Das, V. (1999) 'Tradition, Pluralism, Identity: Framing the Issues', in Das, V., Gupta, D. and Uberoi, P. (eds) *Tradition, Pluralism and Identity: In Honour of T.N. Madan* [Occasional Studies 8], New Delhi: Sage.

Elias, J.J. (1998) *Death before Dying: The Sufi Poems of Sultan Bahu*, Berkeley: University of California Press.

Gold, D. (1987) *The Lord as Guru: Hindi Sants in North Indian Tradition*, New York: Oxford University Press.

Gurumaa, A. (2010) *Rumi's Love Affair*, Delhi: Full Circle-Hind Pocket Books.

Lutgendorf, P. 'SHRI 420' at Philips Filums. [Online]. Available from www.uiowa.edu/~incinema/shri420.html (accessed 3 May 2010).

Madan, T.N. (2003) 'Religions of India: Plurality and Pluralism', in Das, V. (ed.) *The Oxford India Companion to Sociology and Social Anthropology*, New Delhi: Oxford University Press.

Mayaram, S. (2004) 'Beyond Ethnicity? Being Hindu and Muslim in South Asia', in Ahmad, I. and Reifeld, H. (eds) *Lived Islam in South Asia: Adaptation, Accommodation, and Conflict*, Delhi: South Science Press.

Mir, M. (1995) 'Teachings of Two Punjabi Sufi Poets', in Lopez, D.S. Jr. (ed.) *Religions of India in Practice*, Princeton, NJ: Princeton University Press.

Muktananda, S. (1999 [1980]) *The Perfect Relationship: The Guru and the Disciple*, South Fallsburg, NY: SYDA Foundation.

Narayanan, R. (2002) 'Bhakti on Toast', *The Indian Express*, 18 August 2002. Online. Available from www.indianexpress.com/oldStory/7800/ (accessed 15 December 2012).

Oberoi, H. (1994) *The Construction of Religious Boundaries: Culture, Identity, and Diversity in the Sikh Tradition*, Chicago; Oxford: University of Chicago Press; Oxford University Press.

Osho International Foundation (2000) *Autobiography of a Spiritual Mystic*, New York: St. Martin's Griffin.

Rudert, A. (2010) 'Research on Contemporary Indian Gurus: What's New About New Age Gurus?', *Religion Compass*, 4(10): 629–42.

Rushdie, S. (1991) *Imaginary Homelands: Essays and Criticism, 1981–1991*, London: Granta Books.

Schomer, K. and McLeod, W.H. (eds) (1987) *The Sants: Studies in a Devotional Tradition of India*, Berkeley; Delhi: Berkeley Religious Studies Series; Motilal Banarsidass.

Singh, P. (2000) *The Guru Granth Sahib: Canon, Meaning and Authority*, New Delhi: Oxford University Press.

Vaudeville, C. (1997) *A Weaver Named Kabir: Selected Verses with a Detailed Biographical and Historical Introduction*, New Delhi: Oxford University Press.

Index

Abdelmanan Tanandato 142–3, 147
acculturation 14
Adalet ve Kalkınma Partisi *see* Justice and
   Development party (Turkey)
adat 205–6
Adi Granth 238, 241–2, 245
Adishankara 242, 245, 247
Agence France-Presse 143
Ahmad Syafii Maarif 30, 222
Alevi 16, 22
Alexander the Great 3
Ali, Mukti 17–18, 23
Aliansi Kebangsaan untuk Kebebasan
   Beragama dan Berkeyakinan *see*
   National Alliance for Freedom of
   Religion and Faith
Allah: and Hindus 115; knowledge of 82;
   name of 162, 177, 180, 211; prayer to
   80, 190, 243, 245–6
American occupation of Japan 35, 37–9,
   41–2, 47
Anak Muda NU 13, 29
Anand Ashram 217, 220–1, 223, 225–8
Arab: people 187, 191, 206; uprisings 14;
   world 14, 24
Arabic: language 24, 76, 78–80, 82, 84,
   180; script 15, 85, 177–8
Arabization 177, 182, 190, 199
assimilation 4, 177, 179, 181–2
atheism 52–4, 68–9, 104
Aum Shinrikyō 36, 46
Ayat Ayat Cinta 199
azan 115, 165, 184, 192–3, 211

Baba Sheik Farid 244, 247
Baha'i 53, 59, 71
Balik-Islam 139, 140
Bandung 20, 28, 177–8
Bangladesh 28, 124

Bangsa Malaysia (Malaysian Race) 157
Barisan Nasional 154–5, 157, 159, 168
Bernama 210, 212
Bhagavad Gita 238, 245
bhakti 125, 229, 238, 241; *see also*
   devotion
Bigelow, Anna 133
blasphemy 7, 219, 223, 227–8, 230
boundary of religion 3, 5–7, 93–7, 103–6,
   109, 116, 157, 165, 192, 237–8, 245–9
Brahma Kumaris 72, 217
brainwashing 225, 227, 229
Bramantyo, Hanung 199
Broderick Pabillo 147
Buddha statue: 53, 97, 242; 236, 247, 250
Buddhafield 249
Buddhism: in China 56–7, 59, 62–8, 95,
   104; and Hinduism 3; in Indonesia 15,
   191, 217–18, 221; and Islam 180; in
   Japan 5, 35–7, 39, 41–4, 46–7; in
   Malaysia 153, 161; as religion 53–4,
   176; in Singapore 71–2, 75; in
   Southeast Asia 15; and spirituality 237,
   241, 246–8; in Thailand 4, 53
Bulaç, Ali 24–5, 29
Bulleh Shah 239–40, 242, 244, 247

Catholicism: in China 56, 59–61, 68, 104,
   107; in India 236, 241; in Indonesia 15,
   205, 226; in Japan 44; in Malaysia 156,
   160–2; in the Philippines 4, 6, 138,
   143, 147, 149; and pilgrimage 139–40;
   places of worship 140, 148–9; shrine
   138, 145; in Singapore 72; in Turkey
   14
Cemil Aydin 24
Chandran, Premesh 202
Cheng Hoo Mosque 175, 178, 180–1, 185,
   190–2; Foundation 183; in Palembang

175, 178, 185–8; in Surabaya 176, 178–80, 182, 184, 188–9
Chenggiz Khan 3
Cheong, Amy 1–2
children's classes 73–4
China: economy 58, 153, 158; and Hong Kong 105; and Islam 175, 179–84, 187, 192; and Japan 40; post-imperial 52–3, 56, 68; Sea 15; Southwest 5, 52; state-religion relations 51, 53, 104; *see also* People's Republic of China, PRC; *see also* relevant subentries
Chinese Communist Party 52–4, 56–9
Chinese popular religions 53, 59, 64, 67–8, 93, 95, 104–5
Chinese: anti- violence 4, 179, 189; Communist Party 52–4, 56–9; culture 94–6, 106–8, 175, 179–81; diaspora 7, 175–93; ethnicity 55, 94, 97–9, 102; in Indonesia 175–93; language 98, 100, 107, 180; in Malaysia 1, 158, 164, 166; media 66; mosque 175–93; music 67, 181; Muslims 7, 175–93; Muslim identity 176–93; New Year 99, 104; in the Philippines 143; religion 52, 55, 72, 93, 95–6, 103–5, 109; temple 6, 93, 95, 97, 103, 19; in Singapore 72, 80
Chineseness, 175, 180–1, 191–3
Christ 181, 250
Christian Federation of Malaysia 155, 162
Christianity: in China 51, 54, 59–61, 68, 104; gospels 242; in India 116; in Indonesia 17, 181, 217–19, 222, 227; in Japan 35, 37, 39, 42–43; in Latin America 25; in Malaysia 153, 155–6, 159–62; in the Philippines 15, 138–9, 143–4, 146–7, 149; school 160, 250; in Singapore 71–2, 82; spirituality 246; in Turkey 25
Chuan-Jin 1
Ciputat 20, 23, 27
colonialism: American 146; anti- 3, 159; British 2, 4, 104, 114, 119, 153, 158–9, 204–7; Dutch 3, 176–7, 205; legacy 164, 168; pre- states 3, 193; post- 2, 4, 15, 24, 29, 53, 153–4, 157, 207; rule 4, 15, 17, 24 42–3, 82, 158–9; Spanish 143
Communism 22, 53–4
community service centres 81
Confucianism 72
Connolly, William 146
conversion 2, 17, 115, 159, 161, 177, 191, 204, 211

conviviality 4, 7; everyday 2, 113, 116; hierarchized 138–9, 142–7, 149–50; in India 116; Shail Mayaram 3, 5–6; in the Philippines 138; religious 167
cosmopolitanism: alternative 6; discoursive 190; everyday 191; grounded 192; Islamic 13, 18, 21, 175, 193; vernacular 193
Council of Churches of Malaysia 155
cult 36, 51, 56–7, 59, 64, 67, 105, 227, 229

dakwah 153, 159–60, 179–84, 197
Daoism: in China 54, 56, 64, 67–8; in Hong Kong 95, 104; in Malaysia 153; in Singapore 71–2
Dar al-Islam 14
de Certeau, Michel 163
defensive protectionism 148
Democrat Party (Turkey) 16
Democratic Action Party (Malaysia) 154–5
Democratic Party (Indonesia) 28
Democratic Party (Japan) 40
Department of Religion (Indonesia) 219; *see also* Ministry of Religious Affairs (Indonesia)
Derrida 24
devotion 240–2; as *bakhti* 125, 134, 238–41; Catholic 140, 143, Islamic 20, 74, 216
Dewan Dakwah Islamiyyah Indonesia 20
diaspora 7, 183; *see also* Chinese diaspora
Diet (Japan) 39, 42
discrimination 6, 44 93, 190, 250; racial 96, 99, 109
diversity 1–2, 71, 97, 114, 132–3, 138, 159, 203; cultural 14, 19, 62, 109, 176, 182, 188, 190; ethnic 58, 62; ethno-linguistic 129; Hindu 134; Islamic 22, 153, 180–2, 188, 202, 229; management of 2–5, 71; operational 188; organic 176, 188; and pluralism (Michael Peletz) 1–3, 7, 55, 64, 93, 109, 116, 146; religious 3, 14, 35, 51, 62, 72, 145, 149, 153, 218, 228; as richness 6
Diyanet 15, 16, 23
Duara, Prasenjit 68
durga 252
dwifungsi 17

Eck, Diana 109, 146, 148
education: children 71, 76–8, 81, 86; in China 54, 56–7; Christian 61; in India

114, 132–3, 216, 241; in Indonesia 16–9, 28; Islamic 5, 16–7, 20, 24, 74, 80, 205–6; in Malaysia 160, 164; in the Philippines 143; private 17, 23, 25, 27; secular 5, 17, 73, 75, 83, 160; in Turkey 16–7, 25–6; weekend 74, 83; *see also* schools, madrasah
Egypt 14, 17, 24
empowerment 97, 101, 103, 179, 216, 225, 230
enshrinement 36, 41–6
Erbakan, Necmettin 21, 23, 24, 26
Erdoğan, Tayyip 26, 27
ESQ 229
essentialism 193
Estrada, Joseph 148
ethno-nationalism 153, 159
ethno-political discourse 164
ethno-religious: boundaries 7; diversity 6, 158, 164, 165–6; expression 175; homogeneity 7, 158, 165; identity 159, 185; imagination 185, 192; pluralism 157, 159, 166; reality 181, 186, 191–2; solidarities 165, 167
ethnolocality 186–7
ethnoscape 158, 166
European and Asian Mediterraneans 15
evangelism 27–8, 61
everyday resistance 210
Evren, Kenan 22

fatwa: in Indonesia 188, 216, 218, 222, 228; in Malaysia 156, 161, 167
Fealy, Greg 30
Federal Department of Islamic Development (Malaysia) 155, 160
Federated Malay States 158
Feener, Michael 2
Feng shui 106,
fertility 65–6
Fincane Juliana 1
food: Chinese 65, 99, 181; halal 62, 100, 160, 181; Indian festive 94–5, 97, 102–3, 119, 122–4; Middle Eastern 199; Ramadan 197–201, 207, 210–11
foreign infiltration (China) 57
Forum for Inter-Religious Consultation (Indonesia) 17
Freedom House 4
Front Pembela Islam *see* Islamic Defenders' Front
Furnivall, J.S. 3–4

Gaji Pir 113, 119, 127, 132–5

Gan, Steven 202–3, 212
Ganesh 118–20, 122–3, 134
Garib Navaz 115
GDP-ism 58
global city 109, 163, 202, 237
global positioning 175
globalization 19, 75, 85–6, 93, 118, 134, 154, 157, 237
god 227, 239–40, 244–5, 250; as *bhagvan* 125, 128; in China 65, 94; Hindu 113, 134; monotheist 15, 29, 103–4, 207, 218; Shinto 42; Sikh 242; *see also* Allah
gokoku jinja (state protecting shrine) 37–9, 41, 45
Guided Democracy (Indonesia) 16
Gul, Abdullah 26–7
Gulen Movement 23, 29
Gulen, Fethullah 23, 25
guru 115, 225; *bangsa* 18; female 120
Guru Govind Singh 240
Guru Nanak 240, 242–4, 247, 250

Habibie, B. J. 19
hadith 78
hajj 61, 239, 240; *see also* pilgrimage
halal-bilahal 181
halal: Chinese 62, 179, 181, 191; in Malaysia 160, 163, 166–7, 212
Hanafi, Hasan 24
haram 75, 160, 180
harmony 32; ethnic 107; religious 1, 71, 193; racial 157; social 1, 5; normative 2
Hatoyama Yukio 41
HDB *see* House Development Board
Hefner, Robert 3
Hidayat, Komaruddin 20, 27–8
hierarchical plurality 52, 56, 64, 65, 68,
Hindu: caste 114–16, 119, 125, 128; epic 114; festival 118–19, 122, 125, 128, 132; identity 131; Mina community 113, 131; pluralism 72, 125; practices 165, 239, 241, 243; renunciation 243, 253; shrine 113–14, 122, 125–6, 131; spirituality 236–7, 250; temple 115; texts 238, 241–2, 246
Hinduism: and Buddhism 3; in India 53, 118; in Indonesia 15, 176, 218, 221, 226; and Islam 116, 118–19, 122–4, 127, 130–4, 216–17, 237, 243; and Jain 129–30, 133; in Malaysia 153, 161, 164–6, 208; and politics 122, 124; public display of 117, 125; and Sikhism 245–7, 249; in Singapore 71–2
Hindustani 252

Index 261

Hishiki Masaharu 46
Ho, Albertina 224–5, 227–8
Ho, Cheng 179, 181–3, 185, 190
Home Ministry (Malaysia) 162
Hong Kong 2, 6, 148
House Development Board 1, 78
Hui: in Dali 55, 61–2; and Indonesia
 182–3; *see also* Chinese Muslims
Huntington, Samuel 4
hybridity 27, 30, 83, 153, 168, 237;
 intentional 176, 188, 192; everyday
 176, 188, 192
Hyde, Henry 40
hypnosis 225

Ibrahim, Anwar 202
identity: collective 175; contestation of
 188; ethnic 168; formation 19, 22–3,
 30, 175, 181, 183; hybrid 27, 237;
 inclusive 21; Islamic 25, 82–3, 175–6,
 181, 186, 188, 193; Japanese 37, 46;
 manifestation of 175, 178, 187, 192;
 monocultural 149; national 5, 84; plural
 248; politics 115, 159; religious 5, 116;
 religious i. in China 62; religious i. in
 Hong Kong 94, 97, 108; religious i. in
 Indonesia 175, 185; religious i. in
 Malaysia 159, 209; religious i. in
 Singapore 72, 75, 82; religious i. in
 Turkey 23, 25, 30; translocal 186
Idgah 118–19, 124,
Ikatan Cendekiawan Muslimin Indonesia
 19
imaginary homeland 183, 186–7
inclusivity 182, 190–1, 193
Indian Ocean 15
indigenization 51, 190
Indonesia *see* relevant subentries
Indonesian Association for Media
 Development 202
Indonesian Chinese Muslim Association
 176, 178–9, 182, 184–7, 189, 191–2
intangible cultural heritage 59, 65–8
intellectuals: religious 13, 24–5, 29;
 secular 23, 47; *see also* Muslim
 intellectuals
inter-ethnic 1, 4, 153
Inter-religious Council (Singapore) 71,
 161
inter-religious relations 162, 167
International Center of Islam and
 Pluralism (Indonesia) 28, 222
International Monetary Fund 4
Iqbal, Muhammad 24

Islam: political 16, 19, 177; cultural 18,
 20, 22; cosmopolitan 13, 18, 175, 193;
 see also relevant subentries
Islamic Avant garde 20, 23
Islamic Defenders' Front 188, 219, 222,
 228
Islamic discourse 13, 15–16, 22
Islamic law 179; in Indonesia 15–16, 18,
 206; in Turkey 26; in Malaysia 160; *see
 also* Sharia
Islamic liberation theology 25
Islamic Party of Malaysia 154–5, 157,
 161, 207
Istanbul 14, 22, 24, 26

Jain 246–7; in China 53; festivals 118,
 128–30; and Hinduism 129–30, 133,
 245; in India 114–15, 129, 133; in
 Singapore 71; temple 129–30
Jakarta 7, 14, 18, 76, 186, 190, 197, 199,
 213, 216–17; Anand Ashram centre
 220–1; court 227; as global city 202;
 IAIN 17–20, 27–8; mosque 176–8,
 187; National Monument 221–2;
 Ramadan in 200
Jakarta Charter 16, 206
Jal Jhulani 118–19, 125–9, 133
Japan Association of War-bereaved
 Families 39, 42
Japanese Constitution 38, 42, 46
Japanese occupation of Indonesia 206
Jaringan Islam Liberal 28
Java: Central 177, 216–17, 221, 226; East
 18, 178–9, 182, 184–5, 188, 190, 199;
 Islam in 179–80, 182, 185–6, 206
Javanese: architecture 177, 191;
 aristocracy 21, 205–6; culture 21, 176,
 180–1, 185, 187, 221; as ethnic group
 26, 73, 199, 202; identity 187; language
 184
Jesus 181, 240, 242
Jewish 62, 77, 155, 247
jhanki 118, 120–22, 126
Justice and Development Party (Turkey)
 14, 27, 29

Kabir 242, 244–5, 247
Kahn, Joel 158, 210
Kai fong 95–6, 105–6
kampung 1, 149, 159, 164
Kan Naoto 41
Karakoç, Sezai 23
Karaman, Hayderrin 23
Kemalism 15, 22, 29

262　*Index*

Ketuanan Melayu (Supremacy of Malays) 153
Kisakürek, Necip Fazil 23
kiyai 76, 189
Koizumi Jun'ichirō 40
Krishna (deity) 118, 120–2, 126, 128, 236, 240, 244–7, 249, 251
Kung fu 94–5, 100–1, 107
Kurdish 16, 22, 26

laicism 15
Lantos, Tom 40
Lee 1
legitimacy 53, 130, 134, 247; and diversity 1–3, 55, 64, 86, 93, 109, 116, 133, 146–7, 208, 211; Weberian 55, 93
Liberal Democratic Party (Japan) 39–41, 44
liberalism 29, 188, 216, 218
LibForAll 28
liminality 237
Lincoln, Bruce 54
Literacies 71, 73–80, weekday 83–6, weekend 83–6, wars 71, 85–6
literacy 73, 83, 85
living together 3, 6, 116, 130, 133–4, 144; *see also* conviviality
local configuration 182, 192
lok devata (folk deity) 125, 128
love the country, love religion (Ch. *aiguo aijiao*) 58, 60

Macapagal-Arroyo, Gloria 142, 147
Madjid, Nurcholish 17–8, 20–1, 23, 25, 27–8,
madrasah: liberal 75, 80–3, traditional 75–8, weekend 5, 7, 72–86, mosque 80–3; *see also medrese*
Mahathir Mohamad 159–61, 163
Mahbharata 114
Majelis Ulama Indonesia 188, 216, 218–19, 222, 227–8
Malay religion and custom 72, 78, 80, 159, 205
Malaysia *see* relevant subentries
Malaysiakini 197, 199–200, 202–5, 208–12
Malaysian Bar Council 161
Malaysian Consultative Council for Buddhism, Christianity, Hinduism and Sikhism 161
marginalization 21, 144, 150, 166, 220
Marxism 25, 54, 83
Masyumi (Indonesia) 15, 17–18
materiality 181

Maududi, Abu al-'Ala 24, 29
Mayaram, Shail 3, 5–7, 116–17, 133, 238
mazhab 20, 23
Mecca 19, 61–2, 180, 206, 239; *see also hajj*
Medina 21, 25, 239
medium of instruction 75–85
medrese 15, 16; *see also* madrasah
Meiji 37, 43
memorization 77, 79, 84
Middle East 5, 14, 19, 162, 175, 220; architecture 163–5, 176–7; education 74; and Islam 177, 184; migrants 95
migration: and colonialism 2, 158; India 128; Java 26, 182; Malaysia 7, 153, 158–9, 163–4; Muslim 6, 93, 109, 148; Philippines 138–9, 144–5, 147; Turkey 22, 24
Milli Gorus Hereketi 21
Ministry of Culture (China) 66, 67
Ministry of Education (Singapore) 84
Ministry of Health and Welfare (Japan) 42, 44
Ministry of Home Affairs (Japan) 42
Ministry of Religious Affairs (Indonesia) 16, 28, 207–8; *see also* Department of Religion (Indonesia)
minority: cultural 72; ethnic 56–7, 107, 109, 183, 193; in Hong Kong 93–5; and integration 3–5, 147, 211; in Japan 46–7; in Malaysia 165; religious 71, 130, 204, 229
Miyaji Naokazu 41–2
Mohamad, Goenawan 204
Mohamad, Mahathir 159–61, 163
Moon Cake Festival 72
mosque 7, 236–7, 243–4, 250; in China 57, 59–62; in Hong Kong 95, 115; in Jahazpur 124, 127, 131; in Malaysia 149, 155, 159, 162, 164–6; in the Philippines 140–3, 147–8; in Singapore 74, 76–81; in Turkey 16; *see also* Cheng Hoo Mosque
Muhammadiyah 17, 20, 30, 179–84, 188–93, 222
Muharram 115, 119, 131–3
multiculturalism 2–3, 6, 75, 86, 109, 153
murti 128, 240, 242
MUSAID 22
Muslim Brotherhood 24, 27, 184
Muslim intellectuals: Chinese 187; contemporary 13; Indonesian 17–20, 29; new 5, 19, 23–4; Turkish 23, 25; young 30

Musyawarah Antar-Umat-Beragama *see* for Inter-Religious Consultation (Indonesia)

Nahdlatul Ulama (NU): and Chinese Muslims 180, 182–4, 193; in East Java 18, 179, 189–90; as Indonesian Islamic organization 30, 179, 182, 188, 190–1; NGO-affiliate 28; as post-traditionalist 13, 29; youth 13, 20, 29
Nakasone Yasuhiro 39–40
Naksibendi 16, 21, 23, 30
Nasr, Seyyed Hossein 24
Nasution, Adnan Buyung 226
Nasution, Harun 17–18, 23
National Alliance for Freedom of Religion and Faith 222, 230
National Fatwa Council (Malaysia) 156, 161
National Integration Movement (NIM) 220
nationalism: in China 53, 57; and communism 53–4, 58, 183; emergence of 3–4; in Indonesia 187, 204; and Islam 25, 27; in Malaysia 153, 159, 221; secular 15
Natsir, Muhammad 18, 20
negotiations 5–7, 23, 115, 164, 175, 192
Nepalese 95, 101, 108
New Age 237–8, 246
New Economic Policy (Malaysia) 163, 203
New Order (Indonesia) 16–19, 26–8, 175–9, 187–9, 218, 223
Noda Yoshihiko 41
North Korea 40, 42–3, 47, 53

Occidentalist 24, 29
Old Women's Associations 64–6
orthodoxy 3, 7, 60, 68
Ottoman 21, 23, 24
Ozal, Turgut 22–3, 26
Özdenören, Rasim 24
Özel, İsmet 24

Pakatan Rakyat 154–5, 157, 168
Pakdil, Nuri 23
Pakistan 17, 132, 175, 183
Palembang *see* Cheng Hoo mosque
Paltu 242
Pancasila 15, 19, 29, 177, 188, 203, 207, 218, 220, 222
Pangkor Engagement, 233
Panthay Rebellion 61

Paramadina 21, 27–8
Partai Keadilan Sejahtera *see* Prosperous Justice Party (Indonesia)
Parti Islam Se Malaysia *see* Islamic Party of Malaysia
Parti Keadilan Rakyat *see* People Justice Party (Malaysia)
particularism 192
pedagogy 77, 82, 84
Peletz, Michael 2–7, 55, 93, 109, 116, 146
People Justice Party (Malaysia) 154
People's Republic of China 5, 51–5, 58–9, 68, 104–6
Persatuan Islam Tionghoa Indonesia *see* Indonesian Chinese Muslim Association
pesantren 29
pilgrimage 143, 144; economy 143, 145; Gwer Sa La 65–6; Hindu 241, 243; Muslim 19, 61–2, 206, 239; National Shrine of Our Mother of Perpetual Help 138–40; spiritual 239–40; *see also hajj*
place: and body 243; as concept 5, 7; physical 15; pluralist 202, 238; representative 176, 192; sacred 192; *see also* space
pluralism 116, 138, 139, 145–6, 202, 211, 220, 237, 242; accepted 7; active 109; actual 7, 55, 139, 153–4, 163, 168; celebration of; 222; contestation of 228; cultural 153, 162, 179; deep 146; delimited 218–19, 223, 229, 230; and diversity 1, 2, 55, 64, 71, 93, 190; embodied 237–8; everyday 165, 167; fatwa against 188, 216, 218; and festivities 116; ideological 25; Indonesian 21, 29; internal 72, 125; and legitimacy 3, 86, 93, 146, 211; limitations 46, 51, 55, 60, 134, 166, 216, 237; lived 139, 109; management of 157; normative 2–3; ordinary 6, 113, 133–4; performed 116–17; gender 7; *qasbati* 114; and the state 68, 86, 204, 212
Pluss, Caroline 93, 109
politicization of Islam 202, 207–8, 211
politics of difference 59
possession 118, 125,
post-Islamist 13, 15, 29
post-modern 24, 29
post-modern coup (Turkey) 13, 27
post-*traditionalisme* (Postra) 13, 15, 29
preacher 28, 30, 182–90, 227

264   *Index*

primate city 144
priyayi 21, 205–6
procession 65–6, 119, 125, 128–32, 134
Prophet Muhammad 21, 22, 74, 77, 82, 188
Prosperous Justice Party (Indonesia) 27
Protestantism 15, 56, 104, 140, 143, 156, 160
public sphere 5, 13, 15, 26, 130, 149, 153, 168

qasba 113–14, 120, 126, 130–1, 134
Qur'an: chapters 74, 77–8, 82–3, 85 119, 190, 213; reading 75–7, 79–80, 82, 192; school 24, 25; and Sunna 25, 190; *see also* madrasah, education
Qutb, Sayyid 24, 29

racism 1, 162; *see also* discrimination
Radha 240
Rakhmat, Jalaluddin 28
Ram 134, 243, 245
Ramadan 7; at Cheng Hoo mosque 176, 188–9, 191; in Hong Kong: 100, 103–104; in Jahazpur: 118, 122, 124; in Jakarta 197–9; in Kuala Lumpur 199, 202, 20–11
Rasjidi, Muhammad 20
Ravidas 242
reciprocal relations 97–8, 109
Reformasi (Indonesia) 13, 28, 189, 216, 218
Reid, Anthony 3, 71, 149
religiosity: autonomous 217–18; Indic 238; individual 237; Islamic 14, 20, 29–30, 189, 216; in place 118; public 117, 130, 135; state 52, 55, 68; *see also* state religion
religious freedom: in China 51, 54, 56, 66, 104, 105; in Indonesia 219–20, 226, 228; in Japan 42, 45–7; in Malaysia 161
Religious Harmony (Singapore) 71
religious identity *see* identity
riots 4, 153, 184, 189; as *danga* 130–4
Rumi, Jalaluddin 242

Sahajobai 242
Sai Baba 72, 217
Said Nursi, Bediuzzaman 16, 25, 29
saint 115, 134, 251; tombs of 115, 119; *see also* sufi
saint-lovers 240, 250
Salamullah 217–19

Salman Mosque 20
sant 241–3, 247–8, 252
santri 30
Saudi Arabia 20, 177
sectarian 6, 15
secular *see* education, nationalism
secular state 16, 133, 160, 177, 207
secularism 18, 54, 64, 188, 218–19
securitization of Islam 26
semiotics 75, 81, 83, 85
separation of religion and state 5, 17, 38–40, 42, 44–7, 51–2, 54–5, 149
Shankara *see* Adishankara
Shanmugam 1
Sharia 161, 188, 206–7; *see also* Islamic law
Shariati, Ali 24, 25
Shinto 35–9, 41–2, 46–7; state Shinto 35, 38
Shiva 242, 145–6
Sichuan 94
Sikhism: in India 116; in Malaysia 153, 161–2; in Singapore 71–2, 75
Singapore 1–7, 40
Singapore Islamic Education System 80–1
Singer, Milton 116
Sisters in Islam (Malaysia) 208
Sjadzali, Munawir 18–19
Snouck Hurgronje, Christiaan 206
social circle 97–100, 103, 109
South Korea 39–41, 42–3, 47
space: civic 148–9; contested 93, 149, 176, 188, 192; cosmopolitan 175–6, 189, 191, 193; of diversity 2, 3, 68, 149, 159, 164, 193; everyday 118, 163–4; geo-cultural 22; media 167; negotiated 128; "new opportunity spaces" 15, 20, 22, 26; physical 181, 221, 236; pluralist 202, 208, 211; private 225; public 93, 109, 116, 118, 130, 133–4, 149, 160, 175; sacred 76; shared 1–2, 5, 6, 73, 78–9, 133; social 147, 150, 176, 192, 193; transformed 118, 120; urban 133, 139, 149, 154, 163, 165; virtual 154, 156; *see also* place
state religion 15, 53–5, 62, 68, 204; *see also* religiosity of the state
stereotypes 100, 146–7, 149, 188, 193
Straits Settlements 158
Sufi 115, 134, 216, 236, 239, 241–4, 246–9; order (*tariqa*) 15, 16, 23, 217; piety 20, 237–8, 245; songs 240, 246; *see also* saint

Sufism 20–1, 23, 27, 28, 217, 244, 248; neo-Sufism 20
Suharto: fall 26–7, 175, 177, 203; and Islam 16, 19, 207–8, 218; regime 203
Sukarno 16–7, 218, 220
Sultan Bahu 239, 242
Surabaya 199; *see also* Cheng Hoo mosque
symbolic unity 176, 178, 188, 192
syncretism: and Anand Kirshna 224, 227; and Anandmurti Gurumaa 237–8, 241, 245, 250; in Islam 167, 193; and pluralism 146; in politics 154;

tawhid 25, 83
Teja Dashmin 118, 125–6
temple 57, 59, 65, 159, 164, 237, 239, 244, 246; Bai 64; Buddhist 35, 63, 65; Chinese 6, 93, 179–80, 193; Chongsheng 63; Daoist 64; Hindu 72, 114–15, 119–20, 122–4, 126, 128, 165, 242; Jain 129–30; Sikh 162; Tai Kok Tsui; Vaishnavite 120, 122
Tempo 197–200, 202–4, 208, 210, 212–13, 227
Thaipusam 72
Tharman Shanmugaratnam 1
The Sun 202
tolerance 26, 80, 175, 188, 206, 248; and legitimacy 146; limited 54, 64; religious 71–2, 157, 179, 190, 202, 208
Topçu, Nurettin 23
tourism to religious sites 58–66, 95–6, 105–6, 179, 185, 190
translocal imagination 176, 185, 187–8, 192
translocality 175, 186–7
transnational: connections 93, 113, 175, 182–4, 187, 192; imagination 175, 183, 192; movement 47, 134, 184; parallel 5
tribe populations 115
Tunisia 14

Turkey 2, 5, 52, 246
Turkish-Islamic synthesis 22, 25

ulama 205, 207; *ulema* 25
ummah 7, 72, 175
UNESCO 67
United Malays National Organization 207
unity in diversity 71, 162
universal religion 179
Upanishads 245
urban poor 142–4
ustadh 189, 192

Valentine's Day 154–7, 168
Vietnam 53
Vishnu 122, 126, 128
Vision 2020 163
void deck 1, 78

Wahid Institute 28, 219, 222
Wahid, Abdurrahman 25–6, 28, 220–3
wali songo 180
Wawasan 2020 *see* Vision 2020
Weber, Max 2, 17, 55, 93
Wellens, Koen 56
Westernization 18, 22, 25, 85
World Class City 163, 164
world religion day 71

Yasukuni Shrine 5; legal action against 43–6; official visits (*kōshiki sanpai*) to 39–42, 44; as religion 41–2
yoga 217, 228, 246, 249, 252
Yogyakarta 17, 19, 217, 220
Yudhoyono, Susilo Bambang 28, 29

Zahid Kotku, Shaykh Mehmet 21–2
Zakaria, Hazlan 199–200, 209, 213
Zen Buddhism 62, 242, 248
zongjiao 53, 57, 60
Zubrzycki, Geneviève 149
Zulkifli, Arif 213

Taylor & Francis

eBooks
FOR LIBRARIES

ORDER YOUR FREE 30 DAY INSTITUTIONAL TRIAL TODAY!

Over 23,000 eBook titles in the Humanities, Social Sciences, STM and Law from some of the world's leading imprints.

Choose from a range of subject packages or create your own!

Benefits for you

- ▶ Free MARC records
- ▶ COUNTER-compliant usage statistics
- ▶ Flexible purchase and pricing options

Benefits for your user

- ▶ Off-site, anytime access via Athens or referring URL
- ▶ Print or copy pages or chapters
- ▶ Full content search
- ▶ Bookmark, highlight and annotate text
- ▶ Access to thousands of pages of quality research at the click of a button

For more information, pricing enquiries or to order a free trial, contact your local online sales team.

UK and Rest of World: **online.sales@tandf.co.uk**

US, Canada and Latin America:
e-reference@taylorandfrancis.com

www.ebooksubscriptions.com

ALPSP Award for BEST eBOOK PUBLISHER 2009 Finalist

Taylor & Francis eBooks
Taylor & Francis Group

A flexible and dynamic resource for teaching, learning and research.